Bob Drinan

Bob Drinan

The Controversial Life of the First Catholic Priest Elected to Congress

Raymond A. Schroth, S.J.

Fordham University Press | New York 2011

Library of Congress Cataloging-in-Publication Data

Schroth, Raymond A.
    Bob Drinan : the controversial life of the first Catholic priest elected to Congress / Raymond A. Schroth.
        p.   cm.
    Includes bibliographical references and index.
    ISBN 978-0-8232-3304-5 (cloth : alk. paper)—ISBN 978-0-8232-3306-9 (ebook)
    1. Drinan, Robert F.   2. Legislators—United States—Biography.   3. United States. Congress. House—Biography.   4. Catholic Church—Clergy—Biography.   5. United States—Politics and government—1969–1974.   6. United States—Politics and government—1974–1977.   7. United States—Politics and government—1977–1981. I. Title.
E840.8.D75S37   2011
328.73′092—dc22
[B]

                                                                                  2010033726

Printed in the United States of America
13 12 11   5 4 3 2 1
First edition

To

DANIEL A. DEGNAN, S.J.
1926–2007
priest
lawyer
dean and president
loyal friend

JOSEPH A. NOVAK, S.J.
1927–2010
religious superior
inspirational leader
loyal friend

Contents

Preface

The best reason to write a book about Father Robert F. Drinan, S.J., is the importance of his life and career, both in his own time and today. Whether the overall impact of his ten years as the first Roman Catholic priest elected to Congress was positive or negative will be debated for years to come. He decided to answer the question of whether the public roles of the priest and politician are compatible by actually playing both roles. He called himself a "moral architect" and made his reputation as an opponent of the Vietnam War, in his drive to impeach President Richard Nixon, and as a lifelong advocate of human rights. But his defense of legalized abortion clashed with his priestly image and brought on his forced retirement from Congress. The questions raised about church and state, law and morality, by his controversial congressional career and forty years as a law professor and writer remain alive today.

Whenever I have written a book, it has had to be about someone I admired—the men who created and wrote for *The Brooklyn Eagle*; the war correspondent and brilliant radio and TV commentator Eric Sevareid; the authors of the Christian classics; young Jeff Thielman, the Boston College graduate who worked with poor street children in Peru; the presidents, faculty, and students of Fordham University; the missionaries, parish priests, and professors of the American Society of Jesus. And, when Robert F. Drinan, S.J., died in early 2007, I saw that I should try to tell his story.

I hope the reader will find this account, as a friend advised, "critically appreciative, both of Drinan's personal ways, and far more importantly, of his public policy effort."

I knew him because we both wrote for *America* in the late 1960s, just as the Vietnam War heated up; and we both wrote regularly for the *National Catholic Reporter* for some thirty years. In 1995, while I lived at Georgetown University and wrote that biography of Eric Sevareid, and Robert Drinan was teaching in the law school, we encountered each other almost daily in the community *haustus* room, having the same characteristic encounter countless Jesuits have described to me: He zipped in eating a stand-up breakfast or lunch or pulled up his chair coming home late at night, sat down with an ale, and grilled his table companions: "What's new?"

Bob Drinan lived many lives: Jesuit priest, lawyer, teacher, administrator, author, journalist, politician, congressman, advocate. And to those who knew him best, his family and staff, he was a beloved friend and father figure. Although I may have read just about everything he published, particularly the journalism, this book is more an introduction to the man and his work than a definitive study of his output. Legal scholars may some day undertake that task. But he never considered himself primarily a scholar. He wrote—dictating everything—as an advocate, who floated his opinions in newspaper columns and magazine articles, lectures, and interviews, then developed them in books. These he usually ended with a call to action, a plea that the various religious and political leaders join ranks to feed the hungry, end the death penalty, ban handguns, and respect human rights. I have tried to center this book on the identity that Bob Drinan himself most cherished, that of the Jesuit priest. He always believed that the fullest expression of his priesthood was in the House of Representatives. But when forced to choose, he followed his conscience and left the civic world for the religious.

I dedicate this book, first, to Father Daniel A. Degnan, S.J., who died soon after Drinan did. Dan, who came from a large, politically active New Jersey family, entered the Jesuits at St. Andrew on Hudson in 1958, a year after I did. We were friends from that moment on and shared summer vacations at the Cornwall and Sea Bright Jesuit villas. A Georgetown graduate and lawyer when he entered the Society, Dan taught law and served as dean of Seton Hall Law School and then as president of Saint Peter's College. He was a man of high intelligence, great integrity, outspoken opinions, occasional mercurial tempera-ment, and absolute love for his family and a long list of devoted friends.

Joe Novak was formally my religious superior who became my friend. Though his expertise was religious education, for most of his career he was a provincial, and then my superior at Fordham and Saint Peter's College. Without his support I would not have written my books and, with Dan, enjoyed summer weeks at our Sea Bright villa. He honored me by asking for my blessing the week before he died.

I began work on this book on Good Friday 2008. In the first months I discovered obstacles, some blocking the availability of important sources and threatening to sink the project. But I was determined to continue. Late that summer I drove to Weston, Massachusetts, to the old Jesuit seminary where Drinan and most of New England's Jesuits were trained in philosophy and theology. Today it is a retreat center, residence, and health center for retired Jesuits. There I worked my way through the long corridors seeking the men who had known Drinan since he entered the Society in 1942 and others who had played deci-sive roles in his life.

Then, burdened with those obstacles that still stood in my way, I went out to the cemetery, stood at Bob's stone where someone had placed a small American flag, and asked him to help me with this book. My prayer: "Bob, get me out of this." I returned to Boston College, where I would live for the year and work in Boston College's Drinan archives. When I entered the front door, there was a telephone mes-sage telling me that the obstacles had begun to fall away.

St. Mary's Hall, Boston College, May 2009

Acknowledgments

A project as challenging as this requires, in the long run, the efforts of not just the writer, but of a community of persons who believe that the story of Robert F. Drinan, S.J., needs to be told. The hardest part was getting started, overcoming obstacles that had to do with sources, resources, a home base, and personal contacts. So first I must thank my two provincials of the New York province, Gerald J. "Jeff" Chojnacki, S.J., and his successor, David S. Ciancimino, S.J., who gave me the green light and supported me through the year; Donald J. Monan, S.J., provost of Boston College, where I lived, who first called my attention to the Boston College Drinan archives; John Langan, S.J., rector of the Georgetown Jesuit community; Jerome Grossman, one of those most responsible for Drinan's running for office; and Helen Drinan, Robert Drinan's sister-in-law, and her family. Sanford Katz, of the Boston College Law School, was exceptionally supportive. I owe much to the editors of *America* magazine, *Commonweal*, and the *National Catholic Reporter*, where Drinan published literally hundreds of articles, and which published notices of my project that brought forth much precious information. William Lanouette both encouraged this enterprise from the start, directed me to sources, and meticulously criticized the early draft.

Finally, I thank Fredric W. Nachbaur, director, and Eric Newman, managing editor, of Fordham University Press, whose meticulous attention and dedication made this book possible.

The following list is long. It includes scholars and writers who read the manuscript in earlier and later stages, librarians at Boston College, the Woodstock Collection at Georgetown, Weston Center, the New

England Province Archives at Holy Cross, and Hyde Park High School; Jesuits who gave me information, advice, and support and solved my computer problems; old friends and acquaintances of Drinan's who sent me stories of his good deeds; students who helped with research, scanned my lost chapter, and carried heavy boxes; old friends and family who cheered me up when I might have felt down. Those who gave me extended interviews are listed on another page. These others include Joseph Appleyard, S.J.; Shelley Barber; Jim Bernauer, S.J.; Jason Berry; Henry Bertels, S.J.; Nalida Besson; Ben Birnbaum; Jean Blake; Father Laurence Borgh; James Brennan; James Bresnehan, S.J.; Dominique Bruno; Jeremy Clarke, S.J.; Sister Brigid Clifford, S.C.N.; Ellen Clifford; Father John Connelly; Sister Miriam Corcoran, S.C.N.; James Cunningham; R. Emmett Curran; Thomas Curran; John Donovan; Kevin Doyle; Ann Drinan; Betsy Drinan; Michael J. Driscoll; Joseph Duffy, S.J.; Jim Dwyer; Harvey Egan, S.J.; Joe Ekwueme; Fred Enman, S.J.; James Fallon; Maurice J. Fitzgerald, D.M.D.; Joe Galbo; Gary Gilbert; Edward Glynn, S.J.; Ellen Griffin; Tom Fox; Yvette Hanley; Mary E. Hennig; Frank Herrmann, S.J.; James Hitchcock; Sarah Hogan; the John Holl family; David Hollenbach, S.J.; Leon Hooper, S.J.; David E. Horn; Alice Howe; George Hunt, S.J.; Pat Jordan; Gennie Q. Jota; Carolyn R. Jupiter-McIntosh; Robert Blair Kaiser; Gregory Kalscheur, S.J.; James Keane, S.J.; Bob Keck, S.J.; Charles Kelly; James R. Kelly; Paul Kelly; Philip Kiley, S.J.; Colin Kunzweiler; Wiliam Lanouette; Vincent A. Lapomarda, S.J.; Elizabeth Larter; Anne R. Laurance; William Lopa; Gayle D. Lynch; Arthur Madigan, S.J.; Tom Maier; Paul Mankowski, S.J.; Mark Massa, S.J.; John Mayer; William C. McFadden, S.J.; Michael McGrory; William McInnes, S.J.; Peter C. McKensie; William McLaughlin; Ms. Merriman; Tom Mooney; Gustavo Morello, S.J.; Dan Morrissey; John Ward Mullaney; Joseph Murphy; Bill Neenan, S.J.; Joseph Novak, S.J.; Edward T. Oakes, S.J.; Arthur Obermayer; Brendan O'Connell; Sister Elizabeth O'Hara, R.S.M.; Joseph A. O'Hare, S.J.; Claire O'Leary; Carol O'Neil; James O'Toole; Diana Owen, R.S.M.; John Padberg, S.J.; Oliver P. Rafferty, S.J.; Thomas Regan, S.J.; Peter Reichard; James B. Reuter, S.J.; Bill Richardson, S.J.; John H. Robinson; Ross Romero, S.J.; Paul Rothstein; Philip C. Rule, S.J.; José Luis S. Salazar, S.J.; Mary Scobbo; Walter Stimson; Hank

Stuever; Justine Sundaram; Edward Tallent; Vivien Tang; Jeff Thielman; William Tobin; Gilbert Wells; Paul Wilkes; Mike Wilson; James Woods, S.J.; Donna Worsham; and James Zhen.

Finally, while I was enjoying the community spirit and intellectual stimulation of St. Mary's Hall at Boston College, under the rectorship of T. Frank Kennedy, S.J., the year has sent me back and forth among my several homes, where being welcome has helped me carry on— beginning with my family in Trenton, then to Saint Peter's College, Spellman and Loyola halls at Fordham, then Georgetown to the three meetings of the National Seminar on Jesuit Higher Education whose members listened patiently to my progress and problems, and to the Jesuit villas at Chelsea between Sea Bright and Cohasset where I could relax, pray, and write.

Bob Drinan

Introduction

In 1964 Anthony J. LoFrisco was a young lawyer and a 1955 Fordham University graduate who considered himself a very conservative Republican, not someone who usually attended lectures and not someone for whom the civil rights movement was anything he could do more than read about. But when he saw an item in the *New York Law Journal* about an upcoming lecture by a Jesuit, he thought, because he knew Jesuits well from Fordham, he'd drop in. The speaker was Robert F. Drinan, S.J., the dean who was shaking up Boston College Law School and who was already making a name for himself as an advocate for civil rights. In an address to the Congress of Racial Equality at New York's Belmont Plaza Hotel on February 1, Drinan argued that a "strenuous and continuous campaign of non-violent direct action is the only way—at least the principal way—by which the American Negro can attain freedom."

LoFrisco left Drinan's lecture with one idea in his head: Blacks associated with the civil rights movement remained unjustly imprisoned in Mississippi and Louisiana for one simple reason—there were no lawyers to press for their release. Informed that no white lawyer would represent a black man, and there were so few black lawyers, LoFrisco felt that Northern lawyers had a duty to go south and help these innocent men in jail. LoFrisco, who had been married just over a year, told his wife, Eleanor, that he was going to Louisiana and Mississippi for a month with a team from the Lawyers Constitutional Defense Committee (LCDC), and she warmly gave her full support.

Late one night four of the volunteers arrived in a small Mississippi town where blacks had been rounded up and thrown in jail because, allegedly, a riot was "about to" break out. The local judge brushed off the New York lawyers because they were not members of the Mississippi bar and therefore not authorized to practice in the state, so the Brooklyn-born LoFrisco, whose father was a New York City cop, strolled over to the police station, tracked down the chief, and regaled him with stories about the tree that grows in Brooklyn and the Mafia "code of silence." Eventually, LoFrisco promised that he and his colleagues had not come to cause trouble, and that if the chief would just release the prisoners, he would not make a call for federal troops.

The chief stared at him in disbelief. "How could you get the federal troops here?"

"Maybe they'll come, and maybe not. But after I make the call it will be out of my hands."

The chief didn't like his tone and replied, "I think it would be better if you left."

LoFrisco apologized for upsetting him, but he told the chief that if the chief were in jail as those dozen men were and needed *his* help he would make the same effort to help the chief that he was making for those black men. Then he walked out and joined the black supporters of the prisoners in the town square.

Suddenly the group started cheering, the jail doors opened, and the twelve prisoners came running out.

How do we judge the impact of the life of one man on his time? Father Drinan never learned of Anthony LoFrisco's month as a civil rights lawyer, how his words had moved that young, smart Brooklyn lawyer to take some personal risks for racial justice. But this incident is part of the pattern—and the mystery—of Drinan's legacy.

In 1971, twenty-seven young Jesuit scholastics, students at St. Louis University in training to become priests, about one-third of their entire class, were conscience-stricken because, as members of a religious order, they were exempt from military conscription while their fellow students were being drafted to fight and perhaps die in Vietnam. How could they show their solidarity with those drafted and, at the same time, make a dramatic protest against what they viewed as an immoral war? Their answer, they thought, was Father Drinan, who had just been elected to Congress on a platform of opposition to the war. They would publicly turn in their draft cards, risk losing their exemptions, risk being drafted and sent to die. They would turn them in by sending them to Drinan.

It was perfectly logical for Bill McNichols, twenty-one years old, that a priest should be in politics. His father was the governor of New Mexico, and he had grown up to believe that Catholicism had to be expressed in one's public life. So he joined the young Jesuits and helped their leader write a protest letter, as well as mail their draft cards to Washington. Meanwhile, McNichols moved to Boston to study philosophy at Boston College and art at Boston University—in time to learn that he had been reclassified 1A. The New England provincial, Father William Guindon, the same religious superior who had backed Drinan's request to run for office, was committed to defending Bill with Harvard lawyers if he chose to appeal his status. But Bill drew a high lottery number, 287, which made his being drafted only a remote possibility. Meanwhile, though Drinan's mystique had inspired the gesture of the twenty-seven, he felt obliged to return the draft cards. He was a congressman now, obliged to uphold the law.

Robert Blair Kaiser first met Drinan in the fall of 1961 when he was *Time*'s correspondent in Boston and Father William Van Etten Casey, S.J., of Holy Cross College brought Drinan along as a dinner guest to Kaiser's apartment on Commonwealth Avenue. They stayed long after the dinner, talking "brilliantly" late into the night. The following year, Drinan was in Rome and popped in at the Kaiser apartment. Kaiser was then covering the Vatican Council—and had gained a reputation as a host, his Sunday night buffet suppers studded with Council "star" theologians and journalists like John Courtney Murray, S.J., and Gustav Weigel, S.J.; and Protestant scholars like Robert McAfee Brown and Albert Outler. Drinan had come to Rome to gain a feel for the Council, and when he entered the crowd of fifty guests, Kaiser's wife, Sue, planted a big kiss on his left cheek, leaving a big lipstick smear. This Drinan left untouched all night, to the delight of the other guests. "It was, maybe," said Kaiser, "a happy proof that a pretty young woman loved him, and that he was proud of himself that she did."

Drinan knew how to enter a room and become the immediate center of attention. He was also awkward in public, dyspeptic, irritated by anyone who bored him. Confronted with a question that made him uncomfortable, he cut things off, often with a curt reply.

In 1980, during his last year in Congress, Drinan spoke at Rockhurst College in Kansas City; and after the evening event, the Jesuit dean and a small group of faculty entertained him at a local pub where they could eat hamburgers and drink beer and continue the discussion. As the talk warmed up, the dean asked Drinan, known for his support of Israel, if he would also criticize Israel for its treatment of the Palestinians.

"Eat your hamburger," Drinan replied.

In the winter of 1985, Jeff Thielman, then a senior at Boston College, where he was student body president, was trying to decide whether to go to law school or to join the Jesuit International Volunteers in Peru. In Washington to see friends, Thielman, on the advice of Boston College president Don Monan, called on Drinan at Georgetown Law School for some advice. Drinan greeted him warmly, sizing him up with his "intense, steely eyes" as he sat down. He told Drinan his problem.

"Is that all you came to see me about?" asked Drinan. "This is an easy choice. You have your whole life to go to law school and practice law. . . . Go to Peru and don't look back." They talked for more than an hour. Drinan gave him a reading list, including Penny Lernoux's *Cry of the People*, and urged him to keep a journal and to write a book. Jesuits don't publish enough, he added. In his three years in Peru, Thielman built the Cristo Rey Center for the Working Child, which has helped more than 7,000 street children and their families during the past twenty-two years. With a Jesuit collaborator, he turned his journal into a book, *With the Poor in Peru*, and after several years with a law firm, he became a vice president of the Cristo Rey network of schools, which combines intellectual rigor and work experience for boys and girls in poor neighborhoods across the United States. In 1992, as Thielman received his diploma from Boston College Law School, Drinan, on the platform to accept an award, stood up and greeted him warmly, again urging him to "Keep up your good work."

Paul Rothstein first met Drinan when both were teaching at the University of Texas Law School. Rothstein had just finished postgraduate work at Oxford, and Drinan was a visiting professor on leave from his deanship at Boston College Law School. Rothstein, the younger man, saw his new friend as a "bigger-than-life presence, a whirlwind force for good," and he saw past the ever-present Roman collar to the charming, down-to-earth, insightful conversationalist. He also perceived, and had to think hard about, the contradiction between Drinan's liberal stance on abortion and his Catholic priesthood. Over the years, however, he came to understand how "this complex man reconciled (at least for himself) his faith with his politics."

Rothstein and Drinan were kindred spirits because Rothstein was helping with civil rights cases and with the state legislature to push the Texas criminal code into the twentieth century. In their late-night conversations, Drinan shared the two mainstays of his philosophy: "that in a democracy, faith must respect a wide range of legitimately divergent views, and that it is society's obligation to help all those who are less fortunate than we are."

Back in Boston, Drinan invited Rothstein to visit and teach at Boston College; arranged housing for him and his wife, Thelma, and their two children; and found clothing for them when their luggage was lost in transit. When the Rothsteins invited Drinan for dinner during the Passover–Easter holidays, the evening had its comic misadventures—the roast burned and the guest's dining room chair collapsed, dumping him on the floor—but the friendship thrived. In 1979–80 Congressman Drinan hired Rothstein to help the crime subcommittee of the House Judiciary Committee revise the federal criminal code. Rothstein briefed the committee once a week in sessions that put a provision where the law should be changed in the context of the scholarly writings, Senate version, current case law, other parts of the code, and the positions of interest groups like the American Civil Liberties Union, the Justice Department, public defenders, and trade organizations. And then he added his own personal recommendations. Again Rothstein gained deeper insights into Drinan's mind as a congressman: "One was that morality alone was ordinarily an insufficient basis for legislating.

Another was that he had a firm grasp of the practical realities of law enforcement."

Rothstein continued to observe Drinan's struggle to reconcile his belief that abortion was deeply wrong with his role as a legislator in a democracy, to his conclusion that "The wrongness of abortion had to be arrived at by the people's own moral and religious deliberations and free will." By the time Pope John Paul II ordered Drinan to leave Congress, Rothstein was a faculty member at the Georgetown Law Center and invited him to join the school.

The writer Paul Wilkes can't remember exactly when he and Drinan met, and they saw each other only a few times. But Drinan would call Wilkes every week or two, a bit longer when Drinan was overseas, and they would chat mostly about Washington politics. What struck Wilkes most about the calls, which usually came in the early evening, was that the caller was lonely. "This very famous man, House member, distinguished faculty member, author, was calling me, whom he hardly knew. He was never maudlin or whiny, always crisp, but every time I hung up—the calls would last 6 to 7 minutes, no more (two men with short attention spans at work)—I knew I had spoken with a man alone in his room, even with the Jesuit brotherhood, essentially alone with himself."

Robert Drinan was many men. A much longer book, or perhaps several books, may be needed to explain this complex character adequately. This is an introduction to the boy from the Boston town of Hyde Park who moved into the larger world of Boston College in 1938, then into many larger worlds—the Society of Jesus, the Church in Europe, religious journalism, law study in the nation's capital, teaching, academic administration, civil rights, Vietnam, Massachusetts politics, Congress, Central America, Soviet Russia, Southeast Asia, Latin America, book writing. And then twenty-six years of teaching law again, all the while advocating for disarmament and human rights.

Drinan was an idealist who decided in college that he wanted to be a Jesuit and learned that being a Jesuit means "to find God in all things." He was also ambitious and tried to answer the question of whether the priesthood and political power could be reconciled. He found an answer for himself, and for most voters, but not to the satisfaction of religious authorities. And along the way, he touched hundreds, perhaps thousands, of friends and strangers in more ways than he would ever know.

1

A New Beginning

Dottie Reichard, who had run the 1978 campaign, was worried. Something must be wrong, she thought. Drinan had seemed sad, silent, not himself all week. Over the years those close to him had noticed that when these moods came along it was because he was having trouble with the Vatican. Now he had called her twice when she was out. She returned the call. He was in his Waltham office, alone.

"Bad news," he said. "The pope says I can't run again."

Dottie drove to the office, where the two of them became very emotional and wept. But there was work to do. They assembled a core group of friends at Dottie's lovely stucco house on hilly Monadnock Street, just a ten-minute walk from the Boston College campus. Present were Drinan's sister-in-law, Helen; Jerome Grossman, who had gotten him into politics; Tom Kiley, a former Jesuit; John Marttila, campaign manager; and Robert and Ann Carleo. One of them suggested Drinan might leave the Jesuits as a means of remaining in Congress. Kiley said, "You don't know this man. He'll never leave."

Who could run in his place? They called John Kerry and Michael Dukakis and the mayor of Newton. David Frank, Drinan's press officer, heard the news on the radio and called his brother Barney. They called Judith Gilbert, a good friend of the family who had worked in his campaigns. Dottie's phone rang. It was a neighbor, a *New York Times* reporter, calling to warn her that a *Boston Globe* photographer was on the front lawn. How to escape?

While someone slipped out and moved Drinan's car to the next block, Dottie led Drinan through the basement and out the cellar door into the back yard, surrounded by one of those stone walls that New Englanders build to separate their property from their neighbors'. Drinan scrambled over the wall, headed for his car, and disappeared. He had a meeting the next day with the Jesuit provincial, the last of three who had fought the permission battle for him over the years.

Chestnut Hill, 2009

This is the school, these are the streets, trees, homes, and yards that brought Robert Drinan to manhood. These are the doors he knocked on asking for votes, and the men and women who sent him to Congress five times.

Today Boston College, six miles to the west of downtown Boston, spreads over 117 acres in the luxurious Newton–Chestnut Hill area and is still growing. It annexed the campus of the Newton College of the Sacred Heart in 1974, recently added the property across Commonwealth Avenue of the Boston archdiocesan headquarters, and merged with the Jesuit Weston School of Theology, which is moving from Cambridge to Newton. Furthermore, though facing neighborhood resistance, the college plans to add new dormitories so as to bring the students spread out into the neighborhood under the college's care and control. Its 9,000 undergraduates and 4,700 graduate students beat heavy competition to get in. Boston College competes with Georgetown, Fordham, and Notre Dame to be recognized as America's best Catholic university. More than 40,000 cheering alumni pack the campus football stadium for home games.

At the college's front door, Commonwealth Avenue, also known as Route 30, reaches from the Boston Common in the downtown heart of the city out west to the suburb of Weston, where all the New England Jesuits were trained. The slowly rising stretch from Centre Street to the college campus is the dreaded "Heartbreak Hill" of the Boston Marathon. Every morning, shortly after dawn, and on through the day, old men, Jesuit and lay, stooped and straight, young men in sweat shirts or shirtless, young women in shorts and halters with iPods plugged into their ears, and young, sweating, grim-faced men and women in gray shirts marked ARMY run. Some will run the Marathon itself; others are losing weight, waking up, sucking in the beautiful neighborhood.

1938

In September 1938, when young Bob Drinan arrived on that Boston College campus, in the lovely suburban enclave, there were only four buildings—Gasson Hall, Bapst Library, Devlin Hall, and St. Mary's Hall—and, like the community that embraced them, they were all beautiful. The campus, perched on what was called "the heights," was bounded by Commonwealth Avenue on the north and by one of the local reservoirs and Beacon Street on the south. Beacon, lined with mansions of red brick or stone, continued west to Newton's center and stretched back into downtown Boston as well. BRT streetcars began their half-hour run at the Brighton town line and slowly clanged up and down hilly Commonwealth Avenue into central Boston.

So it was—and is today—a neighborhood of hills, tangled, mysterious networks of tree-lined streets with names like Ivanhoe and Mandalay, where a walker might stumble upon a monument dedicated in 1910 by the Daughters of the American Revolution to a signer of the Declaration of Independence, Judge Roger Sherman, who was born a few feet away in 1721. Roads bordered by towering elms, oaks, maples, pines, and fat beeches with four-foot-diameter trunks lead the walker to hidden private schools, a golf course, little lakes, and, for the most part, old homes of the upper middle class and the rich. About 90 percent of the homes that envelop the campus today were there when Drinan arrived. Perhaps then, as today, a solitary swan, surrounded by ducks, would glide on the surface of the Chestnut Hill Reservoir. Perhaps then, as today, flocks of half a dozen wild turkeys paraded through yards, very much at home. Meanwhile, to the visitor who walks the streets, twelve-foot hedges, fences, and stone walls, as well as signs, declare: KEEP OUT.

Bob was by no means overwhelmed by this new environment. His older brother, Francis, was already a sophomore, and Bob had had it in his sights since high school; but it was a far cry from where he had been brought up.

Home

As a candidate for Congress in 1970, Father Robert F. Drinan, S.J., steadfastly refused to talk about his childhood. In a facetious dodge, he told a *Boston Globe* reporter, "I never grew up. I'm Peter Pan." Perhaps there were painful episodes he preferred to forget. Perhaps this reticence was an inherited family trait. Though the grandparents came from Ireland, the Drinans were not curious about their Irish heritage. At the same time, in campaign talks Drinan would occasionally tell audiences that society should return to the days when he'd grown up, when people took care of one another. There is no demonstrable reason why he was reluctant to talk about his past. Possibly, he thought it necessary to ignore it in order to rise above it. Only in the last years of his life, in his newspaper columns, did he open small windows to a private childhood and youth.

Michael and Catherine Drinan, Irish immigrants, had three children: James, William, and Honor. William had a son, also William, who became a religious brother. James married Anne Flanagan, and they had three children—Catherine, Francis, and Robert, the last of whom was born in Roslindale, where the family lived at 979 South Street, in 1920. A few years later the family moved to Hyde Park, described as a blue-collar town, today about a twenty-minute car drive south of the Newton area. James was a very conservative Republican, once relatively wealthy, described as a builder or a salesman, who had dreams of developing the open land around the house; but he lost everything in the Great Depression and later supported his family by measuring windows and doing various jobs.

Their home, No. 7 Fairview Avenue, which stands today, is a two-story, white-shingled eight-room New England structure that dates from the nineteenth century, one of only three houses on the little street, and that leads right from the Turtle Pond Parkway into Fairview Cemetery. James Drinan used his construction skills to add a small wing to the back of the house, and later occupants added a screened porch to the side. With the lawn in front and trees on the side and in back, it was large enough to give comfort and security to a family of five. Catherine, a musician, would later marry a German lawyer, Otfrid Brauns, and move to Frankfurt, where she taught retarded children; Francis, known as Frank, would go to medical school and raise a family of four daughters—Ann, Betsy, Diane, and Susan—and a son, Thomas; and Robert would join the Jesuits and later serve in Congress.

A cousin, Ted Griffiths, recalls that the families would visit each other about once a year. Bob, he says, "seemed to live in a world of his own" but, with his personality, could "take over a room." And, because the father was so strong a Republican, Ted and his family were cautioned not to bring up politics. The mother was "aristocratic" and formal, so much so that she referred to her husband consistently as "Mr. Drinan." Every visit included a musical interlude, in which Frank played the piano, Catherine the violin, and Bob the clarinet. Velia Di Cesare, who grew up in Hyde Park with the Drinans, took piano lessons from Catherine at the grand piano in the Drinan home. She remembers the father for his medium build and ruddy complexion, more English than Irish in body type, and as one who always wore a suit, argued conservative politics on the bus, and advised her to "put your money into land."

Velia says Bob as a young man, before he became a Jesuit, showed no interest in politics at all; but, once ordained, he urged friends to read Commonweal and the National Catholic Reporter and to go to night school at Boston College. When Velia's mother died in 1969, Drinan not only attended the funeral but went to her house to comfort her father, who was blind, and the boy who had been hired to guard the house while the family attended the funeral.

Contemporaries describe the Catholic culture of Depression-years Hyde Park as "poor" but add that they didn't "know" they were poor.

Their salaries as policemen or other public servants might have been $50 a week, but they were all "handy," knew how to build and paint, and they all supported one another.

Grammar School

The Drinans' parish church was St. Anne's, in Readville, a healthy walking distance from their home, but in those days walking to church and school was an accepted inconvenience. It was a basement church, a roof over a basement waiting for an upstairs to be built; but only in recent years has the wish been fulfilled.

The Sisters of Charity of Nazareth, Kentucky, who taught in St. Anne's for ninety years, were much to be admired, according to Frank Donovan, who lived in one of the other two houses on Fairview Avenue, the one down next to the Fairview Cemetery where his father was the caretaker, and who was a classmate of Bob's brother, Francis. But the sisters, like everyone else, were creatures of 1930s Catholicism with its endless list of dos and don'ts. One day the boys and girls on the block went off together to see Lon Chaney in the silent film *The Hunchback of Notre Dame*. When Donovan told his nun, who was also his piano teacher, what they had done, "the fur flew." That was a sin, she said. Victor Hugo's novel was on the church's Index of Forbidden Books; and Donovan had also sinned by taking an innocent young girl to see the movie with the group.

The school on Readville Street was about a ten-minute walk from the church, according to Sister Ann Susan Zilla, who attended in the 1940s. It was a wooden building, eventually replaced by houses, as it moved twice to other locations. With 300 students and about 30 in a classroom, the parish did not charge tuition; it met many expenses through the cooperative efforts of the parishioners. The girls who went to the high school would come back and take care of the church. Most of the men in the parish worked for Westinghouse, the railroad, or the Transit Authority.

The pastor, Father Regan, tall, skinny, and very strict, described as a "tough cookie," would visit classes regularly, single out students, and call on them to stand up and say whether they had gone to Mass the previous Sunday. The seven nuns who taught the boy Bob Drinan for six years, between his fifth and twelfth birthdays, lived in a 1922 convent across the street from the school.

Years later, when he spotted eleven nuns from their order at his lecture at the University of Kentucky in Lexington, he sang their praises in a *National Catholic Reporter* (*NCR*) column (November 25, 1988) as he remembered fondly those who had taught him. Sister Reparata (Hogarty), he said, "looked very old" when he encountered her in first grade. Their order's archives tell us she was forty-five at the time. Sister Mary Hortense appeared "middle-aged and nervous" as she prepared him for first communion. Sister Basil was "rigid and unyielding," while Sister Ruth Angela was "young and sweet." Sister Eulalia was "a bit severe," while Sister Rose Vincent, the superior, was "tall, elegant and stately." Sister Eloise, who taught him to play the piano and the clarinet, was a "lovely lady with a Southern accent."

Sister Mary Hortense, born in England in 1899, kept teaching until 1982 and died a year later. Sister Ruth Angela, after ten years of teaching at St. Anne's, got her bachelor of science degree in general education and a masters in religion education while teaching in four other states and died in 1998 at the age of ninety-one. Meanwhile, Drinan's sister, Catherine, as an alumna of St. Anne's, was chosen to crown the statue of the Blessed Virgin Mary in the May procession of 1939, while Bob was a freshman at Boston College. In the summer of 1953, following his ordination, the new Father Drinan returned to St. Anne's to say Mass for the sisters and join them for breakfast. Sister Basil, whom the young boy had found rigid and unyielding twenty years before, traveled more than an hour from Newburyport to be there.

When Drinan entered his seventies, encounters like the one with these nuns triggered both good and bad recollections which had been buried in the official silence that encased his childhood. In 1994 he met at one of his lectures the granddaughter of a childhood friend who broke open the memory of his first encounter with local bigotry, then wrote about it in *NCR* (October 21, 1994). When Drinan was ten, "Rita"—the childhood friend—invited the neighborhood boys and girls to her mother's birthday party. They were told to wait on the porch until given a name card, then enter singly to greet the mother. One boy, of Italian heritage, quickly perceived that he wasn't going to receive a card. This was an Irish-only–no-Italians-welcome celebration. At seventy-four, remembering this, Drinan realized he had suppressed the fact that Italians had seldom been allowed to become altar boys, that third-generation Irish were prejudiced against Italian immigrants.

Hyde Park High

After six years at St. Anne's and two at Rogers Middle School, Bob went on to the local public high school. Hyde Park High School, which traces its founding back to 1869, now in its third home, completed in 1928, occupies its own triangular-shaped city block, at the rotary of Metropolitan and Central avenues, a long walk north of the Drinan home. Considered one of the more elegant school buildings in the Greater Boston area, recently, with an emphasis on vocational education, it was reorganized from one school into three sub-schools specializing in engineering, social justice, and science and health. In the 1970s and 1980s Hyde Park as a community was radically transformed by an influx of African American families. As neighborhoods became integrated, many white families left town or sent their children to private schools to escape the court-ordered busing of the public schools. In 1974 and 1975 Hyde Park's racial situation erupted. Today there is scarcely a white face in the huge school, except for some of the teachers'.

But in 1934 everyone was white, as were most residents of Hyde Park and nearby Roslindale, Readville, and Mattapan. The visitor strides down long, broad, quiet, high-ceilinged hallways and tries to imagine the school's impact on Bob Drinan. His brother, Frank, was already there and writing sports stories for the *Postscript*. One of the school's most distinctive features was its military drill regiment, which had been winning championships in Boston's parade competitions for ten years and which included a drum and bugle band. Sports included football, track, baseball, and girls' basketball. But Bob, who was neither a military marcher nor an athlete—although he was a sports fan—

began feeling out those activities by which he would define himself in later years.

Hyde Park was known as a good school with good teachers. Bob waited a year before he joined any activities, then emphasized the intellectual organizations, like the French Club, of which he became vice president in his senior year, and the Classical Club, of which he became president. Then journalism, including the *Postscript*, where he was business manager; the *Courier*, a magazine that made its first appearance in his senior year; and the yearbook, *The Bluebook*. As a senior he also joined the Social Committee. Oddly, there is no evidence of his writing. He seemed satisfied to keep a low profile rather than to express himself in print, contributing as an editor or manager. But he was far from unnoticed by his peers.

When the graduating class of 1938 was polled on its "favorites," its members voted Bette Davis and Spencer Tracy their favorite movie stars, Tommy Dorsey their favorite bandleader, *Gone with the Wind* their favorite book, and Robert F. Drinan Most Likely to Succeed.

Under Bob's smiling senior portrait the yearbook listed his farewell quote as "What a shame B.C. isn't co-ed." In the judgment of one of his Boston College classmates, Bob's high school quip had to be a bit of kidding. In their group, he said, "We didn't have girlfriends. Most of us married the girl we took on our first date."

The documents from Hyde Park High School offer but one hint of the larger world into which their graduates were about to move. If Bob read his brother's 1936 yearbook he must have paused over two prize-wining essays by his peers on "Can America Remain Isolated from International Problems?" The "Yes" author, Aldona A. Burdulis, said that we should mind our own business. France and Germany have always been hostile to each other, "like a wife quarreling with her husband." The greatest reason for neutrality is that we have troubles of our own. "Why do we allow our fine country to be undermined, by gangsters, murderers, crooks, kidnappers, hit-and-run drivers, drunks, reds [Communists], dope-peddlers, divorcees, gigolos, crooked politicians, tired business men, lazy bums, swindlers and immoral men and women? . . . Why can't we shoot on sight these hateful criminals?"

In the "No" essay, Ruth Logan answered that the United States "[is] not a self-contained, economic unit, that no nation is or ever could be entirely independent in our modern world." We depend on world trade for our livelihood, Logan wrote. Recalling the nursery rhyme taught all children in the 1930s, she concluded that America must conquer its fear of engaging the world, that we cannot become like little Jack Horner who sat in the corner eating his pie.

In about twenty years, young Drinan would have answers for many of Burdulis's questions, once he decided what to do with his life.

Boston College

In June 1938 Joe Louis knocked out Max Schmeling in the first round at Yankee Stadium, a sign to those who interpret world news through sports events that American democracy had struck a blow against Adolf Hitler's schemes of world domination. But in July Hitler built a concentration camp at Mauthausen and in September the Munich agreement gave the Sudetenland to Germany. Meanwhile Italy revoked the citizenship of those more than 10,000 of its 44,000 Jews who had entered Italy since the end of World War I in 1919 and ordered them to leave. And the *Boston Globe* (September 1–3, 1938) published three analyses by Joseph Alsop and Robert Kintner on American foreign policy. President Franklin D. Roosevelt, wrote Alsop, was both strongly pro-British and pro-French and intensely anti-fascist. Furthermore, according to Alsop, FDR suffered from the same messianism that had inspired his predecessor Woodrow Wilson, being possessed of a mission to "make the world safe for democracy." At the same time, among the public, Alsop wrote, the commitment to isolationism was fading. Pacifism had lost influence and young liberals now talked of "collective security." What might check this rise of interventionism? Perhaps the Catholic Church, whose intense anti-Communism caused it to back Generalissimo Francisco Franco over the Loyalists in the Spanish Civil War, would openly oppose an alliance with the Soviet Union in a European conflict.

The campus spirit at Boston College when Bob arrived was optimistic. In 1913 the college had moved its operation from the deteriorating and congested downtown neighborhood of South End, where it had been established in Immaculate Conception Parish in 1864, to the rural area in Newton known as Chestnut Hill. The archdiocese of Boston had preceded the college by building St. John's Seminary and moving the archdiocesan headquarters onto a hilly estate at the intersection of Lake Street and Commonwealth Avenue in neighboring Brighton, just east of and across the street from Boston College's campus.

When Boston College's seventy-one seniors moved to the "heights" that March back in 1913, a single stately building, then called Recitation Hall, welcomed them. There the president who had bought the land and planned the buildings, Father Thomas I. Gasson, gathered them in the rotunda and told them that, in the paraphrase of the historian Thomas H. O'Connor, this edifice would be a "source of strength to the church, a source of joy to Boston Catholics, and a bulwark of service to the nation." The other buildings were St. Mary's Hall, the Jesuit residence (1917); Devlin Hall, a science building (1924); and the John Bapst, S.J., Library, named for the missionary who was tarred and feathered by a Know-Nothing mob in Maine in October 1854. In 1860 the Jesuits sent Bapst, who never fully recovered from the trauma of his lynching, to the new scholasticate, the College for Young Jesuits, in Boston. That little school became Boston College in 1863. The following year Bapst was named rector and president, and the first lay students were admitted.

In Myles Connolly's once-popular novel *Mr. Blue*, the young hero, a romantic Catholic who gives away a fortune in the 1920s, peers out over the Boston College campus from the Newton Reservoir across the street. The college "with its solid Gothic tower, stood black against the last smoking flame of a November sunset . . .". Blue says, "That up there is no mere group of college buildings; that up there is a hearth and home for a Lost Cause that is never lost, the citadel of a struggle that shall outlast the hill and the rocks it stands on."

These four buildings, plus a small Philomatheia Club house to the north and a little museum on Hammond Street to the south, framed by two athletic fields below, constituted the entire campus. By 1938 the prospering Boston College had added graduate schools of arts and sciences and education, the law school (1929), an Intown College (evening school), a nursing school, a graduate school of social work, and a school of business administration. Its academic jurisdiction also extended to the College of Liberal Arts in Lenox, which was the Jesuit novitiate and juniorate called Shadowbrook, and the School of Philosophy, Literature and Science and of Theology at Weston, the four-year seminary where Jesuits completed their course.

The Heights, the student newspaper, told its new readers that Boston College's educational standards "rank with the finest schools in the country" and that it had been called the "Oxford of America" for the structural beauty of its four Gothic buildings. The tower building, once known as Recitation Hall and today as Gasson Hall, the paper wrote, was best seen from the other side of the reservoir below. In the rotunda, murals and statues honor Jesuit saints, and a statue of St. Michael the Archangel conquers Lucifer in the soft light filtered through the stained-glass windows. The student chapel in St. Mary's Hall has the air of a small medieval church; the main hall in the library doubles as an assembly room and theater. And the reception room displays paintings by Benjamin West, Guido Reni, and George Inness. A feature of the orientation schedule was free time to simply wander for a week and explore the beautiful buildings. What the campus lacked, however, was a formal dining room. At noon the students, all commuters, gathered, sitting or standing, in a big room in the basement of Recitation Hall and ate the peanut butter and jelly sandwiches they had brought from home.

To be admitted, freshmen took an entrance exam based on the syllabi of all the Jesuit high schools in the country. This included identifying selected passages from English, Greek, and Latin literature, including, for example, *Hamlet,* Gray's "Elegy in a Country Church Yard," Webster's "First Bunker Hill Oration," Dickens's *David Copperfield*, Bryant's "Thanatopsis," Caesar's *De Bello Gallico*, Cicero's "Orations against Cataline," Xenophon's *Anabasis*, and Homer's *Iliad.* Standard high school reading in the 1930s, some of these showed up in the Jesuit seminary courses in the 1950s, and today they gather dust on library shelves.

Partly because of the opening of the new business school, enrollment was up to 1,374, including 317 seniors, 356 juniors, 328 sophomores, and 373 freshmen. Of those new freshmen, 276 would graduate and two would die. The class would shrink not just through academic attrition but because, foreseeing the war, students began leaving to join the Army Air Corps and Navy rather than accept possible slaughter as infantrymen. The majority sought the bachelor of arts degree, though interest in "more practical studies" like social sciences, education, and history was rising. The days ahead brought the outdoor Mass of the Holy Spirit, a three-day religious retreat, and the first home football games.

In reality, once a freshman started classes, how great was the challenge? It depended where he came from. If he came from Boston College High School or Boston Latin School, he may have been disappointed. Those students, it is said, walked the corridors talking Greek and Latin to one another as if they were their native languages. Paul Kelly, who graduated from Boston Latin School at sixteen in 1945 and arrived at Boston College a few years behind the Drinans, found that his first two years at Boston College repeated what he had covered at Boston Latin, where he had gotten low grades and flunked at least one course a semester. At Boston College the courses were all easy; they were taught mostly by Jesuits who just stood there and lectured and, contrary to the Jesuit teaching handbook, the *Ratio Studiorum*, provoked no class discussion. Still, Kelly earned grades in the high 90s and joined the Society of Jesus when he graduated.

Bob Drinan, A.B. English major in honors courses, paid his $280 annual tuition and fees and adapted to a daily almost-two-hours-each-way commute in which he took a trolley from Hyde Park and transferred at Forest Park to another trolley that churned slowly west on Commonwealth Avenue to Lake Street, the end of the line. In his first semester he reported to five courses a week—English, Latin, Greek, history, and religion—and the same for the second semester. The religion syllabus included the divinity of Christ, the Church, existence of God, creation, Redemption, grace actual and sanctifying, the commandments, and sacraments.

Of the roughly fifty Jesuit faculty only a dozen had Ph.D.s, and among the fifty-seven laymen, including fellows and tutors, eleven. Boston College had endured an embarrassing controversy at the turn of the century when Harvard Law School declined to accept graduates from Jesuit colleges; this was not anti-Catholicism, Harvard said, it was just that the standard—and "antiquated"—Jesuit curriculum, particularly in science and mathematics, did not produce the broadly educated person Harvard required. Jesuit philosophy Professor Timothy Brosnahan, formerly of Boston College and then of Woodstock Theology School in Maryland, joined Harvard President Charles William Eliot in a duel of magazine articles. In time the Jesuit-school graduates gained entrance to Harvard Law; but the episode highlighted the deficiencies in the Jesuit system, particularly the prevalent notion that the Society's course of seminary studies, with its three years in philosophy and four years of theology, adequately prepared a man to teach at a university in the twentieth century. In effect, the Jesuits, including those at Boston College, were teachers but not publishing scholars in the full sense of the word.

The Report of the Commission on Higher Studies of the American Assistancy of the Society of Jesus, 1931–1932, also known as the Macelwane Report, by a committee of six headed by Father James Macelwane of St. Louis University compared the standards of Jesuit institutions of higher learning with those of other secular and Catholic colleges and universities and found the Jesuit schools wanting. The other schools hired the best faculty, who researched, wrote, and published; and they had well-organized procedures and trained leaders. Only 9 percent of 621 Jesuits surveyed had Ph.D.s and published research. The committee recommended that all Jesuits get Ph.D.s and that admission standards be tightened; Jesuit institutions had too many "pious but useless men." All scholastics should be at or near universities with graduate programs. Thirty years would pass before these ideas took hold. The Society's bureaucracy would move slowly while Drinan was still in training, but he would have to find ways to compensate for the institutional foot dragging.

Drinan limited his freshman activities to three—the sodality (which just about everyone joined), which enriches student piety usually through Marian devotions and guest speakers; the Marquette Debating Society, which was for underclassmen; and the band, which gave him a chance to use the clarinet lessons Sister Eloise had given him at St. Anne's and the opportunity to play the clarinet at football games. He also joined the staff of *The Heights*, but whatever his contribution, he got neither a byline nor a masthead spot in his first year.

Viewed through the lens of the student publications, the out-of-class intellectual life was potentially rich. *The Heights* on October 10, 1938, ran two essays debating the status of the Sudeten struggle. One writer, moved by a lecture by Father J. M. X. Murphy, sympathized not with the Czechs but with the Germans, Poles, and Hungarians under Czech domination. The other concluded that the adage "The sun never sets on the British Empire" was no longer true—Germany, under Hitler, would consume all of Europe. Meanwhile, the Fulton Debating Society, for the juniors and seniors, concluded that Hitler wasn't so bad; just as Texas and California became part of the United States, so would Sudetenland become part of Germany.

Throughout the four years Drinan spent at Boston College, three motifs dominated the pages of *The Heights*, and, to a lesser extent, those of the *Stylus,* the literary magazine. The first was football. In the 1930s football was the fire and the glue, the public reputation and the basis of community, in several of the Catholic and Jesuit universities. Notre Dame had Knute Rockne, Fordham had Vince Lombardi, and Boston College briefly acquired Frank Leahy, who had come from Notre Dame through Fordham. At Boston College the B.C.–Holy Cross game was the biggest event of the year, and in Drinan's sophomore year the team went to the Cotton Bowl in Texas.

The second, along with reports on dances and debates, was the continuing reinforcement of the Catholic culture that permeated the students' daily lives. Religion courses were ranked as the easiest; and, until reforms following the Second Vatican Council in the early 1960s, when the influence of modern scripture scholarship and of the new theology developed in France and Germany took hold, Jesuit colleges passed along the faith through exercises and activities outside the classroom.

The third theme often blended with the second. Deep down in the student collective consciousness was the realization that their generation might well go to war. In various ways they fought off that awareness, and popular culture gave avenues for escape. The popular musical of Bob's first semester was Nelson Eddy and Jeanette MacDonald's Technicolor version of Victor Herbert's *Sweethearts*. Bing Crosby was the students' most popular singer and "swingin'" Sammy Kaye's the favorite band. Fred Allen, their most popular comedian, was the biggest distraction from their Sunday night homework. But the looming war and the issues it raised wouldn't go away.

The October 1938 *Stylus*, in anticipation of the 1940 presidential election, polled the entire senior class on whether they would support a Roosevelt third term, whether they would vote for another New Deal candidate, and whether the United States should unite with England and France in a common front against Germany, Italy, and Japan. They found that 80.5 percent of the class opposed a third term for FDR, and 56.2 percent would vote against any New Deal Democrat who ran in his place. On joining with the other democracies, the overwhelming majority, 93 percent, said no. Why? Aiding the British would make the British "more cocky" was among the answers, along with We have little in common with France and England, and We have enough troubles at home. A fourth question asked about the chief fault in the American economic system. A third of the respondents blamed low wages and resultant low buying power.

Today historians credit FDR with successfully leading the country out of the Great Depression. The young men who answered the survey had little money; they had come from towns like Hyde Park where the Depression had hit hard. Drinan's classmate Joe Nolan recalls that Bob had a great deal of nervous energy and was always alert, upbeat, and exciting with ideas; but his working-class origins showed. He always wore the same double-breasted brown suit. But this was the status of nearly all the Boston College boys in those years. Overwhelmingly Irish—there were seven Sullivans in the class—they had imbibed a deep hatred of England and did not see FDR as their savior. The

America First Committee of 1940–41, which opposed aiding the Allies, and the Lend-Lease Act would gain a following on the campus; and Charles Lindbergh, one of the Boston College boys' icons, had a strong campus following. Drinan's friend Robert F. Muse joined the America Firsters and Bob Drinan sympathized with some of their ideas, but he did not join.

Meanwhile, the religious and quasi-political aspects of student activities sometimes overlapped. The sodality, for example, established committees that systematically examined the Boston newspapers for evidence of propaganda against the Catholic Church or "unfavorable attitudes" toward Catholics. The press, said a *Heights* writer, gave favorable coverage to Jews persecuted in Germany but passed over the persecution of Catholics in Spain and Russia.

In early January 1939, Catherine Baroness de Hueck spoke on campus. She had grown up associating with the Russian royalty until driven out as a refugee following the Communist revolution, fled to Canada, and established a series of centers called Friendship House, dedicated to religious devotion and social reform. She traveled to Jesuit campuses delivering her spiritual and political message. Her American Friendship House was in New York City, in Harlem; and at Fordham and Georgetown she did not hesitate to scold the Jesuit fathers whom she saw as slow in integrating their campuses. "A prayer-life is the basis of an active life," she told her Boston College audience. Drinan, whether he was present or not—and most likely he was—would make the adage his own.

The same week the famous British author Father Owen Francis Dudley, puffing angry clouds of tobacco smoke from the pipe clenched in his teeth, warned the students against the Communists and the Jews. Neville Chamberlain was a true leader of the English people, he said; Anthony Eden was a creature of the "Jewish-controlled press." Americans say they would never submit to a dictator, he told the boys, but they were already controlled by the so-called Jewish press (*Heights,* January 6, 1939).

In April, as if in response, the Jewish law students in the Boston College Law School Evening Division formally answered Cardinal William O'Connell's plea for support for European Catholics displaced by the war by donating to his cause. "We affirm our faith in the Father-hood of God and the brotherhood of man," they said, "and we make this gift as brothers to aid a common cause." A *Heights* editorial on April 21 answered, "In these words they express the spirit of Christian charity and Americanism."

As the year ended, *The Heights* reported that Muse, the popular debater and hockey star, had been elected the next year's president of the Marquette Debating Society and that his friend Robert F. Drinan, who had been an active member of Marquette and of *The Heights*, had been named secretary. Because they had read the book in high school, the two had gone to see *Gone with the Wind* together. In the last scene, when Rhett Butler (Clark Gable) delivers to the whining, clinging Scar-lett O'Hara (Vivien Leigh) the famous line "Frankly, my dear, I don't give a damn!" and walks out of Tara, the startled freshmen turned to each other and exclaimed, "He *said* it!" With the use of the word "damn," cinema had taken a bold risk, and the integrity of the book had been preserved.

Father Shea

For Drinan, the most memorable experience during sophomore year was his encountering Richard Gregory Shea, S.J., the English teacher who, in his Bapst Hall classroom, put all his energies into teaching his pupils—who included Bob's friend and *Stylus* writer Joe Nolan—the fundamentals of clear English prose. Shea made them write every day "two shorts and a long," referring to paragraph lengths. Shea would take the essays home and grade them, returning them not always the next day, but inevitably with a huge pile of papers that he could barely carry, all marked up with corrections.

Shea taught sophomore English, which was then called Rhetoric, and Latin in the honors program. Drinan remembered him as a "relent-less workhorse" who tried to form all his students in the same mold. He assigned two or three themes a week, with much memorizing of passages from prose and poetry and instant class translations of Latin passages. Shea demanded grammatical correctness—tight prose and commas in all the right places.

In an article in *Boston College Magazine* following Shea's death in 1984, Drinan remembers Shea tracking his writing in *The Heights*, his careless reference to a certain Catholic women's college as "exclusive," without justifying that adjective. An examination of *The Heights* from 1938 to 1942 shows no Drinan bylines; Shea was probably referring to articles for which Bob, as a copy editor, was responsible. Shea tracked Drinan's debating skills as moderator of the Marquette Debating Society. Like any college boy, Drinan did not always welcome these criticisms, but also like many college students, he was grateful for them many years later.

Drinan's comments on Shea might apply to other Jesuit professors as well:

> Fr. Shea was not a scholar or an intellectual. He was a priest trained in the long Jesuit course who did not need a graduate degree to be professional and an expert at what he did. He loved the writings of Cardinal Newman, G. K. Chesterton, Francis Thompson and Daniel Webster; as a result, he communicated that enthusiasm to his class. But his emphasis was on the rhythm and the rhetoric, not on the historic meaning of the work. He gave the course in English in order to teach us how to write. If I had not had that course I am not certain that I would ever have learned how to structure sentences, develop paragraphs and put together articles and books.

The writer Drinan remembers for having influenced him the most was John Henry Newman. He learned to recite Newman's 1842 sermon "Second Spring," on the restoration of the Catholic hierarchy in England, and he read his *Apologia Pro Vita Sua* and *Idea of a University*. Many years later, as a lecturer at Oxford, Drinan visited Newman's home and his grave (*NCR*, February 21, 2001).

Drinan wrote the Shea article five years after leaving Congress, during years when he was finding his voice again, recovering through his writing the public platform he had lost in leaving Capitol Hill. But as a young college writer, he seems to have done most of his writing for class and as a rewrite editor, cleaning up the prose of others, for *The Heights*.

Joe Nolan recalls that another extracurricular activity which must have been most formative in Drinan's world outlook was the informal seminar conducted every other Friday at the home of Lee Bowen, the outstanding medieval historian, trained at Johns Hopkins. There they drank beer and read a book on the medieval guilds that tended to disparage modern technology. Their talks led them into a critique of capitalism and contemporary economic issues, including discussions on functionalism, the sociological theory that analyzes society in terms of how each institution functions to achieve the community's common goals. In the yearbook, the class historian quipped that what distinguished Drinan from his contemporaries was his being the most outstanding "functionalist." This, says Nolan, was most likely an "in-joke" reference to Bowen's influence on Drinan.

In Drinan's sophomore year, a *Heights* editorial reminded the paper's readers that the second week of November 1939 was Catholic Book Week. Catholic writers—like Christopher Dawson, Owen Francis Dudley, and Jacques Maritain—were said to offer "true answers" for problems of the day, unlike the popular writers of the day—Will Durant, Margaret Mitchell, and John Steinbeck.

The following week Father Daniel Lord, S.J., perhaps the best-known Jesuit in America—renowned for revitalizing the sodality of the Blessed Virgin Mary movement by publishing a flood of books and pamphlets with catchy titles like *Murder in the Classroom* and *Has Life Any Meaning?*—brought his traveling road show to Boston College for an eight-college sodalist convention. Lord's method was to write musicals and stage them with student casts. He trained thousands of priests and nuns at Summer Schools of Catholic Action and published a sodality magazine, *The Queen's Work*. Rather than argue about racial equality, he simply put black as well as white faces on his stage. If asked about the war, he said he could never kill anyone and would refuse to serve. Influential in Hollywood, he advised Cecil B. DeMille on *King of Kings* and wrote the first version of the Motion Picture Code. With his Boston College group he sat down at the keyboard and played popular songs they could all sing. Then, as the crowd relaxed, they opened up to talk. A lot of his routine was simple catechism and his brand of common sense. So as students stood up and revealed that for some time they had been harboring "false opinions," he corrected them kindly.

On Friday, December 1, 1939, *The Heights* announced on page one that "The biggest day of the year is here." The next day Boston College, bragging a record of eight wins and one loss, would play Holy Cross in Fenway Park, and the winner would receive a bowl game bid. The night before the game, a band of Boston College students slipped onto the Holy Cross campus and raised the Boston College maroon-and-gold flag over its football field.

The whole issue talked sports, and among the players profiled was Lou Montgomery, the "Brockton Flash," from Roxbury, one of the two black students in the class of 1941. The other, Cornelius Vincent, also from Roxbury, a graduate of Boston Latin School, played the trumpet in the band, excelled in public speaking, and was considered Boston College's "most traveled" student. During summers he took jobs as mess or cabin boy on ocean liners. Although he was a year ahead of Drinan, they must have known each other as members of the band; he was Drinan's first black schoolmate. Perhaps his experiences with these two young men influenced Drinan's eventual devotion of much of his life to the civil rights cause.

Before a crowd of 45,000, Boston College beat Holy Cross 14–0 and won a trip to the Cotton Bowl in Dallas, Texas. The 5'8", 150-pound Montgomery, known as "Dynamite Lou" and "Hula Lou" for his ability to slip through a wave of opponents, was the first black man to wear a Boston College football uniform. At that time many Southern schools had in their contracts a "Jim Crow" clause that prohibited black team members from playing either in away games in the South or in home games against Southern teams. Boston College went along. A Jesuit explained this policy to appalled students as their "tradition." As a result, Lou Montgomery couldn't play against Florida in Fenway Park, against Auburn in Fenway, against Clemson at the Cotton Bowl in Dallas, and at the January 1, 1940, Sugar Bowl against Tennessee in New Orleans. Montgomery told a *Boston Magazine* sportswriter in 1987, "Some of the guys didn't take it well. They talked about striking or going up to the game and at the last minute saying 'If he don't play, we don't play.' But when they asked me, I said no."

A crowd of more than 5,000 gathered at South Station to cheer for the team leaving for the Cotton Bowl. The next day the *Boston Globe* reported, "The loudest cheers were sounded for Little Lou Montgomery, the brilliant Negro halfback, who voluntarily withdrew from the trip in order not to embarrass Boston College or himself." Somehow *The Heights* and the *Sub Turri,* the yearbook, did not write about Lou's story.

Asked about his greatest disappointment as an undergraduate in an interview for *Boston College Magazine* in 1982 (Summer), Drinan the clarinetist recalled that the band didn't go to the Sugar Bowl game in 1941.

1940

In February 1940 the war was back on the editorial page, with an emphasis on war's "tragedy," as expressed in the verse of Rupert Brooke and other World War I poets. The writer mourned lost men who "poured out the red sweet wine of Youth," and the "betrayal of the ideals of Versailles in the ignominious terms of surrender." In April, Boston College president and rector William J. Murphy, S.J., delivered a long address at a communion breakfast that was reprinted in *Vital Speeches.* The "common schools," he said, had failed to teach morality to young people. The new field of "social sciences seeks its meaning it knows not where," he continued, adding that education without religion is knowledge without meaning.

At the end of Bob's sophomore year, 1940, his brother, Frank, graduated. Bob had followed his brother's footsteps in two activities. Both gave priority to the sodality, whose purpose was the spiritual development of its members, and both worked for *The Heights*, although Frank, for his last two years, focused heavily on his pre-med program. The yearbook quipped, "It really is a treat to see his 6′3″ frame curled around a microscope." Frank had also been named to the elite Cross and Crown, the society for those most outstanding in both academics and service. For Bob that remained something to reach for.

Junior year opened with a letter from the dean, John J. Long, S.J., warning the students that "The world around us stands in the path of a huge avalanche of human sorrow, tears, and dread . . . cynicism, and despair." The answer for this world, according to Long, was in the "virtue most characteristic of Christianity," the virtue of restraint. By restraint he did not mean passivity but the "VIA MEDIA" between extremes. The alternative, he concluded, was the "VIA PERDITIONIS" (*Heights*, September 27, 1940).

The same issue, which listed Drinan on the masthead as a special editor, noted that 1940 was the 400th anniversary of the Society of Jesus with an editorial that called attention to the martyrdom of Father Miguel Pro in Mexico in 1927 and the deaths of many Jesuits in the recent Spanish Civil War. Editorials the following month promoted the sodality and the annual October retreat. On November 15 the editorial writer reminded students that the football team started every Saturday with Mass and communion to pray for victory and protect them from injury. So far, the prayers seemed to be working. A December 6 editorial sang the praises of scholastic philosophy, "the only refuge of the modern wanderer in a sea of despairing thought." In December, with Drinan shifted from special editor to the rewrite staff, the editorials decried the proliferation of "indecent literature" on Boston magazine racks and the poor student attendance at First Friday devotions.

This was also the year for Bob to plunge into the philosophy requirements, including a philosophy oral exam, followed by senior year classes on medieval and modern Catholic literature—where he earned his highest grades. Senior year would deal with the special ethics issues—socialism, divorce, education, civil society, and war—on which he would build his future.

On October 28, 1940, Franklin D. Roosevelt, who was in the midst of a hard campaign against Wendell Willkie for a third term and was annoyed that Fordham's president, Robert I. Gannon, S.J., had invited Willkie to a Fordham football game, got himself invited to the Bronx campus, as commander in chief of the armed forces, to review the Fordham ROTC. After some joshing with Gannon—who, FDR knew, hated him—the president got serious in his address to the crowd. He had been on the phone all day with the War Department and had decided to order universal conscription the next day. He described his review of the ROTC to the young men before him as a "muster," a word that goes back to colonial days, "when every able bodied man had the obligation to serve his community and his country in case of attack." The visit lasted only as long as it took for FDR's car to drive up the elm-lined path to the Edwards Parade ground in front of the soaring Gothic tower that crowns Keating Hall to give his short talk and drive off. But it was a jolt of realism to young men who had many less serious things on their minds.

At Boston College, by January 10, 1941, although the rumor mill had buzzed that Coach Leahy was looking for a new home, the editorial page returned to criticizing Great Britain, which was, it said, "not a democracy, but an Autocracy, with a history of aggression in India, Ireland, Africa and North America." America, it concluded, "has a democracy that has been wrought in the 'toil and sweat, blood and tears' of self-sacrificing patriots." It is not clear whether the writer knew he was quoting Winston Churchill.

In an exceptional move, the editors gave Al Arsenault, their sports columnist, a full page and a half over two issues to spell out what he considered the "crisis in Catholic education": the move from a "cultural" program based solely on the liberal arts and built around the emphasis on scholastic philosophy, which includes religion, to specialization. He recalled Father Timothy Brosnahan's debate with Charles W. Eliot, president of Harvard and champion of the elective system, as the "final cry of despair" against the modern trend that no longer "develops leaders from the best men" but, with its business and technical schools, just molds businessmen. Arsenault called upon Catholic educators to convince students that specialization would never make a true leader of men and upon students to "write, talk, and argue to the best of their abilities." The editors of the Georgetown *Hoya* were so impressed with Arsenault's polemic that they reprinted it. Nevertheless, to a scale that a student in the 1940s could never foresee, government money made available to American universities after World War II and the huge growth of the college-age population accelerated the spread of specialized, commercial, professional training until the liberal arts, particularly philosophy, were all but marginalized to the brink of extinction.

Meanwhile, the anti-Britain editorials continued, Frank Leahy signed a contract for five years (up to that time the longest granted by Boston College), and stories began to appear about alumni, like John McLaughlin, '40, on his way to advanced flight training at Pensacola. In February 1941 the paper asked students, "Do you think college students should be deferred from Army service until they finish school?" Some suggested that the unemployed be drafted first, others that the students should go now because they needed the time to learn to fight well. Bob Drinan replied, "No! Because it [military service] looks like the only job there will be after college." The answer, like his high school yearbook quip, seems facetious, perhaps a comic mask for his own plans, which were beginning to form. When the dean's list was published in March, he had received third honors for his 87.5 grade point average. Although he had entered into honors classes, this is the first indication of his average going above the required 84.5. His singular intellectual accomplishment of the year had been, with his friend Frank Nicholson, to direct discussion sponsored by the philosophy academy of St. Thomas Aquinas' *Summa Contra Gentiles*.

The *Heights* anti-war editorial of March 14 was particularly harsh. H.R. (House Resolution) 1776, the Lend-Lease bill, committed America to "all-out aid to Britain" and "sold the American public down the river." FDR, with his "intoxicating, soothing tones," had become a "dictator." A letter on March 21 chided the editor for the editorial's insulting language that "would disgrace even [William Randolph] Hearst." (The four student signers included a "Robert A. Drinan." Our subject is Robert F.; no Robert A. has been found.) The last editorial of the year, entitled "America First," imagines a future in which England has fallen and the German Reich rules Europe. All the more reason to stop aiding Britain right now and fortify our shores against invasion, it argued. In the yearbook, the senior class voted "Li'l Abner" its favorite comic strip, Camels its favorite cigarette, "We're in the Army Now" its favorite song, and Charles A. Lindbergh its Man of the Year.

By September 1941 Father Anthony G. Carroll, chemistry professor, had joined the Army as a chaplain, the largest class in history had enrolled, and Robert F. Drinan, now in his senior year, was among the seniors selected for the Order of the Cross and Crown. Chosen by the dean, they served as ushers for concerts and on the committee to plan the annual Fathers' Day. In November he joined the yearbook as managing editor. Five former members of the class of '42 posed on page one in their Navy uniforms. Justin McGowan, football and track star, was drafted. The usual half-page ad for Camel cigarettes featured an endorsement from the man who tested the Army's tanks: He crashes the M-3 into a crater and through a brick wall, then feels like relaxing with a Camel. "They're EXTRA MILD and have FLAVOR." The soldiers tell him, "That's the old army spirit."

Wartime

On December 11, four days after the attack on Pearl Harbor, President Murphy called the entire student body together, told them to remain calm and carry on with their studies, then formed a series of committees to help students deal with the impact of the war—conscription, civilian defense, and changes in the curriculum. Freshmen were to be allowed to finish in three years. There were no midterm exams or senior theses. The classics were replaced by science courses. As a large number of students were entering officer training, they needed courses in navigation, nautical astronomy, radio communications, Morse code, aeronautics, and spherical trigonometry. Some wondered whether the campus would be transformed into a training camp, as it had been during World War I, governed by military regulations and law. In those days 800 student-soldiers were in uniform, and everyone lived in barracks, learned drill, and went to daily Mass. But in the end, none of them had gone to war.

On December 12, 1941, *The Heights* had no gripes. "There is no point in bemoaning the whole affair," the editorial said. Once we know the war is just, it goes on, "we cannot allow ourselves to be diverted by recoiling from the brutality of war." At the same time, as if they foresaw Hiroshima and Nagasaki, they added, "There are military objectives in Japan. It is not necessary that civilians be deliberately bombed."

In a December 24, 1992, Christmas reminiscence in the *Boston Globe*, Drinan recalled the 1941 Christmas Midnight Mass, when the Drinan family knew that Frank would probably be drafted and that Bob was considering the priesthood. They were relieved that their authoritarian pastor would not be giving his usual twenty-five-minute sermon. Rather, a new young priest from Latin America spoke briefly and held their attention. He concluded, "God is calling us to sacrifice and to suffer."

In response to the crisis, Boston College shortened its academic year, cut down philosophy requirements, and moved the yearbook deadline up so that the books would be available before graduation, knowing that by graduation many seniors would be gone. But when the noted English author Martin D'Arcy, S.J., arrived in January and conducted a roundtable discussion with the members of the Cross and Crown, including Drinan, he discussed the war aims in terms of defeating Japan. A February 12 editorial asserted that Christ "taught vigorous and cheerful defense of the institutions that ensure that men shall be able to utilize their freedom and opportunities for salvation." But until the end of the year the paper's headlines were a mix of prom plans and stories about both Jesuits and students leaving Boston College to serve as chaplains or to fight, usually in the Navy or Army Air Corps.

By May 1942 Hitler had invaded Poland, Denmark, and Norway and marched into Paris and had been bombing London since the previous summer. In August Roosevelt and Churchill had met on a warship in the Atlantic and announced the Atlantic Charter. In September Hitler ordered all Jews to wear a yellow star. And in January 1943 the first American forces had arrived in Great Britain. This was a day the editorial writers of *The Heights* in their wildest dreams had never envisioned. They did not discuss it. They simply saw themselves in a war in which God was on America's side and that must be won.

The Invitation

Bob Drinan found himself at a crossroads. Since Pearl Harbor, the now-250 members of his senior class had been scrambling to enter military officer recruitment programs, mostly to escape being drafted into the infantry. He himself had in his pocket an application to a naval officer program. He had also been accepted to the Maryknoll Order, an association of missionary secular priests who had spread their work to Latin America and China and publicized it through the lively and idealistic *Maryknoll Magazine*, which was widely read in Catholic families. It was a way of life with a powerful attraction to religious young men who thought big.

Bob had never been a friend of Father Shea, whose rigor and discipline made him more the object of awe than a pal to students. But in March he made an appointment to meet Shea in one of the parlors that line the long corridor inside the front door of St. Mary's Hall. He explained his alternatives to Shea, who listened, then, without arguing against his tentative Maryknoll decision, said, "I would be honored as a Jesuit if you were to enter the Society of Jesus. You have talents which could benefit the Church if you became a Jesuit. I want to invite you to join."

It seems to have been a bold move on Shea's part, but these invitations were very much the custom of the Society in that generation. Teaching high school during regency, the three-year period of training between philosophy and theology, the Jesuits kept alert for young men they might recruit and, if they did not enter the Society after high school, wrote them letters while they were in college, reminding them that God was calling them and they should take up their cross. Also during college, a priest who heard the confession of a young man might invite him to talk about his vocation after the sacrament. Drinan did not consider Shea's approach a recruitment or sales pitch, "just three sentences enunciated by Fr. Shea." Shea assured him that he should feel no obligation to serve in the military before entering the seminary. Unbeknownst to Bob, Shea himself, like several other Jesuits on the faculty, was planning to enter the service as a chaplain.

The academic year rushed to a close. The yearbook listed the usual favorites: song, "Deep in the Heart of Texas"; films, *How Green Was My Valley* and *They Died with Their Boots On*; Man of the Year, General Douglas MacArthur; and Woman of the Year, Madame Chiang Kai-shek. The book published twenty-three pictures of classmates already in uniform, some officers and overseas, and of two of the Jesuits who had worked at Boston College and were now on active service. One listed but not pictured was Joseph T. O'Callaghan, S.J., who had been a track and tennis star at Boston College and a teacher at Holy Cross. He had dropped out of graduate studies in mathematics at Georgetown the year before Pearl Harbor to become a Navy chaplain. In 1945, on the *U.S.S. Franklin*, he was awarded the Congressional Medal of Honor for his heroic leadership fighting fires and leading men to safety when Japanese bombers almost sank their ship.

The group picture of the forty-two classmates who had entered the seminary was unusually crowded. It was bandied about that a large number of them had acquired their vocations after Pearl Harbor, but that this did not apply to the two, Frank Nicholson and Robert Drinan, who were headed for the Jesuit novitiate at Shadowbrook.

Their decisions had clearly evolved to those who had known them as the years went on. After graduation, Joe Nolan and Drinan got together at Drinan's home in Hyde Park. As they sat on the lawn, Bob asked Joe whether he gave the impression that he was trying to avoid the service. The idea still bothered him. Joe himself went into the Navy, then joined the FBI, and then joined the Boston diocesan priesthood and became a well-known liturgist and Boston College theology professor.

Finally Bob Drinan said goodbye to his family in Hyde Park and took the train to Shadowbrook. His mother, who is described as very sweet, hospitable, and charming by Bob's contemporaries, had long suspected that this is what he would do. His father did not understand.

2 Breaking out from a World Frozen in Time

During the 1942 spring semester the war mobilization moved swiftly. Day after day, when Father William Leonard, S.J., a theologian and liturgist who had enormous influence on the boys, especially on Bob Drinan, called roll in class, someone would answer, "He's gone, Father." Following Pearl Harbor, Leonard himself had twice asked the provincial for permission to join the Army as a chaplain and had been refused. The third time, because enrollment had fallen so drastically—it dipped as low as 200—that there was less need for teachers, the provincial said yes. In April a group scheduled to graduate in 1943, whose classes had been accelerated so they could leave then, asked Leonard to preside at a farewell Mass. Leonard, who would become a pacifist while overseeing the burial of thousands of young men in the Philippines, did not preach of the glories of battle. He tried to express what parents and teachers were thinking as they watched their sons and students march away:

> You must not think that Alma Mater looks impassively on your going. Rather she is like Rachel, bewailing her sons and refusing to be comforted, because they are not. We who have taught you and given you our best and come to love you, we shall miss your bright faces, your boyish honesty, your unspoiled goodness. We shall look for the happy day when you will come back to us for the years of peace.

The following summer, in July 1943, some 430 to 500 troops moved onto the Boston College campus and the Jesuits moved out of St. Mary's Hall into six houses on the periphery to give the troops offices and lodging. At 8:00 A.M. the troops marched to class for four hours, six days a week, of engineering and languages. At night they assembled again for a study hour. Three-quarters of them were non-Catholic; but over three months they got used to the sight of these men in black habits, some wearing capes, and the Jesuits were challenged to learn that their world might have to change.

Meanwhile, Bob Drinan moved into a world frozen in time and, during much of the year, frozen in ice and snow. In the group picture of those who joined the novitiate with him he is 5′10″ tall, the face is more slender and pointed than he appears in his high school and college pictures, and the cheekbones are more pronounced. His forehead is high, his hair already receding.

Shadow Brook (later Shadowbrook) was the estate of the Episcopal priest, philanthropist, and civil rights activist Anson Phelps Stokes, originally purchased in 1892, above the 200-acre Lake Mahkeenac surrounded by the southern Berkshire hills, between the Massachusetts towns of Lenox and Stockbridge. According to Stokes's wish, it was the largest private home in New England and the second-largest in the United States. Later it was the summer "cottage" of Andrew Carnegie. To the Jesuit superiors who bought it for $200,000, it was ideal for molding young men fresh from the outside world into obedient soldiers of Christ. "There is not a single soft or enervating line in it," wrote a correspondent for *Woodstock Letters*, the Jesuit journal that recounted Jesuit history as it happened. It suggested the "perfection of Divine workmanship," and there was about the property "an air of deep seclusion; not a house can be seen, and one gathers the impression of complete isolation."

While the center housed the classrooms and ascetories—study halls in which each novice or junior had his own tiny desk, chair, and kneeler—the west wing had the fathers' room and the east wing the dormitories for novices and juniors, those who were just getting started in their first four years. In the twentieth century up through Vatican Council II in the early 1960s, the formation strategy, very strictly during the novitiate and slightly modified through philosophy and theology, was to isolate the young Jesuits from worldly distractions. Only in this way could they focus rigidly first on developing spiritual discipline, the ability to meditate fruitfully; to live simply, free of the material paraphernalia of books, magazines, records, radios, favorite sweaters, hobbies, sports heroes, family and friends that clutter the mind. They would replace previous affections—or rather place them in a new perspective—with the history and lore of the Society of Jesus to the extent that every expression of the religious superior is interpreted as, somehow, God's will.

Bill Leonard went through his training in the 1920s, Drinan in the 1940s. During that time the novitiate schedule and its atmosphere changed very little, if at all. Leonard, in his memoir, *The Letter Carrier* (1995), described the Irish Catholic culture from which he and Drinan came. He was grateful to have inherited the 2,000-year-old Christian tradition, but,

> I see now that as the tradition reached me it had been filtered through the Counter-Reformation. As a result it was triumphalist, ultramontane, autocratic, intransigent, legalistic, given to peripheral and sometimes weakly sentimental devotions rather than to biblically oriented prayer, definitely low church in its staple parish ritual, heavily reliant on an *ex opere operato* theology of the sacraments. [The sacraments have their effect regardless of the worthiness of the priest who administers them.] It had been seriously damaged, as well, by Jansenism, imported from France by way of Ireland, and certainly not mellowed by being domesticated among the Boston Puritans. (Sunday baseball, even of the sandlot variety, was still frowned on in my boyhood.) Personal and family morality was strong, and there was a general expectation that public servants would not become poorer during their term of office, and sometimes one even sensed an amused admiration for their peculations or their dubious strategies at election time. Culturally, great store was set by conformity to the community mores (even in the novitiate, how often we were told not to be "singular") and on respectability. We thought a great deal about sin, death, judgment, hell. Authority had been canonized and pronounced infallible—or at least irreversible. Due process was known only to civil lawyers. Patriotism was enthusiastic and unquestioning; I doubt if most people

would have espoused in theory the "my country right or wrong" doctrine, but they were the same people who in the next twenty years would listen eagerly to Father [Charles] Coughlin and [Senator Joseph R.] McCarthy. The sobering and chastening lessons of Vietnam and Watergate were still in the future.

Leonard also listed some of the intellectual and personal treasures which emerged from the same Catholic culture that would be a source of inspiration to both Drinan and himself: Edward Skillin and the editors of *Commonweal* magazine; Pope John XXIII; the publishers Frank Sheed and Maisie Ward; Boston's Cardinal Richard Cushing; Father Michael Walsh, as president of Boston College and Fordham; and William Guindon, the New England provincial who would pave the way for Drinan's move into active politics.

But there used to be a sentiment that every young man must participate in the war of his generation, that those who were too young for World War I and too old for World II had missed something essential in forming their character.

Leonard came to feel that when asked, "Where do you come from?" he would answer not Boston, but "from World War II." But during Drinan's three years of isolation at Shadowbrook, for the first two years with no access to newspapers or the radio news, with only one or two visits from family allowed each year, and with incoming and outgoing mail opened by superiors, the world turned upside down. However, it did so, for the most part, outside his vision and hearing. During his one year of juniorate, which included college-level studies, he had limited access to news. America began to bomb Germany. The battle of Stalingrad waged for more than four months. Roosevelt, Churchill, and Joseph Stalin met at Teheran and Yalta. General MacArthur returned to the Philippines. Roosevelt died, and Truman became president. When Drinan later moved to the slightly larger world of Weston, he did so in time to read that America had dropped the first two atomic bombs, on Hiroshima and Nagasaki.

Meanwhile he submitted to Shadowbrook's daily order, never doubting that this was the best way to use the talents God had given him. He lived in a barn-like dormitory, the cots about three feet apart, with forty other young men, with no curtains separating their beds and only "modesty of the eyes"—that pious discipline by which each one, lest he be distracted, keeps his eyes to himself—to grant privacy to those sleeping, undressing, and dressing, on every side. Indeed, there was little or no more privacy in the seminary than in an army barracks. All shared the same washroom, a long trough with a row of spigots and only cold water with which to wash or shave. Toilets and showers were in stalls in the basement three floors below.

They rose at 5:00, made a "visit" to the chapel, and prayed for an hour kneeling by their desks in the ascetory. Then Mass, breakfast, and *manualia*, each one to household chores like waxing the floor or washing the breakfast dishes for the roughly 125 priests, novices, juniors, and brothers who filled the house. Then followed an hour-long conference from the novice master on some aspect of the Constitutions, which are the Society's rules, largely written by St. Ignatius; two hours of Latin and Greek; fifteen minutes of free time; and a fifteen-minute daily examination of conscience in which each one privately reviewed how the day had gone so far, whether one had broken any rules or failed to be as virtuous as possible before lunch.

They filed silently into the dining room in their habits and sat eating in silence while one of them delivered a prepared sermon from the refectory pulpit or read aloud from a religious book while the prefect of reading called out corrections in pronunciation ("The WORD is impri-MAH-tur!"). Next came forty-five minutes of outdoor recreation, in which, no matter what the weather, they walked around the grounds in "bands" of three, as designated by the beadle. This was the *numquam duo* ("never two") rule, designed to mix up or rotate social groups and to prevent "particular friendships," a bond between two friends that might become intimate and threaten the unity, or conformity, of the group.

Holidays—which were Thursdays, or a long list of religious feasts, or when the novice master, sensing that the boys were getting "tight," decreed them—were opportunities to let off some steam through sports. Depending on the facilities, weather, and customs of the novitiate, in New England, New York, or Maryland they would swim in a pond or pool, ice skate, ski, play soccer in the rain and snow, or play softball or a form of touch football called "flag" ball. In a rule that is based partly in decorum and partly in reinforcement of chastity, the word was *Noli tangere*: no one is to touch another. Rather than tackle or even touch the man carrying the football, players would grab the cloth that hung from his belt. Basketball presented special problems, especially for aggressive athletes who liked to rough it up under the basket.

The afternoon required another hour of Greek or Latin and twenty-five minutes of "spiritual reading" from Thomas à Kempis's *The Imitation of Christ*, a manual intended to indoctrinate young monks in the Middle Ages, in which the author cautions the monks that every time one ventures out into the world he "comes back less a man." Finally, a second half-hour meditation, followed by supper. Outdoor recreation after dinner required that during the *ultima quadrans*, the last ten minutes, everyone speak only Latin. After all, Latin was the official language of the house, except for conferences and private meetings with the master, and once the young men got to Weston, the philosophy and theology classes and oral exams would be in Latin as well.

At 7:30 the spiritual reading would be from the life of some (usually Jesuit) saint, followed by thirty minutes of free time (free time was doled out in short increments to teach the novices not to waste a minute). Then they prepared "points," an outline of the next morning's meditation, examined their consciences again, recited the Litany of the Saints in chapel, and retired to the dormitory for lights out at 9:30. There, three times a week, they self-administered a penance called the "discipline." Together, at the ring of a bell, they whipped their bare shoulders with a knotted cord for the length of time it takes to say one "Hail Mary"—about ten seconds. Then they went to bed.

The Long Retreat

For Drinan, and for all Jesuits, the central experience of Jesuit life was the Spiritual Exercises, usually made in the first October, then repeated during tertianship, a final year of formation, a year or more after ordination. The Exercises, written by Jesuit founder Ignatius Loyola himself, are based partly on some traditional medieval practices and partly on his own experience of conversion after having been wounded at the battle of Pamplona in 1621. Though written in a manual, they cannot be merely read but can only be done—and done under the direction of one trained to listen carefully and interpret the movements of the Spirit in the exercitant's soul.

Extended over thirty days of silence, they are divided into "weeks" not of seven days but according to four subjects: self-examination, the public life of Christ, the passion of Christ, and the risen Christ, along with a concluding meditation "to obtain the love of God."

Though adaptable to almost any time and circumstance, today the Exercises are usually experienced as they were when Ignatius directed his first companions one-on-one. But in the pre–Vatican II Society, the master delivered the points for each meditation to the room full of thirty novices, then saw them privately later. The first week clears the deck, empties out the bad experiences and sins that might stand between the novice and God's grace, and presents a vision of the whole world yearning to be saved. The second contemplates gospel incidents in an imaginative, almost cinematic, way by picturing Jesus preaching to the crowds, curing a leper, or instructing his disciples. In the third the exercitant tries to enter into Christ's suffering, not in a morbid way, but to sense and identify with Christ's willingness to endure pain and death for our sake.

The final and shortest "week," on the risen Christ, sends the Jesuit out into the world with an energizing vision meant to carry him through the rest of his life—that of God constantly at work in human society, revealing Himself to us through the love of our fellow men and women. This is called "finding God in all things."

This insight—that God lives and acts in the many gifts of creation, including not just the lovely countryside and the stars or the rivers, jungles, and forests of the New World but especially the teeming streets of the big cities—is the key to that distinctive Jesuit spiritual attitude called contemplation in action. Ignatius insisted in his negotiations with Pope Paul III that, unlike the monastic orders, Jesuits would not be required to pray the "office," the daily readings of the Psalms, together in the church choir. Rather, in their private meditations, they put themselves in the presence of God and retained that sense of His presence throughout the day—whether teaching the classics to young boys, caring for prostitutes in their shelter in Rome, paddling down the Mississippi or the Amazon, or attempting to impeach President Richard Nixon.

Each Jesuit is expected to repeat this happening in an annual eight-day retreat made either on his own or with a director. Bob Drinan was faithful to this rule and wrote about individual retreats over the years. It is reasonable to conclude that the climactic vision of his very first fourth "week" with the Spiritual Exercises planted the seeds of a spirituality that finally drove him to run for Congress at the height of the Vietnam War.

In fact, in his seventies and eighties, Drinan returned again and again to these early spiritual experiences as a way of explaining who he really was and what drove him to the stands he took. In 2000, when the Irish Benedictine Abbot Columba Marmion (1858–1923) was beatified by Pope John Paul II, Drinan recalled reading his three spiritual books, beginning with *Christ and Life of the Soul* in the novitiate, and making Marmion's emphasis on Christ's words "Love one another as I have loved you" the center of his own spirituality (*NCR*, November 3, 2000).

Not an athlete, Drinan missed some of the usual opportunities to let off steam, but he did cherish one privilege that gave him some time to be alone and to do something different: his little job as a promoter for the popular Jesuit-edited devotional magazine *The Messenger of the Sacred Heart*. This afforded him a tiny office space, a cubicle, that allowed him the privacy he needed to read.

Bill Leonard, reflecting on the juniorate years, wrote:

> At an age when our peers at home were choosing a career, marrying, raising a family, making critical decisions, directing subordinates, handling money and property, we were without options, protected, watched over. It was a life-style, as Father John Courtney Murray later pointed out in a famous "exhortation" to the community at Woodstock [on the dangers of the vows], that could have prevented us from ever

achieving a responsible maturity. It could also—and did in some instances—produce a cramping, legalistic mentality or even a sad scrupulosity, incapable of distinguishing between right and wrong, unable to come to a healthy decision. The Second Vatican Council, emphasizing an almost forgotten evangelical doctrine of responsible freedom for all human persons, would change much of this, but the change would not come until forty years later.

About ten years after leaving Shadowbrook for Weston, shortly after his ordination in 1953, Drinan revisited Shadowbrook. In private conversation with one novice, he asked him frankly, "Do you like it here?"

The novice replied that he did.

Drinan replied, "I couldn't wait to get out."

"The spirit of the world" becomes the "enemy"

During the war, Father Zacheus Maher, who had been appointed a "visitor," the title of one appointed by the Superior General of the Society of Jesus in Rome to visit and analyze a situation and make recommendations to Rome, took up residence in St. Andrew on Hudson, the New York novitiate, and in January 1943 wrote a thirty-eight-page report on what he saw as the predominant weaknesses in American Jesuit lifestyle. His leading point was that the recently deceased General Wlodimir Ledóchowski had prayed that "we might be less *effusi ad extoriora* [absorbed in external, material things], less caught up with sports . . . and more embracing of mortification." Maher praised the accomplishments of American Jesuits, including the New England province's new school in Iraq, the Fordham intellectual quarterly *Thought, Jesuit Educational Quarterly, Theological Studies*, and Daniel Lord's *The Queen's Work*. But "the spirit of the world"—American popular culture—was undermining traditional Jesuit spiritual life.

He warned against sunbathing, wasting time at football games, and reading sports pages or listening to games on the radio. Magazines, novels, movies, and visiting externs (non-Jesuits) and associating with girls undermine chastity. Jesuits should not wear brightly colored sweaters at recreation. The customary penances—like *pedes,* where one gets on hands and knees during a meal, crawls under the table, and kisses the feet of the one on the other side—were being neglected. He deplored smoking, not because it endangered health but because it symbolized worldly pleasure. Jesuits' only worldly pleasure was to listen to the news only fifteen minutes a day—except during the war, when time was extended. Finally, even though there was a manpower shortage during the war, male secretaries and cooks must be found to work in Jesuit houses. Meanwhile Maher was disturbed by what he called a "group spirit" that was starting among the younger men during philosophy—men with "inferior ideals" who expressed themselves forcefully but lacked "modesty in managing the body."

At the end of his second year, 1944, Drinan took his first vows; after one more year of college work, he left Shadowbrook for Weston.

On March 9, 1956, at a Shadowbrook dinner, a junior delivered a sermon honoring the fourth centenary of the death of St. Ignatius entitled "Go, Set the World on Fire," words reputedly said by Ignatius to Francis Xavier when he sent him to Japan. That night, about half past midnight, Father Bill Carroll thought he smelled smoke. He had been wrong before, but not this time. At the bottom of the stairs he was confronted by a wall of flame. The house was a fire trap. Most escaped. Some were badly injured leaping from the roof or windows into blankets held below. Three priests and a brother perished as the mansion burned to the ground. Drinan, of course, was long gone by the time of the fire, but it had a profound impact on his fellow Jesuits.

Indeed, this accident was both a trauma and a turning point for the New England province. The hundred novices and juniors were spread out to other houses in the New York and Maryland provinces. The close bonds that had held them as a family at Shadowbrook were stretched, but, cast into the "outside world," they learned to live with and befriend a Society bigger than the New England countryside.

Weston

Today what was known for almost a half century as Weston College in the beautiful hill country ten miles and a twenty-five-minute car ride west of Boston College is known now as both the Campion Renewal Center, named for the English martyr Edmund Campion, with its program of retreats for both laypersons and members of religious orders, and the Campion Health Center, an infirmary for Jesuits recovering from illness or surgery and a residence for assisted living. Many of the men who go there know that this will be their last earthly home. In the graveyard behind and below the house, rows and rows of tombstones, marked with the dates of birth, entrance into the Society, and death, with flags planted for Memorial Day, stretch out across a vast green lawn.

The Society purchased a local estate, with a mansion house known as Fairview, in 1921. By coincidence Mrs. Grant Walker, widow of the estate's owner, was the niece of Father Joseph Coolidge Shaw, the Jesuit uncle of Colonel Robert Gould Shaw, who led the 54th Massachusetts Regiment of black soldiers during the Civil War and who died in battle with his men. The property consisted of one mansion house with eighteen rooms and three frame buildings that had a combined fifty-four rooms among them. The mansion, which would lodge the faculty and superiors and perhaps three scholastics, had beautiful oak stairways, many bathrooms, and space to be converted into a chapel, fathers' recreation room, and library. In December 1921 and January 1922 the first class arrived from St. Andrew on Hudson.

More groups arrived from the New York and New England provinces while, next to the mansion, a huge five-story, three-winged institution rose around an enormous chapel and a towering central rotunda.

A 1930 *Woodstock Letters*, the Jesuit history journal published at Woodstock College, describes a visitor's arrival. "Approaching the College by way of Concord Road our first view through the maples, elms, and pines that shade this winding road is of the east side of the building and takes in the fifty-foot limestone pillars with their massive bases. They mark the building as being of Georgian style. The pillars are fifty feet high and four are found at the end of each of the triple wings."

The main part of the building, constructed of limestone and marble, went north–south with three parallel wings running perpendicular to it: theologians to the north, philosophers to the south, and the chapel and classrooms in the middle. Bill Leonard, who arrived in 1929, mentioned that his class, accustomed to the warm golden oak chapel of Shadowbrook, found this spacious silver-and-stone chapel far less inviting. They nicknamed it "The Temple of Reason," and Cardinal William O'Connell remarked that it was not a "chapel," but a "basilica!"

Consistent with the policy of controlling the young Jesuits' formation by limiting the sources of new ideas, known as "distractions," philosophers and theologians were not permitted to socialize with one another except for designated days called fusions. But, in addition to a house built to hold 300, the property included a golf course, a baseball field, tennis courts, an old wooden handball court, a pond, and a farm. In 1946 a pool was added. What more could a young man want?

In all, the Weston course consisted of three years of philosophy, interrupted by three years of teaching in a Jesuit school, concluded by four years of theology, with ordination at the end of the third year. An undated yellowed document in the Weston archives lays out the rules for packing one's trunk for the move from Shadowbrook to Weston. It may not have applied to Drinan's class, but it gives a picture of what the standard Jesuit was permitted to own in the early 1940s: two hats, one for winter, another for summer; three changes of underwear; three suits; four dress shirts; six pairs of socks; six white handkerchiefs and six colored; one winter coat and another for summer; four pairs of pants; one pair of slippers and pair of gloves; one habit and cincture. Furthermore, a brother, not the scholastic, would pack the trunk. Thirty years later, in one of those clever answers that did not answer a personal question, Drinan said he wore his black clergy suit as a congressman because it was the only suit he had. If so, this is where that habit began.

He had his own room for the first time in three years, but with no sink. The sinks, showers, and toilets were in a room at the end of the hall. Morale was high. Among his fellow philosophers were his friend and comrade in the course Frank Nicholson, Richard G. Philbin (brother of the man Drinan would defeat in his first congressional race), and Walter Abbott, who would become an editor of the Jesuit-edited opinion magazine *America* and edit the extremely influential first collection of the documents from Vatican II, which would help provide the theological rationale for Drinan's decision to run for Congress.

The daily order was only slightly less oppressive than Shadowbrook's, with the usual round of retreats and devotions; English allowed only on Thursdays and feasts, Sunday afternoons, and villa; during class shows, no sets were to be constructed, the "rule of touch" was to be enforced, and no Negro* characters could be portrayed. Perhaps this was because the role would require blackface makeup, perhaps because "minstrel" characters were seen as demeaning. If so, the Society in Weston was ahead of its time. Scholastics could smoke only in their own rooms or on a walk or when cigars were given out on feast days, of which there were seventeen—for example, for the Immaculate Conception on December 8 and St. Ignatius on July 31.

Drinan was regarded as a serious student, but the intellectual level of the education was not high. Philosophy classes were taught in Latin. The professors were mostly beginners who lectured by reading their notes (or notes borrowed from manuals of other professors) aloud as the students, sitting at long, narrow tables called forms, scribbled them down, then had to memorize formulaic answers to feedback during harrowing Latin oral exams.

The course descriptions in philosophy resembled those in the Boston College catalogue, except here the students were twenty-five-year-old men. Courses included the philosophy of knowledge, general metaphysics, and a fair amount of science—chemistry, biology, astronomy—along with those philosophical and ethical questions raised by the science of the day. But all these were treated in isolation. There were no opposing points of view; the library was locked, one needed permission to get in, and there weren't many books when one did gain entrance. Considered a classic in those days was James Walsh's *The Thirteenth, Greatest of Centuries*, a rhapsodic catalogue of the glories of the Middle Ages, written by a former Jesuit, a physician who helped found the Fordham Medical School. Marx, Darwin, and Freud were mentioned mainly to have their ideas brushed aside.

---

* When I use the term "Negro," which is not employed much currently, I am reflecting the usage in the documents of the time.

"Urgent mission in the temporal order"

When Bob Drinan arrived in 1945, the house, built to accommodate 300, held 191, including 47 who were faculty, five of whom were in the infirmary, which was in the old mansion. One contemporary described him as having a "sparkling personality." Another, who observed him during most of his formation, including the novitiate and his career at Boston College, says people liked Bob because they knew he was very smart, he made his points in argument with a big smile, and then he stuck to his point of view. He had many friends because he had good insights on whatever they were talking about and he "didn't try to overwhelm you." He had a good sense of humor, and most of his jokes were about their daily life, kidding the older Jesuits, teachers, and authorities. Though not a "jock," as a good alumnus he kept his interest in Boston College football and baseball. But it was finally time for him to express himself in print.

Only a limited number of periodicals were available in the library—the *Catholic World, Dublin Review*, the *Month, American Catholic Quarterly*, the London *Tablet*, the *Irish Monthly* (nearly all the faculty and students were Irish), and the standard *Messenger of the Sacred Heart*. In 1946, his second year, Drinan joined forces with Richard W. Rousseau, S.J., and produced a mimeographed in-house publication of about a dozen pages, *The Weston Quarterly, A Journal of the Philosophers*. Their introduction asserted that "Jesuits have always been writers," with models like C. C. Martindale, an Englishman, and Daniel Lord.

The goals of this journal were to defend the Church, teach the truth, and, through promoting a "sound spirituality," to "make sinners good men and good men saints." That their "models" in the articles visited Boston College when Drinan was there suggests that Drinan wrote the introduction. His own article "Catholic Action and the Social Question" asserted that "no one will deny that the church has an important and urgent mission in the temporal order." He quoted Popes Leo XIII, Pius X, Benedict XV, and Pius XI as those who promoted "Catholic action." Why, then, he asked, was this political teaching of the Church overlooked? Because so few knew the true role of the Church, because the faithful were widely ignorant of the economic problems for which the Church had the answer, and because "secularizing" was destroying the traditional ethos of Western culture. At this time Drinan would know that the social encyclicals of Popes Leo XIII and Pius XI, particularly "*Quadragesimo Anno*," supported the rights of working men to organize into unions, to strike, and to receive a living wage. He may not have known that through Catholic advisers these principles influenced Franklin D. Roosevelt during the New Deal.

The January 1947 issue described the arrival of the first thirty-two scholastics at Weston in 1922. They stepped off the train into a terrific snowstorm and had to walk four miles in their best clothes to Fairview in snow. Drinan reviewed a book by Michael Tierney, *Aristotle's Politics and the Western Tradition*, and concluded that only a return to the Western tradition could save civilization from barbarism. In the May 1947 issue, an anonymous writer called for a greater effort in converting Jews. And Drinan argued that scholastic philosophy was not "sterile"—it had resisted utilitarianism and opposed the absolutist concept of the state, Manchester liberalism, and Communist collectivism. The articles, not remarkable in themselves, are important because they point to a moment when Drinan first began to publish his thoughts for others to see—and he quoted popes to validate his argument. When he announced his decision to run for Congress, he quoted the General of the Jesuits.

"Villa"

For two weeks each summer, usually late June or July, the New England scholastics either enjoyed or endured their annual "villa" (vacation time) at Keyser Island, not actually an island but a peninsula jutting out from the coast of Norwalk, Connecticut, into Long Island Sound. At a mansion there a handful of Jesuits doing pastoral work lived year-round; but the visitors lived in barracks, where each had his own room, an old mattress, but no sink, and the toilet at the end of the hall. Though it was vacation time, the usual regimen commanded the day with its 6:00 A.M. rising, Mass, meditation, examination of conscience, and so on, and they wore their formal habits to dinner. But they also swam out to the raft, played softball, ran the circumference of the "island" in fifteen minutes, bowled, played croquet, and sat on the porch.

In 1948 they arrived to find a television set in the living room. They watched the Red Sox play the Yankees, boxing matches, and the nomination of Harry S. Truman at the Democratic National Convention in Philadelphia. But the set was weak, the picture fuzzy, and they had to keep adjusting the antenna. On feast days they performed at dinner, sang selections from *Oklahoma!*, served cordials after dinner, and gave out cigars. On movie nights they watched *Sun Valley Serenade, Topper Returns*, and *Song of Bernadette*.

Some had a good time. Many hated the place with its boredom and the usual isolation. It was not Drinan's kind of place because it offered few intellectual opportunities, except for the visits in 1947 and 1948 by Jesuits John LaFarge and Wilfred Parsons. LaFarge (son of the distinguished American painter and stained-glass artist of the same name), who had become a Jesuit after having been ordained a diocesan priest while studying in Europe, had as a result of working in the black parishes of Maryland become an advocate for racial understanding and an editor at *America*. Parsons, also an *America* editor and political writer, lectured the young men on national and international affairs. Drinan made contact with LaFarge, wrote to him with ideas, submitted a version of his "Catholic Action" piece, and finally published his first *America* article, during his Georgetown Law School experience in 1949. And briefly he gained permission to escape the "island" for a trip to New York to talk to a possible benefactor of a Jesuit project.

A major event at the villa was Baghdad Day. In June of his last year each man received his *status*, a letter telling him where he would work and spend the next several years of his life. Sometimes the men volunteered or were consulted about where they'd be sent. Often they were not. The essence of the Jesuit vocation is to "go to various places," sent where the superior determines one is needed. In the 1930s, at the request of the Chaldean patriarch, who had graduated from the Jesuit university in Beirut, the Society established Baghdad College, built a campus along the Tigris with more than a dozen buildings, and eventually established Al-Hikma University as a higher-education extension of the college high school.

With textbooks in Arabic and English, and following the government-dictated curriculum, the university delivered a version of the Jesuit education to a Muslim culture—including science labs, debate teams, yearbooks, and basketball, soccer, handball, track, and tennis teams, plus pouring on the personal attention to every student. In Drinan's time it was staffed by twenty priests and five scholastics, and, given Drinan's 1942 decision to join a missionary order, he would have been a likely candidate to join the staff. The Jesuits loved it there and were enormously proud of their mission in the Middle East, which extended the Society's and the Church's influence on an exciting frontier. A dinner on Keyser Island on Baghdad Day celebrated the newly assigned Baghdad men.

As a matter of fact, Drinan's yearning for distant lands had not died out. According to an undated letter from these years, he wrote to the provincial and asked to spend the rest of his life as a missionary in Japan. His health was good, his eyes didn't need glasses, and he was "good enough" at languages. He said he knew life was hard there because his brother, Frank, a doctor, had worked there for two months. But he had always been inspired by St. Francis Xavier, who had evangelized Japan and died on an island waiting for a chance to spread the faith to China. Bob Drinan wanted to follow in Xavier's footsteps. We can only imagine how history would have been different if he had been sent to Iraq. Or to Japan. But he and Frank Nicholson faced a different future. While everyone else was going to teach high school, they were on their way to Georgetown Law.

In 1946 Drinan's mother died. We know little about her, but she has been described as beautiful, charming, gracious, and formal, the kind of woman who welcomed guests, and who, more than her husband, understood why her son yearned to become a priest.

Georgetown "Gentlemen"

When the two New Englanders, Nicholson and Drinan, arrived in the nation's capital in the hot summer of 1947, Georgetown Law School, which had opened in 1870 in the American Colonization Building on Pennsylvania Avenue, had moved four times and was now at 506

E Street in downtown D.C., near the courts, on Judiciary Square, and about five blocks from the Capitol. At the time of its founding, like most American law schools, it didn't even require a high school diploma or an entrance exam for admittance. From the beginning the twenty-five students who would attend its evening classes were told that the school's goal was for them not merely to master the law but to learn history, the operation of governments, geography, literature, and the passions of the human heart—and also to become "gentlemen."

For Francis Edmund Lucey, S.J., who was appointed regent in 1931 and would be the de facto dean and effective policymaker until 1961, the school's purpose was preeminently spiritual, in that he saw all civil law as founded ultimately in natural law—God's law. He asserted Georgetown's identity as a Catholic law school and staffed it for a long time almost exclusively with Catholic professors who were Georgetown Law alumni.

Lucey, who had not a law degree but a Ph.D. in sociology, shepherded the school through the low enrollments of World War II, fought for higher academic standards, revised the curriculum, reduced teaching loads so faculty could specialize and publish their scholarship, and strengthened the library, all the while placing Georgetown in opposition to the secular mainstream of American legal thought.

He built up strong relations with the government. New Deal figures and federal judges came to ceremonial banquets, and he founded an association of law alumni to support the school. In 1935 he required a college degree for admission. He charmed students and encouraged warm student–faculty relationships, and he was solicitous toward Nicholson and Drinan. He was particularly solicitous toward Drinan, to the extent that he wrote him a three-page, single-spaced, small print, paternal letter after he returned to Weston, filled with local news and encouragement to specialize in moral theology and canon law. Indeed, when Drinan later became dean of Boston College Law School, some of his reforms—only some—resembled Lucey's.

But Lucey could be cold and harsh to faculty who he thought opposed him. Yet, understandably, when in 1934 he decided he would take courses from his own faculty to earn his own law degree, everyone gave him A's.

During World War II enrollment dropped—from 641 in 1941 to 208 the following year. But when the war ended, prosperity returned. Eighty percent of the 1,000 students who entered with Drinan and Nicholson were veterans, and two-thirds of them were Catholics. The first-year students in Lucey's Jurisprudence course paid attention as Lucey lined up his quotes from eminent jurists, explained their systems of thought, rebutted "adversaries" like Kant, Hegel, and Oliver Wendell Holmes Jr., and finally presented the Church's natural law position.

Meanwhile the school was becoming known as the Georgetown Law Center, a vague title that allowed the school to expand and experiment, as the students established their own student government, African Americans and women were admitted, a Thomas More chapel opened, and students made annual retreats.

Ultimately, Drinan does not seem to have embraced the "Catholic truth versus secularism" stance that Lucey personified. Rather, he was particularly interested in the relationship between church and state. So, while the Supreme Court was hearing *McCollum v. Board of Education*, wherein Mrs. Vashti McCollum, the wife of a University of Illinois professor and an atheist, objected to the public school plan according to which students were released from class to attend religious instruction, leaving her son, age ten, alone, Drinan "observed the entire litigation in closest detail."

On December 8, 1947, he went down to the Supreme Court and heard the oral arguments. On March 8, 1948, the Court ruled 8–1 that the practice to which Mrs. McCollum objected was unconstitutional because it used the public school building once a week to teach religious courses on school time. Drinan's analysis of this case would be prominent in his first book, *Religion, the Courts, and Public Policy*, in 1963. He wrote that the case would continue to be the "great divide in church–state relations for many years to come." It created a "new liberty" by which a plaintiff can by invoking the Establishment Clause petition for the elimination of a practice whereby the state morally or financially aids religion.

He also used his Washington years as a chance to make social contacts. At a legal fraternity dinner he engaged Supreme Court Justice

Wiley B. Rutledge in conversation about the 1947 *Everson v. Board of Education* ruling, in which the Court had authorized public funds to finance transportation to Catholic schools, and he wrote about the case ten years later. All the while he was cultivating the editors of *America* with articles, comments, and ideas. Robert C. Hartnett, the editor famous for his opposition to Senator Joseph R. McCarthy, liked Drinan and asked the New England provincial to allow him to spend the summer of 1950, his last year in law school, at *America*, assuring the provincial he would look after the promising young man's spiritual and social welfare. The provincial turned him down, wanting Drinan to "rest."

In his personal life, the three years at Georgetown gave Drinan a second home to which he would soon return. He received his bachelor of laws degree in 1949 and his master of laws in 1950 and was admitted to the District of Columbia bar.

But his time at Georgetown also juiced his ambition, his hankering for bigger challenges and farther places. He asked permission to spend the rest of his theology, four years, in Europe. And after one year back from Georgetown, he asked to study French history and law in Montréal during the summer. We can only guess why the answer, repeatedly, was no. It could have been the insensitivity of superiors to the desires of young men anxious to break out of the mold. It could also have been that they had his life planned without telling him, as men were commonly sent places without being consulted.

Back to Weston

The train ride at the end of regency back to theology studies, for both the men at Weston and those at Woodstock College in Maryland, was always a long and gloomy one. Teaching high school is usually the most exhilarating experience of a young Jesuit's life. After seven years in obedient isolation the teacher is surrounded by adolescent boys who challenge him to teach them something, who test him, connive to "break" him, and often idolize him. Some would become friends for life; he would officiate at their weddings and baptize their children.

He had loved them, and now he was headed back to the woods, where he would sit in a big classroom and again absorb lectures in Latin. Unbearable—except that it would lead to the priesthood. Drinan never had the high school teaching experience, but thirty years later he would crown his life in the law school classroom.

Paul Kelly, who was a philosopher, a beginning student, at Weston in 1952–54 while Drinan was a theologian approaching ordination, knew and admired him from a distance, meeting him only when the "grades" between the different ends of the house were lowered for fusions. To Kelly, Drinan was already well known because between 1951 and 1954 he had published five articles in *America*, the *Catholic World*, and *Commonweal*, as well as pieces in *The Boston Pilot* (the diocesan Catholic paper) and other publications. And his peers referred to him as "Bobby D." At Weston he also led the social order academy, a group that studied the social teachings of the Church.

A number of his peers did not share Kelly's awe at Drinan's publications and referred to him as a "popularizer" who wrote for the "people," rather than for fellow scholars. But a study today of the list of Drinan's contemporaries at Weston reveals only a few who excelled as scholars or writers in their later careers.

Weston had changed little in his absence, except for an influx of some new faculty and theology students, many from the New York and Maryland provinces, as well as men from Malta, Mexico, Colombia, Jamaica, French Canada, and the Philippines. Two among the faculty made a special impression. John C. Ford with his colleague Gerald A. Kelly wrote frequently on issues of sexual morality and composed a series of "Notes" on moral theology that summarized the latest studies on moral issues in the leading theological journal, *Theological Studies*. His courageous article "The Morality of Obliteration Bombing" (*Theological Studies 5*, 1944) stated, a year before Hiroshima, that the mass bombing of cities was "an immoral attack on the rights of the innocent." He later became very conservative and was influential in convincing Pope Paul VI to go against the recommendation of his appointed committee and condemn contraception absolutely in his 1968 encyclical, *"Humanae Vitae."* Nevertheless, his position on bombing was one Drinan would embrace.

Enter Berrigan

A popular teacher was John J. Walsh, who, teaching theology for the first time, was "into it" in a way that held his students as he dealt with Christological questions such as how to reconcile the humanity and divinity of Jesus and what we mean when we say that Jesus is a redeemer or savior. Walsh took an interest in Daniel Berrigan, who had just finished his regency at St. Peter's Prep in Jersey City, New Jersey, and found the intellectual atmosphere at Weston to be stifling. Berrigan had written an article on the Church, inspired by some ideas from Henri de Lubac, for the *Modern Humanist,* an in-house journal edited by the theologians, and Walsh convinced him to publish it outside and to apply for studies in Europe. Berrigan published a later version of it in his book *The Bride: Essays in the Church.* He was on his way to a creative and controversial career.

But to Berrigan most of the teaching at Weston represented the last gasp of the nineteenth-century philosophy and theology, taught by men from their own notes, who had been trained in Rome and were simply passing along what they had been taught in studies. One of the most conservative was Father Philip Donnelly, who regularly attacked the ideas of French and German theologians like de Lubac, Congar, Danielou, and Rahner—soon to be recognized at the Vatican Council as the most influential theologians of the time—whom he dismissed as adversaries.

Berrigan characterized the place in his autobiography, *To Dwell in Peace*:

> Those years have the air of a predawn: a darkness with, here and there, a shaft of light breaking through. And ghosts abroad. Theology as presented was a strange exercise indeed, an *omniumgatherum* culled from times primitive, medieval, eras of reform and post reform. And then a heavy infusion of the safe and sterile nineteenth century, with its loyalty oaths and rounding on the heads of modernists, Americanists, et al. (111)

The scholastics knew little of the signs of the times.

> We were like the crew of a ship of fools: we were reassured by our captain. All, we were told, with a trimmed sail here and a good wind there, was well. And we were bound, straight as an Iroquois arrow, toward disaster.

To ward off disaster for a while, a group of theologians formed their own study group and read articles from *Commonweal* and *Cross Currents*, meeting weekly in one of the cabins where they could cook a meal and talk freely, raising questions they could never pose in class.

Drinan did not take part in those discussions. Chances are, suggests Berrigan, that Drinan's mind was so logical, organized, and syllogistic that he was comfortable with the method used in class. Given that Drinan later expressed satisfaction with his theological training, he may not have been interested in "cutting edge" conversations. But Berrigan's impressions of Drinan, who was a year behind him, were positive. He had a good sense of humor, liked to joke, worked very hard, and clearly aspired to be the best.

But Drinan was engaged in one extra activity that profoundly affected his social philosophy: He taught religion to juvenile delinquents and adult prisoners. Twenty-five years later, prison reform would be another of his driving issues as a congressman.

For both Drinan and Berrigan, the great moral issue of their time would be the Vietnam War. But they would oppose it with different strategies. Drinan would break the presumed barrier between priest and politician to run for and win a seat in Congress. Berrigan did not foresee Drinan's move into politics, but he thought a political position would limit one's freedom to preach and say what he believed. In February 1968 he flew to Hanoi with a peace group to witness the results of the American bombing campaign and returned determined to take dramatic action against it. In May, with his brother, Philip, a Josephite priest, and seven other Catholic activists, he raided a draft board in Catonsville, Maryland, and burned 380 files in the parking lot with homemade napalm.

Becoming a Priest

After his ordination on June 20, 1953, at Weston, Drinan and his colleagues spent another year on theology, this time exercising pastoral ministry in a variety of places—parishes, retreat houses, hospitals, and military bases. Then, in 1954, Drinan went to Florence—to Villa St. Ignazio, Firenze, Italy—for the period called tertianship, meaning the third probation. Frank Nicholson, who had earned a Harvard doctorate in law, went to Wépion, in Belgium.

But the climax of theology was the ordination itself, followed by the first Mass, which was to be in St. Ignatius Church, on the Boston College campus, on the corner of Commonwealth Avenue and St. Thomas More Drive, right across from the site for the new law school building. As Drinan began looking forward to his first Mass in May 1953, he received a rare letter from his father, dated December 4, 1952. The letter is both affectionate and laced with clues on the distance between the father and son.

James Drinan wrote to thank his son for a birthday card and congratulate him on his November 22 article in the *Pilot*, in which the younger Drinan explained to the huge Catholic readership of Boston what moral and legal rules govern—or should govern—the interrogation of witnesses before a congressional committee. The unstated context was the hearings of the House Un-American Activities Committee (HUAC) on the supposed influence of Communists in government and public life. After a dispassionate analysis of how a committee works and what protection a witness has against self-incrimination, Drinan argued that "A witness's reputation is such a precious thing that it should be clouded only when absolutely necessary." Thus a man who left the Communist Party some years before should not be forced to disclose that unless it can be proven that the good of the republic requires that he do so. About twenty years later, Congressman Drinan was named a member of that congressional body, by then renamed the House Internal Security Committee, and helped lead the effort to abolish it.

The father, however, worried that Communists were indeed in high places and speculated happily that with the election of Dwight D. Eisenhower as president they would be driven out and FDR's New Deal and Truman's Fair Deal would be wiped from public memory. "All the Socialism and the other cracked schemes must go," he wrote. "Man must earn his living by the sweat of his brow." There was news from the parish and the family. His sister, Catherine, had a new job and two good girl roommates. But . . . "Business with me is and has been so bad I hate even to think of it. . . . I am so tired and depressed that silence seems the best course. . . . Can't you make a plausible excuse and come home for Christmas dinner?"

James, of course, was alluding to the strict rules at Weston in those days that limited the contacts between young Jesuits and their families, many of whom lived in the Boston area. The theory behind the policy, of course, was based on the ascetical principle that "apostles" must separate themselves from their families in order to commit themselves fully to the Society's works, wherever they might be sent. But because Drinan has told us virtually nothing about his relationship with his father, we can speculate that he might not have wanted to go home.

Drinan made every effort to have his first Mass, in June 1953, celebrate those ideals which he wished to represent as a priest. He invited John LaFarge, who could not come because of a previous engagement; William Kenealy, dean of Boston College Law School, who came but declined the honor of being a deacon because of a physical handicap; Monsignor Francis J. Lally, editor of the *Pilot*; and Father Hartnett, in the role of archpriest, who wished to present a special gift on behalf of the *America* staff, a $25 gift certificate. Bill Leonard really wanted to be there too but had a conflict. Finally, the homilist was John Wright, bishop of Worcester, a friend of the family through Frank Drinan. Wright was known at the time as one of the more progressive members of the hierarchy.

The following September, Drinan received a prescient letter from Ray Bernard, S.J., managing editor of *Social Order*, at the Institute for Social Order in St. Louis:

> May I say, in all sincerity, that people quite well equipped as you are with a professional training, face a danger of maintaining a professionalism even while studying in other fields and perhaps being known as the "lawyer priest" or "artist priest," instead of exploring the richness

of the priesthood? I don't know whether I should have any such fear about you, because I believe you have a sort of universal interest in things and not an absorbing passion for one rigid science, and you have a sense of the human.

There was a tension, Bernard seemed to be saying, between professionalism and priesthood. And Bob Drinan needed to be careful about that.

3   **Moving Up**

After ordination, in the pre–Vatican II course, the fourth year of theology was usually a mixture of the two worlds—taking some more courses in preparation for the climactic *ad grad* oral exam, in which a panel of professors grills the young priest on all he was supposed to have learned during the seven years of philosophy and theology and grades him from a six to a ten. In the minds of some examiners, these final orals were not just a measure of whether the young Jesuit had learned his philosophy and theology well enough but also whether he showed exceptional skill in this kind of encounter that would mark him as a future religious superior. And in those days there was no distinction between the religious superior and the president of a Jesuit university. One man filled both roles—and not always well.

Drinan's grades were consistent from his freshman year at Boston College to his last year at Weston. He entered and left Boston College as an honors student, graduating *cum laude*, and left Weston with the same *cum laude* mark. That's B's rather than A's. But an analysis of his early writing suggests that the grades were a result of his priorities. Like many excellent students, he decided early that he was in the long run going to profit more from following his interests in extracurricular activities, most of which were intellectual, than from cramming for Latin oral exams. Unlike his peers, he ended his course having published articles in *America* and other national Catholic magazines.

The fourth year combines academic with pastoral tasks, like saying Masses at local parishes. Drinan had consulted Jesuit friends studying in Europe and had settled on the Jesuit house in Florence for tertainship, for that "third probation," or practical test, during which the tertian makes his second long retreat, repeating the novitiate experience of the thirty days. The idea was that one's spirituality had probably grown rusty during the years of study and teaching and the engine had to be retuned before admission to final vows, the ceremony that, according to church law, binds one to the Society.

The record suggests that three things happened to young Drinan in the roughly five years between his approaching ordination and his arrival at Boston College as a law professor. First, he finally broke out of the isolation of rural Weston into an international setting, one that he had requested several times and finally achieved. Second, he got the ego boost an ambitious young man needs by writing for *The Boston Pilot, America, Commonweal*, and the *Catholic World*. Third, these scholarly articles in the "popular" press planted the seeds for ethical, moral, and legal positions he would take more than a decade later.

One position, for example, was that civil law should be based on morality. In "The Supreme Court Confronts Segregation" (*America*, March 25, 1950), we see what becomes standard structure for articles on court cases: He states the original complaint, gives the background on similar cases, and then analyzes the ruling.

In 1943, Elmer Henderson, a Negro, on a train from Washington to Birmingham, Alabama, was denied a seat in the dining car because the seats reserved for Negroes had been given to white people who had arrived earlier. Henderson's suit eventually reached the Supreme Court. Drinan observed that the Court by implication had asserted for half a century that the separation of Negroes and whites is a reasonable arrangement. He concluded, "The time has come to re-examine the concept [of "separate but equal"] and to discover that there is no basis for it in fact, history or law. Furthermore, the classification is not only unreasonable but immoral. It is the product of passion and prejudice and unworthy of Americans, to whom racism is odious."

His "Is Pacifist Larry Gara a Criminal?" in the *Catholic World* (March 1951), about a professor convicted for advising a student to follow his conscience and not register for the draft, concluded that "civil law cannot violate a certain conscience even if the bases upon which that conscience is formed seem to the ordinary person very flimsy." Fewer than twenty years later priests and other counselors would face a flood of young men sorting out their reasons for wanting to avoid service in Vietnam.

Most interesting is "The Supreme Court and Religion" (*Commonweal*, September 12, 1952). Here, Drinan rejoiced that the recent ruling in *Zorach v. Clauson* had "cut the heart out of the 1948 *McCollum* decision and transmitted the explosive question of Bible reading in public schools." He reminded his readers that "*McCollum* outlawed released-time religious education when this took place on the premises of the public school." The issue in *Zorach* (April 28, 1952) was the allowance of released-time religious education but off the premises.

Drinan argued that before *McCollum* the Court had had a history of decisions favoring religious liberty but, perhaps because of poor research, had forgotten its own tradition. "The philosophy of law of the Supreme Court cannot without some oversimplification be reduced to an easy formula; it generally reflects the pluralistic culture of the nation and the varied backgrounds of the justices." The dominant philosophy during recent decades, he said, was that of octogenarian Dean Roscoe Pound of Harvard Law School.

> The core of Pound's doctrine is that the law is a social instrument designed to effectuate the greatest possible harmonization or accommodation of conflicting views and interests. It can be argued with credible evidence that this philosophy is the legal equivalent of James's pragmatism and Dewey's instrumentalism. As such it contains dangerous elements inconsistent with traditional notions of the bases of democracy. Pound's jurisprudence is perhaps underpinned by relativism in morals, but it has nonetheless advocated a stern sense of justice and has in no small way done away with some of the conceptualistic thinking which dominated the nineteenth century legal world. In any event the Supreme Court has employed Pound's harmonizations-of-interests tests in the field of religious liberty. The result has been satisfactory.

The idea that the law represents a "harmonization" of interests in a pluralistic society prepared the way for Drinan to tolerate legalized abortion, as an action that Catholics may deplore but that the society at large demands.

Zorach also meant that "the state may accommodate its public institutions to the religious needs and aspirations of the American people." In Drinan's Constitution, the church and state are separate but friends. The Constitution guarantees religious freedom; but, as his studies in Europe would remind him, religious freedom should include a provision that Catholic families who pay taxes to support the public school system should also, if their conscience requires them to send their children to private schools, receive state support for their children.

Italy

The academic year 1954–55, Drinan's tertianship in Florence, was an opportunity to relish at the age of thirty-five the sights and sounds, the art and history, that other American university students were gobbling up in the "junior year abroad" programs of the 1950s. This was also the time in which the American Jesuits, particularly in the Northeast, were finally sending their men to doctoral programs at leading Ivy League and European universities, determined to raise their schools' academic standing. Along with his spiritual training, Drinan also charmed several convents by saying Mass for the nuns, and he flew back and forth between Florence and Morocco to say Mass for American troops stationed in North Africa.

Also in 1954 his father died, dropping dead on a transit platform. We can presume he mourned his father's passing. But, if he shared his sorrow, any record is lost.

Meanwhile he strengthened his ties with *America* in five articles on Italian politics and culture. "Italy's Hopes and Needs" (April 2, 1955) depicts the state's and the church's continuing struggles to recover from the devastation of World War II. There can be no religious revival, he wrote, without economic progress: "Grace presupposes nature; grace works against difficulties where a man is obliged to lead a life below the dignity of the son of God. Poverty can be so crushing that it almost snuffs out the flame of divine love in the soul." He argued that the United States should revise its immigration laws to admit more Italians. U.S. immigration policy, he said, "judged by the principles of justice and charity, seems hard to reconcile with natural moral law."

In "A Letter from Florence" (May 21, 1955) he noticed that American novelists—Hemingway, Steinbeck, and Dos Passos—were popular in Italy, as were Bishop Fulton Sheen's books and Thomas Merton's *Seven Storey Mountain*. But where, he asked, were the Italian Catholic writers? This dearth of Catholic writers was due, perhaps, to the diminished influence of Catholic universities and the "secularistic attitude to literature which is all but universal in the university life of Italy." Catholics, he feared, were developing a "ghetto" mentality and "retreating from the main currents of intellectual life."

An odd piece, "The Weeping Madonna of Sicily" (May 28, 1955), reported on a sick, pregnant young girl in Syracuse who, in 1953, saw tears streaming from the eyes of her plaster statue of the Blessed Mother. Chemical analysis confirmed that the fluid from the statue contained the elements of human tears. The local bishop suggested that Mary wept because there were so many Communists in the diocese. After investigations, Pope Pius XII declared that Mary, now in Heaven, cannot shed tears; but she could cause tears to appear in the statue to remind us that she is our loving mother. Though he always put "tears" in quotation marks, Drinan disappointed the reader hoping for a note of skepticism. Given that the "weeping Madonna" had recalled many souls to the Church, "then is it not a plausible supposition that our Lady herself caused these 'tears' to flow?"

In "Crisis of Italy's Contemplative Convents" (August 27, 1955), Drinan was shaken by the decline of cloistered convents and monasteries, wracked by poverty and sickness, mostly the result of damage, disease, and skyrocketing inflation caused by the war. Drinan stressed, in accord with Pius XII's Christmas message, that those who are citizens of the world really do depend upon the prayers of contemplatives who spend their lives "doing reparation for the sins of humanity." Drinan concluded that American Catholics, who have abundant riches and who find that their contemplative vocations are soaring, should send contributions.

Finally, his report on the meeting in Florence of the International Union for Freedom of Education urged that the United States learn from the example of virtually all the European nations that provide financial support to private schools. The free school is the "logical derivative of democracy," Drinan wrote, so the state is obliged to "avoid all discrimination between state schools and private agencies of education."

Return to Boston College

Boston College had thrived since Drinan's departure in 1942. In 1941, Cardinal William O'Connell had purchased the Louis K. Liggett estate, bounded by Hammond Street, Beacon Street, and Tudor Road, next to the main campus, and had given it to the college to develop over the years as the business school and for capacious student residence halls. Then the college added two major academic buildings: Fulton Hall, begun in 1947, and Lyons Hall, begun in 1951, both on the main campus in fairly close harmony with the original four Gothic halls. *The Heights* proclaimed that Lyons "included a modern cafeteria with seats"—a dig at the standing-room-only eating room in the Gasson basement.

The curriculum held steady, except for dropping the Greek requirement for the A.B. degree in 1935 and Latin in 1958. When the college in 1949 acquired the property of the smaller of the two city reservoirs directly below the heights and drained it, the whole complexion of the campus changed. Now there was an extended fence with several entrances along Beacon Street, and room for more schools, classroom buildings, and sports buildings, including fields, a stadium, and a hockey rink. As the college met the demand for more dormitories, it assured its neighbors that the semi-monastic rules—rising at 7:15 and retiring by 11:00—would keep the youths under control.

Its theological reputation weathered a storm stirred by Father Leonard Feeney, S.J., a well-known Catholic poet who had taught at the college in the 1930s. Feeney was a charming and witty raconteur—he loved to do Katharine Hepburn and Eleanor Roosevelt imitations—and a popular spiritual guide at the St. Benedict Center in Cambridge, frequented by Harvard Catholics. One was the young Avery Dulles, a U.S. Navy veteran who was trying to decide what to do with his life. He later became a Jesuit theologian and a cardinal. Feeney gained a large following, but he preached the strictest interpretation of "Outside of church there is no salvation," and two of his followers, Boston College professors, were spreading that doctrine to their classes. When they accused the college of heresy for not agreeing with them, both men were fired. In 1949, Feeney himself was dismissed from the Jesuits and excommunicated from the Church.

The law school, founded on Beacon Street downtown in 1929, required at least two years of college for admission. It moved three times and was in the process of moving to its new home in Thomas More Hall on St. Thomas More Drive, across from St. Ignatius Church, when Drinan arrived in 1955. The dean then was William J. Kenealy, S.J., who had taken over in 1945 when he returned from his wartime Navy chaplain's duty.

Drinan returned to Boston College as a faculty member at the law school at a turning point in the history of the American Catholic Church, marked by the publication of Monsignor John Tracy Ellis's landmark essay "American Catholics and the Intellectual Life" in the Fordham journal *Thought* (1955). Ellis had the courage to say that, while the Church had prospered, its intellectual accomplishments were inferior. Although the Society of Jesus had begun to send its more talented men for doctorates at the best secular universities, Ellis's criticisms applied to the Society's colleges as well.

Between 1955 and 1970 Drinan would work with three presidents—Joseph R.N. Maxwell, S.J. (1951); Michael P. Walsh, S.J. (1958); and W. Seavey Joyce, S.J.(1968)—each of whom would be for him a source of either support or irritation.

Father Maxwell brought to his presidency, at the age of fifty-two, leadership experience as dean of Boston College, president at Holy Cross, and rector of Cranwell Prep in Lenox. He had to struggle with the enrollment drop caused by the Korean War, but during his tenure faculty norms for promotion were developed, and, with the talents of Bill Leonard and the writer Francis Sweeney, S.J., the college took on a heightened atmosphere of culture and intellectual endeavor. Today the distinguished lectures they initiated are commonplace, and celebrities have agents who sign them up for thousands of dollars a talk; but in the 1950s they were events that signaled a Catholic institution's commitment to bringing in the outside world. So, Boston College welcomed Adlai Stevenson, G. Mennen Williams, Frank Sheed, and Robert Frost, who was invited to celebrate the diamond jubilee of the *Stylus*, of which both Leonard and Sweeney had been moderators.

Drinan immediately established a good relationship with Maxwell; and though Drinan was just a first-year teacher, they talked regularly about how things were going downtown at the law school. Within a year, Kenealy was out, off to Loyola New Orleans Law School, and Drinan became dean.

Dean

Back at Weston, Paul Kelly, who had gone to Japan for regency, was thinking of leaving the Society and sought out moral theology professor John Ford for advice. Ford asked Kelly to write an essay on why he might leave; then, at a second meeting, to test him, said he had lost the first paper and asked him to write it again. The arguments proved to be consistent, and Ford was convinced Kelly was acting in good faith. Ford said there were three reasons men left: never had a vocation; lost the vocation through neglect; had a "temporary vocation" to stay just a while. Kelly, he said, was in that third group.

Ford agreed that Kelly should leave the Society, but he insisted he go without saying goodbye to anyone. Kelly argued that he had to say goodbye to certain friends. Ford went along but also, on the grounds that Kelly had forgone a scholarship to graduate school to join the Society when he left Boston College, offered him a scholarship to a Ph.D. program in philosophy at Louvain or Toronto or St. Louis, with a teaching position at any Jesuit university in the United States. They settled on Boston College Law School. Before he left Weston, Kelly felt obliged to say goodbye to an elderly Jesuit who used to run the movie program for the scholastics. The old man broke into tears and said, "I wish I had your courage when I was your age, but I didn't and stayed. For the rest of my life I've lived a life of mediocrity, waiting for the end."

In 1957 Kelly settled in at Boston College Law and quickly realized that the new dean was determined to make his mark. At orientation Drinan used what is now an old ploy of telling the students to look to the right and left and realize that those next to them might well disappear soon if they did not measure up.

To Kelly, the dean was someone he had known, as everyone had known him at Weston, as "Bobby D," and he started saying "Bobby D" around the school. Drinan called him in and said, "At Weston, Paul, we met a few times, that was all. Here, though, this isn't the Weston Social Order Academy. I'm the dean, not 'Bobby D.'" There wasn't much contact the first two years, although Kelly took Drinan's course on family law. His style was Socratic, instilling a creative tension into the classroom, asking tough questions, demanding that everyone be prepared. The word was out that the dean was hiring the best professors he could find, including Warren Abner Seavey from Harvard, and he demanded that faculty publish. To that end, he established two scholarly publications: *The Annual Survey of Massachusetts Law* and the *Boston College Industrial and Commercial Law Review.*

He also listened to students. When Kelly was elected senior class president, Drinan called him to say that, because Kelly was a former Jesuit, he and Kelly should get along fine. Kelly reminded him that he might be a former Jesuit, but his job was to represent the class. Drinan bent and told Kelly he would be a good lawyer, a representative for his clients. They did get along fine.

As an administrator, Drinan developed a style both highly personal and public. He arrived at his office, a large box-like room down the main corridor to the left of the entrance, sometime before 9:00 A.M., by coming up the back stairs from the parking lot through a private door. There he would toil—when he wasn't on the road or teaching his course on family law—sometimes all day and into the night. At the age of thirty-six, Drinan, because of his position, was now, though a very private person, also a national public figure; and, in an era when deans had sweeping discretionary power, he used that power liberally to craft the school according to his hopes—and also according to his own ambitions.

The position allowed him to reveal aspects of his personality in brief encounters that left deep impressions. One day in the late 1950s a young Korean graduate student, Kwang Lim Koh, appeared in Drinan's office with a problem. He had his Harvard degree but not an American law degree. He had to return to Korea, but he might want to come back to practice law in the United States. Drinan, rather than send him down the hall to the admissions office, simply replied, "Mr. Koh, you are in and I am happy to have you study here!"

Koh took his courses and, three years later, returned to Korea to work on a friend's political campaign in Seoul, but called back to the States to ask if his law grades had arrived. He passed, and his party won the election and appointed Koh acting ambassador from Korea to the United States. That fall, with his wife and six-year-old son, Harold (forced to wear a tie for the occasion), Koh revisited Drinan in his office. Overwhelmed, Harold asked his father whether Dean Drinan was like Dean Martin. "No, Harold," he replied, "Dean Drinan is much more important." Forty years later Harold Koh, at this writing U.S. assistant secretary of state for human rights, appeared as a guest lecturer in Professor Drinan's Georgetown University law class. Drinan recalled the necktie and the little boy's discomfort in the office listening to the grown-ups. To Koh, the incident typified Drinan's instinct for seeing every scene "from the perspective of the smallest and meekest person in the room."

Around the same time, Sheila Mullen Twyman, a shy first-semester Boston College undergraduate, was making her way across the campus loaded down with more books than she could possibly carry. A priest passed her and offered to help. Sheila's shyness stemmed at least in part from a speech impediment, a stutter, that made it very hard for her to converse. What would she do if the priest wanted to talk? But he simply helped her with her books and quickly sensed that he shouldn't draw her into conversation. It wasn't until later that she realized the dean of the law school had carried her books and that he was a very kind man.

Judge Henry W. McCarr of Minneapolis remembers warmly the cocktail party Dean Drinan held for a seminar of visiting prosecuting attorneys on the lawn of Boston College Law School in 1969. McCarr had come to lecture on the grand jury but was slightly overwhelmed by the collection of leading professors from the best law schools in the East, while he had come from the little-known night school of the St. Paul College of Law, which had but one claim to fame: An alumnus was Warren E. Burger, then the Chief Justice of the United States.

As the guests gathered in a circle, they began to introduce themselves, each emphasizing the fame of the school that had produced them. McCarr shrank back a bit as one after another proclaimed: "I'm from Harvard, I'm from Yale, I'm from Columbia," until they got to him. McCarr meekly uttered, "I'm from the St. Paul College of Law . . ." when Drinan broke in, raised his glass, and announced, "That's where the Chief Justice of the United States came from and that's a lot more than any of us can say for ourselves." That quashed the bragging, and, though McCarr never saw Drinan again, he kept him in his heart and prayers. That's how Drinan's legions loved him.

But kindness alone doesn't transform a law school. There were no secret elements in Drinan's formula; but it's rare that one administrator can successfully pull together the several rules for educational leadership.

First, assemble the best possible faculty. In an era before search committees were the norm, Drinan had a knack for meeting someone, grilling him (or her), sizing him (or her) up, and offering the job. Francis J. Larkin, whom Drinan hired as his associate dean, called the method "spontaneous, intuitive, visceral . . . and usually followed by a happy ending." Sanford Katz, who was among the first Jewish professors Drinan hired, had quit the law faculty at the University of Florida when the dean failed to heed a faculty request to give sanctuary to a black professor who had been threatened. Drinan had pursued Katz for several years, seeing him as his possible successor and coveting his expertise in family law. Katz knew that the "interface between religion and law" was for Drinan a lifelong concern and that family law, with emphasis on the mutual rights of divorcing couples, the role of therapy in possibly saving marriages, and the welfare of children who were often the victims of divorce, should be a primary concern. As chairman of the family law section of the American Bar Association, he was also founder and editor of the *Family Law Quarterly*. And Katz, whom Drinan had looked to in several ways to continue his ideals, followed Drinan as *Family Law Quarterly* editor for thirteen years.

Meanwhile, Katz was instrumental in hiring John Flackett, who, like Anthony LoFrisco, had struggled for civil rights with the Lawyers Constitutional Defense Committee in the South and who had also spoken on behalf of the black professor at the University of Florida. Enthusiastic about Drinan's use of the law for social justice, Flackett worked on the death penalty, corrections, and prison reform. The two men would often talk until midnight, and Flackett would leave bursting with new ideas.

Second, attract the highest-quality students. At a 1967 reception following a talk at Scranton University, Drinan met Edward Leahy, a senior headed for law school. He had applied to six schools, not including Boston College. "Write to me when you hear from them and tell me what they say," said Drinan. All ultimately offered scholarships. Drinan brought Leahy to Boston, sat him down in a class, and met with him for half an hour afterward, spinning out tales of his travels around the country recruiting the best and named faculty whom Leahy had never heard of, such as Sanford Katz and Mary Ann Glendon. Then he looked at young Leahy and said, "I want you to come to Boston College." He came. But the dean also insisted that these "best" students be challenged when they came. Good grades were hard to earn. A's were very rare. The top student in Leahy's class ended with a grade point average of 6.3, just above a B. Leahy went on to clerk for Justice William J. Brennan Jr., becoming the first Boston College law graduate to clerk at the Supreme Court.

When George V. Higgins was fifteen, he wanted to teach English and write novels, but his father was convinced that he should be a doctor. At Boston College his A's in English and a losing battle with chemistry, plus his winning an *Atlantic Monthly* contest and serving as editor for the *Stylus*, moved him back to writing. After graduation in 1961, he signed on with the *Providence Journal,* then with the Associated Press. The thrill of covering trials led him to become a lawyer.

Yale accepted him, but the financial aid officer told him to sell his car in order to be eligible. Higgins balked. One day, researching an AP story in the law library, Higgins ran into Drinan. "Come here," said Drinan. On finances, he said, "Don't worry. We'll figure it out." Higgins rose quickly through the justice system to become an assistant U.S. attorney and then a lawyer in private practice in 1974. By then he had published *The Friends of Eddie Coyle*, in 1972. By 1991 he had written fifteen books and sold about two million.

Third, remember the famous Oliver Wendell Holmes Jr. quote: "A man must share in the actions and passions of his times, at the risk of being judged not to have lived." "Serve" was one of Drinan's key words. The law was to serve justice, the lawyer to serve society. The great passions and actions of the late 1950s and 1960s were civil rights and the peace movement. Drinan threw his personal and institutional resources into both. Larkin points to the school's commitment to clinical, or hands-on, legal education, the clinic in Waltham known as the "laboratory"—the National Consumer Law Center—which fostered internships in municipal, state, and federal agencies. Meanwhile, there was no substitute for scholarship on the part of the faculty. In this way Drinan raised the moral and intellectual climate of the institution.

As another gradual step in raising the school's academic reputation, Drinan phased out the evening division by simply not offering the core courses at night.

Drinan's leadership style at either Boston College or later in national politics was not all grace, charm, and smooth diplomacy. One day, after losing a vote on a faculty committee in which Sanford Katz participated on the winning side, Drinan, disappointed, scolded Katz, reminding him that he had been brought to Boston College Law School to excel in scholarship—not faculty politics. It wasn't that Drinan thought Katz was neglecting scholarship but that Katz had disagreed with him on a political issue. Disagreement was akin to disloyalty.

John Robinson, who later became associate dean of Notre Dame Law School, first met Drinan in 1961 when Robinson was a Jesuit novice and Drinan took the trouble to talk with him again and again, although Drinan was on retreat and the young man did not realize he was interrupting him. The two men kept in contact, meeting from time to time for dinner over the years. Robinson admired Drinan for his kindness, intelligence, and idealism. But, said Robinson, echoing the experience of others,

> He was not particularly patient with individuals who disagreed with him or with arguments that led to a supported conclusion that he thought was wrong. Perhaps the single-mindedness that gave him both the energy and the force to get so much done worked against his being open to points of view he did not share. Perhaps not. But once he had made up his mind on an issue, he showed little interest in suggestions that perhaps he ought to change his mind on it. This made him a reliable political ally, but it worked against him in the halls of academe.

Nevertheless, Drinan, in every way possible, was transforming what had been a small, local Irish Catholic institution into one that was more "modern"—interracial, ecumenical, mixed, and national. And, in his mind, he was not just educating men and women to pass the bar exams; he wanted to empower agents of social change. He told his audience at the University of Michigan Law School in June 1959:

> The lack of vision which can be perceived in the legal profession cannot be corrected by another course in law school or by the addition of a seminar in professional responsibility. It can be corrected only by new depth in all the training in the law school—a depth based on the fact that lawyers have been the makers of symbols and fashioners of ideals in American society as of no other society in the world.

His heavy speaking schedule fed his public reputation. Averaging nine to a dozen major addresses a year, he lectured on civil rights, religion and education, church and state, at meetings of the Congress of Racial Equality (CORE) and the American Civil Liberties Union, to Catholic theology conventions, in synagogues, and in various cathedrals as homilist at the annual Red Mass, a liturgy for judges and lawyers usually attended by a cross-section of political and religious leaders. And wherever he went, he both learned something about another local or national community and left behind a strong impression about both Boston College and himself.

In 1963 he published his first book, *Religion, the Courts, and Public Policy*, a study of court cases on government support for religious and private schools, prayer and Bible reading in the classroom, church-related colleges, and Sunday laws from the standpoint of the three major religions, all topics he had been writing about since law school and that were gist for his many *America* articles over the past few years. At 259 pages the book is a bit longer, and more supported with scholarly apparatus, than his later books, as well as less polemical than the two short books to follow on dissent and against the Vietnam War.

While his approach was balanced, new themes emerged: The relationship between the state and religious education should be more one of cooperation than one of separation. He concluded with some practical advice for each religion. Catholics, he said, should avoid the temptation to oversimplify the issues and not become obsessed with their own rights. Above all, they "should not contemplate the use of the power of population or politics to secure the ends which they may seek." Jews, on the other hand, should recognize that "the moral health of the nation may be endangered by that divorce of religion from society, which may result from the continuous application of the doctrine of absolute separation of church and state."

Boston College Begins to Shine

In 1958 Michael P. Walsh, S.J., a biologist and above all a man of broad vision and enormous political skills, assumed the presidency of Boston College at a time when Catholic higher education and the Church worldwide were in the throes of revolution. In 1959 Pope John XXIII convened an ecumenical council, Vatican II, the first since Vatican I in 1870. He was "opening the windows" to let in a breeze—or winds—of change, the intellectual history that much of Catholic education had excluded, the impact of Darwin, Marx, and Freud, and also John Dewey, thinkers usually categorized for years as "adversaries" in those required philosophy classes. The American Catholic intellectuals were engaging in some self-criticism, by now a response to Monsignor Ellis's article in *Thought*.

In the 1950s and 1960s, Catholic scholars, many influenced by French and German theologians like the Jesuits Teilhard de Chardin, who synthesized an evolutionary worldview with his Jesuit spirituality, and John Courtney Murray, who, in *We Hold These Truths* (1960), reconciled American democratic theory with Catholicism, were beginning to bloom. A turning point would be the 1967 meeting by twenty-six presidents of Catholic universities and other intellectuals at Notre Dame's villa in Land O' Lakes, Wisconsin, to draw up the academic world's response to the Vatican II document *The Church in the Modern World*. The group's manifesto, "The Nature of the Contemporary Catholic University," declared that the Catholic university must "be a university in the full modern sense of the word, with a strong commitment to and concern for academic excellence." In practice this meant, among other things, that faculty at Boston College, Fordham, Holy Cross, Loyola, Notre Dame—indeed, all Jesuit colleges and universities—must have Ph.D.s, publish books and articles, and compete and cooperate with other members of their profession just like faculty at the top secular schools.

Walsh, a self-proclaimed workaholic who spoke softly, holding a cigarette to his lips, shook up the faculty and reduced the combined philosophy and theology requirement, where many of the courses were taught by less competent Jesuits. Intellectually below par, these courses alienated the better students. He required all faculty to publish. He also appointed Drinan to head the committee to plan the 1963 centennial celebration. The series of events opened with the great Swiss theologian Hans Küng speaking on "The Church and Freedom" and the awarding of an honorary degree to Nathan Pusey, president of Harvard, whose university a half-century before had declined to recognize the Boston College degree for law school admission. The day concluded with an academic convocation in Alumni Stadium addressed by President John F. Kennedy, who expressed his pride as a Catholic in Pope John XXIII's recent encyclical *"Pacem in Terris."*

Race and Abortion

Each year Drinan moved closer to the cutting edge of controversy, closer to conflict. In February 1964, in an address to CORE in New York City, he told his audience that Negroes should not be inhibited from nonviolent, direct, nonlegal protests out of reluctance that they might offend the white majority. "Any adverse reaction among whites may be an asset and not a debit." Nor was there a good reason why children should not participate in the Negro's march for justice. How should the Negro respond to the white question "What does the Negro want?" They must, Drinan insisted, ceaselessly explain, elaborate on, and reiterate their dreams and aspirations.

Drinan's much-debated position on abortion, as it evolved by the time he ran for public office in 1970, was that, in the words of one of his political sponsors, "abortion is a sin, but not a crime." In other words, in a pluralistic society a religious minority has neither the right nor the opportunity to impose its morality upon the larger community. But in his sermon at the Red Mass in St. John's Church in Bangor, Maine, on October 2, 1960, Drinan praised the history of law in Maine for being based on religion as the principal source of morality of its people, and he acclaimed its jurisprudence in that it "guarantees the sacred right to be born to every child by placing the severest sanctions on the taking of the life of an unborn child."

At the Kennedy Compound

According to Albert R. Jonsen in *The Birth of Bioethics* (1998), during the summer of 1964, as a Jesuit graduate student at the University of San Francisco, he met Joseph Fuchs, S.J., a distinguished German theologian from the Gregorian University in Rome, who invited him to join a meeting organized by R. Sargent Shriver, the Kennedy siblings' brother-in-law, at the Kennedy compound in Hyannis Port, Massachusetts. Senator Edward M. Kennedy was running for reelection and Robert F. Kennedy was running for the U.S. Senate in New York, and they hoped to come up with a stance on abortion acceptable to both Catholic teaching and the public at large.

They flew to Boston to meet Drinan, who drove them "at breakneck speed" to Hyannis Port, where they met Dr. Andre E. Hellegers; Father Richard A. McCormick, S.J.; and Father Charles E. Curran, professor of moral theology at Catholic University. The Kennedy brothers attended the discussion only briefly, leaving the theologians, who, other than Drinan, were the top moral theologians in America, and especially Fuchs, a leader on the international scene, to struggle with the problem. McCormick, recalls Jonsen, "was particularly articulate." He built on John Courtney Murray's distinction "between the moral aspects of an issue and the feasibility of enacting legislation about the issue." The group concurred, almost a decade prior to *Roe v. Wade*, "that the translation of a rigorously restrictive ethic of abortion into law was unlikely to be enforceable or achieve its positive goals without significant social evils."

In the end, the theologians, all of whom agreed that abortion was immoral, proposed restrictions in line with those proposed by the American Law Institute's model statutes, drafted in 1962, and by that time enacted in about a dozen states. This model permitted abortion if a licensed physician believed "there is substantial risk that continuance of the pregnancy would gravely impair the physical or mental health of the mother, or that the child would be born with grave physical or mental defect, or that the pregnancy resulted from rape, incest, or other felonious intercourse." Drinan stated at the 1964 meeting, and later, beginning in 1967, his dissatisfaction with the law's imposing these choices. For him, one way of avoiding the law sanctioning abortion under several often ambiguous circumstances was for "the law to withdraw its protection from all fetuses during the first twenty-six weeks." But this was not the consensus of the group.

Three years later, addressing the International Conference on Abortion in Washington, D.C. (September 6–8, 1967), on "The Right of the Fetus to Be Born," Drinan analyzed the various attempts in American and other laws to radically change the emphasis from the right of the fetus to be born, from allowing the death of the fetus only to protect the *life* of the mother, to (1) laws that would allow abortion for stated medical reasons, or (2) laws to allow abortion on request. In the latter, abortion would be a crime only when performed by persons not licensed to practice medicine. Allowing abortion for a variety of medical reasons, said Drinan, "for the first time in American jurisprudence singles out certain types of individuals whose lives can be taken not because of any offense they may have committed but only because their existence is inconvenient to others." There was an implication in his address that it might be better to allow abortion on request rather than have the state involved in any way in determining the life or death of a fetus.

A year later, in an address to the American Catholic Theological Society in Washington, D.C., his position had shifted. He found support for his new stance in the Vatican II "Declaration on Religious Freedom," which says that the freedom of man must be respected as far as possible, and "curtailed only when and in so far as necessary." Under what circumstances should Catholics attempt to regulate abortion by law in a pluralistic society? The Declaration states that in spreading the faith Catholics must avoid any appearance of coercion. Yet it also says that the "protection and promotion of the inviolable right of man ranks among the essential duties of government."

If Catholics were to be engaged in this argument, Drinan said, they must be well informed. But we do not know whether there are 200,000 or 1,200,000 illegal abortions a year. We do know that 80 percent of those aborting are middle-class married women who simply want to dispose of an unwanted or inconvenient pregnancy. They should realize that defeating the suggested new Model Penal Code that legal scholars had recently proposed, permitting certain kinds of abortion, will not solve the problem. They should seek to obtain a legal regulation of abortions that would minimize the number of fetal deaths but not impose sectarian beliefs on others.

Drinan proposed withdrawing criminal sanctions and replacing them with laws that would regulate abortions in other ways: prosecuting illegal abortionists, a mandated waiting period with counseling, a thorough survey of the scope of the problem. He concluded that there was no one "Catholic position" on the jurisprudence of abortion law and one was free to advocate prohibition, the Model Penal Code, or abortion on "request," which would remove the law from the issue.

In the *National Catholic Reporter* (June 19, 1968), in a letter written between the two talks, Father William Hunt, a theologian at Saint Paul Seminary, accused Drinan of abdicating his responsibility, giving in to abortion on demand, presuming that that is what pluralism required. In other social issues, Hunt said, for example open housing and gun control laws, we fight to have the moral principles of the right to live where one wishes and to be free from gun violence written into law. Why not fight abortion on demand? "Involvement of the Christian in the secular order does not mean attempting to predict the inevitable or waiting for the polls to decide in advance. It means working for a world which is more truly human."

Inner Turmoil

Drinan has been described by those who knew him both in the Society and by laypersons as a friendly man with a gift for making "friends," but with few, if any warm friendships. He was a "community man," in that while he was serving in Washington he returned to Boston almost weekly to see his constituents, and he always visited the Jesuit communities in New England during holidays, including the sick and old at Weston, and made the rounds. But few would say they knew him well. He was less a "community man" in that he seldom had time for relaxed small talk; he was noted for eating breakfast or lunch standing up, often in attendance but always in a hurry. During his deanship his constant travels, including teaching a course in Dallas while commuting back to Boston and teaching another course in Israel, separated him from the Jesuit community in St. Mary's Hall.

In St. Mary's Hall the large rooms were on the main corridors, but he lived in a comparatively small (about fifteen feet by eighteen feet) room on the second floor, with a sink in a walk-in closet, on a dark corridor with a window overlooking a garden, and the bathroom down the hall. The men seldom if ever visited one another's rooms and said private Masses each day before dawn in a series of tiny chapels spread around the house. His office was "off campus" in the sense that it was out the front gate and down the street, a half-block away from St. Mary's, which, because the religious rector and the university president were the same person, housed the college administrative offices as well as the residence. So he was isolated by both temperament and ideas from the older fathers who ran the institution, many of whom did not share his ambitions for the college or for himself or his political ideas as they became more and more public.

A *Boston Globe Magazine* profile by Robert L. Levey (October 29, 1967) was an apt portrait of the Boston College Law dean as he approached the turning point in his life:

> His policies have measurably improved the Law School: the law aptitude scores of entering classes have moved from below 500 (43rd percentile) to about 600 (89th percentile), thus ranking Boston College Law School as 15th among 138 schools in the nation. The class is so talented, says Drinan, that "anybody who studies will not flunk." About 10–13 percent of the freshmen class do flunk out, but about 85 percent of the graduates pass the bar exam. Teaching church–state relations and family law, he would pace restlessly back and forth, removing his ball point pen from his pocket and replacing it. Though a patient listener in some circumstances, in class he is impatient, refusing to "suffer fools gladly." The students refer to him as "Boss," respect him for what he has done for the school, hold him in some awe, but refer to their experience as students as "punishing" or "horrible."

Drinan delighted in pouring out his ideas to the interviewer. He spread out on the desk recent articles and texts of speeches, reminded Levey that he learned on the debating team to take every side in an argument like abortion, and floated his proposal that "maybe the law should withdraw." As chairman of the Massachusetts State Advisory Committee to the U.S. Commission on Civil Rights, he was very critical of his fellow Bostonians on their racial attitudes. "Racism is everywhere," he said. "It is another public sin, like graft and corruption." He was persuaded that American society owed reparations to today's Negro. On family law, he had a lot of "new" practical ideas, like a mandatory reconciliation system for couples facing a divorce, making them talk things out before approaching the lawyer or judge.

In reply to questions on his family background, on the origin of his ideas, he, as usual, revealed little. When a friend asked in a group if priests should be allowed to marry, Drinan replied, "That would be fine, but I want it to be retroactive." This was interpreted as a surprising, mild irreverence. But many a true word is said in jest. He had said in 1938 that he wished Boston College were co-ed.

His inner life showed itself to some degree in a series of notes made during annual retreats, or just in daily meditations, between 1966 and 1968. Jesuits keep what in some provinces is called a "light book," a day-by-day collection of the results of prayer and self-examination. They are, for the most part, written not for the world but for one's own reflection, signposts on spiritual progress or defeat. As a literary genre they are, like some of the Scriptures, not to be taken literally. The word "death," for example, does not necessarily mean actual, physical death; it may refer to spiritual "death" or dryness, or the need to "die to one's self," to conquer the ego.

The entries are all in phrases, not sentences; in abbreviations, if not in code, so some are ambiguous and can be interpreted and misinterpreted in many ways. (They have already been published, in more detail, in a Brown University honors dissertation on Drinan's first campaign. The interpretations here differ on some points.)

Some examples, the first from 1966:

> The desire to be 1. + be 1 on a permanent basis? This granting—or is it mere surface attraction to W. who are lovely—pretty—to? . . . . Do I know my problems?

From 1967:

> Depr so P. N. to wake up. Love—dif—forget. Lack of Conf. Will I ever be happy again? Profound moral confusion—over something so trivial—really closer to God. . . .

> Retreat at Weston. A real desire to repent and really to die. Newman—"If you are at peace with venial sin be certain that it is their company + and in their shadow mortal sins are lurking."

The desire to be totally different, intensely spiritual—but how—how find and fill other needs (?) the incessant activities of mind, adm, people.

From 1968:

> Gd Friday, 12 April 68. Why has appeal, allur of rel ex gone? 13 years Without a Voice! My determination re future of BC!! Lies—mismanagement—Deception—Hypocrisy

> Slander behind back—the agonies of the reform that are needed. Sweep incompetence out!!!

> May 68 Keep cool

> All of life everywhere is sad and filled w/ rejections

> WHY the nagging fear of not getting the praise we crave?? So small—subjective—selfish

> If only I could pray—be pure—a vision

> This (summer) could change my life—make it spiritual!!

> Loss of buoyance and nerve?

> Aloneness deepens

> But is it a new dark night of the soul?

Several things are going on. In the years ahead Drinan would write articles several times about his spiritual retreats. His attraction to "W" is clear enough. As one of his law school colleagues observed, it is an attraction that dies about three weeks after you are in your grave. Depending on how and when the Jesuit is trained, the spiritual life is still a constant struggle to retain one's ideals and keep one's life on track. Drinan's ambitions, it appears, included becoming president of Boston College, and when Mike Walsh resigned in 1967 and was replaced in 1968 by W. Seavey Joyce, S.J., the dean of the business school, not by Drinan, he had to rethink his future. The key phrase is

"13 years Without a Voice!" He had been at B.C. for thirteen years and was successfully transforming the law school, but he was not satisfied. The feeling that he was surrounded by lies and incompetence could have been the result of his long absences and isolation. It could also have been true.

The irony is in his conviction that the summer of 1968 may change his life. He was hoping it would make him more spiritual, but for many politically committed men and women like himself, it was the summer that changed the world.

4   "The World Turned Upside Down"

When General Cornwallis surrendered to General Washington after the Battle of Yorktown in 1781, the band struck up an old march, "The World Turned Upside Down." There would be a consensus of not just historians, but most of those who actively participated in the action and passion of America in 1968, that the song symbolized not yet another victory but at least another revolution: political, cultural, and in many ways religious. There was a string of events during the 1960s that those involved will remember as long as they live—including where they were and what they were doing when tragedy struck.

The frustrated jottings in Drinan's Weston spiritual retreat notes during those months are partly a product of those days when the whole world, including a number of belief systems, seemed to be falling apart, and here he was, a priest and a dean, apparently powerless to do much about it. The Church had completed the landmark Vatican Council II, but its reforms were just sinking in, and in some quarters of the Church's governance, officials were dragging their feet. At Boston College, the process begun by Mike Walsh of handing over ownership of the institution to a board of lay-dominated trustees was not complete; and, because Drinan had supported Walsh in this move, it remained as one more factor isolating him from many of the senior members of the Jesuit community, anxious to hold on to what they considered their patrimony.

In January 1968, the North Vietnamese launched the Tet Offensive, during which nearly 70,000 North Vietnamese troops, many of whom had infiltrated the South through a network of tunnels, brought the war from the countryside into the cities. They even invaded the U.S.

Embassy in Saigon and held it for seven hours. Although the American and South Vietnamese forces may be said to have "won" the weeks-long battle, in that "only" 1,100 American and 2,300 South Vietnamese were killed, compared with 40,000 Viet Cong and North Vietnamese, as a psychological blow it marked a turning point in the war. The famous photo of the Vietnamese security official summarily executing a captive with a bullet in the head, including the blood spurting from his skull, prompted Robert F. Kennedy to stand up in the Senate and ask what America had become. In March, he announced his candidacy for the presidency.

In February, CBS News anchor Walter Cronkite, a veteran war correspondent, went to Vietnam and reported to his "CBS Evening News" audience that the time had come for the United States to negotiate a withdrawal. In March, troops under the command of Lieutenant William Calley massacred more than 500 Vietnamese civilians, including infants and elderly people, in the little hamlet of My Lai. In April, Martin Luther King Jr., who was in Memphis planning for the Poor People's March on Washington, was shot to death while standing on his motel balcony. Hearing the news in Indianapolis, Robert Kennedy delivered a spontaneous eulogy, calling on the audience to "tame the savageness of man and make gentle the life of this world." The student strikes in France spread from Paris as millions of workers joined throughout the country. On June 5, having just won the California primary, Robert Kennedy was shot by Sirhan Sirhan, a twenty-four-year-old Palestinian living in Los Angeles, and died the next day.

In July and August, race riots broke out in Gary, Indiana; Miami, Florida; Chicago; and Little Rock. In Iraq, the Arab Socialist Ba'ath Party staged a coup, drove out the Jesuits, and set the stage for Saddam Hussein's eventual ascent to power.

In August, the Soviet Union invaded Czechoslovakia to put an end to the growing democratic movement called "Prague Spring." For thousands of Americans at the Democratic National Convention in Chicago and millions watching the news on TV, the trauma was the police attack, with clubs and tear gas, over three days, against the thousands of young demonstrators who had come to protest the Vietnam War. More than 100 were sent to emergency rooms and 175 were arrested.

In the eyes of some, the "young hoodlums" had gotten what they deserved; in the eyes of many, America had become a police state.

Meanwhile, in the parallel world of the Church, three events set the tone for the future understanding of how a believer should relate to the church and state authorities.

In May, nine Catholic activists led by Daniel Berrigan and his brother, Philip, a Josephite priest, plus seven others, entered a draft board in Catonsville, Maryland, seized 400 files of young men classified 1-A (for immediate service), and burned the files with homemade napalm, in mockery of the U.S. napalm bombings in Vietnam. This action was the fruit of a process begun in the early 1960s, inspired by Dorothy Day's Catholic Worker movement and influenced by Thomas Merton's spirituality, all loosely called the Catholic Left.

Dorothy Day (1879–1980) grew up in San Francisco and Chicago, where she read books, like Upton Sinclair's *The Jungle*, that stirred her social conscience. In New York she wrote for socialist publications and in 1927 became a Catholic, baptized her daughter, and left her common-law husband. With Peter Maurin, a French immigrant inspired by the idea of a social order based on Gospel principles, she founded the *Catholic Worker*, a radical newspaper that was part of a movement dedicated to pacifism, labor, and service to the poor.

Thomas Merton (1915–68), born in France of a New Zealander father and an American mother, after a dissolute life in Europe and England came to Columbia University in New York, where he read himself into the Catholic Church and later joined the Trappist monastery Gethsemane Abbey in Kentucky. His autobiography, *Seven Storey Mountain*, followed by *Seeds of Contemplation*, made him one of Catholicism's most influential writers. Though a cloistered monk, he wrote on social and political issues and opposed the Vietnam War.

Narrowly defined, the Catholic Left consisted of about 230 activist men and women, mostly laypersons, but including many priests, about seven of whom were Jesuits, willing to take nonviolent action and face arrest in order to draw attention to civil and human rights and what they saw as the immorality of the Vietnam War.

On July 29, Pope Paul VI issued the encyclical *"Humanae Vitae,"* reaffirming the Church's opposition to all contraception except the "rhythm method," which limits sexual intercourse to periods when the wife cannot conceive. A papal commission, consisting of priests, moral theologians, and married couples, appointed by Pope John XXIII and reaffirmed by Paul VI had recommended a change in Church teaching that would allow married couples to practice contraception under certain circumstances. But, partly because of the intervention of John Ford, who saw any break in the continuity of papal teaching as a threat to all Church teaching, the pope moved back to continuing the ban. From the encyclical's publication many moral theologians took exception to its conclusions, arguing that its natural law argument failed to take into consideration the full context of the marital relationship and advising Catholic couples that they should follow the voice of their conscience. The result was the alienation of married Catholics who had found that birth control deepened their love and strengthened their families. Some continued to go to Mass and receive communion; others fell away. That same summer, the United Nations celebrated World Population Day, and world leaders proclaimed that individuals have a basic human right to determine freely and responsibly the number and timing of their children.

In December, Thomas Merton died in Bangkok. Though a cloistered monk vowed to a life of silence and prayer, somehow Merton was allowed to become a writing machine. From his daily journals to his condemnations of nuclear weapons, Merton poured out books and articles that joined the contemplative and political lives. At the same time, he was partly responsible for the post–World War II surge in American monasticism while, as Drinan lamented, the contemplative life was drying up in Italy. In his last years Merton was moving eastward in his religious philosophy. Mohandas Gandhi, he said, was one of the few who understood the Gospel ethic and could apply its principles in a way that was thoroughly religious and political at the same time.

With each of these events—from the bombing of Vietnam to the renewed ban on contraception—Drinan had to chart his course to establish greater public influence. But the underlying question of the mid-1960s was: Just what is the proper role for the priest in this post–

Vatican II world? In his writings and lectures he was already supporting conscientious objection and the right to demonstrate and break an
unjust law in order to protest what one viewed as a social evil. He
did not shrink from being called a liberal, but, perhaps by personal
disposition, he could not personally identify himself as a member of
the Catholic Left. As a law professor and a priest, he was not ready to
go to jail, but he sensed that he had to do more than teach and talk.

What Is a Priest?

Just as Drinan, ordained at Weston in 1953, spent his year in Italy and
took his first deep drink of a foreign mindset, Daniel Berrigan, ordained the year before, went to France. Like the other American Jesuits
in those years, he traveled to military bases in Germany preaching and
giving retreats. But he soon became aware of how sheltered his life
had been. "Arriving in France was like landing on a fresh-air planet
after being locked up all my life in a capsule. The American church, at
the time, was an Irish ghetto. I had never been politically aware before," he wrote. "I arrived so American, such an idiot. . . ." He was
radicalized by his discovery of the worker-priests, an organization of
more than a hundred priests in France and Belgium. Most had been in
the resistance and/or in German prison camps during World War II
and had recently joined the workforce, not as preachers but as co-
laborers, to regain the lost working class for the Church.

Berrigan's time in France coincided with the French Foreign Legion's loss of the battle of Dien Bien Phu and of France's forced withdrawal from Indochina. Also, the Vatican suppressed the worker-priest
movement on the grounds that its vocation—that is, working in a factory—allegedly compromised the role of the priest. For example, the
priest would join the union and participate in a strike—all rights guaranteed by the papal social encyclicals of 1891 and 1931. But what if
the union were Communist-dominated and what if the strike turned
violent? And, to a certain kind of piety or cultic understanding of the
priesthood, which sees the priest primarily in his liturgical role, could
the same hands that were covered with grit and grease or that shoveled

manure on a farm also hold the host at Mass? According to a Catholic educator who worked with Berrigan after his return, he became obsessed with two issues: "alleviating poverty and breaking down the traditional structures of the priest–layman relationship."

Matthew O'Connell, S.J., a professor at Woodstock College in Maryland, which, like Weston, prepares young Jesuits for the priesthood, wrote in "The Priest in Education: Apostolate or Anomaly" (*Theological Studies* [1965, 26, 65–85]) about attempts to resolve the problem of the "hyphenated priest," the tension between the priesthood and other jobs that priests take on. He dealt immediately with the priest-scholar, probably because in the 1960s there was some fall-off in the number of Jesuits who wanted to be university professors, even though the Society was attracting several medical doctors and lawyers. He began with the example of Christ, who was seen as prophet, priest, and king, which today would mean a minister of the word, of the sacraments, and the authoritative guide for the faithful. The solution is for the priest not to partition his priesthood off from other aspects of his life. Instead he must integrate the two and not let one swallow up the other. He must remember that in the eyes of men he cannot escape the new *persona publica*, the new personality acquired by ordination. If his life is discordant with his message, the message is diminished. Nor can he draw a line as if there are parts of life in which the Church has no say, because "the church's field of operation is as broad as life itself."

But there is a hierarchy within which the forms of the priest's ministry may live. The first is preaching the Gospel; the others may not swallow up the first. But which works most to embody the human values that need to have put upon them the mark of Christ? O'Connell listed science, literature, philosophy, theology, poetry, and art because these disciplines most need to hear the words of redemption. As a contrary example he added, there is "no need of priest garbage collectors because there is no crisis here." He did not say that a priest is too good to pick up garbage. There are other possible ways for priests to work that need more time and experimentation—for example, in city planning, technology and politics.

In contrast to O'Connell's article, William H. Cleary's edited *Hyphenated Priests: The Ministry of the Future* (1969), a collection of essays by ten Jesuit priests, is personal, practical, and built around the theme that all priests can, should, and indeed must develop a profession—an identity—along with the sacramental or cultic identity specific to the priesthood. Cleary had invited Drinan to contribute; he was to explain how he harmonized priesthood with law studies and politics. Drinan promised to do so and said he spent the whole weekend trying. But he gave up, then told Cleary that he could not figure it out in time. Cleary was taken aback, and the book was published without Drinan's contribution.

Perhaps he really couldn't come up with a rational explanation, or perhaps he prudently calculated that whatever he said could be used against him politically. Most likely he read *Hyphenated Priests*, because many of the authors were his contemporaries, including ten *America* editors. They included a journalist, a sociologist, an economist, an aerospace engineer, a missionary, a doctor, a lawyer, a poet-novelist, a concert pianist, and a theologian. Two essays are especially pertinent to Drinan, who saw himself as a writer and a lawyer.

The young poet-novelist, John L'Heureux, did not shrink from incompatibility, or tension, between the two roles; but, for him, the hyphen was not a negative force but the person himself, the priest-writer, who sometimes acts as a priest and sometimes as a writer. Yet, he insisted, whatever he may give to people in his writing, he must also regularly say public Mass, administer sacraments, and preach. "Otherwise he might as well be a social worker." Another tension: The writer is egocentric; he looks at the world and judges it. "The priest's psychic force must bend outward." How does he bring these two outlooks into one? L'Heureux answered:

> The priest must love his world, he must cure it with the care of Christ. The writer must show the world its image: keeping in mind the extermination camps of World War II, the mass rape of the American Negro, the cultured inanity of the diamond and liquor advertisements of the *New Yorker*, the shame of Vietnam and the terrifying heroism of Czechoslovakia, he must say: Here you are, change or despair.

Charles Whelan, like Drinan directed by his provincial, went to Georgetown Law School in 1951, received his LL.B. in 1954 and an

LL.M. in 1955, and was admitted to the District of Columbia bar in 1954. Eventually he joined the bar of the U.S. Supreme Court. After ordination he worked in parishes and hospitals and as general counsel for what was then the U.S. Catholic Conference. This was the beginning of his interest in church–state issues. He became an associate editor of *America* and a longtime professor at Fordham Law School. "The world will not be saved without the Mass and sacraments," he wrote, "but neither will it be saved by them alone."

In short, when Drinan moved step-by-step from priest to lawyer to politician, he was a pioneer, but not a lonely one. Meanwhile, of the eleven writers and one editor of the book, only three later left the priesthood.

Exodus

As if all these tensions were not enough, the time also marked the rapid decline in religious vocations and membership in the Society. Between 1958 and 1978, the number of American Jesuits peaked at 8,338 in 1960, then fell to 7,055 in 1970. About a third of the novices left within their first two years. During these years, the seminaries moved from the country to urban university campuses, and many of the barriers intended to protect the young men were gone, But the exodus included leading seminary professors, who, perhaps experiencing the freedoms of the reformed Vatican II Church for the first time, rethought their lives and reached out for more—and to marry before they were too old to raise a family. And, perhaps, as John Ford told Paul Kelly, some men were called only for a short time and would continue their service as laymen. (Drinan's generation survived a little better. Of the forty-nine novices with him at Shadowbrook in 1943, thirty were still Jesuits in 1980.)

Francine du Plessix Gray, in *Divine Disobedience: Profiles in Catholic Radicalism* (1971), summed up the chaos and the wonderful excitement of those years:

> The Catholic Church can be compared to a zoo of wild beasts, held in captivity for over a millennium, whose bars Pope John removed. There

are as many pacifists among the rampaging animals as there are liturgical innovators and structural reformists. Before the Second Vatican
Council pacifists were a rare species. They have proliferated since the
Council ended in 1965. Pope John's encyclical *Pacem in Terris* issued a
clear call for total pacifism in the nuclear age. An important Council
edict, "The Constitution on the Church in the Modern World," called
for clearer government recognition of the rights of conscientious objec-
tors. And by 1967 Jim Forest estimates that he was counseling some
200 Catholic C.O.'s a month at the Catholic Peace Fellowship. But by
that time a schizophrenia had set into the American Catholic Church
concerning the Vietnam War. The Pope had condemned it. Progressive
theologians such as Notre Dame scripture scholar John McKenzie, Boston College Law School dean Robert Drinan, and the Berrigans, as well
as the progressive Catholic press—*Commonweal, Jubilee, Ave Maria*,
the *Critic*, the *National Catholic Reporter*—had called it the most immoral war in our history. The lines were drawn: the pleading Pope
versus the timid, property-loving American bishops; the lonely young
curates radicalized by ghetto work versus their cautious, Bingo-mad
pastors; the Catholic intellectuals versus the war-mongering, law-and-
order Catholic masses; *Commonweal* versus the *Brooklyn Tablet*; the
guerrillas versus the gorillas. It was going to be, as Daniel Berrigan
said, "some beautiful polarization." (94–95)

Law and Order

Drinan responded to the public call for "law and order," which
stemmed from the public anxiety engendered by the black militant
and student demonstrations, with his second book, *Democracy, Dissent,
and Disorder: The Issues and the Law* (1969), and to the Vietnam crisis
by speaking at Boston College about the moral issues involved and by
going to Vietnam.

This second Drinan book broke from the first in that its discussion
was more immediate, more "popular," addressed to a specific public
attitude on a contemporary controversy, and shorter, and, for the most
part, free of extensive documentation. It must be said—and those who

have read his books will agree—that, as a writer, Drinan was not a notable stylist. He wrote to promote his ideas; and somehow he lacked what it took to express his ideas with imagination, grace, felicity. Perhaps it was because, though he joined the newspapers in high school and college, he didn't publish articles until he was almost thirty, and although his highest grade in college was in English literature, his flood of books and articles have few references to fiction, poetry, theater, or film. So his articles, which later become, sometimes with few changes, book chapters, followed the format of the classroom or civic event lecture.

Democracy, Dissent, and Disorder begins: "There exists in many American minds a hitherto suppressed but now more and more unavoidable fear that the peaceful and proud America which everyone has known up to the present day may have lost its way." Clearly he was talking about black riots and demonstrations, the rise of crime and juvenile delinquency, the breakdown of the family, and the rejection of accepted moral standards that many felt resulted from failures of law enforcement; the solution, therefore, was to clamp down.

Two prime examples, of course, were the riots in Washington and across the country following the assassination of Martin Luther King Jr. and the eruption of violence at the Democratic National Convention in Chicago. In 1968 Richard M. Nixon and Spiro T. Agnew tapped into this anxiety in a "law and order" campaign and rode that anger into the White House. Drinan's response, many chapters written as talks during the election year, was that the enforcement of laws, particularly criminal law, would not by itself solve the problems that stemmed from other ills in society.

By no means did Drinan deny that the problems were real. He specialized in family law because personally he had strong feelings about the breakup of the family. At that time every fourth marriage ended in divorce. To him, there appeared to be a fantasy that spouses have an "almost absolute right to separate from any marriage that has not lived up to their romantic expectations." Meanwhile many people called for more severe punishments for juvenile delinquents—"a position which is in contradiction with the assumption that delinquents are the unwitting and inculpable victims of a divorce in the family."

The American student revolts were to some degree inspired by the 1968 student strikes in France; and the governance of the universities, controlled by absent trustees who disregarded student opinion, had invited student rebellion. Did this mean that students may use force, break the law? The end does *not* justify the means, Drinan said. Then he spelled out guidelines for rebellion: Exhaust all possible alternatives, consider and attempt passive resistance, and assure that the objective to be attained is significant enough to justify "the dislocations to the public good brought about by the temporary upheavals."

Drinan listed other problems without legal remedies: psychological abuse of prisoners, punitive laws dealing with alcohol and narcotic addiction, the commitment of mentally retarded persons, and safeguards for the aged in nursing homes. He challenged the dogma that America was incapable of conducting an immoral war and that every child must be taught both to respect the armed forces and believe that America has acted morally in every war it has fought. In fact, he said, the United States "breeds lawlessness by indulging in lawlessness." He cited the 421-page 1967 report by Clergy and Laymen Concerned about Vietnam, which documented violations of the Hague, Geneva, and Nuremberg conventions in international law in at least a dozen areas, including care of the sick and wounded, the rights of noncombatants, and the plight of refugees.

Drinan asked whether America, which has the historical reputation for absorbing its revolutions, "can absorb another tidal wave of dissent and disorder." In response he argued that today religious groups *must* speak out on moral issues. They worked together successfully assisting displaced persons after World War II, repealing the unjust racial-quota immigration law, and passing the Civil Rights Acts of 1964 and 1965. When he spoke about religious cooperation he used the expression "churches and synagogues." During these years the ecumenical aspect of his personal spirituality and politics played an increasingly larger role.

The *National Catholic Reporter* gave *Democracy, Dissent, and Disorder* a feature review. In the *Boston Globe* (December 7, 1969), Leonard W. Levy, a Pulitzer Prize winner at Brandeis University, had a little fun. He called it a "seditious tract," "which should earn him an honored place on the roll-call of native sons of this commonwealth, like Sam Adams, Theodore Parker, and Roger Baldwin, who have been 'libertarian rebels.'" It was a slim volume that "pack[ed] a megaton wallop." It was as wise and illuminating as it was outrageous and infuriating. With reference to both Nixon and Thomas Paine, he concluded, "It is a book especially for that morally paunchy lot, the silent majority, and for those who serve as summer patriots and sunshine soldiers in the cause of liberalism."

Going to Vietnam

By the spring of 1969 the American Catholic bishops, cautious as ever, still could not make up their minds on whether the Vietnam War, according to traditional Catholic Just War Theory, should be labeled "unjust." To some degree America's initial involvement in Vietnam had been a "Catholic" enterprise, in that it had the full support of New York's Cardinal Francis Spellman, influenced by the fact that Vietnam's President Ngo Dinh Diem was a Catholic. About one-tenth of the nation's population was Roman Catholic, partly because of the influence of French Catholicism during its colonial period. About one million of South Vietnam's Catholics were families who had fled North Vietnam to escape Communist persecution, and now South Vietnam must be rescued from Communism. But by April 1968 the National Conference of Catholic Bishops (NCCB) stepped back from its blanket anti-Communism and noted that the conflict had "spawned great injustices and immoralities and greatly troubled the consciences of many bewildered sons of the Church." The bishops deplored the deaths, destruction, and uprooting of whole populations and called the war of "questionable legitimacy," but not yet "unjust." In November 1968 they called for amending the Selective Service Act to allow for selective conscientious objection, but they continued to agonize over the war without condemning it.

Drinan seized an opportunity to gather evidence that might further reveal the true nature of the war. Sponsored by the Fellowship of Reconciliation and the newly formed ecumenical organization Clergy and Laymen Against the Vietnam War, he joined a study team of eight distinguished clergy and civic leaders—Methodist Bishop James Armstrong, Anne M. Bennett, Allan Brick of the Fellowship of Reconciliation, Congressman John Conyers Jr. of Michigan, English Congregationalist pastor Peter W. Jenkins, American Civil Liberties Union Executive Director John de J. Pemberton, Rabbi Seymour Siegel, and Rear Admiral (Ret.) Arnold E. True—for a May 25–June 10, 1969, study visit to Vietnam. Their purpose was to investigate the treatment of political prisoners.

To read their forty-page report in the present day—in the context of the Iraq War and the controversies surrounding the treatment of prisoners at Abu Ghraib and Guantánamo Bay; the debate over terminology like "harsh interrogation techniques," "waterboarding," and "torture"; and whether political prisoners have the right of *habeas corpus*—is to realize how deeply rooted the culture of abuse can become, especially during a war that lacks the support of the people and when a government makes its decisions based on the crassest of utilitarian logic.

The study team met with South Vietnam's President Nguyen Van Thieu, the minister of the interior and his staff, U.S. ambassador Ellsworth Bunker and his staff, religious leaders, lawmakers, intellectuals, attorneys, students, representatives of a spectrum of political opinions, and scores of political prisoners.

In a report to the *Washington Post* (June 24, 1969) Drinan described Thieu, a convert to Catholicism, as "gentle and amiable." But he also found Thieu evasive as he finessed the group's four questions. Buddhists had not been imprisoned unjustly, he said. A grenade had been found in their meeting place. Religion was not being repressed; they were violating the laws on the size and frequency of demonstrations. On abuses in military field courts, he said the law allowed the government to disregard rules of evidence in wartime. On the suppression of newspapers, Thieu said Vietnam already had too many newspapers.

The members of Drinan's group visited three major prisons, including the escape-proof Con Son Island, and the national police headquarters. When they felt they were being blocked from places they wanted to see, they insisted until they gained access. They granted the difficulties under which the South Vietnamese government operated. It was wartime, the country was poor, and their constitution, which granted all the traditional liberties, was only two years old—and a recent law had nullified some human rights. Nevertheless, they concluded in a message cabled directly to President Nixon: "Speaking of peace or in any way opposing the government (in South Vietnam) easily brings the charge of communist sympathy and subsequent arrest. . . . There must be no illusion that this climate of religious and political suppression is compatible with either a representative or a stable government."

Along with the routine research and interviews, the visitors got their share of dramatic moments that would remain embedded in their memories. In response to the pope's plea for peace in Vietnam, 2,000 students, mostly Buddhist but many of them Catholic, held a peace procession, after which hundreds of the marchers were arrested. During the visit to Con Son Island, a Buddhist student stepped out from the mass of the prisoners and called out that he was there because he refused to be drafted, because he "[didn't] want to serve the United States."

They met with a group of leaders from old-line political parties no longer allowed to function, men who had opposed the French and were ardent nationalists and now saw the Americans as merely replacing the French. These men, who had endured imprisonment for twenty-five years, warned the team that America makes a mistake when it confuses Vietnamese Communists with European Communists. A leading nationalist handed the study team a three-page paper arguing that the whole cross-section of the population must be given a voice. A student leader who had been imprisoned twice for peace activities said that no truly representative democracy could come into being as long as U.S. troops were present and U.S. policy was being imposed: "The Americans must depart leaving us to decide our own future." Drinan, the teacher and family lawyer, must have choked up when he saw fifty women, some with babies, living in a space forty feet by thirty feet; two students, unsentenced detainees, who showed "leftist tendencies" in their student newspaper articles; forty-seven children under the age of eight, in one room forty feet by twenty-five feet; one child, four years old, in prison because he was accused of stealing a necklace; two prisoners who had been in solitary confinement for six months for refusing to salute the flag.

The prison authorities denied that there were any "tiger cages," cells with bars in the roof that resembled the cages for tigers in zoos; but one prisoner took a team member aside and assured them the cages were there, "You looked in the wrong place." Physical abuse included beatings with sticks and clubs, on the back, legs, hands, genitals, and soles of the feet. A key water torture was "waterboarding," or simulated drowning. And the most common torture was tying the victim's hands behind him and hoisting him up by the wrists, stretching the arms and body in excruciating pain—a method that dates back to the Inquisition.

Furious, Drinan published his reaction to what he had seen in *America* (June 28, 1969), the *Boston Globe* (June 28, 1969), and the *New Republic* (July 19, 1969). On May 23, he said, a highly placed U.S. State Department official told him that South Vietnam had been decreasing its number of political prisoners. He went to Vietnam anyway, and returned to tell the State Department that the official had "lied." There were 35,000 political prisoners and their number was rising, he said, and one-third of the prisoners had never been accused of anything or given a sentence. Rather, Drinan continued, the political imprisonment was the result of the so-called "pacification" program that ferreted out civilians suspected of being "disloyal" and handed them to local "kangaroo courts." He attacked the system of torture and the marginalization of citizens who were loyal but had something critical worth saying.

Independent of the study team, Drinan suggested in *America*: release the long-term prisoners who had not been charged with crimes, grant due process to those charged and hear their cases, and protect the Buddhists and those whose conscience prevented their participation in the war. He repeated the John F. Kennedy quote he had used in other articles: "Those who make the peaceful revolution impossible make violent revolution inevitable."

On June 10 and 11, 1969, the study team gave its report to the State Department and the White House. Neither responded.

Drinan was so depressed when he left the handsome offices of the State Department that he could not speak for half an hour. He didn't know what to do. He ate his usual quick lunch and hastened to a two o'clock appointment with a senator. He shared his frustration with a few congressmen. They were not surprised. He saw what he thought students see in their government policy of lies. It was the "ultimate form of corruption."

He concluded his *New Republic* article: "I shall never forget these encounters. They have probably done more than any other event in my life to galvanize my determination to work for a government which will be honest in its communication with its citizens."

Just how he would do that was not yet clear.

Enter Jerome Grossman

Jerome Grossman, a tall, imposing man who in his youth had played tennis, baseball, and football and run track, was also a successful Boston businessman, president of the Massachusetts Envelope Company, and had been active in the peace movement since the 1950s. Unlike some peace activists, however, he was determined to work through the Democratic Party. In 1968 he worked for the presidential nomination of Senator Eugene McCarthy of Minnesota and was on the scene in front of the Hilton Hotel during the Democratic National Convention in Chicago when, as the demonstrators chanted, "The whole world is watching!" the police attacked and drove demonstrators and spectators crashing through the plate-glass front window of the hotel, sending them cut and bleeding into the hotel lobby. Grossman was so depressed by the ultimate November choice between Vice President Hubert H. Humphrey, whom he saw as a hawk, and Nixon that he could vote for neither. But he kept working to stop the war.

On April 20, 1969, at a Brookline meeting of MassPax, a Massachusetts peace organization he founded in 1960, Grossman proposed a novel tactic: a series of monthly national strikes, demanding the withdrawal of American troops from Vietnam, in which all opposed to the war would refuse to work on that day. For every month that the troops remained, the strikers would add one more day. Each month they would conduct a "market survey" to determine if there was enough public support for them to try again. Fellow activists Sam Brown and David

Hawk convinced Grossman to change "strike" to "moratorium," lest the public confuse their actions with student strikes, which had less support. The heart of Grossman's plan was not a major demonstration but a mass process in which anti-war citizens would fan out into their neighborhoods and knock on doors, making the case against the war and signing up their fellow citizens to participate. As plans developed, however, the door-to-door campaign was combined with the mass rallies. In Boston, on October 15, 1969, they would do both—hold a mass meeting for hundreds of thousands during the day on the Boston Common and a neighborhood meeting at Boston College that evening.

Meanwhile, back on the Boston College campus, the administration was engaged in a mini-war of its own. In September 1969, as reported in *The Heights*, Drinan, increasingly frustrated by what he considered the failure of leadership at B.C., used the occasion of an address on the role of the professional school to the university academic senate to lash out at what he considered the overconcentration of power in the hands of the president, Father W. Seavey Joyce; the treasurer; the trustees; and the board of directors. In his judgment, students and faculty should have a voice on financial matters and the alumni ought to have a voice in choosing a representative on the board of directors. More and more the actual work of the dean's office was falling to his assistant Richard Huber, as Drinan's off-campus commitments made more demands on his energies. His off-and on-campus roles would soon come together as he prepared his homily for the Boston College Moratorium Mass on October 15.

As October 15 approached, the Harvard faculty voted 391–16 to support the moratorium. Senator George McGovern of South Dakota, who had in Chicago briefly stepped into the breach created by the death of Robert Kennedy, was scheduled as the main speaker for the mass rally on the Boston Common. Grossman was his designated host. After his group picked up McGovern at the airport, at City Hall Grossman's responsibility as host was handed over to, as he remembers it, "Mayor Kevin White's chief assistant, a pudgy, fast-talking young man with a New Jersey accent" named Barney Frank.

When they rode up Beacon Hill to the Common, where more than 100,000 people were chanting "Peace now," Grossman asked the driver to pull over to a subway stop. He told McGovern that he belonged back in his neighborhood spreading the word to his neighbors about the war.

Grossman was also scheduled to speak at Boston College that night. Earlier the campus had devoted itself to a "teach-in," a folk concert, and a Mass for Peace, for which Drinan delivered the homily. During the afternoon some students spread out to canvass the community. The main event that night was a dinner, followed by a rally in Roberts Center. There William Sloane Coffin, Yale University chaplain, told a crowd of what *The Heights* guessed was 6,000 that "silence becomes treason when a good American dies in a bad cause."

Echoing the results of Drinan's report on Vietnamese prisons, the son of the South Vietnamese opponent to President Thieu condemned the South Vietnamese regime for holding more political prisoners in jail than the North held in total. Jerome Grossman, introduced as the Newton Adult Moratorium Coordinator, took the stand. He remembers the auditorium jammed with nine or ten thousand people. As he started to speak, he could already sense the anger in the crowd. He remembers, "They did not cheer my words and those of the other speakers—they roared their feelings. I held on to the lectern against the torrent of anger and at that moment believed that there was no way the war could continue."

But did the moratorium do any good? From what Grossman heard from sources in Washington, Nixon and his national security adviser, Henry A. Kissinger, were at the point of using the most extreme measures to achieve what they considered a "win." The critical situation called for something very different, very dramatic. They needed a candidate to run against the entrenched Democratic warhorse, who uncritically supported the Nixon administration's Vietnam policy, in his Third District in 1970.

Grossman noticed there was this Jesuit at the dinner that W. Seavey Joyce had held before the rally and that he and his wife had attended. The priest, finding a seat next to a young Vietnamese man whose father was in a jail in Vietnam, was "unusually kind and considerate to the young man. There was no question as to where his sympathies lay on the war."

5   A "New Politics" Candidate

Like Jerome Grossman and all those who were across from Grant Park at the Democratic National Convention in Chicago in 1968 during the police attacks, Arthur Obermayer, a scientist, intellectual, philanthropist, and activist, was determined to do whatever he could to make sure that something like this could not happen again. For the previous ten years he had been president of the Moleculon Research Corporation of Cambridge, which had been doing secret work for the Department of Defense and the Atomic Energy Commission. Because he was concerned about the U.S. defense posture, he did not want to see national resources wasted on useless programs. In practice, this meant finding a peace candidate to run for Congress in Massachusetts' Third Congressional District, a collection of towns to the west of downtown Boston that included Newton and Boston College at its eastern border.

For Grossman, the success or failure of the moratorium was critical because Congress was debating the war that very night in Washington. Nixon had told the electorate in 1968 that he had a "secret plan" to end the war; but it was actually a plan to escalate it. The so-called secret plan, prepared by Henry Kissinger without the knowledge of Defense Secretary Melvin Laird, called for massive bombing of Hanoi, Haiphong, and other targets in North Vietnam, including the dike system; mining harbors and rivers; a ground invasion of North Vietnam; and specifically bombing the Ho Chi Minh Trail, which in places ran along the border between North and South Vietnam. Central to this escalation was the proposed use of nuclear weapons. Kissinger was reported to be pushing the "nuclear option." Nixon may have been ready to avail himself of that option until the moratorium, among many factors in the growing opposition to the war, made him back off. The fact that that idea was even under consideration was all the more reason to elect to Congress a spokesman who had the intelligence, courage, and eloquence to help put the brakes on a potential nuclear holocaust.

Meanwhile, Drinan's interests and areas of expertise were broadening, to the point where, although he had zero political experience and had never even registered as a member of a political party, he could at least appear to be as well informed as any candidate for office. At Boston College he put special emphasis on racial issues. He had become chairman of the Advisory Committee of Massachusetts to the National Commission for Civil Rights. His support of black students led to the creation of a black studies program. Drinan condemned the de facto segregation in Boston's school system and challenged Boston College students to become involved with CORE and the NAACP. In his last year as president, Mike Walsh established a $100,000 scholarship fund to attract black students. This was the basis of the Black Talent Program set up by Walsh's successor, W. Seavey Joyce. Other schools were following suit. On some campuses, the sudden influx of black students initially raised more tensions and questions about how the white and black students should be integrated. Some schools hired a black student adviser to track the black students academically, and some black students demanded a "black corridor" in the residence halls so they could live with people like themselves. This, of course, was contrary to the purpose of their having been recruited to a previously "white" college.

At Boston College, black students presented demands to the board of directors for a 10 percent black representation in future student bodies, creation of a community center in the black neighborhood of Roxbury, two cars for an organization called the Black Student Forum, an all-black dormitory, and a flexibility in academic rule that would allow them three years to adjust to college requirements. Black enrollment was now a very low 137.

In November 1969 Drinan drew national attention when Tufts University brought him in, in his role as head of the federal Civil Rights Commission Advisory Committee of Massachusetts, to resolve a civil

rights dispute. Tufts was building a dormitory, and 400 students supporting the Afro-American Society, which represented the 150 blacks
on campus, were demonstrating to demand more jobs for black workers on the construction project. Black students interrupted work by
occupying the construction site when only five blacks and two Puerto
Ricans were employed out of 104 workers. Drinan's committee held a
public hearing, which, at the black students' request, toured the construction site. Drinan called for the construction company to publish a
list of the jobs available as they mediated a solution.

After this, Drinan's eyes were on the war.

In 1968, while Grossman was busy on the McCarthy campaign, Newton, the wealthy suburban home to both Boston College and Grossman,
was added to the Third Congressional District, which Philip Philbin, a
war hawk and current vice chairman of the House Armed Services
Committee, had represented with little opposition for twenty-eight
years. Those sympathetic to Philbin appreciated his attentiveness to
constituent service—his birthday cards, his appearances at weddings,
wakes, and funerals. But he was not issue-oriented, and he was an
unswerving supporter of the war. He was also a Roman Catholic with
a brother who was, with Drinan, a member of the Society of Jesus, and
Philbin may have thought that out of loyalty to a fellow Jesuit, a Jesuit
would not oppose him.

Two anti-war candidates, Thomas Boylston Adams and Joseph
Bradley, mounted campaigns against Philbin for the Democratic nomination in 1968. Grossman made a modest attempt to get one of them
to drop out in favor of the other, but they both held on, split the liberal
vote, and handed Philbin renomination with 48 percent. So Grossman
and Obermayer approached the 1970 primary convinced that the right
candidate could take out Philbin for the nomination and, because the
district was strongly Democratic, beat the Republican opponent in November. Grossman already had a brigade of young volunteers he'd organized for the moratorium; they would be ready for the primary and
the November election. Grossman also wanted a victory in order to
convince the powerful but cautious Massachusetts Congressman

Thomas P. "Tip" O'Neill that the anti-war liberals had broad support and that Grossman's strategy was relevant to other campaigns.

If it became necessary, Grossman was ready to run himself, though he was not confident that a wealthy Jewish businessman could carry the Catholic and Protestant towns, and he might lack the support of the Kennedys, given that he had supported Ted's Democratic primary opponents in 1962 and 1964. Obermayer, as soon as he got back from Chicago in 1968, worked for Joe Bradley and watched him lose. Then on December 2, 1969, Douglas Stewart, a classics professor at Brandeis University and a former Jesuit seminarian, called Obermayer's attention to an article in the December 6 *New Republic*, "From the Streets to the Polls," by Yale University professors James David Barber and David R. Mayhew on organizing an anti-war campaign. The authors argued for early organization, the selection of a candidate determined to stop the war, and "leg power"—personal contact with the voters.

The authors zeroed in on Philbin, whose district "[nested] among one of the most thickly settled hotbeds of student power in the United States—the Harvard–MIT–University of Massachusetts–Brandeis complex." They concluded that the finale of the drama

> require[d] a special dedication which may be too much for the older generation. It means hour after hour of work few will notice. It moves beyond the excitement of provocation to the exhaustion of persuasion. There will be speeches by those who have never made speeches, lonely encounters with hostile voters, cold feet and missed recreations, chances taken in a cloud of uncertainty. No one can say how it will turn out. But if the alternative to politics is acquiescence to killing and dying, we have a responsibility to try politics.

In a way they could not have foreseen, the authors caught the spirit that would drive Drinan's campaign.

Obermayer, who was chair of the peace group Newton Coalition for New Politics, and Stewart recognized that while often a candidate puts himself forward and looks for a constituency, they already had a constituency—the anti-war forces, ready to work for the right candidate. Obermayer asked, "How about Father Drinan?"

Two days later at a monthly meeting at Obermayer's house, the suggestion was greeted with enthusiasm. Obermayer, who had heard Drinan speak at the October 15 moratorium, asked a B.C. professor, Gary Brazier, to approach Drinan and sound him out. Drinan was cautious but open, aware of his liabilities and of booby traps (surprise opposition tactics); but he asked Obermayer to put the invitation in writing. Then on January 12, 1970, Drinan met in his Boston College Law School dean's office with Obermayer and a three-person committee consisting of Peter O'Malley, a Catholic; Kenneth Wilson, a Protestant; and Obermayer, a Jew. Drinan had done his homework and was warming to the invitation. But, asked the committee, did he have the Church's permission to run?

Drinan replied that he did. Furthermore, he was willing and anxious to run because he was convinced that this was the way he could do the most good in his life.

To reinforce his point, he read a statement by Father Pedro Arrupe, the much-respected superior general of the Society of Jesus, in which, in an interview with the Spanish magazine *Indice*, he urged the Society's members not to avoid political involvement when such involvement was deemed necessary to combat social injustice. It is not surprising that Arrupe would have strong feelings on political and social justice issues. Trained as a medical doctor, he was superior of the Jesuit community in Hiroshima when American planes dropped the first nuclear bomb in 1945. He and his community spent all their energies and opened their house to the wounded and dying. "We reject the idea," Arrupe said,

> that Jesuits must systematically avoid all political involvement. Modern man rejects such an idea. . . . How, for instance, can a Jesuit priest remain passive in the face of racial injustice, or in the face of institutionalized violence? To remain inactive would mean betraying our calling in life. . . . In the past we failed many times to fulfill our mission, particularly in the social field, because of lack of freedom or because of political allegiance with the world and the powerful . . . but now the Jesuits must act, by word and deed; preach the social doctrine, act in the name of divine law, which surpasses human law.

Most likely Drinan had not read them the entire article, which concluded, "Freedom from factional politics is a basic condition of our boldness in taking the action needed in the supra-political field of man and mankind." Arrupe did not say that Jesuits should run for political office.

Permission

The two most controversial issues in Drinan's career were his support for legalized abortion and the fact that by running for Congress he raised, and answered to his personal satisfaction, the question of whether a Catholic priest should so formally identify himself with one political faction and thereby risk separating, perhaps alienating, himself from many of the people he was ordained to serve. And the "hyphenated priest" debate, though answered in many theological essays, was not dead. Indeed, one of the unforeseen by-products of sending more young Jesuits into Ph.D. programs in the 1960s was that some could not balance or mesh their dual identities as priests and scholars, and left the priesthood.

A few days after the meeting, in January 1970, Drinan wrote to Kenneth Wilson, expressed his enthusiasm, and assured him he had consulted a high-ranking lawyer with the American Civil Liberties Union who assured him there was "absolutely no church–state problem" with the notion of Drinan's running for or holding public office and that the Constitution's Article 6, Section 3, which says, "no religious Test shall ever be required as a Qualification to any Office," should be "decisive and definitive." Drinan added the observation that the Third District was ripe for a registration drive, in that the eastern area tended to be a bedroom community for those who worked in Boston and that those potential voters might have a higher educational level that might make them liberal and thus opposed to the war. He tacked on a handwritten note that Grossman had just phoned him and would support him.

Grossman had concluded that Drinan was the best candidate for four reasons. First, he was impressed by what he saw at the Boston

College moratorium dinner—Drinan's speech and his record on human rights. Second, there was Drinan's reputation as a scholar and speaker. Third, Drinan had put Boston College Law School on the map. Fourth, "he was a one-man ecumenical movement in a state where ecumenism was then rare." Finally, Grossman said, "in [his] Jewish naïveté" he imagined that Drinan could deliver the Catholic vote, while he could deliver the Jewish vote.

Off and Running

On January 21, Obermayer took heart from a page-one story in the *Wall Street Journal* on conflict in Latin America, particularly Brazil, between the authoritarian governments and the progressive forces in the Catholic Church. The Church was seen as a "solid bulwark of resistance" to an increasingly stern military rule. Archbishop Dom Hélder Câmara, the hero of the young Latin American priests, held the Church responsible for having acquiesced in the "social disorder" for centuries, but now the common people were awakening to their plight. The progressives found support in Pope Paul VI's 1967 encyclical "On the Development of Peoples," calling for social justice where a certain "type of capitalism had institutionalized misery and deprivation." In 1968 the Latin American bishops meeting at Medellín, Colombia, thrust the Church into political issues by aligning the Church with the poor. In short, there was an international precedent for the Third District's bold stroke in running a priest for Congress.

In a sense, we might interpret Drinan's decision as an anticipation of the day, five years later, at the Society of Jesus's 32nd General Congregation in Rome, a turning point in the Society's history, when the delegates and Pedro Arrupe would commit the Society to the dual, simultaneous pursuit of faith and justice as a "faith that does justice." Decree 4—not formally a juridical decree but one that the Jesuit historian John Padberg calls "a message of guidance and inspiration to Jesuits everywhere"—had its roots in Vatican II's Schema 13 and liberation theology. It says, "There is no genuine conversion to the love of God without conversion to a love of neighbor and, therefore, to the demands of justice." With his usual frankness, Arrupe warned his brothers that if they followed the spirit of the decree some of them would be killed. Indeed, as the 1970 *Wall Street Journal* article reported, Hélder Câmara's young aide, a priest sociologist, had his throat cut and his body riddled with bullets, and thirty-two clerics were reported to be on a right-wing "death list."

On the Boston College campus, in November 1969 activists had focused on the nationwide strike at General Electric, affecting 15,000 workers at 280 plants in twenty-three states. When recruiters arrived at Alumni Hall to interview students who might want to work for GE, workers and student allies picketed the building, and six students were charged with forcing their way into the placement offices to interrupt the employment interviews. (Tried the following February, they received suspended sentences.) In December 1969, Daniel Berrigan had come to the campus and read his poems. In response to student protests, the University Academic Senate reduced ROTC to an extracurricular activity to be financed by the federal government.

Then, in the first week of February 1970, the Board of Directors appointed Drinan the university's vice president and provost. In effect, it gave him jurisdiction over development, public relations, and alumni relations. From today's perspective, it seems a surprising appointment in that, although the title appears to have made him a likely successor to the president, the duties didn't seem to mesh with the role of a Boston civil rights crusader and outspoken opponent of the Vietnam War.

Drinan admitted to *The Heights* that, yes, liberal Democrats had approached him about running for Congress and that he had not yet dismissed the possibility of running; his decision would depend on "considerations to be made by the local Democratic party." What this meant was that he had to be nominated by the local caucus within two weeks in order to run against Philbin in the primary.

A group of citizens calling themselves The Third District Citizens Caucus (3DCC) assembled their delegates for the nominating caucus at the Concord–Carlisle Regional High School, in the middle of the district, on Saturday, February 21. Having been preparing for the meeting since December, they had sent extensive questionnaires to all the prospective candidates in both parties, asking them to name their five most important issues, in order of importance, and to spell out their stands on withdrawal from Vietnam, pollution control, and poverty in the United States and abroad. Finally, they decided to consolidate their efforts behind one trustworthy anti-war candidate. They interviewed twenty such candidates and cut the list to four finalists who would speak at the caucus.

Three came to the meeting ready to address the caucus. The winner would need two-thirds of the votes. Any citizen in the district could take part. The youngest participant was sixteen and thus not yet even able to vote, and about 2,000 showed up, 852 of whom were voting delegates.

Each candidate had twenty minutes in which to speak. Of the four, Drinan, forty-nine, was the oldest; two were in their thirties, including H. Chandler Stevens, thirty-five, and Gordon Martin, who dropped out. A surprise candidate, John Kerry, twenty-six, was running strong and picking up support as others dropped out. Stevens, an MIT Ph.D., was a state representative and an adjunct professor at Brandeis. Kerry was a Yale graduate, young and handsome, a Vietnam War hero, planning to marry in May. He saw the Vietnam War as a mistake and a cause the United States could not win. He pledged to force industry to clean up the polluted environment, stop building cars, and build better public transportation. His eloquent speech, said a *Boston Globe* columnist, "almost stampeded the caucus." He was ahead in the voting until the Newton delegation reported in.

Drinan had his reputation for improving Boston College Law School, including editing the *Family Law Quarterly* and writing for *America*. He had membership on seven state and national committees and had written three books, including *Vietnam and Armageddon*, scheduled to be published that spring. A witness told *The Heights* that the very mention of Drinan's name at one local meeting "electrified with anticipation" those in attendance.

In Drinan's speech he confronted directly the atmosphere of fear and intimidation that the Nixon administration had employed to silence those who opposed its policies.

For almost a generation, an obsession about communism has so be-
mused the American mind that it has long since been patently "un-
American" to raise the question whether this country should any
longer "contain" communism. I say, boldly and unequivocally, that the
policy of containment has failed and that an entirely new foreign policy for America is the first imperative of a society of free men. . . .

I advocate, therefore, not merely the cessation of all hostilities in
Vietnam but an imaginative and massive program to bring about disarmament. I urge all Americans to divest themselves of the "mind-set"
against communism which has made impossible any re-examination
of America's foreign policy in the past generation.

Drinan also assured his audience that he was uniquely qualified to
challenge the anti-Communist myth and "its contamination of American life." He proposed himself as "a new moral and spiritual voice." In
other words, it would be difficult for his opponents to call a priest who
knew his theology a Communist.

The speeches and debate went from 9:00 A.M. until 6:30, when
Grossman noticed that some of his Drinan supporters were beginning
to leave. So he locked the doors and brought the discussion to a vote.
In the fourth ballot Kerry rose and moved that the assembly nominate
Drinan.

Kerry and Stevens served as co-chairmen of the Drinan for Congress campaign with Obermayer as treasurer. In March the leadership
selected John Marttila, a thirty-year-old disillusioned Republican who
had a reputation for running successful campaigns among ethnic
groups in Detroit, as campaign manager. Marttila brought with him
twenty-six-year-old Dan Payne, who would serve as press secretary and
flood the media with position papers. In Drinan's back yard, Robert
Cook, a student at the law school active in his campaign, also issued
press releases, the first describing Drinan as a "New Kind of Candidate": "One of the most unusual candidates for Congress in this or any
year is a Catholic priest. But beyond his very visible collar, Father Robert Drinan is much more." Cook's other responsibility was to drum up
support for Drinan among the Boston College students. Everyone who
attended the caucus had paid a $2 registration fee and many had added

contributions. Every delegate received a letter a week after the convention listing the dozen-plus jobs awaiting them—sign painting, holding coffee parties, telephone canvassing, and soliciting donations. The campaign's secret weapon was this army of 2,000-plus (and growing) volunteers revved up by this "new" candidate who appealed to their ideals.

All three principal figures—Grossman, Obermayer, and Drinan—however, were guilty of a few miscalculations. Both Grossman and Obermayer, as Jews looking in on the Catholic Church, overestimated the enthusiasm among Catholics for a priest candidate, and they thought their man was a bit better known than he actually was. They spent $15,000 on a comprehensive poll only to be advised by the poll analyst: "If you haven't gone too far with this effort, I recommend it be dropped." A *Boston Globe* poll published in May said that 54 percent of the constituency of the Third District had never heard of Drinan. And Drinan himself, accustomed to dealing with people from the status of a dean or a provost, and though charming with younger people or prospective faculty members he was recruiting, would reveal shortcomings in his dealings with people who challenged or bored him. A public person is by definition a target for those who oppose what he symbolizes, and Drinan began getting middle-of-the-night phone calls from people who didn't like him. But he declined to be intimidated.

Rome Steps In

On February 25, just a few days after Drinan's nomination, Father Paul Lucey, assistant to Father William Guindon, the New England provincial who had given Drinan the green light on running, was stunned to receive a cable from Father General Pedro Arrupe in Rome to Guindon in response to the news reports of Drinan's candidacy, telling him that Drinan's running was contrary to his directives and that "Drinan may not run for office and if elected may not serve." Thus began a behind-the-scenes struggle, which sometimes broke into the

headlines, between Church and Society authorities in Rome and Drinan's supporters in the New England and other Jesuit provinces over
his continuing role in politics—a struggle that would culminate in
Pope John Paul II's intervention in the spring of 1980.

Guindon was a very open man, supportive of younger Jesuits with
good ideas, who, by nature, enjoyed a good argument as a way of
getting at the truth. His assistant, Lucey, recalls that "It was an exhilarating experience to be working with Bill. He had built a wonderful
staff. We were very active and outspoken. Every time we had a staff
meeting there were raucous goings-on. They were wonderful meetings." A member of Guindon's staff said, "It wasn't fighting, it was just
a discussion." Part of the Jesuit myth is that all Jesuits salute and shout,
"Yes, SIR!" whenever a superior makes a decision. In reality, they are
free to use "representation," meaning that, after prayerful consideration, they may list their objections and ask for reconsideration. And
so that's what the American Jesuit provincials involved did with Father
Arrupe in the weeks and months leading up to Drinan's candidacy—
and in the following years.

Because Guindon was away, Lucey answered on his behalf, saying
that Drinan thought he had all the permissions necessary; that his
candidacy was consistent with the criteria adopted at the recent province congress on "the Christian reform of social structures"; that the
group nominating Drinan was not, strictly speaking, a party but a reform caucus; that a "distinguished monsignor" close to Cardinal Richard Cushing, archbishop of Boston, told Drinan his candidacy would
be "beneficial to the church"; and that the candidacy was not in any
way contrary to the rules of the Society or canon law.

Drinan wrote to Guindon, saying that he was "thunderstruck" by
Arrupe's intervention, that even the American Civil Liberties Union
found no problems with his running, and that it was too late to stop
now because 3,000 people were already engaged in the campaign.

On April 10, Guindon followed up with a seven-page letter to Arrupe in which he stressed that the province consultors were unanimous that nothing should interfere with Drinan's race and that scandal
and damage to the good name of the Society and the Church would

follow upon any appearance of ecclesiastical interference with the American democratic process.

Guindon's argument was at once highly personal, idealistic, and tough. It was personal in that he told Arrupe honestly that he found himself in a "quandary of obedience" for the first time in his life, "having to choose between the Superior's expressed wish and my own conscientious judgment." He wanted to save Arrupe any embarrassment that Drinan's candidacy might have caused him, but he had a morally unanimous opinion of everyone he contacted that he should not direct Drinan to withdraw from the race. It was idealistic in that, in his view, putting this man in Congress was the best way to bring the Church into the modern world, to fight against war, racism, and starvation. It was tough in that he sensed Drinan's real opponents were anonymous persons pressuring the general in Rome rather than openly confronting Drinan himself. Anonymous sources, said Guindon, are people who are afraid to take responsibility for acting openly. Their behavior is "despicable and unworthy of any Jesuit." Drinan had identified one of his open opponents as his former Weston professor John Ford, a strong supporter of "Humanae Vitae" and adviser to the Washington, D.C., archbishop.

Arrupe consulted widely, writing to all the American provincials for advice and to the bishops of the two dioceses, Boston and Worcester, that were in the Third District. Arrupe wondered whether Drinan should consider "qualified exclaustration," a temporary leave of absence from the priesthood, to run for office. But Guindon rejected that idea, again because, in his view, interference from Rome would result in scandal. Very likely Drinan, who was attached to his public image as a priest, agreed. Arrupe also expressed the wish for Drinan to come to Rome, but the archives of the New England province do not explain what happened to that suggestion.

As the weeks went by, Drinan fed Guindon more reasons supporting his case to pass along to Arrupe, like the decree on the choice of ministries from the 31st General Congregation emphasizing working through international organizations; examples of other priests in government roles, including Father Theodore Hesburgh, national chairman of the Commission on Civil Rights; that it was customary for law school deans to run for public office; and that the province congregation, with Drinan participating, had voted 54–6, with 3 abstentions, against asking Rome for guidelines on seeking public office.

After a long silence Drinan wrote to Arrupe on June 26, sending him editorials from *The Boston Pilot* and *Worcester Catholic Free Press* and reports on his personal interview with Bishop Bernard J. Flanagan of Worcester and Guindon's conversation with the chancellor of the archdiocese of Boston. Flanagan, cordial and receptive, volunteered to write a letter to the priests of the diocese indicating his approval. Cushing's "approval" came second-hand; Cushing told someone who told Drinan that his candidacy was a "great idea." Drinan included for Arrupe a copy of his just-published *Vietnam and Armageddon*, reminding Arrupe of his visit to Vietnam.

Arrupe Replies

On July 9 Arrupe thanked Drinan for the book and reminded him that he, too, had visited Vietnam in 1969 and narrowly missed being bombed. Arrupe had obviously been doing a lot of thinking and listening. Though he failed to get anything in writing, he accepted Flanagan's conversation and Cushing's second-hand enthusiasm as permission granted, though somewhat indirectly, and as fulfilling canon law. In the future, he said, because modern communication makes the world smaller, these local issues would require more involvement by the general. But he joined his prayers to Drinan's in the hope that his candidacy would promote the public morality of "your own country and to some extent of the whole world."

How did it happen that Arrupe moved from opposition to acceptance?

One of Drinan's supporters in Rome was Father Vincent O'Keefe, S.J., formerly a Woodstock College scripture scholar and briefly president of Fordham University before being elected Arrupe's general assistant—in effect, his number two man. O'Keefe and others saw Arrupe arguing from a European, specifically Spanish, context and not being fully familiar with the American understanding of the relationship between church and state, the nature of political parties in America, or the practical workings of American democracy.

At some time during a process that took several months, O'Keefe brought Drinan to Rome to meet with Arrupe's key advisers so they could understand one another. Then the American provincials—specifically Guindon; Father James Connor, the Maryland provincial; and Father Robert Mitchell of New York—remained involved and added their support. They pointed out that Drinan was not just any American Jesuit but one with a great legal mind, with an unusual background and experience, and, as Guindon and his advisers continually emphasized, that it would not look good from the American point of view for Arrupe, a foreigner, to seem to be interfering with the American political process. But the final touch, according to O'Keefe, which won Arrupe's acquiescence, if not his heartfelt approval, was the American group's argument that Drinan would never win anyway. "He didn't have a chance."

According to O'Keefe, Cushing approved of Drinan's running but would not say so publicly lest he appear to be formally endorsing a candidate. But Cushing's personal support of Drinan might be suggested in that in earlier years he used to sign his notes to Drinan as "Your devoted admirer," and in that the official Boston diocesan newspaper, *The Boston Pilot,* for which Drinan wrote and over which Cushing had control, saw no contradiction in a priest's running for Congress.

The Controversy

In 1992 Paul Mankowski, a Jesuit graduate student at Harvard, was given access to Jesuit archives in order to research an article on Drinan's congressional candidacy and voting record on abortion. He photocopied many pages of documents and, rather than write the article, passed them on to an historian at St. Louis University, James Hitchcock, author of *The Pope and the Jesuits* (1984), which attacked Drinan and portrayed the Society as in many ways antipathetic to traditional

Catholicism. When Drinan published in the June 4, 1996, *New York Times* a controversial op-ed piece on the procedure known by some as partial-birth abortion, Hitchcock produced a long essay in the July 1996 *Catholic World Report* purporting to demonstrate that, based on the documentation supplied by Mankowski, Drinan ran for Congress "in direct defiance of orders from Rome." The article tracks Arrupe's continuing attempts to stop Drinan from running again and concludes with generalizations, some on the mark, on how the Drinan phenomenon was a symptom of what Hitchcock termed the misguided "reforms" of the 1960s.

In summary, Hitchcock described the correspondence between Arrupe, Drinan, and Guindon on whether Drinan had the permission to run and the circumstances under which Drinan may have been able to run for office. It is reasonable to conclude, based on what Hitchcock read, that Arrupe did not want Drinan to run. In fact, Arrupe said publicly on several occasions that, although he strongly urged Jesuits to fight for justice, he did not think they should participate in partisan politics as candidates for office, that the party politician priest would not be free to be the priest-prophet.

Arrupe never took back these convictions. In the spring of 1971, after Drinan had been elected and had taken office, Arrupe visited the United States and met with the young Jesuits, including novices, at Weston. During the question period, one of the novices asked Arrupe what he thought of Drinan's being in Congress. Arrupe's response, says Michael Boughton, S.J., who was present, "was very friendly and calm, but very clear: he did not approve of priests serving in elective office, and he did not agree with or approve of Bob Drinan serving in elective office." Jaws dropped; some of the novices did not agree with their general. Well then, someone asked, how did Drinan get to be in Congress? Arrupe responded that it had been worked out at the local level. Apparently it was Arrupe's leadership style to trust the provincial on the scene to make a prudential decision with which he himself did not agree.

Today, forty years after Drinan's first election, the New England Jesuits' strong conviction that the Church of 1970 must be extremely sensitive about Rome's apparent meddling in American politics may seem surprising. In context, however, it may be significant that the campaign and narrow victory of the first Catholic president, John F. Kennedy, were still only a ten-year-old memory, and the assassinations of both John and Robert Kennedy were as if yesterday. And it may be part of the New England temperament, which Jesuits necessarily share, to insist on running their own affairs.

Some may be surprised that once the beloved General Pedro Arrupe said what he wanted, the New England leadership acted to the contrary. But representation, the policy that one may, after consultation with other Jesuits and superiors, challenge the superior's decision, is not well understood. Each side in such a dispute must withdraw, pray, consult, and come back. The New England religious superiors who argued with Arrupe were conscious that they were arguing not so much with a boss as with a brother. Whether their decision was right or wrong in the long run remains to be seen. The original decision of Church authorities to merely tolerate Drinan's running rather than endorse it would dog him to the end of his congressional career.

The Outside World

On May 4, about eight weeks after the nominating convention, the national mood went through another convulsion that further alienated the younger generation. U.S. forces in Vietnam invaded Cambodia; campuses across the country erupted in protest; college presidents, including several from Jesuit universities, signed a public protest; and at Ohio's Kent State University the National Guard opened fire on a line of student demonstrators, killing four and wounding nine, one of whom was paralyzed. Across the nation, student strikes closed hundreds of colleges and high schools. The reaction to the tragedy gave the Drinan campaign 1,000 volunteers to knock on doors and telephone 85,000 voters out of about 200,000 who were registered.

The background of the Kent State killings coincided with a major survey conducted by Oliver Quayle and Company, a New York political consulting firm commissioned to do both an "objective" and a "subjective" analysis of the Third District. The Quayle staff conducted 412 in-person interviews, eliminated many, and based their findings on 251 regular Democratic voters. The voters answered 132 closed-end questions (multiple choice) and 14 open-ended questions (in their own words). The interview period, April 18–29, also corresponded with the first observance of Earth Day, the return from the moon of the *Apollo 13* astronauts, and, most important, the announcement of the National Conference of Catholic Bishops that they disapproved of Catholic clergy running for public office.

The Quayle firm was to both describe the survey findings and advise the campaign on how to respond to its findings. Presented with a list of eleven political leaders, including Nixon, Edward M. Kennedy, and Philbin, voters who recognized Drinan saw him as extremely liberal. To offset this, Drinan was advised not to change his positions but to use words like "sensible" and "responsible" to soften his image and appear more moderate. Philbin was generally liked and respected, so he was not to be personally attacked. Although he was a Democrat, the Quayle firm advised that Philbin be described as a Nixon supporter, whenever possible, as "out of step" with Massachusetts' U.S. senators, Edward W. Brooke (a Republican) and Ted Kennedy. But Philbin was "old"—seventy-one—and had been born in the nineteenth century. The pollsters recommended that Drinan and his literature mention Philbin's age in every speech and publication. And they did.

The Quayle report was emphatic in its conclusion that the main issue was religion: "Unless this issue is handled properly the rest will be of little importance." Voters surveyed said that if the candidate were a Protestant there would be no problem, but if the candidate were a Catholic priest a third said that would make a difference, and 75 percent would be less favorably inclined to the priest candidate. On whether a priest should run for office, 45 percent said no. This, said the Quayle report, "[was] deeply disturbing." The district, the report said, was 75 percent Catholic and its authors speculated that a great number of them might be influenced by the statement of the National Conference of Catholic Bishops that clergy should not run for office. This, the report said, was Drinan's number one problem. In fact, 52 percent of Catholic voters held the same opinion. Thus, the Quayle report concluded, Drinan was dealing not with bigotry but with people who had an image of what a priest is and what he should or should not do.

The Quayle group's advice was that the best way to change the priest's image was through the Catholic Church's hierarchy. Drinan was to take his case to Cardinal Cushing and Jesuit Father Guindon and get them to take up the cause. As a follow-up, a well-known priest in each part of the district should send a letter not endorsing Drinan but saying that it would be perfectly proper for voters to cast their ballots for him. An analysis of how the primary voters broke down showed, under religion, that 22 percent of Catholics supported Drinan, while 79 percent of Jewish voters were for him. The Quayle people were adamant: "When only one Catholic voter in five is behind a Catholic priest, something is wrong. This is the number one problem confronting Drinan. If he gets this vote he can win the nomination, without it he is an also-ran."

Typical of Drinan's Jewish supporters—along with Grossman and Obermayer, and Law School faculty members like Sanford Katz—were two Boston College professors, Seymour and Paula Goldman Leventman, both sociologists specializing in race, minorities, and social stratification. They were savvy on college politics, sensed Drinan's unsatisfactory relationship with President Joyce, and knew that Drinan loved to be the center of attention and aspired to the college presidency. From their observations, when Drinan failed to gain the presidency in 1968 he began looking for alternatives. Paula sent Drinan a memo encouraging him to run for office and Drinan called her back. Newton had just been added to the Third District and had the highest local percentage of Jewish residents. Jews are liberal and get out the vote, said Paula. They are concerned with social justice because they have suffered persecution. That the Jews would support Drinan so enthusiastically was not surprising. He had been reaching out to them, speaking in synagogues, for thirteen years. And on so many issues their principles coincided with his.

The idea of getting the Catholic clerical establishment to back Drinan's right to run would get nowhere, based as it was on the image of the Church as a cohesive community, whereas, in reality, the Catholic population had been assimilated into its various secular, middle-class communities. To some degree Catholics might have been influenced by the bishops' declaration against priests' running for office; but most may not even have read about it. And this was the generation that had heard the pope's encyclical condemning birth control, *"Humanae Vitae,"* and had gone their own way, supported by their confessors, on whether to use artificial birth control.

The Quayle group concluded that, aside from religion, the five main issues were taxes and spending; Vietnam; crime, drugs, and disorders; ecology; and the cost of living. Drinan was advised to avoid the economic issues—these were not his expertise—but to tie them in to larger issues. On Vietnam a majority favored bringing the troops home within eighteen months. On crimes, drugs, and disorder, most voters felt that Drinan, who had written a book about these issues, was better equipped to deal with them. Referring to the Cambodian invasion, the authors said, "What has occurred in the past several weeks among the college generation is the culmination of years of alienation from government and the established order." Indications were that the adult population was impressed by Drinan's credentials. The message to convey to voters was that "here is one man who has spent his life working with young people and a man who can relate to them and make them feel they are part of the system without giving up authority." He should contrast himself with Congressman Philbin, "who at 71 years old neither understands nor cares about the student generation."

It is worth pointing out that, compared with other Jesuits, Drinan had less experience with young people than his peers. He had not taught high school during regency but had gone to law school. He had never taught college students. He had never taught anyone until he arrived at Boston College Law School, and once there he immediately became dean. So his students were all graduate students, who were generally older. Yet the implication that he had his finger on the pulse of the young may have been borne out by his writing.

On drugs, Drinan was advised to stay away from the issue of liberalizing drug laws. On ecology, Drinan should sponsor an ecology day in Newton or Fitchburg to clean up the city. He should ride in a special car that emitted little or no pollution, and, if he could get a reporter to spend the day with him, he should pick up a piece of garbage here and there and deposit it in a trash can: "It would make a nice paragraph in the article." Race was mentioned by only 22 percent of the voters as a major concern, and race and education were seen as issues Drinan was more equipped to handle than Philbin. But only 3 percent of the Massachusetts population and only 1 percent of the Third District was black. Drinan was advised to use this issue sparingly: "The voters certainly are not of the opinion that they should do more for the Negro."

Finally, the public perception of Drinan was that he was "highly educated and bright" but that politics and religion should not be mixed, that he should choose one or the other. The Quayle group said Drinan should portray himself as a "man on the go with modern ideas." If a reporter was scheduled to be with him on a particular day, he should try to schedule as many events on that day as possible: "Reporters are always impressed with how much a candidate can do with his time." And he should make sure not to be late for scheduled appearances. Drinan's other main perceived weakness was his "too-liberal, academic" image. To counteract this perception, he should keep his answers short and simple: "The last thing he wants to do is intimidate his voters with words."

The report concluded with fourteen points and recommendations, the most salient of which were: (1) convince the electorate that it was proper for a priest to be in Congress, (2) emphasize Vietnam, (3) work secondarily on pollution and crime and drugs—with emphasis on "cooling it" with students, and (4) hit Philbin as too old and out of step.

The last assessment: "Father Drinan can certainly win this primary and achieve, if he will forgive the phrase, a political miracle."

6   The "Miracle" Election

In a February 16 letter to his would-be constituents on Boston College Law School stationery, Dean Drinan invited voters to the February 21 caucus in Concord and reminded them that his new book, *Vietnam and Armageddon,* would appear on May 6 as an "outline of a new challenging foreign policy for the United States in the 1970s." And, he asserted, his visit to Israel in 1964 made him highly qualified on Middle Eastern affairs. In a subsequent letter he pointed to his article in the current *Theological Studies* on abortion for those who had questions on that subject, which was not a big campaign issue but was roiling offstage.

But as the campaign progressed, on a talk show, during a debate, and in interviews, both publications would give him some close calls. One would imperil his progress, and both would challenge and raise questions about his skill as a campaigner and spokesperson.

To those who recall the religious issues during the presidential campaigns of 2004 and 2008, when some American bishops sought to deny the Eucharist to candidates who favored keeping abortion legal, it may be surprising to remember that in 1970 abortion was not an overriding issue. Senator Edward M. Kennedy was roundly booed at a Cambridge voters' meeting for opposing looser abortion laws. But Drinan was spared such treatment. Of course, all this preceded the Supreme Court's 1973 *Roe v. Wade* ruling, which, on the basis of a newly developed constitutional right to privacy that had been employed to support the legality of contraception, struck down state laws that made abortion illegal. Since that time, Church strategy has concentrated on effecting *Roe*'s reversal, including the hope that conservative presidents would appoint justices who would reverse the landmark decision.

In 1970, however, in the Quayle survey only 2 percent of those interviewed saw abortion as a campaign issue, and the Quayle report did not even include it among voters' twenty leading concerns.

Nevertheless, in the years leading up to his candidacy in 1970, Drinan's legal philosophy on abortion had been evolving: from one in which religious faith was seen as the principal source of public morality, the strongest source of all our moral convictions, to one that removed the government from influence on what was later considered one of the great moral issues of our time. One adviser who worked with him for more than ten years referred to this "evolution" in his thinking as his "ten positions on abortion." During an interview with a *Boston Globe* reporter in 1967, Drinan showed the writer a recent *America* (February 4, 1967) article, "Strategy on Abortion," in which he suggested that Catholics opposed to the legalization of abortion should not get cornered into discussing the emotion-laden, extremely rare cases but rather meet the opposition with a positive stand concerning abortion following rape or incest and concerning deformed infants, so as to isolate these cases, rather than let these rare cases become propaganda for general legalization.

For example, in Drinan's view abortion opponents should present a carefully drafted bill that would allow immediate medical assistance to a rape victim to prevent pregnancy; a state fund to support a defective child; and a "therapeutic" abortion, certified by three medical specialists, when the mother's life is in danger. Then he wondered aloud to the reporter whether the state should have any role in abortion at all. Meanwhile, all his articles held to the moral principle that the happiness of one human being can never take precedence over another human's right to exist.

But by the time his "Jurisprudential Options on Abortion," a development of his earlier presentation to the American Catholic Theological Association, was published in *Theological Studies* (March 1970), his position had become broader and much more complex. Nevertheless, while presenting the pros and cons of different theories, he was careful to return to and conclude on the same strong stand, that abortion is immoral. Perhaps anticipating *Roe v. Wade*, he predicted that in the 1970s "those opposing abortion on moral grounds will confront several

legal–moral dilemmas which are now just beginning." The new struggle was no longer about modified abortion law, he said, but about
"abortion on request to any person who desires it for any medical
or social reason." Now, he suggested, Catholics should think of ways
traditional Catholic moral principles might be interpreted to permit
abortion in certain instances and restrict the evil results of allowing
many abortions.

In his major polemical writings, Drinan, ever the college debater,
structured his arguments logically, laying out a series of positions on a
controversy. Then he slid in provocative or hypothetical ideas without
making it clear where he stood. For example: There are those who say
this; there are those who say that. Perhaps this, and maybe that. Those
who know more than I about this say this or that. However, perhaps,
as a lawyer rather than a professional theologian, he wrote with the
Vatican's Holy Office looking over his shoulder. The process by which
Rome would silence a controversial priest usually began with scrutiny
of his published work.

Perhaps, said Drinan, an ecumenical effort among Catholics, Protestants, Jews, and nonbelieving humanists could create a consensus on
the immorality of "terminating the life of a healthy fetus in the womb
of a healthy mother." (Indeed, many of Drinan's proposed solutions to
complex political problems involved dialogue and cooperation among
religious leaders.) He called attention to a medical phenomenon that
got very little recognition among Catholic scholars: that one-third of
all embryos "die"—meaning that they are expelled—before they are
born. Perhaps the mother, by the use or non-use of medical means,
could allow the "withering away of the fetus within her." Perhaps.

The heart of the article was its consideration of the three legal
proposals to regulate abortion. One was to prohibit all abortions. The
second was to allow abortions where pregnancy threatened the physical or mental health of the mother, resulted from rape or incest, or
resulted in a fetus that is predictably deformed. The third way was to
withdraw all criminal sanctions and allow physicians to decide. Drinan
listed the strengths and weaknesses of each position.

First, a law prohibiting all abortions would protect life as a nonne-
gotiable item. It would have the advantage that thus the government

would teach, by law, the integrity and inviolability of every human or potentially human life. "It can also be argued that society needs dubiously enforceable laws—like those against gambling, prostitution and narcotics—to protect men from their own weaknesses. But many object that, since the law is unenforceable, when many demand abortion as a right it breeds contempt for the law. And Catholics are accused of forcing their moral views on non-Catholics."

Second, a law allowing only certain "hard case" abortions, for example that involving the deformed fetus, would put the state in the position of deciding whether the unborn person is to live or die. This would imply that parents have a right "to prefer bright and healthy offspring to retarded and defective offspring." Drinan, it appears, could never accept that.

Finally, perhaps all criminal sanctions against abortions should be abolished. But this would teach society that abortion is a neutral event with no moral difficulties. The good effects, however, would mean that unlicensed abortionists could be put out of business. Such an approach would also provide an opportunity for in-depth counseling; a law could require a "cooling off period." If there was any doubt as to which of these options Drinan preferred, he removed it in an April 17, 1970, *Commonweal* article. Governor John A. Burns of Hawaii, a devout Catholic, had allowed a bill decriminalizing abortion to become law without his signature, with the simple statement that abortion was a "matter of conscience." Without saying, "I prefer abortion on demand," Burns eliminated the alternatives, and he added that Catholic clerical spokesmen were wrong to "intervene in the political order" and stated that no attempt to prevent a change in abortions laws would succeed. This became Drinan's position.

The Barry Farber Show

All this background made Drinan's behavior on a late-night New York radio talk show in early 1970, a month or two before these articles and the book on Vietnam were published, seem puzzling.

From 1964 to 1970, Father William Tobin was the assistant director of the Confraternity of Christian Doctrine for the archdiocese of New York, the ecumenical liaison for the Council of Churches for the City of New York, and, with a doctorate in canon law from the Gregorian University, a part-time judge on the New York Metropolitan Tribunal. He was also assistant director of the Family Life Office, which put him in charge of the first "pro-life" effort to counter the strong movement in the New York state legislature to liberalize abortion laws. WOR's Barry Farber was one of the most popular of the New York evening talk-show hosts, with an audience spread out over thirty states.

Farber invited Tobin and two proponents of the legislation for the two-and-a-half-hour session, and Tobin invited Drinan to join him. Why would Tobin ask Drinan? Perhaps he remembered Drinan's appearance on David Susskind's TV show in the spring of 1967, when he had appeared as a defender of the Church's position.

Tobin had admired Drinan when he was dean of the law school and Tobin was chaplain for the Catholic students at NYU Law School and he would invite Bob down to speak. At that point Drinan's "pro-choice" reputation had not been established. His articles looking for "common ground" between opponents and proponents of criminalization emphasized the "inviolability" of the fetus. His "sin, not a crime" formula was not yet well known. Why would Drinan not beg off? Perhaps his tendency to say yes to invitations and the attraction of being heard by so many listeners played a part. As Tobin recalls that night, he and Drinan strongly supported the traditional Catholic position, stressing that the issue was not the "why" of what was being done but the "what," the fact that a human life was being taken. As the evening progressed, the conversation became heated.

Suddenly, during a commercial break, Drinan stood up and headed for the door. Tobin caught up with him and asked, "What are you doing?"

"I'm leaving," Drinan replied. "These people are idiots and speaking irrationally."

"Bob, it's a two-and-a-half-hour show. We have time to make our points at length. We can even refer back to statements they made earlier in the show, and point out how they contradict themselves. It's not like a brief TV or radio interview." Drinan returned, and when it was over Drinan and Tobin felt they had discredited their opponents.

Why did he try to walk off the show? It may be that he was overwhelmingly irritated by what he perceived as the stupidity of the other participants. Even his admirers have described Drinan as an "intellectual snob" who "did not suffer fools gladly." Once Drinan had made up his mind, he often had little patience with opposing ideas. Maybe, also, he was disturbed by the duality of his own position—telling a radio audience that the law should protect unborn life while telling his Newton constituency that abortion is a "sin, not a crime." Did Farber have listeners in the Third District?

On Foreign Policy

Vietnam and Armageddon would emerge months later at a critical moment in the campaign when his opponents would actually read it and distribute free copies to the press to demonstrate that, in their view, Drinan's foreign policy views were not just anti–Vietnam War but far to the left of where any other candidate in 1970 was willing to go.

He began the book by regretting Vatican II's acceptance of the "possession of nuclear weapons whose only purpose is to destroy entire cities or extensive areas," while nevertheless condemning their use. He castigated the American Catholic bishops for their failure in 1968 to see the immorality of the Vietnam War. He quoted with approval the Catholic Peace Fellowship rebuke of the American Catholic hierarchy for telling Catholics they may "conscientiously support" the war while offering no comment on how the war was just or how napalm bombing and crop poisoning and the high civilian casualties could be viewed as acceptable.

On the morality of war in general, and the question of whether Christian nations must allow themselves to be annihilated rather than participate in war that would bring about the deaths of millions of people, Drinan quoted with approval his old Weston professor John Ford's position that "if the alternative to the immoral use of atomic weapons were subjugation to an atheist regime or the extinction of the human race, the followers of Christ should abandon themselves to divine Providence rather than forsake these [Christian moral] imperatives."

Drinan called for a third Vatican Council that should "ban all war on the grounds that no version of Christianity can possibly tolerate as morally acceptable the deaths of vast numbers of persons which is inevitable in modern war." He quoted with approval Cardinal Joseph Ritter, who proposed at Vatican II "the absolute condemnation of the possession of arms which involve the intention or the grave peril of total war." Nor did Drinan believe that the violation of territorial integrity—invasion—was sufficient reason to declare war.

In a chapter on Judaism and the morality of war, he wrote that "the whole thrust and ideology of Judaism are, of course, contrary to armed violence of all types" and praised the "virtual unanimity in the Jewish community against America's war in South Vietnam." He noticed the apparent contradiction between American Jews' Vietnam policy and their attitude toward the six-day war that Israel waged against the Arabs in 1967 and the future wars that might be necessary to protect Israel. But he seemed to doubt that the deaths of thousands of and perhaps ten million Arabs could ever be justified in a future war in the Middle East. In an October 2, 1970, *Commonweal* review, Tom Forest, a peace activist, was "astonished and excited" by Drinan's proposal for unilateral disarmament, but he found a logical breakdown in Drinan's reluctance to apply the same norms to Israel.

In a chilling paragraph, Drinan spelled out what he thought few readers realized when they cheer for war: In World War I only 5 percent of the casualties were civilians. In World War II, the number was 48 percent; in the Korean War, 84 percent. In Vietnam, 90 percent. In a future Middle East War, even fewer than 10 percent of the casualties would be soldiers. "The possible or potential millions of civilian casualties staggers the mind and the imagination."

The key chapter was "Is Pacifism the Only Option?" The time had come, Drinan wrote, for Christians to stop imagining a "just war" and to advocate a policy of passive resistance or militant nonviolence toward a conquering foe. Assuming that the next war, by current strategy, would be a nuclear war, it did not follow that, if we lost 20 million Americans in a "first strike" by an enemy, we must retaliate on the same scale. Rather, in Drinan's view the policy of "massive retaliation" was an incitement to massacre as much as a policy of deterrence.

We should unilaterally disarm, Drinan stated, concluding that, "if conquered by a superior military force, the American people will become totally ungovernable" and drive out the aggressor "by highly sophisticated techniques of nonviolence."

Drinan recommended, however, while still endorsing the pacifist strategy, that Americans propose intermediate policies in dealing with the Soviets, who, he stated, did not plan to dominate the world.

First, reeducate young Americans to be members of "one world." Second, reduce the international sale of American weapons. Third, unilaterally disarm—Stalin and Khrushchev's Russia is not that of the Russian Revolution but a conservative, class-ridden regime. Fourth, create new political directions—a new political party dedicated to peace.

The Plan

Meanwhile, old friends and new followers, thrilled by the possibility of a new kind of politics, flocked to Drinan's side. He had consulted his college friends Robert and Mary Muse on his decision to run, and they were the first to host a fundraising event, in their beautiful old home in Chestnut Hill. The commentators in the press reopened the question of whether students could be counted on. How dedicated was the younger generation to political reform?

John Marttila resigned from his Republican Party job and made his way to Boston. For two days he sat alone in his hotel room preparing a plan by which he would organize the Boston neighborhoods and lead this priest whom he had not met to a primary victory and then to Congress. The search committee for the campaign manager met in a packed conference room on a snowy day in the Boston College Law School conference room. Marttila's interview audience was between forty and sixty people, a signal to him that this really was a bottom-up operation. Though he had devoutly religious Jewish friends, Marttila had no religion of his own and had never met a Jesuit. He was impressed by Drinan's dynamism, energy, and humor. The grilling lasted three hours. At the end Drinan, with his usual instinct for people, told Marttila, "You're my choice," before the group's voice weighed in.

The plan consisted of three steps. First, the volunteers, who numbered about 3,500, canvassed 45,000 households, representing 75 percent of the potential voters, and recorded their background and attitudes toward issues like the war. Second, the information for 40,000 households was put on punch cards and processed by computer to give the respondents' positions on various issues, for future reference. Third, persons seen as potential voters received pamphlets on Drinan's positions, and potential strong supporters received a phone call from Drinan. Because the canvass had revealed which issues concerned which voter, the voter received Drinan material on whatever mattered most to him or her.

But the great phenomenon of the campaign was the community of campaigners. Marttila, in the eyes and prose of an October 18 *Boston Globe* article, was a gunslinger from the Old West: "tall, broad shouldered, mustached, long blond hair." He gave the impression of a "man able to carry out assignments and inspire others to do theirs." His travels for the Nixon administration to attract minority voters convinced him that the administration had done "terrifying" damage to low-income people.

What Marttila remembers most is not his skillful direction of the campaign but the personal education he received. Young Jesuits have some freedom during their summers, and 1970 was one of those years in which the seminaries had moved to the cities and the young men were fanning out to have some political influence of their own. About a half-dozen Jesuits in training headed for Boston to work in Drinan's campaign. One, Tom Kiley, wrote ahead from the Midwest to volunteer. Marttila, inundated with requests, figured he had his quota of young Jesuits, so he crumpled up Kiley's application and tossed it into the wastebasket. Kiley showed up anyway and took charge. In time the contributions of young Jesuits became part of Marttila's conversion process—not to Catholicism, but to the level of moral commitment Drinan could inspire.

Kiley had spent two years at the University of Dayton before joining the Detroit province of the Society. After four years as a Jesuit at the University of Detroit, he was inspired to offer his services to the Drinan campaign. For the first several weeks, before moving into an off-campus apartment with another Jesuit volunteer, he lived in St. Mary's Hall, the big community, where he could indulge the Jesuit tradition more common in the 1960s and '70s than today, of late-night sessions over a few beers in the *haustus* room. Drinan, his blue eyes set back, beaming with purpose and intelligence, was very exciting in those sessions. Sometimes he had grabbed a sandwich. Often he had not eaten. He grilled everyone about what had happened during the day, pressed them on the issues, Kiley recalls. Drinan's commitment to the issues was an extension of his persona, his Jesuit identity.

Kiley brought experience in organizing with him from Detroit. He had been accepted at Georgetown Law School, but he had put that off to work for Drinan. Like all the other young Jesuit volunteers in the campaign, Kiley ultimately left the Society of Jesus—not because of the campaign but because in those years many left for many reasons, including to marry and to seize the opportunities the Church's new open door to the world offered. Reflecting on the issues again, he found himself a bit to the right of Drinan on abortion, but he sensed that if Drinan had taken any other position he would have lost. He also stayed committed to Drinan and kept working for him in subsequent campaigns.

Of the 3,500 volunteers, half were over thirty, which means the rest were high school students, college students, and young adults at work or in graduate schools. Anne Marie Goggin, student president at Regis College, a small Catholic women's college on a beautiful rural campus west of Boston College and very near Weston, asked Drinan to give their graduation address. Drinan used the occasion to condemn arms manufacturers as "merchants of death" and garnered a headline in the *Globe*. This was fine with Goggin. Drinan invited her to volunteer. She started working. The campaign helped her to find herself, to discover what she wanted to do with her life. It led her to see that law school could be a tool with which to help people.

Working on the campaign, she met John Hurley, a Boston College law student back from his tour of duty in Vietnam, looking for a way to oppose the war, who had joined the Drinan team. As happened with several volunteers, the campaign led to romance, and Hurley and Goggin married and remained Drinan friends for years.

Tom Vallely graduated from Newton High School with a mixed record and no clear idea of what he wanted to do with his life. Somehow the Vietnam War struck him as right, an example of America's effort to do good in the world. He was not motivated to go to college, partly because of some learning disabilities, so he joined the U.S. Marine Corps. On August 13, 1969, twenty miles south of Danang, when his unit was ambushed, he collected hand grenades from the wounded and tossed them into the enemy gun emplacements. And he won the Silver Star. In a November 21, 1970, *America* magazine article, he recounted how he moved from warrior to a Drinan peace campaigner.

> Like last week, 43 men were killed in Vietnam. I remember when 43 men were killed in a day. You ask yourself: Why do I have to kill these people? Why do my friends have to die? Why are we here? Well, our two governments sent us. When you capture one of these people, you don't even want to hit him, he's so scared, so nervous. Then I read the statistics—about the political prisoners, the government, the deaths. So I thought I'd do something about it, I suppose. Maybe we owe something to the friends I left there, the friends in my company.

Back in Newton, working on a highway construction project, twenty years old, and coming from a family with lots of local political connections, he wanted to do more with his life. He had read about the Citizens Caucus while in Vietnam. So, though skeptical, he went to check it out. As it happened, the campaign, overwhelmed with volunteers, was looking for someone who was "not a hippy." Ex-Marine Tom stood 6′1″ tall, was well built, with a short haircut, the kind of man with whom you would not want to start a fight. He became Drinan's "body man"—his driver, the constant companion who controls, to some degree, the details of the candidate's schedule. He answered questions like: Where are we now? Who are these people? How do they relate to me and one another? Who are the key persons in the Fitchburg fire department?

He recalls Drinan affectionately as "not articulate," nowhere near possessed of the eloquence of John Kerry, who went with Drinan from meeting to meeting and delivered introductions far more thrilling than the talk that followed. Drinan was an "intellectual snob" who would "put people in a box," classify them, if he resisted their ideas. Drinan was, by consent of his best friends, the "world's worst driver," who once drove a car up onto a sidewalk. So Tom drove. With a fairly high-pitched voice, Drinan was not a great speaker. But he was concrete, detailed, and, above all, "inspirational." Young people were hungry for his message.

Typical among the enthusiastic volunteers was Christiane Joost-Gaugier. A Harvard student, she was studying for her Ph.D. and teaching at Tufts University. She found Drinan's candidacy attractive because he was against the war—he had committed himself to the anti-war movement when others had copped out—but he was pro-America. His argument was that the war was legally wrong. She hosted several parties and dinners for Drinan at her house, and she brought him vitamins because he was campaigning so hard that she feared he would wear himself out. Her main job during the primary was to go door-to-door collecting signatures on petitions. There were lots of rumors spread by the opposition, and even liberal Harvard professors were opposed to a priest's running for office; but she did get Newton women to sign. She recalls an open meeting, with 200 to 300 audience members, at which Drinan spoke and the atmosphere was very tense because the word had spread that someone in the audience might have brought a gun; but Drinan won them over with his oratory.

Jan, an Amherst graduate and VISTA volunteer, and her husband, Harold W. Attridge, a Ph.D. candidate in New Testament at Harvard, turned their tiny Watertown apartment into an election day center for Drinan's campaign. They had married in June 1968 when both were twenty-one. Harold had a Marshall Scholarship in England and Jan had joined him there; but they had to return from England in 1968 because the draft law had changed, and so Harold joined the military reserves. While in Cambridge they had several Jesuit friends who introduced them to Drinan's cause. Jan had met Congressman Philbin once, remembering him as a large florid, "old," big man with a big mane of white hair, known for taking care of his constituents. To her, he represented the "past."

For Jan and Harold, the issue was the war's cost, its waste of resources, with the body bags on TV every night. Drinan, in contrast to Philbin, was a young firebrand. His voice rang with conviction. He was not a great orator, but he projected conviction, energy, and integrity. Every Saturday and Sunday in Watertown they went from door to door, informally asking how the voters would react to the idea of a priest's running for office. Watertown had a heavily Armenian constituency, many of whom supported state Representative Charles Ohanian, an independent candidate of Armenian descent. The Attridges had expected no opposition from the Catholics; they did encounter some, but it helped that Drinan was not a parish priest but a professor, already fairly well known as a speaker and writer.

When Mark D. Gearan was in the eighth grade he biked to Drinan's headquarters and bike-delivered campaign literature in his Garner neighborhood. When he was old enough to drive, he drove Drinan. On the road, "Tell me something I don't know," Drinan would tease and challenge his young staff members. Gearan went to Harvard College and Georgetown Law School, interned in Drinan's Washington office, and courted his staffer Mary Healivy. Drinan, like a father to his staff, celebrated their wedding and the births of their two daughters.

A Sketch of the Campaigner

A composite image of Drinan the campaigner drawn from the recollections of several colleagues who knew him well presents a complex personality whose most notable ability was to inspire a generation of liberal intellectuals and young people through his idealism and well-informed intelligence. In face-to-face contact he had a knack for getting and remembering names, so that people who met him only briefly would consider him their "friend." If he met a law professor at a convention one year who had recently married, Drinan would meet him the following year and the next and ask, "How's your bride?"

Drinan the campaigner-politician had rough edges. He could be abrupt. If, in the middle of a conversation, he discovered he was talking to someone who was not a constituent, he would break off the conversation curtly. His tight, wound-up mannerisms could turn people off. In discussion he could take a flat-out position and that was it. Women were attracted to him, and he was attracted to them, but he was not smooth or "debonair" in dealing with them. One woman inspired by his public presence found him "blunt," not really understanding women in a personal relationship. Another remarked that he shared the common practice of politicians "working a room" of looking over one's shoulder at the next quarry, a "more interesting" person on the other side of the room, while supposedly talking to you. Unlike Bill Clinton, whom this volunteer had met, Drinan did not look you in the eye. He would give you about thirty seconds of full attention and move on, perhaps not self-aware enough to know that one has to work on a relationship. Jerome Grossman acknowledged that Drinan, like every politician, had weaknesses; but he was the only politician who, in vote or opinion, never disappointed him.

Meanwhile, the alternate spiritual fuel of the campaign was poured out at Marttila's home at Newton's 53 Vernon Street, a half-hour walk north of Boston College, between a Presbyterian church and a middle school, where almost every night at nine o'clock, the volunteers ended the work day with a party. Across the country, student activism was on the wane, but not in Massachusetts' Third District. Why? A rare chemistry of a group of very young but very talented professionals, an issue like Vietnam that made some absolute moral demands, a believable idealist candidate at the center, and several thousand others ready to work for their beliefs.

The Other Candidate-Priests

The religious issue, often focused on the meaning of the priesthood, would never go away. Drinan told an interviewer that he had not decided whether he would wear his clerical collar if he went to Washington, but past behavior left no doubt that he would. His decision was ironic, in that he was seen as a very liberal priest; but many liberal Jesuits had stopped wearing clerical garb in professional situations five years before. To them the collar signified the "cultic" concept of the priesthood, a symbol of pre–Vatican II clericalism where, at the sight of the collar, the traffic cop declined to give "Father" the speeding ticket and the usher at the movie theater moved "Father" to the head of the line. Some Jesuit college professors wore "civilian" garb lest they alienate non-Catholic or ex-Catholic students who already saw the teacher as an authority figure and might not welcome additional symbols separating them from their professor. Besides, the Jesuit in the shirt and tie wanted to be respected because he knew his trade and taught well, not because he was a priest. Drinan offered several reasons for wearing clerics. Some were facetious, like "It's the only suit I own." More likely, it suited the identity he chose to project.

In 1970 a record number of clergymen decided that they also belonged in elective politics. In 1788 Thomas Jefferson, in a draft of the Virginia Constitution, said that the principle of separation of church and state meant that clergymen could not hold elective office. James Madison answered that the exclusion of clergy from office would violate their religious freedom, and Jefferson changed his mind. In 1822 the French-born Gabriel Richard was the first priest elected to Congress, but as a nonvoting delegate from the Michigan territory, not a state until 1837. An August 10, 1970, *U.S. News & World Report* survey found sixteen ministers and priests seeking major office—three for the U.S. Senate, eleven for the House, and two for governorships.

Among these, five other priests, most likely inspired by Drinan, threw their hats into the ring. In Wisconsin, Father Robert Cornell, a Norbertine priest associated with St. Norbert's College, was running as a Democrat for Congress, against the wishes of his local bishop but with the support of his religious superiors. In the Bronx, Father Louis Gigante, a popular neighborhood activist and brother of an alleged Mafia racketeer, was also running for Congress. In a district in Ohio, Father Joseph B. Lucas, a teacher at Youngstown University, was one of several Democrats pursuing the congressional nomination. In Grand

Rapids, Michigan, Father Stephen Vesbit, a pastor, dropped out of his congressional race for lack of support.

The most interesting race, however, was in adjacent Rhode Island, where another Jesuit, John L. McLaughlin, forty-three, a former associate editor of *America*, who had left Rhode Island to join the Jesuits and had not voted there in twenty years, had secured the Republican nomination for the U.S. Senate. In fact, the incumbent senator, John O. Pastore, with twenty years in the Senate, had been reelected with 82 percent of the vote, and it was hard to find a sacrificial victim to run against him—until McLaughlin thought he would like to be a senator. McLaughlin, although he had originally contemplated challenging Pastore for the Democratic nomination, sided with Nixon on most issues, except on the antiballistic missile (ABM), which he said had value only for its pork barrel contracts. McLaughlin handled the priest identity issue less adroitly than Drinan. Lest voters think he was abandoning a parish for Washington, he stressed that he had never been a parish priest and had publicly administered the sacraments only "from time to time." He had applied to Father William Guindon, the New England provincial who had given approval for Drinan to run, for permission but had been quickly refused on the grounds that Guindon already had a dispute over Drinan's running and needed no more controversy.

McLaughlin's campaign strategy featured walking tours. In shape from his daily jogs, 6'1" tall, with reddish blond hair and a strong voice tinged with a whiff of an upper-class accent, he looked good as he set out to shake 1,000 hands a day. Like Drinan, McLaughlin visited Vietnam and came out against the war. He even wrote an *America* article criticizing the bombing strategy. But unlike Drinan, he was unable to engage the public on other issues where he could show some expertise or enthusiasm. He kept pleading with his audience not to make an issue of his priesthood and in doing so kept calling attention to it. Russell J. McVinney, the bishop of Providence and a longtime friend of Pastore's, made a big point of declaring that McLaughlin was running without his permission. In the end, McLaughlin simply failed as a politician in his attempts to make himself really known and respected. He ended up with 31 percent of the vote. Nixon brought him to the White

House as a speechwriter, he moved into the Watergate, and he was eventually called back to the province by the New England provincial. He left the Jesuits, married, and achieved fame as the bombastic host of the "McLaughlin Report" political talk show.

As primary day, September 15, came into view, each campaign worker received whole or part of an extremely detailed twenty-page manual with explicit directions on what to do. Its tone was both pragmatic and hortatory. The managers appealed to the idealism and generosity of the workers. The ward chairman was to activate the precinct chairmen and equip them with computer printouts for their precinct, four colors of markers, poll workers, and voters' lists for poll watchers. The precinct chairman was to supervise canvasser-pollers, headquarters staff, and polling staff. All phone calls to headquarters were to be brief: "These phones *must* be kept as free as possible." Neighborhood captains were to first call the "neutrals" to ask if they had decided, then call the "projected favorables." If they favored Drinan, stress the importance of the primary vote. If they were still neutral, give Drinan's position on *their* issues. Try to coax undecided voters into the camp, but do not annoy them away. The manual concluded: "We cannot overemphasize to you the importance of your job. The whole campaign is aimed at getting every favorable voter to the polls. If we do that, we will win."

The Campaign Heats Up

Drinan campaigned energetically. He was up early and by 8:00 A.M. had read and digested five newspapers and showed the staff he was raring to go. In his speeches Drinan emphasized that Philbin was the go-along member of the Armed Services Committee who had never raised his voice against either Presidents Johnson or Nixon in the conduct of the war. But he also attacked Philbin's reputation as a faithful servant to his constituents. Besides reminding his audience that Philbin was seventy-one, he ridiculed what he considered Philbin's inadequate letters responding to their questions. Philbin described himself in his campaign as a mainstream Democrat who had brought jobs, especially military contracts, to the district. The complicating factor in the race was the presence of Ohanian, who had declined to follow the caucus rule that all the candidates support the winner.

September 15 was a cold and rainy day, but the turnout was strong. Drinan won with 46.9 percent of the votes (28,605); Philbin got 35.6 percent (22,133); and Ohanian trailed with 18.4 percent (11, 434). But the general election would be rougher and closer.

The Drinan candidacy was a gamble from the start. The Quayle consultants' report did not promise a "miracle." The authors privately recommended that Grossman pull the plug, then concluded the report saying a "miracle" was possible. In the end Drinan had done much better than anticipated in the Catholic neighborhoods. The combined impact of the caucus meeting and the primary convinced political observers that they were witnessing something special, even unique, in the combination of innovative polling, computer technology, youthful energy, and a very different kind of candidate. But in the six weeks between the primary and the general election, a number of local and national surprises and slips almost sank the ship.

First, Philbin, bitter in defeat, blamed the rain for keeping his voters home and decided to run again as a "sticker" candidate, a form of write-in voting in which the voter attaches a sticker to the ballot or machine. He charged that "ultraliberal extremists" and the "minions of new wealth" had poured thousands of dollars from outside Massachusetts "in a golden stream" into Drinan's campaign. Ohanian threw his support to Philbin. Both Ohanian and Philbin took the line of argument that they were protecting the people from the effects of a Drinan victory. Drinan, Philbin said, was moved by "unstable ambitions." Without his influence, Philbin said, the district would lose the advantages of his seniority in Congress, especially in defense contracts.

The *Boston Globe*, in an October 8 editorial, reminded its readers that the *Wall Street Journal* had the previous month (a week before the primary) called Philbin a "party hack" who in taking his seat near the Speaker's rostrum "almost always falls asleep." The editorial went on to speculate that much of the vote that would normally be expected to go to the Republican candidate, John A.S. McGlennon, would go instead to Philbin; it would be ironic if Philbin ended up thereby helping

Drinan. The editorial cartoon depicted Philbin as an overweight soldier in World War I attire, his helmet on the floor holding his cigar, a pop-gun rifle in his left hand, and his severed head resting in his right hand. The head is saying, "I'd like to re-enlist."

That fall, the unemployment situation worsened. Massachusetts had lost 45,000 manufacturing jobs within the past month, thanks to the national recession, cutbacks in defense spending, and a slash in federal research funds. Some of the wind had gone out of the Vietnam issue when Nixon proposed that a cease-fire be negotiated in Indochina to end the war. Nixon campaigned vigorously throughout the country for a Republican Congress, emphasizing his "law and order" issue and calling for the "Silent Majority" to stand up against lawlessness. At home, Drinan lost a friend in church politics when the ailing Cardinal Richard Cushing retired, to be replaced by Archbishop Humberto S. Medeiros, fifty-five, who flew in from Texas. Now a man who did not know Drinan would be asked again and again whether he thought priests belonged in elected office.

On a Monday night, October 5, during a late-night talk show from Worcester, a caller asked Drinan whether he would endorse Ted Kennedy in his race for reelection to the Senate. In fact, Drinan was already on record as having endorsed him; but, on the talk show during which he got hostile questions on religious issues, he had become irritated with a woman caller who repeatedly asked whether he was "backing Teddy Kennedy." Drinan stalled, said he wasn't in a position to answer that because he hadn't been elected yet and was just a private citizen.

"Would you vote for him?" the caller asked again.

"I'll come and vote according to the way my mind and conscience dictates."

"What do you think of him?" she pressed. Drinan kept beating around the bush.

The next day Drinan met with reporters at the State House to try to explain. He said he felt the woman's hostility and didn't want to "dignify her" with an answer. The woman, he said, was "nagging, hysterical . . . pushing . . . monstrous. You instinctively pull back in situations like these."

More likely, Drinan feared being pulled into an extended discussion of Chappaquiddick, an auto accident and the events surrounding it that took its name from that of the island off Martha's Vineyard where it took place. The previous summer Kennedy, following a party, drove his car off a bridge into the water and his passenger, Mary Jo Kopechne, died. At the State House press conference, Drinan not only endorsed Kennedy as "eminently qualified, intellectually, morally, ethically, and in every other way to be in the Senate," he criticized the retired Edgartown judge who had recently called into question the completeness of Kennedy's account of the incident.

Assessing Drinan's position in view of recent developments, *Globe* columnist Carol Liston on October 8 said that Drinan was used to "rough hewn politicking conducted behind oaken academic doors." But his "volatile personality" had not equipped him "to win the hearts and votes of thousands of citizens with very disparate needs and attitudes." Marttila recalls a moment in the Howard Johnson's restaurant over Route 90 when Drinan displayed his personal combative instincts spontaneously in a public place. The president of the International Brotherhood of Engineers in America (IBEA) walked in and stopped by Drinan's table. Drinan's instinctive reaction was to see him as one of those who had been raising the priesthood question to suggest that Drinan did not belong in Congress. Rather than fake cordiality, Drinan got up, confronted him face-to-face, and, while jabbing his index finger repeatedly into the man's chest, gave him in a loud voice a "If you ever call into question my faith . . ." chewing out.

Robert Cormier, in a May 1971 *St. Anthony's Messenger* article, said that Drinan, campaigning twelve to eighteen hours a day, "was like a tiger let out of a cage. He purred and he growled." A campaign worker said, "He'd enter a room and immediately there was a reaction. He either turned people on or he turned them off. Maybe it was the collar or the man himself." Not all students loved him. At Brandeis University, a group from the Students for a Democratic Society (SDS) who resented his participation in the Center for the Study of Violence, which they thought passed data on ghettos to the police, heckled him and called him a "fascist liberal."

Drinan snapped back, "Do you think I'm naïve or corrupt?"

"Corrupt," they replied.

"Thanks," said Drinan. "I'm pretty bright, and it would hurt if you thought I was stupid."

McGlennon, the Republican candidate, could take a "safe" position on Vietnam, agreeing with Nixon's intent to have the troops out by the end of 1971 but insisting on "flexibility." Drinan's preference was to bring the troops home and give asylum to any South Vietnamese who needed it. But on a practical level he backed the Hatfield–McGovern plan, which also would have gotten the troops out by the end of 1971. Drinan, said Liston, was not "unstable," as his critics said, but unorthodox. Drinan had demonstrated his weakest campaigning on the talk show. Rather than simply endorse Kennedy, he showed a "mixture of irritation, stubbornness, weariness and political inexperience. . . . Some say it was insincerity. Most likely it was the candidate's lack of political grace."

But Drinan's opponents got the most mileage out of *Vietnam and Armageddon*, which Drinan had assumed would get him votes. Acid-tongued conservative columnist William F. Buckley Jr. in his September 26 *Globe* column called the Jesuit priest "the greatest threat to orderly thought since Eleanor Roosevelt left this vale of tears." He went on, "Fr. Drinan, as a lawyer and a trained Jesuit, is capable of being foxy, though one suspects that he is not quite lucid enough to know when he is being foxy." His example was Drinan's argument that Catholics who accepted the arms race were like Germans who accepted Hitler's atrocities. Drinan's logic, said Buckley, was that 99 percent of the American people agreed that unilateral disarmament "would bring instant chaos and misery to the world." And, perhaps anyone who favored unilateral disarmament was "stark mad."

Buckley worked his way through the arguments on passive resistance and concluded that he wished "Fr. Drinan were running for office in Czechoslovakia." Buckley continued, "We can, then, simply assume that the poor gentleman is simply addled by idealism." Alas, said Buckley, "Fr. Drinan does not leave us with the kind of satisfaction we would have in dealing with Peter Pan. The question was raised, well Father, do you think we should abandon the military even where Israel is involved?" Buckley took Drinan's answer to be a "ho, ho, ho, huh, huh, eh, eh . . ." stand by our commitment to the Jewish state. Buckley's zinger: "The Elmer Gantry of disarmament hath spoken." Buckley's column must have been a basic document for Drinan's opponents; but their use of the book did not rise to the level of Buckley's exegesis. Rather, they took quotes out of context and distorted their application.

Carol Liston on October 22 hit Drinan's opponents hard. McGlennon's wife, Mary Jane, at a meeting of the Congregational Church in North Leominster, claimed that Drinan said, "If a law is unjust then not only should we, but we must break that law." In fact Drinan was referring to the Nuremburg principle, which posited that a citizen in conscience has an obligation to oppose laws that allow one's nation to commit atrocities, like the murder of millions of Jews.

Drinan's approval of the Catonsville protesters' burning draft records as an act of conscience was interpreted by his opponents as a call for all young people to become lawbreakers. Drinan's book, said Liston, was "the concerned musings of a man who fears that Vietnam could bring the United States to disaster and how he thinks that disaster could be avoided." Meanwhile, "The tactics used against Fr. Drinan are base. They echo the McCarthyism of the '50s and the Agnewism of today—trying to destroy a man by false charge and ugly innuendo."

As a result of these charges, Drinan, a law school professor and dean, had to go on TV and radio saying he was not a law breaker. The same week, the Boston College theologian Mary Daly appeared at a Massachusetts Organization for the Repeal of Abortion Laws (MORAL) rally at City Hall Plaza to say that "The Catholic church has no right to impose its views on the public. The question of abortion should be decided by the woman herself." And, as noted earlier, Ted Kennedy faced a hostile audience in Cambridge at the end of October when he said, "No, I don't believe in abortion on demand."

C. E. Fager, in *Boston After Dark*, observed on October 27 that there was "no question that Drinan does call for some form of unilateral disarmament, but McGlennon's use of the book is disgraceful, worthy of no one in public office." On the other hand, one of Drinan's close aides told Fager that "the man who wrote that book couldn't possibly get elected in this district . . .". Yet Fager felt that Drinan did not own up to his statement on page 142 that "the destruction of draft files by the Catonsville Nine . . . may be a dramatic 'homily' against the evils of militarism, and the sincerity and heroism of those who participate in such activities is beyond dispute." Now Drinan called those actions "foolish" and "counterproductive." Challenged on unilateral disarmament, Drinan retreated to "I disown that idea." Drinan, said Fager, often told his audience that what he really wanted to do was "to get back to the kind of world I knew when I was young. When I was young, young people wouldn't think of experimenting with dangerous drugs; when I was young we took care of our old people . . .". Fager asked, Where and when is this world in which Drinan grew up? For anyone familiar with Drinan's reluctance to discuss the details of his childhood, that précis of his childhood rings an odd bell.

Fager was one of Drinan's most persistent and intelligent questioners. One day, as reported in the *Christian Century* of September 9, he followed Drinan on the run, taping him in spare moments. Drinan reaffirmed his conviction that "The American bishops are spiritually and intellectually bankrupt." He called for a corporate tax on the local level. He defended Daniel Berrigan's burning draft records as "symbolic speech" and his escaping the law by going underground as a way of teaching. On Vietnam, he suggested that 75 or 50 percent of all students should refuse induction on moral grounds and that he would help defend them in court.

The public campaign ended the Sunday night before election day in a debate at the Brotherhood of Temple Shalom in Newton. Drinan invoked the name of his host as the theme of his remarks. He said he believed in a government that would help those who could not help themselves, in a "brotherhood of man . . . the idealism of the story of Ruth and the Good Samaritan." McGlennon replied that the public "is not my brother's keeper, if he can keep himself," adding that problems should be solved not by "big government" but on the community level. Drinan, reported the *Globe* on November 2, "called for halting the ABM, biological and chemical warfare and removing 'some or all' of the 316,000 U.S. troops in Europe." On the Middle East, Drinan tried to be even-handed; he supported arms for Israel as a way of maintaining the balance of power and Israel's territorial integrity; at the same time, he said, it is easy to condemn terrorist tactics, but we should realize that the refugee problem was breeding terrorists. McGlennon recommended "an independent state of Palestine" for the refugees and opposed the invasion of Cambodia as well as the SST (supersonic transport) and the ABM. In foreign policy, McGlennon was narrowing the distance between their positions. When McGlennon, who said he had read Drinan's book three times, brought up unilateral disarmament, Drinan replied that he was only "postulating" about an alternative position to the arms race.

Marttila's polling suddenly revealed a significant slippage in the last two weeks of the race. As well, a *Globe* poll showed that Drinan's backing among Democrats had fallen from 56 percent to 49 percent and among liberals from 66 percent to 60 percent. He responded by intensifying the campaign and enlisting Ted Kennedy, who had a big lead in his Senate race, to come in and campaign. By then he had already had the endorsement and assistance of former U.S. Attorney General Ramsey Clark; Senator Eugene McCarthy of Minnesota; Senator George McGovern of South Dakota; the economist John Kenneth Galbraith; former Supreme Court Justice Arthur Goldberg; Senator Edmund Muskie of Maine, who had been his party's vice-presidential nominee in 1968; and seventeen unions, including the United Auto Workers, the International Chemical Workers of America, the International Ladies' Garment Workers' Union, and the Teamsters.

Globe reporter Theresa McMaster wrote on October 29 that the contest which had promised to be the most issue-oriented had disappointed everyone by deteriorating into a personality clash. Drinan "has been caught in the shifting sands," had shifted from opposing the Vietnam War and promoting a "politics of love" to defending the Nuremburg principle "which basically calls for mankind to break unjust laws." Drinan talked fast and waved his hands, distracting the listener from what he was saying, and peppered his speeches with so many legal explanations that his views lost clarity. McGlennon, on the other hand, McMaster said, was direct and determined to avoid a personality clash. He emphasized the "war at home"—violence, bombings, and unrest. Philbin, on the other hand, called Drinan and his supporters "conspirators," and his friend Ohanian told guests at a

Philbin dinner in Clinton that "to send Robert Drinan to Congress would be frightening."

But even as Ohanian was speaking, the Drinan forces returned to the techniques that had worked for the primary but redoubled their efforts. The candidate made the rounds of rallies, dances, cocktail parties, garage sales, lox-and-bagels breakfasts, and ham-and-beans dinners, as well as large, formal meetings. The campaign's TV spots, prepared by a professional ad agency, appeared on "The Tonight Show" and during Boston Bruins hockey games. The campaign spent $100,000. On election day, November 3, the staff had breakfast at 5:00 and then set to work. Poll watchers checked to see if the expected voters appeared. If someone failed to show up, they called that person's home to see if the voter needed help. They would not, however, drive voters to the polls, because Drinan personally believed that the democratic act of actually voting was an individual responsibility.

When the polls closed at 8:00 P.M., Philbin had 45,378 (26.6 percent); McGlennon had 60,575 (35.6 percent); and Drinan, 63,942 (37.8 percent). It was a close race, and more people had voted against Drinan than for him. Interpretations vary. Drinan took five towns: Newton, Waltham, Gardner, Watertown, and Westford, three of which were contiguous on the eastern tip of the district. In the long run, many saw the victory more in terms of what it proved about political organization than as a triumph of ideas. Grossman told *The Nation* in a December 21 article that it was both. It was "a laboratory experiment that worked." But the participants were peace-minded voters who had organized on the basis of that belief.

That night Drinan told his supporters gathered to celebrate the victory in the Newton Armory—displaying jubilant signs: "Our Father Who Art in Congress"—that the voters had repudiated three things: the war policies of Nixon, the economic policies of the Republican Party, and "the campaign tactics of fear and smear followed by both the losers in this race." He went on to say: "This victory tonight means that groups of peace-loving citizens in caucuses like that which met on February 21, 1970, in the Third Congressional District must be the new and dynamic method by which to transform the nation. The people themselves must rise up, and, by exercising their right under the Constitution to recall Congressmen every two years, create an entirely new Congress." Marttila reinforced that theme later: "Drinan and all of us think we have found a method of restoring in our times government to the people."

7   The Age of Less-Great Expectations

During the first week of January 1971 Father Robert F. Drinan moved into another new world, one that called for him to assume a new role and a new identity. And the decade of American history into which he was carried had begun to accumulate its own unforeseen peculiarities. Dubbed in 1976 by author Tom Wolfe "The Me Decade," the 1970s had a new ethos that grew in some ways out of an idealistic, positive, revolutionary movement—the morally based protest against the Vietnam War—that had propelled Drinan into office. But now it was beginning to shatter. James T. Patterson, in *Grand Expectations: The United States, 1945–1974*, wrote that the spirit which had animated those expectations after World War II had begun to sour. People were becoming more anxious and contentious. This was not because they were worse off absolutely—most people managed as well or a little better economically, especially in the mid- and late 1980s; but, because of their very high expectations, they became frustrated. The United States, so powerful for much of the postwar period, seemed adrift, unable to reconcile the races (or the classes or sexes) at home or to perform as effectively on the world stage. Patterson quotes a woman: "Sometimes you get the feeling nothing has gone right since John Kennedy died. We've had the Vietnam War, all the rioting. . . . Before then you were used to America winning everything, but now you sometimes think our day may be over" (782–83).

In August 1973, the Subcommittee on Intergovernmental Relations of the U.S. Senate commissioned the Louis Harris firm to survey popular attitudes toward the government, to measure the responsiveness of the government to public standards and expectations. The survey also asked government officials how well they felt they were meeting public needs. In the fall of 1973, for the first time since the 1968 assassinations of Martin Luther King Jr. and Robert Kennedy, a majority of Americans (by 53–37 percent) felt "there is something deeply wrong in America," that those were no ordinary times of crisis. This conviction permeated every social class and geographical area. Government leaders, those polled felt, were "corrupt and immoral." Most alienated were blacks, residents of big cities, rural residents, and people age fifty and over. In 1970, in one congressional district, the Drinan campaign had been able to confront an earlier stage of this alienation; now, particularly because he saw himself as a symbol of moral values, his challenge was to deal with it in a much larger and more complex milieu on a national level.

During Drinan's first term in Washington, although the number of troops fighting in Vietnam had been reduced somewhat, Nixon's promise of "peace with honor" remained a distant goal. In February 1971, the United States mounted a South Vietnamese–led invasion of Laos that failed miserably. Nixon responded with massive bombing strikes. At the 1972 Munich Olympic Games, the Palestinian extremist group Black September killed two Israeli team members and took nine hostages. In Northern Ireland, on Sunday, January 27, 1972, British soldiers opened fire on unarmed demonstrators in Londonderry, killing thirteen people. In reaction to this "Bloody Sunday," the underground Irish Republican Army (IRA) swelled with recruits. At home, Lieutenant William Calley went on trial for the 1968 murder of 102 Vietnamese men, women, and children at the village of My Lai. He was convicted of premeditated murder and sentenced to life imprisonment at Fort Leavenworth; however, Nixon ordered Calley released from the stockade and held under house arrest at Fort Benning, Georgia. In June the *New York Times* and *Washington Post* published what became known as the Pentagon Papers, a secret government history of the conduct of the Vietnam War that contradicted the upbeat stories the government had been telling the American people. Nixon sought an injunction to halt further publication, but the Supreme Court ruled 6–2 that Nixon's effort constituted "prior restraint," a "flagrant, indefensible" violation of the First Amendment.

In February 1972 Nixon, after long-secret preparation by Henry Kissinger, flew to the People's Republic of China in a week-long, bold diplomatic move to reset what he considered the "balance of power" that maintained international equilibrium, by playing off China against the Soviet Union and softening China's possible reaction to his escalation of the war in Vietnam. Three months later Nixon journeyed to Moscow to sign the Strategic Arms Limitation Treaty (SALT I), limiting the future buildup of intercontinental ballistic missiles (ICBM) for five years and restricting the deployment of ABMs on both sides. But his management of the Vietnam War deteriorated. As he withdrew troops, those who remained felt worse about being there. Desertions increased to an average of seven per one hundred soldiers. Between 1969 and 1972 enlisted men more than 1,000 times "fragged"— attempted to kill—their officers rather than follow orders. By 1971 an estimated 40,000 of the 250,000 American men in Vietnam were heroin addicts. That year 1,000 veterans camped out on the National Mall in Washington, called out the names of their dead buddies, and threw their medals on the Capitol steps.

The Church

The changes in American culture from the 1960s through the 1970s were mirrored in the Catholic Church. The years of the civil rights struggle coincided with the Vatican Council, and Catholic and Protestant churches cooperated in working for social and racial justice. Frank Drinan, as an example, was active in the Catholic Interracial Council and must have had a significant influence on his brother's racial ideas. But there was a negative side to the shift from communal values to autonomy, to the individualism that accompanied the '70s sense of alienation. Many big-city middle-class Catholics didn't want blacks in their neighborhoods, rejected priests like Drinan who preached tolerance from the pulpit, abandoned their parishes, and fled to the suburbs. In Cleveland, parishioners told activist priests, "Mind your own business, Father." In Boston in 1974 a parade of women marched past their church praying to keep their schools segregated. When the priest told them they should not pray for that, they shouted back, "We deal with God directly." On Vietnam, Catholic opinion went along with the general public, although a handful of young men associated with the *Catholic Worker* burned their draft cards.

The most lasting shift followed *Roe v. Wade*'s legalization of abortion in 1973. Initially prominent Catholic laymen, including Senator Edward M. Kennedy, deplored the decision, but by the 1980s Kennedy was "pro-choice." In general Catholics knew abortion was wrong but were not comfortable with its being totally outlawed. Only 36 percent of Catholics agreed with *Roe v. Wade*, but 56 percent were willing to leave the question of abortion to women and their doctors. The "personally opposed, but legal" stance became the standard politician's response to Catholic and non-Catholic audiences, and they knew their constituencies well. As James O'Toole pointed out in *The Faithful* (2008), "The faithful remained faithful," but they had also, to some degree, "lapsed." They accepted the new liturgy, went more often to communion, joined charismatic groups, and sought spiritual advisers. They also stopped going to confession, made their own decisions on birth control, and favored the ordination of women. They cheered the pope, but they disregarded his ideas and commands. O'Toole concluded, "These were, without doubt, exciting times to be a Catholic, but they were also times of uncertainty. The institution of the church was challenged, and the consequences of its weakened position became only too apparent as a new century opened."

It seems that, though often considered a radical or maverick, Drinan read his time well and spoke for it in more ways than his critics realized. On one level he embodied the simple piety of Shadowbrook, while on another he embraced the autonomy of the new era. Popular culture responded with its own apt American portraits. The film *Dirty Harry,* with Clint Eastwood, seemed to speak for those alienated urbanites who wanted to take the law into their own hands to tame their neighborhoods. A TV series, the sitcom "All in the Family," featured a middle-class Queens, New York, family led by Archie Bunker, a lovable bigot. Both fed on the frustration and anger of ordinary 1970s Americans. *The Godfather*, which grew into a trilogy, depicted, and for a while glorified and romanticized, a criminal underworld as a representative American family institution.

Ironically, as the 1972 election came onto the horizon, the Nixon administration, in putting the first stages of the Watergate break-in and cover-up in motion, had begun to mimic a criminal organization. It also manipulated its Vietnam strategy to influence the electoral returns. From the first moment of Drinan's candidacy, the Newton political leaders and Drinan had sought out one another with one goal in mind—to stop Nixon and halt the "madness" of his war. How Drinan was going to do this was not clear, especially when his new role as a congressman made so many other demands on his talents and time.

Old Georgetown, His New Home

One source of consolation and stability for Drinan would be his return to the Georgetown Jesuit community, where he had lived during his law school years. The Jesuit community consisted of three linked ancient brick buildings forming one side, overlooking the Potomac River, of an almost two-centuries-old quadrangle. The opposite side was originally a student dormitory, now offices, and the front was Healy Hall, harboring the administration, the president's office, classrooms, the Gaston Hall auditorium, and, originally, the library. President Patrick Healy had deliberately designed this signature building to look out over the city, as a sign of where the apostolate should be directed. In the center of the quad stood Dahlgren Chapel, the symbol of the university's religious life. Ryan Hall, which housed the high-ceilinged Jesuit dining room on the first floor, students on the second, and Jesuits on the third and fourth, jutted out from the community wing, with balconies on the end overlooking tennis courts, the Potomac River, and the grandly arching Francis Scott Key Bridge. From the top balcony it seemed one could almost reach out and touch the planes that took off from National (now Reagan) Airport down the river and roared by overhead.

Drinan's room in Mulledy Hall was larger than his room in Boston's St. Mary's Hall, but plain and spartan enough for him to witness to the public that he was living the Jesuit lifestyle and subject to the usual religious discipline. As in every Jesuit house, throughout the living area there were small private chapels where, before the practice of concelebration—priests saying Mass together as a group—took hold in communities, the men would say private Masses, usually at 7:00 A.M. or earlier. Drinan said his at seven o'clock.

Next to the dining room was the centralized *haustus* room, also called the Georgetown room, through which everyone naturally passed on the way to meals, the front parlors, the rector's office, the house library, the house chapel, or the corridor to Healy. This was the social hub, where someone who missed breakfast, lunch, or dinner could grab a snack, or those who wanted to eat breakfast and read the *Washington Post* at the same time could spread out their paper and feed both mind and body undisturbed. Here regulars gathered after 10:00 P.M. and later to drink a bottle of ale or beer on tap, tell stories, and sometimes laugh or growl about what was going on outside. In this room Drinan was a frequent, if brief, visitor. He would return home after a twelve- to eighteen-hour day in the office, pour his ale, spread peanut butter or mayonnaise on his crackers, sit down, and ask, "Well, what's new?"

The community, like all the major, large Jesuit university communities, was still going through the tensions of adapting to the challenges of Vatican II: wearing or not wearing clerical garb, sharing the governance of the university with laymen, allowing laypersons as guests in the dining room. But there was a special guest dining room on the side that community members like Drinan could use for special events.

Consistent with the time, Georgetown students had, a year before, added a second newspaper, *The Georgetown Voice,* to rival the traditional *Hoya.* More than the *Hoya,* the *Voice* wrote about the university's relationship to politics and to the city. And campus memories still lingered from the march against the Pentagon in 1967, the smoke curling into the sky from downtown Washington when the black neighborhoods broke out in riots following the assassination of Martin Luther King Jr., and the 1968 funeral of Robert F. Kennedy.

Drinan Meets the Press

On January 7, 1971, described by Donnie Radcliffe in the *Washington Star* the next day as "the congressman-elect with his collar on backwards," Drinan, with quick wit and a broad grin, gave his first formal news conference since moving into the Cannon House Office Building three days before. What should we call you, they asked. "Bobby," he replied with a smile, then corrected himself a few minutes later with the old line about the lawyer who said, "I don't care what they call me as long as they call me." The reporters experimented. One called him "Congressman"; most stuck with "Father." As expected: What will you wear and where will you live? "These are the only clothes I have," he answered; and he would live in the Jesuit community, as he had during law school. Although his $42,500 salary would be given to the Jesuit community, as his vow of poverty required, he had permission to use some of it to provide services for the people of his district.

Later Drinan acknowledged to Robert Cormier that he wore the collar to attract attention. How many reporters were at the press conference? More than forty. "I'm not kidding myself," he said. "They were there because I'm a priest. Curiosity—what's he like, what's he going to say? But think of what an opportunity that represents! The white collar grabs their attention and they find themselves listening to what I have to say, and reporting it all over the country. That's what's important."

Pressed later by Cormier about being a "priest-politician," Drinan simmered, but he held back his annoyance and then offered a dictionary distinction: first, a politician is one versed in the art or science of politics; second, one primarily interested in political office for selfish interests.

"Maybe there are too many of the second kind and not enough of the first," Cormier quipped.

"Maybe there are too many people talking about the second kind and not enough [about] the first," Drinan snapped. "All right," he concluded. "I'm a politician and glad of it. Which doesn't make me any less a man. Or a priest." It was impossible to separate the priesthood from the man, the reporter decided. And Drinan didn't seek a separation.

Already, questions centered on the 1972 election. Drinan told the *Washington Star* he was convinced Nixon could be beaten, because of the economy and inflation, the "crisis of confidence" caused by the war, the eighteen-year-olds who were getting the vote by virtue of the Twenty-sixth Amendment to the Constitution, and the efforts of the young people who had elected him. Yes, he would support Senator Ted Kennedy for president. He proposed fighting the unemployment that would follow the phasing-out of the defense industries by retraining thousands of persons to fight pollution, build houses, and solve the problems of the cities. Upstairs in his office the reporter found him comfortable, unruffled by his sudden responsibilities. According to his secretary, because he was a bachelor Drinan had time to open his own mail and even personally sign some of the 1,000 invitations going out to his open house. How long did he plan to serve in Congress? "I'll be around here for 28 years," he said. "That's a custom in our district." Taken seriously, that would mean that Drinan, who had called Philbin too old at seventy-one, would stay until he was seventy-seven. In 1971 the average age in Congress was about fifty-two.

The congressman's home away from home on the fifth floor of the Cannon Building in some ways replicated his life in his dean's office on St. Thomas More Drive at Boston College. And, in spite of his reluctance to talk about his original family, a sign of his fidelity to his current family was the picture of his brother Frank and sister-in-law Helen's family prominently displayed. He recruited his staff with the same confident aplomb with which he gathered faculty, students, and staff—and, inevitably, disciples—for the law school and the campaign. It was hard to avoid the biblical motif in his "Come, follow me" invitations. Elizabeth Bankowski was working in the law school library when he stopped by her desk, gave her some political literature to read, and later invited her to join his staff. He didn't know her well. How did he know that she was the right person? She followed him to Washington and took charge of his constituent relationships, which, in light of his campaign criticisms of Philbin, with almost weekly trips to Boston, he made an effort to maintain and satisfy.

The Washington office had about ten full-time workers and another ten interns and volunteers. He had brought them together by meeting them, liking them, and asking them to join. Somehow he saw something in them that they did not see in themselves. He would say "Go, do this," and they would go. They were overwhelmingly young, and the group took on the aura of a family who loved and served their "father"—in two senses of the word—even as, through constant exposure, they became more aware of his flaws and limitations. In his office, which had a back door that allowed him to escape an unwelcome visitor, he wore a Hawaiian shirt and took off his shoes. Although he wore the collar, he did everything to avoid being looked upon as a priest. He never discussed religion. When asked to say a Mass at a social gathering, he resisted, lest he impose on anyone present who did not desire or understand the Mass. He would lose his temper, become short with people who bored or annoyed him, and quickly usher them out of his office. Few knew him intimately, and he did not invite personal probing; but some knew him well enough to sense a visible struggle within himself to be a better person. Yet, all the while, he was the best person to work for.

He found himself warmly received by his congressional colleagues. As he strode through the halls of Congress, said Cormier, he was instantly recognized because of the collar, and the greetings made him feel at home. His seat on the Judiciary Committee fit his talents, and the committee's concentration on prison reform, civil rights, and immigration matched his priorities.

A Visit Home

At 4:00 P.M., on April 17, a typically cold, gray winter afternoon, Congressman Drinan and Bruce Holbein, his law student aide in his early twenties, stood hatless in the wind outside the entrance to the DuPont plant in Leominster as the front doors opened and the workers poured out, headed for the parking lot across the street and home. "Meet and shake hands with Congressman Drinan," said Holbein. "Meet Congressman Drinan." One by one they took his hand and he said, "Good to see you." Enjoying himself, Drinan looked for details that would allow him to connect with the individual. "Hard day?" he asked a small, round-shouldered woman.

"I'm glad it's over, Father," she replied and trudged on.

Drinan stayed until they stopped coming, then turned to his car and drove off. Why today? There was no election coming up until next year. But this was a factory he had not hit during the first campaign. He would be running again, as congressmen do every two years. He had to establish himself.

Later that morning at the district headquarters, he met with seven constituents who had made appointments, allowing each one fifteen minutes. One wanted to discuss his applications for school. The next had a service-related disability. He had contracted asthma but was not receiving benefits. Next was a mother who had lost her son in Vietnam. The next wanted to teach in a foreign country. Another needed advice on an exam he had to take as part of his education. Another wanted to talk about her nephew getting out of the service. What can a congressman do for each of these persons? Every member of Congress knows that his or her ability to serve successfully and be reelected hangs largely on the handling of these cases. Often the member's office will refer the constituents to an agency or to someone else. Or aides will make phone calls on their behalf, or the member will actually draw up legislation for the benefit of one man or woman.

Between January and April 1971, Drinan co-sponsored about a hundred bills, which means he added his name to what was often a long list of co-sponsors of a colleague's bill. He sponsored, or initiated himself, six. In one bill, Drinan joined seventy-seven others to support New York Congressman Ed Koch's bill to require that the Voice of America (VOA) undertake Yiddish language broadcasts to the Soviet Union. The United States Information Agency (USIA) responded that, of Russia's three million Jews, only 40 percent understood Yiddish. Koch and fifteen others, including Drinan, threatened to cut all funds for broadcasts to Russia unless the VOA complied. Drinan's bills included a proposed tax reduction for blood donors to nonprofit institutions, help for a blind man to receive disability insurance, and help for handicapped dependents of military personnel.

Founded in 1964 in Kansas City by Robert Hoyt, editor of the local diocesan paper, the *National Catholic Reporter* had quickly become what many Catholic journalists had hoped for but never accomplished, an independent, lay-edited, influential national voice, with emphasis on investigative reporting, on the issues and controversies of the day. To many readers, particularly clergy, its outstanding feature was that if Church officials, including bishops, abused their power, the whole country would soon read about it. Two of its best moments in its early years were its powerful editorial condemning the Vietnam War as immoral and its publication of the full text of the Vatican's Pope Paul VI–appointed committee of theologians, including laypersons, to examine the teaching on birth control. The commission recommended that birth control, under certain circumstances, be permitted; but following the intervention of John Ford, S.J., the report was buried and the 1968 encyclical *"Humanae Vitae"* reaffirmed the condemnation of artificial contraception.

In February Hoyt was beefing up his list of columnists to include Eugene McCarthy, the theologian Charles Davis, Garry Wills, and Michael Novak, and he invited Drinan to join them with a column every other month. Drinan jumped at the invitation. He was an enthusiastic *NCR* reader and he had no shortage of things to say. Meanwhile he continued to write articles for *America*.

Anthony Frisoli

Drinan had a soft spot in his heart for immigrants. He had written an *America* article during his tertianship in Italy proposing that U.S. immigration quotas be rewritten to make room for more Italians. A few years later, on August 21, 1954, he wrote "Deporting Our Subversive Aliens" for *America*, in which he observed that "Most legal comment on the question of aliens is unanimous in the view that American law, both past and present, is harsh, inconsistent and unreasonable in many of the restrictions on aliens." Criticizing the McCarran–Walter immigration law, he quoted then-Archbishop Cushing's testimony to the President's Commission on Immigration that the McCarran–Walter

Act "[failed] to provide for an independent, fair hearing, for the people who [were] threatened with deportation," and it should be purged of its "several un-Christian and un-American provisions."

In Drinan's 1971 legislative file, the fattest folder, H.R. 6742, dated March 24, 1971, is devoted to one man, an Italian immigrant, Pasquale Antonio Frisoli, known as Anthony, seeking permanent residence. It is worth attention not because of its impact on history or immigration policy; rather, it illustrates what many congressmen will go through on behalf of a constituent. Drinan was no exception.

We can picture Drinan opening his own mail on a late March morning and reading, "Dear Father Drinan: I am in desperate need of your help." The missive concluded, "Please Father, won't you help me and let Mr. Frisoli remain here in the United States and become a permanent resident here in Massachusetts so that he along with his daughter can live a normal life, rather than go from Country to Country in desperate pursuit of happiness." The Waltham constituent was Frisoli's cousin Olga E. Trivisano. With her family, Trivisano was profoundly committed to Frisoli, thirty-six, who had come to America by way of South Africa with his five-year-old daughter, Maria, on a visitor's visa in 1968.

An Italian, he had worked as a garage mechanic in Swaziland, South Africa, where he had married a South African and they had had their child. But his wife had worked in a casino and gone to soccer games and gone swimming rather than care for the little girl. They divorced and a nun and priest helped care for the child; Frisoli then took her to Italy, briefly, to see his sick father. In Massachusetts he worked at a garage but was told by immigration officials that he had to return to Italy when his visa was up. A lawyer, for $1,500, promised him either a "special worker" status or a special bill in Congress to legitimize his status. Congressman Philbin introduced the bill and had his stay extended to February, then to March 1971, then to April, because Congress adjourned at the end of 1970 without voting on the bill. Drinan picked up Philbin's task and reintroduced his bill to give Frisoli more time.

The Trivisanos cared for Maria as if she were their own child, determined to sacrifice their own businesses if necessary, as Frisoli went to work each day, then was sidelined for nine months by an auto accident in 1970. All this time he refused to ask for government assistance. While their friends urged them simply to bribe the immigration authorities, as so many immigrants apparently did, they wanted to prove that the U.S. government could be just and fair. Trivisano offered to tell Drinan the names of those who protected illegal immigrants.

Drinan's staff investigator, Jean Crosby, wrote, "It is a sad story, but whether sad enough to get special consideration on it, I don't know."

As the clock ticked and the months passed, the case became more complicated. Perhaps because Frisoli's English was not good, Trivisano insisted that all communication with him go through her; otherwise, she said, some message might so upset and depress him that he would kill himself and the child. Drinan, who had yet to meet Frisoli, seemed determined to save him. He stayed on top of the material and scribbled notes on the memos. Some new facts, he said, were irrelevant, but "*so interesting.*"

On September 29, 1971, Drinan met with Trivisano and wrote to her about strategies. Frisoli could apply for preference as a skilled auto mechanic, of which there was a national shortage, although the quota for immigrants from Italy with this occupation was already oversubscribed. Next, if he believed there was any chance that returning to Italy would endanger him or the child, he should document that. Drinan twice mentioned that marriage to an American would be an answer—he didn't exactly urge him to marry but surely dropped a big hint. Testimonies as to Frisoli's character, industry, and extraordinary skills as an auto mechanic and a parent poured in. They came from teachers, a priest, his employers, his former boss in South Africa, his upstairs neighbor, and Maria's pediatrician. In addition there was a letter from five-year-old Maria to President Nixon directing him to stop the war because of the killing, prevent drugs because they made sick people kill people, stop air pollution because some day all of us would die, and "let Anthony and Maria become Americans."

On October 15 Trivisano wrote to Drinan, disheartened that the federal bureaucracy was unable to do anything to save this poor man and his child. She had mentioned the "getting married" business to Frisoli, to which he had exclaimed, "Look at the mess I'm in already, and do you think I've gone completely mad?" But, Trivisano thought, maybe he would change his mind when he calmed down. Also, he "would like very much to meet you in person." Other strategies were considered: rewriting his qualifications to stress his experience with diesel motors and foreign cars, upgrading his current job title, and having him train other mechanics. But the Department of Labor replied that it could not certify that there was a demonstrable need for Frisoli's abilities, that such qualified auto mechanics were not then already available in the United States. Finally, on November 18, 1971, Congressman Peter W. Rodino of New Jersey, chairman of the Judiciary Committee's subcommittee on immigration, wrote "Bob" that he was sorry, but "the facts do not warrant favorable consideration of this legislation."

Drinan, rather than give up, got Rodino to put off a final decision until the beginning of the next congressional session and asked the law firm of Joseph T. O'Neill to take Frisoli's case. In February 1972, O'Neill weighed in and informed the Immigration and Naturalization Service that Frisoli could prove that he would be subject to persecution on account of race, religion, or political opinion if he were returned to South Africa or to Italy. For the next three months Frisoli became more difficult. He failed to come up with any such evidence that he would be persecuted and, although demanding more and more services from O'Neill, declined to pay any of his bills.

On November 1, 1972, according to a memo from Crosby to Drinan aide Liz Bankowski, Trivisano reported that Frisoli had married the week before, on the Monday before his scheduled deportation day. The next day immigration officials arrested both Frisoli and his bride, holding her in handcuffs for three hours. They picked up Maria at school and told her that if she did not go with her father they would send her to South Africa, where she was a citizen, alone; then they put Frisoli and Maria on a plane to Italy. Trivisano was in constant tears. Drinan's scribblings on a separate page say, "fraudulent marriage . . . turned over to District Attorney . . . ."

Crosby concluded: "Thought you should have this info in your file, in case they should come back to us."

The War Comes to Washington

On April 23, 1971, about 1,000 members of the Vietnam Veterans Against the War ended a week of meetings, testimony, and demonstrations in which 700 of them, including John Kerry, before about 500 spectators, approached the wire fence hastily erected in front of the Capitol before the statue of Chief Justice John Marshall and, in twos and threes, hurled their Purple Hearts, Silver Stars, discharge papers, and commendation medals over the fence.

Joseph Bangert, a twenty-two-year-old Marine, dressed in his jungle fatigues, returned six medals, including a Vietnamese Cross of Gallantry. He said he had wanted to return them in Vietnam when he realized that the "political force" he was fighting was actually the Vietnamese people. The people were struggling against the aggressor, "and we're the aggressor."

At a special Senate hearing that day attended by George McGovern and Walter Mondale, the veterans testified about what they considered the previously unreported side of the war. Naval veteran Dale Grenada, twenty-five, testified that on his destroyer he had been ordered to shell and destroy a suspected Viet Cong village. When spotter planes reported people fleeing from the shelling across open fields, they "switched to fragmented shells and began to chop the people up." Then they fired phosphorous shells and incendiaries to burn what was left to the ground. Grenada said the only difference between himself and Lieutenant William Calley was that Calley could see the people he killed.

The veterans tried to hold their final memorial service in Arlington National Cemetery, but the gates were locked against them. But that night more than 3,000 people, including about 600 active-duty servicemen, 250 in uniform, assembled at Washington National Cathedral. Army Sp. 5 Charles T. Baient, who was still on active duty, told the gathering that most of the nearly 3 million Americans who had fought in Vietnam were unwilling draftees taken from their homes for reasons never explained to do the dirty work in a war they did not want: "Those of us fortunate enough to come home alive and unwounded can wash the blood from our hands, but not from our minds. We are the ones who have had to be in holes in the ground, covered with wounded brothers' blood, listening to his screams of pain, listening to him ask why, and cursing those who sent him to die." With Yale University chaplain William Sloane Coffin, Bishop J. Brooke Mosley of Union Theological Seminary, and Dean Francis B. Sayre Jr. of the cathedral by his side, Drinan said the American conduct of the war had been "barbarous" and called for Congress to set up a $50 billion reparations fund to be paid over the next five years to "all peoples of Indochina."

Drinan told the *Washington Star* that as a freshman congressman, "I'm like a novice in a religious order," and he would have to work his way into the framework, though he would vote in favor of a modification of the seniority system. But three days after the memorial service, he did not sound like a novice when in the April 27 *Hartford Courant* Patricia Stewart portrayed him as "Priest-Legislator Battles System." With the event of the Vietnam veterans' week still ringing in his head, Drinan told a student audience at Hartford's Trinity College to take power, "start a national movement today or tomorrow." He criticized his fellow members of Congress, accusing the institution of "lethargy or apathy." This rendered him "more than a little depressed." He split his colleagues between the "100 very fine" congressmen and the "old men" who held the power. The average age of House committee chairmen was seventy-one, while the average age of the citizenry was twenty-five. He was toying with the idea of a constitutional amendment to lower the age of eligibility to hold federal office from twenty-five to twenty-one. On Vietnam, he urged that Americans all "face up to our guilt and insist that our G.I.s and generals confess. . . . This is a hideous, insane, and genocidal war, we've never done a thing like this in two centuries." He told his audience that during his 1969 trip to Vietnam a Vietnamese lawyer told him of thousands of dossiers filled with evidence of American atrocities that could be presented to some future trials perhaps modeled on those held at Nuremberg.

As a young priest, one of Drinan's first articles concerned the rights of citizens questioned by congressional investigative committees. To his Trinity audience he described himself as the "one good guy" on the House Internal Security Committee (HISC) and dubbed Nixon's attorney general, John N. Mitchell, "much more dangerous" than FBI Director J. Edgar Hoover. The current atmosphere of surveillance, he said, was "very gruesome." In fact he had been appointed to the committee, formerly known as the House Un-American Activities Committee, two days after proposing legislation that it be abolished. His opposition was based on his belief that the purpose of congressional committes should be legislative rather than judicial, and the committee in question had taken over the functions of judge, jury, and "executioner" by destroying people's reputations.

In May, Drinan had a dust-up with Richard H. Ichord, chairman of HISC, who objected to Drinan's informing the public that a witness, Richard Diao, who was testifying about Red China was on the staff of Voice of America. Diao had asked that his job not be disclosed, but Drinan thought the public should know, so he went on ABC's evening news program the next night and told them. In June Drinan said he wouldn't run for the Senate, because the only black senator was his Republican Massachusetts colleague Edward W. Brooke, and he didn't want to "pit a Jesuit Democrat against a black Republican." On July 3 he introduced his amendment to the Constitution lowering by three years the age of eligibility to hold a House seat (from twenty-five to twenty-two) and to hold a Senate seat (from thirty to twenty-seven).

A few days later, on July 19, he told the New York Times that "My spiritual life is the most enjoyable thing I do, I suppose. When people allege some conflict of interest, I try to figure out what their cobweb . . . what is their preoccupation." The same day, twenty-seven Jesuit scholastics from St. Louis University in the Missouri province mailed Drinan their draft cards. Their logic was that, in opposing the war, they should not cooperate with the Selective Service in any way, which meant they would neither carry their draft cards nor accept their seminarians' exemption from military service. It was an interesting, probably unique approach. They were challenging the government to draft them and send them to Vietnam or to prison. If the government took the bait, they would have to figure out their next move. The seminarians may not have known that Drinan, during his election campaign, had said he would help defend in court—get lawyers for—student protesters who refused to serve on moral grounds.

The young Jesuits also sent letters to Drinan, Pope Paul VI, and several American bishops in which they chastised themselves for being idle. "We have watched as men our own age are forced by their government to commit murder or face imprisonment while our bodies are immune to conscription, hidden behind our clerical exemption." They were violating the law, but "we believe that this law in our land is the law of death."

It is not clear what they wanted Drinan to do with their cards, but he returned them. "Because I have chosen to seek radical change in America as a congressman," Drinan wrote to them, "I have sworn to uphold the Constitution and to avoid forms of civil disobedience." A spokesman for the group, James Ayers, said the group was "encouraged" by his response and "understood" his position.

Mississippi

Between the second week of October and the first week of December 1971, Congressman Drinan, as of October 4, already had twenty-five commitments, some of which lasted several days and which flew him to various parts of the country. They included, for example, a meeting of the members of the visiting committee for Harvard Divinity School; an all-day conference on "Choices of Our Conscience" at the John F. Kennedy Center; a board meeting of Americans for Democratic Action; a three-day inspection of Soledad, San Quentin, and other California prison sites; Judiciary Committee hearings in California; a White House Conference on the Aging; and an address at the Jewish Center Forum in Cincinnati. On October 29 he flew to Greenville, Mississippi.

Five months before, in New Orleans, a young Georgetown student journalist, Jason Berry, twenty-two, eager to make his mark as a writer and political activist, headed, against his parents' advice, for Mississippi to work as a volunteer for the first black candidate for governor of the state. The candidate was the mayor of Fayette, Charles Evers, brother of Medgar Evers, the civil rights leader who had been murdered in 1963.

Berry knew that before Charles Evers had run for office he had been a Chicago gangster. He did numbers running and ran a brothel. But his brother's assassination had turned his life around. He returned to Mississippi. For much of his life he had dreamed of killing whites, killing one big racist every day, and he had collected some guns for the job. But something kept telling him that was not the way. He wrote in his autobiography that he would sit at his brother's desk and listen to a voice that said Medgar wouldn't like that. Instead of killing people, he should get them registered to vote.

Drinan could hardly have imagined more hostile territory. Berry loved Mississippi, but he described it well in his memoir, *Amazing Grace*:

> Mississippi has more recorded lynchings than any other state, is considered the state most brutal in opposition to civil rights legislation and its implementation, and has an unparalleled history of racist demagoguery. Mississippi is the land where the Pulitzer Prizes are anathema and where the nation's fourth Nobel winner in literature, William Faulkner, was hated even after he won the prize.

Drinan was flying in from Washington to speak at a Charles Evers campaign rally in Greenville, a town known, said Berry, "for its civility in race relations." Having linked up with Berry in a bar, the forty-eight-year-old tough politician Evers took a liking to the young man and made him his press secretary; and so on the final week of the campaign they drove across the state to meet a group of local journalists, including the famed Hodding Carter III, and Congressman Drinan in the local courthouse. They arrived to find it packed with black people, the journalists all squeezed into the benches in the front row.

Evers's speech was a spellbinder, in which he listed the sins of the white oppressors, like the Delta planters and Mississippi's U.S. Senator James O. Eastland. The Princeton graduate Carter leaped to his feet and yelled, holding back his tears. Drinan, says Berry, "hung on Evers' words." Then Evers turned toward Carter and told his audience how this white man's newspaper had told its readers that it's wrong for white folks to hate black folks and that "black folks and white folks have to work together."

Drinan, visibly moved, rose to speak. He had come to tell them they could win: "It can be done." His own campaign was the proof. People said a priest could never be elected to the House, but thousands of volunteers had poured into the raining streets and gone door to door, asking those who had not voted to go to the polls. He concluded, "I know you can do the same for the courageous Mayor Evers and all the candidates on the Mississippi Loyalist Democratic ticket."

He was wrong. Evers lost the race for the governorship by 424,000 votes, claiming only 22 percent of the vote. But it was a start. Of the 300 candidates for local office on Evers's Loyalist slate, 51 were elected. This was a 50 percent increase in the number of blacks elected four years before. Evers ran as an independent for the Senate seat vacated by Eastland in 1978 and came in third, splitting the Democratic vote to allow a Republican, Thad Cochran, to win. Berry went on to write a series of books on the South and was the first journalist to expose, in the *National Catholic Reporter,* the pedophile scandal in the American Catholic Church. Berry met Drinan a few times after that. They talked in 1987 when the younger man was working on the pedophile series. It was not a pleasant exchange. Drinan "fumed," upset that the priesthood was getting this kind of scrutiny. "A gay priest is not a term with much meaning to me," he said. He meant, concluded Berry, that a priest is just a priest.

8

One of Drinan's Jesuit friends was Mike Lavelle, dean of Cleveland's John Carroll University Business School, who would occasionally invite him to speak—for example, at the annual Bench and Bar alumni dinner in the spring of 1972. Lavelle was never known to be cowed by negative reaction to his straightforward presentations on social justice. Mary Kay Kantz, whose husband, Paul, was a John Carroll alumnus of the 1960s and worked there for thirty years, remembers the night vividly. The audience was politically and religiously conservative, well-off, with many not pleased with the evening's speaker; some were still grumbling about liberal Jesuit political science teacher Paul Woelf, who had run unsuccessfully for Congress recently. And they had the same "What's a priest doing running for Congress?" idea about Drinan.

Others in the audience had not heard of Drinan before but were shocked and disgusted by his attack on the Vietnam War. He came on strong. Mary Kay and Paul sat up front, and they could see that his eyes were piercing and blue. "There is a fire in his eyes," Mary Kay thought. Several times Drinan caught her eye and seemed to be speaking directly to her. She would have followed him to the ends of the earth—while others in the audience would have strung him up.

As the 1972 presidential campaign picked up momentum, Mary Kay volunteered for Senator George McGovern of South Dakota and headed for the local shopping center, her kids in tow, to pass out campaign literature as shoppers called her a "dirty commie."

Years passed. Mary Kay went to law school nights at Cleveland State University, and Drinan spoke there about a year after he left Congress. In 1980 he had been instructed to leave Congress by Pope

John Paul II, who was determined that priests not hold political office. Mary Kay looked into his eyes, and the fire was gone. She returned home and told her husband in tears, "There's no light in his eyes any more. There was no light in his eyes." Fifteen years after that, Drinan returned to speak at John Carroll again, and much of the spark had returned. Mary Kay reminded him of his appearance in 1972. "I want to thank you. I heard you speak in this very room 25 years ago, and you radicalized me."

Drinan laughed, shook his head, put his arms around her shoulder, and replied, "No, I didn't. I Christianized you!"

As 1971 played out, Drinan, still in his first year as a congressman, doggedly and single-mindedly pursued the issue that had brought him to Congress—ending the Vietnam War—all the while paying due diligence to the needs of his constituents. He averaged about a dozen major speeches a year—preaching at Masses, addressing high school and university graduations, talking in synagogues and in church halls. Letters poured in on the strife and famine in Pakistan, and above all on Vietnam. Between March and April 1971 he received—and answered within a few days—more than one hundred letters, many of which expressed in highly personal and emotional language the moral horror of average voters and distinguished public figures, including the president of Holy Cross College, John Brooks, S.J., on Pakistan, and friend and sponsor Jerome Grossman, who concluded in a February 11 letter, "Continuation of the present policies will kill us all." The letters came in all forms, from a postcard crammed to the margins with the tiniest possible script, key words underlined in red, and "Personal and Important" in capital letters on the front, to long, scholarly treatises, sermons, and a report on the South Vietnamese "tiger cages." The writers reminded Drinan that they had voted for him and now urged him to make even more effort to deliver on his promises. Some asked, What more can we do? He told some to join Common Cause, the private nonpartisan association he considered most effective.

The radio commentator Paul Harvey addressed his long letter, "Dear Mad Monk." (Drinan seemed to have acquired that nickname early in his term.) Harvey was worried that the Vietnam War would lead to a nuclear conflict. He boiled his strategic advice down to: Don't invade North Vietnam and give no air support if the South invades the North; don't get mired in Thailand; get troops out by June 1, 1971, and air support out by December '71. He added a prescient comment: "I'm intrigued by your desire to elect a new Congress in 1972. Since you are essentially a gadfly, I can easily see why you would suggest it." Drinan answered generously, made no reference to "Mad Monk" or "gadfly," and urged Harvey to write frequently. Certainly Drinan considered himself much more than a "gadfly." Nevertheless, he did show a propensity for proposing legislation that had little chance of passage but that made a moral point to which he sought to call attention. Such "symbolic" legislation could also plant a seed that might blossom in later laws and allowed the congressman to point out to his constituents that he had proposed a law addressed to their problem.

Most eloquent was a long public letter, published in the *Boston Globe* on April 19, 1971, from the eighty-three doctors and staff of the 91st Evacuation Hospital, Chiu Lai, Vietnam, addressed to President Nixon but also sent to Drinan:

> First of all, let us discuss the moral aspects of the war itself. As staff members of a hospital in an area not yet "pacified," we are daily witnesses to the carnage and brutality wrought upon human beings, both military personnel and civilians. How does one explain to a man without legs, maimed for life, that he has played a part in an effort to stop the "communist aggressor"? How does one console a mother who just lost a child in a village sweep, having previously lost her husband and her first-born son? Will a man be able to tell his adopted son, the war having made that the only choice to have an heir, that what we did was right? And we justly destroy these countries, displace and disintegrate families, and kill thousands of innocents in order to wipe out an internal "enemy" whose ranks are maintained by birth and environment rather than conscription? . . . This is a nation tired of the decades of war it has endured, and tired of the continuing American presence . . . .

Tom Sewell, a reporter for the *Boston Herald Traveler*, forwarded Drinan a copy of a telegram sent to Nixon, signed by 120 journalists, saying, "The war in Indochina is wrong and each day our military remains there is a further crime against mankind."

Many letters focused on the proposed Vietnam Disengagement Act, which called for the withdrawal from Vietnam of all American forces by December 31, 1971. This was one of at least seven proposals concerning Vietnam that were the subject of hearings held by the Senate Foreign Relations Committee, chaired by Senator J. William Fulbright of Arkansas, on eleven days between April 20 and May 27, 1971. Those who testified during the five weeks included Senator George McGovern; Senator Mark Hatfield of Oregon; Senator Adlai E. Stevenson III of Illinois, son of the former governor and 1952 and 1956 Democratic presidential candidate; John W. Gardner, chairman of Common Cause; W. Averell Harriman, former under-secretary of state and former governor of New York; Senator Walter Mondale of Minnesota; and John Kerry, representing the Vietnam Veterans Against the War.

Kerry summarized the Winter Soldier Investigation, the title of which was a takeoff on Thomas Paine's line in his Revolutionary War pamphlet "The Crisis" deploring the "sunshine soldier and summer patriot" who would not fight for the American Revolution. At an earlier public forum in Detroit, the veterans had graphically described crimes they had witnessed and shameful deeds they had done.

> They told stories of times they had personally raped, cut off ears, cut off heads, taped wires from portable telephones to human genitals and turned up the power, cut off limbs, blown up bodies, randomly shot at civilians, razed villages in fashion reminiscent of Genghis Khan, shot cattle and dogs for fun, poisoned food stocks, and generally ravaged the countryside of South Vietnam in addition to the normal ravage of war, and the normal and very particular ravaging which is done by the applied bombing power of this country.

These crimes, not the "Reds," threatened this country, said Kerry. Nothing happening in Vietnam threatened America, except what we (the soldiers) were doing, and nothing was worth the death of another

American soldier. The war continued, he said, because President Nixon had said he did not want to be the "first president to lose a war." Kerry then added, "How do you ask a man to be the last man to die for a mistake?"

Reflections

On July 1, Drinan sat down with his tape recorder and composed some "reflections" on his first six months in Congress. The resulting essay was basically a promotion of Common Cause, but along the way he revealed something about his expectations for churches in public life. Up to then, most of his public complaints had been about the lethargy of his secular colleagues; but on this day he laid his criticism on the leaders of the church, who were "unwilling to have their voices heard in the Congress of the United States." In his logic, the 535 members of the House and Senate "[formulated] the public morality of America." Therefore, he found it "appalling" how few Christians and people of other faiths made any effort to influence those key 535. True, some churches had spoken in support of the several amendments to cut off funding for the war, but Common Cause was responsible for changing more votes than any church lobby.

The relative silence of Catholic officials on the war was "almost thunderous," he said, and it gave the impression that those Catholics who were vehemently anti-war did not represent majority Catholic opinion. True, the hierarchy of many churches, including the Catholic bishops, opposed continuation of the draft; but a real broad-based ecumenical lobby could have at least terminated the draft by July 1, 1972, rather than a year later. Statements of the bishops on government aid to Catholic schools, abortion laws, and obscenity are well known, but we know of no national Catholic lay organization to demand the end of compulsory military training. Lobbies, Drinan said, can do both good and harm: Environmentalists stopped construction of the SST; the farm lobby got subsidies for farmers not to farm for the sum of $4 billion per year; but Common Cause had generated hundreds of thousands of letters to Congress pleading for a change in the seniority system, an end to job discrimination, an expansion of the food stamp program, and aid for the working poor.

On August 5, a month later, Congressman Drinan testified at length before the House Foreign Relations Committee Subcommittee on Pacific and Asian Affairs. The transcript of his testimony is an unusual document that does not dwell upon the moral horrors of the war but presents a sociopolitical analysis of how the United States became involved, based on the writings of Alexis de Tocqueville, C. Wright Mills, G. William Domhoff, and Seymour Martin Lipset, who maintained that the keystone of democracy was a pluralistic distribution of decision-making power—whereas in the current situation a governing elite had separated the people from the decision-making process and undercut the role of the people as the ultimate decision-making force in a democratic society.

Drinan summarized Domhoff for the committee, pointing out that the social upper class, owners of large amounts of corporate stock, had come to dominate foreign policy decisions through special appointments to committees and by financing major nongovernmental opinion-forming institutions, all to make the case that Congress, the military, and public opinion had lost all control of foreign policy formation. Drinan's main point, one that he returned to again and again from different directions, was that Congress had become "a rather impotent body." The executive branch "can get its way with Congress on foreign affairs any time it wants to with patience, tact, research and vigorous leadership by the President."

The executive branch got its way in Indochina by holding back information, spoon-feeding the public misinformation and propaganda, and invoking patriotism to ostracize dissenters. Drinan's answer: "What must be done now is not to point fingers at particular participants but renew America's great experiment in democracy." Congress must "resist all elitist tendencies in foreign policy management and reassert the proper role of Congress and the people in foreign affairs."

Drinan returned to this theme in a November 28, 1971, address at the Ford Hall Forum, calling upon Congress to "assert itself" in 1972.

In his view, Congress had demonstrated its subservience in its November 17 rejection, by a vote of 238–163, of a proposal to end the war by June 1, 1972. Its biggest problem, as he had said many times, was seniority, old men controlling committees, then the lack of initiative by congressional leaders, like Carl Albert, Speaker of the House, and majority leader Hale Boggs. The only solutions would be to "recall" these old-timers in the 1972 elections. Clearly, as he had said in Mississippi, his own election, an insurgency against what he described as an old, out-of-touch congressman, was the model for other states and districts.

On January 7, 1972, W. Seavey Joyce resigned the presidency of Boston College. Opposition had been building for months. By general agreement, Joyce was well liked, but his skills in budget and crisis management were below what the times required. Apparently he had hoped that if he appointed Drinan a vice president for development, Drinan's national reputation would energize alumni and public relations; but Drinan's stronger drives had led him into national politics, to some degree as compensation for his not having been named president in 1968. A member of the Boston College search committee for Joyce's successor, Father Frank Mackin, S.J., had been much impressed by an unsuccessful candidate for the Fordham University presidency, Father Donald Monan, S.J., dean of LeMoyne College in Syracuse. Mackin tracked down Monan, who was on vacation, and got him to apply to Boston College. Monan, who assumed office in September 1972, completed the restructuring of the trustees to a board of thirty-five with fifteen Jesuits and became the most successful president in recent times, earning Boston College a reputation as a national university and an intellectual powerhouse, with some help from a successful football team. Drinan must have looked at Boston College as his "road not taken" and Congress as the road destiny had laid out.

Again Arrupe

As 1972 progressed and Drinan floated the idea of recalling ineffective congressmen, one Church leader had his own candidate for recall. During a January 10 interview on NBC television, Cardinal John Krol of

Philadelphia, president of the American Catholic hierarchy and one of its most conservative members, said Drinan should resign from Congress. The previous fall the Synod of Bishops, said Krol, initially had affirmed the conclusion of the Vatican Council that "the priest is not to invade the competency of the laity. He is not to enter the world of partisan politics. He must not be an agent of a dividing faction—that is the point." For a bit, Krol tried to avoid mentioning Drinan by name, but the reporters pressed. In the light of that teaching, was Krol saying that Drinan should resign? Krol conceded, "In the light of this teaching I would say that Father Drinan is in politics. Yes." Krol also expressed doubts about priests who engaged in protests that got them jailed. "Men of this caliber—and sincere conviction"—should find ways where they don't put themselves in a position where they are bearing "silent witness." Three weeks passed before the Society responded, but, in a February 5 interview with the *Globe*, Father Guindon, the New England provincial, came on strong. Krol's statement, he said, was "completely impertinent." Drinan had his (Guindon's) permission "based on a specifically Christian ground."

But since the previous December the discussion between Rome and Boston and Washington on the same topic had been heating up. Father Arrupe had concluded, considering what he was told by the American hierarchy and his interpretation of the Bishops' Synod of the previous year, that the "exceptional circumstances" which would allow a priest to run for office did not exist because, he had been told, the Boston area already possessed "outstanding and qualified Catholic laymen well suited" to serve in Congress.

Drinan was dumbfounded, especially given that he had met with Arrupe in May 1971, well into his first term, and taken from him what he interpreted as encouragement and approval. To Drinan's defenders, Rome was again thinking in terms of European political parties that did not correspond to the American system. Also, they might ask, if Boston has all these "well qualified" laymen, why don't they run for office? Furthermore, because the district had been realigned, now called the Fourth District, new volunteers had begun working months before, committing time and money to the cause. In another long letter to Arrupe, on January 29, Guindon warned him of the scandal that interference with Drinan would cause, especially to the younger priests of the province and the young people of the country who saw in Father Drinan a "fearless leader seeking what is really the reform of social structures." Drinan was unique, he said; no layman possessed the training and expertise that would make him the ideal representative of the people. He pleaded with the general to let Drinan work this out "in the context of his own conscience from now on."

Arrupe responded that Canon 139 par. 4 of Church law required the approval of both Archbishop Humberto S. Medeiros of Boston and Bishop Bernard J. Flanagan of Worcester. Informed in mid-March by Flanagan that neither he nor Medeiros approved of Drinan's candidacy for reelection, Arrupe informed Drinan that he could not approve either. Drinan, during this period, as during his first campaign, became distracted and, in the view of some friends, seemed to not realize the precariousness of his situation, as he put off answering Arrupe's letters and convinced himself that, because congressional terms are deliberately very short, it is implicit when one runs for the House of Representatives that to run once is to keep running. Therefore, as he saw it, his original permission applied to future campaigns as well.

Finally, in a six-page reply to Arrupe on April 11, Drinan made his ultimate plea. He reviewed his motivations for running, his opposition to the war and the draft, consistent with the American Church's concerns, and reported on his recent session with Bishop Flanagan. Flanagan had told him that the original permission remained valid and continued "as long as the office continues," and that the fact of the election itself fulfills the requirement of canon law for an "extraordinary" situation. Medeiros said that, although he had reservations, Cardinal Cushing's permission endured. Drinan concluded, as evidence of his moral leadership, that in May the House would vote on a measure sponsored by Senator Mike Gravel of Alaska and Drinan that would end the war and bring home the prisoners of war. On May 29 Arrupe replied that, after considering prayerfully all the circumstances, "I too shall not give a positive approval for your candidacy, but at the same time I shall not prevent your placing your name for reelection."

While all this was going on, a Drinan-related debate brightened the pages of the liberal Catholic biweekly *Commonweal*. Peter Steinfels took as a springboard for his March 31, 1972, column a February 3 article in the English-language edition of the official Vatican paper *Osservatore Romano* by Reverend Donald W. Wuerl, secretary to Cardinal John J. Wright, the former bishop of Worcester who had preached at Drinan's first Mass. Wuerl argued that the priestly role of prophet demanded freedom from party and electoral ideology. He added that there was "one case where a priest office holder has already found it necessary to reject the teaching of the church on abortion."

Steinfels replied that, misled by a "non-fact" in James Hitchcock's *Decline and Fall of Radical Catholicism*, Wuerl was wrong on three counts: (1) Drinan had not rejected the church's position on abortion, (2) Drinan's position was on abortion laws, (3) Drinan had evolved his position out of consideration for pluralism in society. Steinfels pointed out that in Italy the Church was deeply involved in party politics, "stoking up its Catholic Action committees for the Christian Democrats." Wuerl responded that, as proof of Drinan's having rejected the Church's position, the bishops had labeled abortion "murder," and to disagree with the bishops on a secular legal question is to reject the Church's teaching. Steinfels shot back that Wuerl implied that Drinan, a legal scholar, when the distance between the Gospel message and the teaching of the American bishops on the legal import of a moral judgment was vast, was not free to disagree with the bishops on a law. Steinfels himself was not an enthusiast for priests in public office, but he concluded that priests and bishops constantly meddle in politics and that what the hierarchy really feared was a priest-politician with ideas of his own.

Drinan's struggle for the Church's tolerance of his role was a close call, and Drinan might have asked himself how often he would have to run the same gauntlet and how long he could depend on the steadfast support of his local Jesuit superiors. The evidence suggests that he blocked most of those questions from his mind. He loved the role he was playing, he saw himself as a moral exemplar, especially on justice issues; and, in spite of legislative defeats and disappointments, he would be in Congress as long as his health and political skills lasted.

In March an interfaith consultation on Soviet Jewry at the University of Chicago's Center for Continuing Education brought together again

Mayor Charles Evers of Fayette, Mississippi, and his supporter Robert Drinan. The goal of the two-day meeting was to "call on the conscience of mankind to make known its profound concern about the continued denial of the free exercise of religion, the violation of the right to emigrate, and other human rights of the three million Jewish people in the Soviet Union and of other deprived religious groups and nationalities" (*New York Times*, March 20, 1972). Drinan used the occasion to urge President Nixon to speak out on these issues during his upcoming Moscow visit, and he urged passage of proposed legislation to give Israel $85 million in order to help that country absorb 40,000 immigrants with newly issued visas who were expected to come from the Soviet Union. A Nixon spokesperson said that the administration had responded generously to Israel's needs. Drinan said that this small amount did not represent the solidarity that should exist between all those, Christians and Jews, who "worship the God of Abraham, of Isaac and of Jacob." Drinan also said he planned to visit Israel in May.

In his keynote address, Evers called on Jews and blacks to "join hands" in the fight against racism in all its forms. Evers defined separatism broadly as "no education, no participation in city government, poor black mothers washing and ironing, and City Halls controlled by mean white folks." With typical frankness, Evers had criticisms for both sides. He pointed out that recently blacks had excluded a white person from a political caucus in Gary, Indiana. And, not to pass over the faults of his present audience, he mentioned country clubs that admitted Jews only. "We've got to be very careful that once we're free, we don't become oppressors ourselves. We blacks have got to remember the same thing."

Shortly after Drinan mentioned to Arrupe his bill with Gravel to end the war, the House shot it down. But in May, Drinan was chosen by his peers as chairman of the Massachusetts delegation to the Democratic National Convention, and by the end of June the House Democrats were fighting among themselves over the extent to which they should reform the party and its procedures in this presidential election year. The reforms called for a radical change in the party's National Committee, with meetings twice a year and new room for women, blacks, young people, and Spanish-speaking Americans. The party establishment was already in shock over rules that drastically cut the number of House members attending as delegates from eighty-five in 1968 to forty-one, and of senators from forty to seventeen. House members from the big-city machines and the South were convinced that the combination of new rules and the selection of then-frontrunner George McGovern as the presidential nominee would spell disaster for the party in November.

At a meeting on June 28 of the Democratic Congressional House Caucus, Representative Frank Annunzio of Illinois proposed a motion to reject the proposed reforms. Speaker Albert urged the motion's rejection, calling it "counterproductive," as did majority whip Thomas P. O'Neill. But the motion carried 105–50. The resolution was purely advisory and would have no effect on the delegates who would vote on the proposed party reforms at the convention in July. But to new House members, like Drinan and New York's Bella Abzug, this was all the more evidence that leading Democrats were "out of touch." Said Abzug, "They feel threatened." Drinan told the *New York Times* on June 29, "What right do they have to do this? Where are their suggestions? Where have they been all this time?"

On July 16, Drinan formally announced that he would seek a second term.

At the Convention

In the political summer of 1972, religious issues emerged in a variety of ways. Drinan's opponents and critics attempted to depict him not just as a liberal Democrat but as a dangerous radical. To some he was another lawbreaking Berrigan, but one who wore his clerics as a defense. According to his FBI file, in 1971 a suspicious nun wrote to J. Edgar Hoover and, because of some of his "un-American and unorthodox" views, expressed doubt that Drinan was really a Catholic priest. Perhaps, she suggested, he had been "planted" in the Church to harm it. Those Catholics already opposed to a priest's participation in politics would remain opposed, and those who were uncomfortable with Mc-Govern as well as with Drinan, who supported McGovern's nomination for president, would have two reasons to not vote Democratic. Meanwhile, the Third District had been redrawn and renamed the Fourth District, with the addition of Brookline and Framingham. Brookline, like Newton, had a large Jewish population, and they were beginning to ask themselves, all things considered, what was "good for the Jews." Perhaps a fellow Jew could represent them better than a Jesuit priest.

Convicted of mutilating draft records at Catonsville and sentenced to three years in Danbury Federal Prison, before he was incarcerated Daniel Berrigan went underground for several months, making surprise appearances in church pulpits before the police could arrive. Drinan, pressed to comment on his exploits, declined to condemn Berrigan's "teaching methods" while declining to break the law himself. Paroled after eighteen months in Danbury, Berrigan appeared at the *Commonweal* office in Manhattan for a long interview that appeared on July 14, prior to the Democratic convention.

On the war, Berrigan said he discerned a difference between the Nixon administration and the basic American moral sensitivity.

> It seems to me the Administration has been able to do two things—one of them quite evil and immoral and one of them, in spite of itself, quite moral and quite hopeful. The first has to do with the spread of corrupt language and corrupt attitudes sponsored by Mr. Nixon. The second has to do with the inevitable and very slow rise of true consciousness in opposition to him.

On the convention, he focused on McGovern but said, "I'm not looking on McGovern as a kind of messiah who would find me his home chaplain after election. I think that as a priest I would have to remain a critic of whatever system is in power, because that system couldn't be equated with the Kingdom of God."

An editor pushed him on abortion. Did he find it incongruous that the "overriding issue of the moment" had to do with the fate of the unborn when there was such callousness to the life of the born—in Vietnam, the Third World, and American ghettos? Berrigan told the anecdote of the "hysterical statement" on abortion on the Fordham Jesuit community bulletin board from Cardinal Terence Cooke of New York, which, ironically, was issued on the letterhead of the Military Ordinariate. Berrigan said he tried to be as sensitive as he could to both issues—violence against human life at any point. But the Church, he felt, was excessively interested in control, and it was simpler to deal with infants than with adults.

On the future of the priesthood, an editor suggested four types of ministry: the parish priest, the professor, the priest who participates in government, and the priest, like Berrigan, on the fringe, in a countercultural movement. All these forms, Berrigan replied, may develop from a superficial understanding of the Gospel; but "a pure political solution in electoral politics is a dead end." It suffocates, he said, the independence of the Gospel.

> And that's the one—the political priest—that I would have the least patience with, as having least connection with a real tradition. You see I can't conceive of any possible utopia to which I would give allegiance that I want to give to the Gospel. And I think that's exactly what electoral politics demands of a man. In substance, that's the kind of acceptance that he has to give to this American system. And I wouldn't give it to the American or the Russian or the Cuban or the Vietnamese, or any other.

* * *

Massachusetts' 153 delegates and alternates to the Democratic convention, led by Drinan, were uncommonly young and diverse. They were committed first to McGovern, second to Congresswoman Shirley Chisholm of New York, the first black woman elected to the House.

The *Commonweal* correspondent's July 28 report on the convention began:

> Four years ago I stood up in the press gallery, behind Hubert H. Humphrey as he quoted the healing love prayer of St. Francis of Assisi over the political and moral shambles of the 1968 Democratic Convention. The words were oil, but they did not heal. They seemed merely *words*—words from a man who used words with so little reverence for

their power that the convention would have been better off with a moment of silent prayer.

The significant thing about McGovern, said the writer, was that he was not a messiah. There is no white horse. Rather, McGovern, whose father had been a Wesleyan pastor, believed that all men were decent and good if only given a chance to follow the better angels of their nature. McGovern did not, on other occasions, hesitate to quote Jesus, who stood up in the synagogue and said, "The Spirit of the Lord is upon me, because He has anointed me to preach good news to the poor," which McGovern adopted as the charter for Christian social action. Obviously McGovern and Drinan were in many ways kindred spirits.

Later in the campaign columnist Michael Novak speculated in the August 25 *Commonweal* that in the 1972 election, consistent with Nixon's plans, half or more of the white urban Catholics would vote Republican, while educated white suburbanites and blacks would go (or stay) Democratic. Novak hoped that Catholic college students would canvass for McGovern—"to build a new progressive coalition of white ethnics and blacks, to tackle the problems of our cities in an inclusionary way." But Novak's wish went unheard. A Hart poll of 300 Catholic voters in late September, reported in the *Washington Post*, found that 60 percent of Catholics over the age of fifty found the country "on the wrong track," but they preferred Nixon to McGovern 54–31 percent, while they had gone 78 percent for John F. Kennedy in 1960 and 76 percent for Lyndon B. Johnson in 1964. The respondents agreed that the Democratic Party was better for the poor, young, old, and minorities; but Watergate was not yet a scandal to them, and they trusted the Nixon administration on the war.

Although Drinan returned from the Miami convention satisfied with the candidates, he had to watch the ticket self-destruct when Senator Thomas F. Eagleton of Missouri, the vice-presidential nominee, revealed his history of depression and shock treatment. Drinan, most likely with his Jewish constituency in mind, favored Senator Abraham Ribicoff of Connecticut to replace Eagleton when the Missouri senator's departure from the ticket became inevitable. McGovern got refusals from a number of possible replacements, then settled on R. Sargent

Shriver, a Catholic, former director of the Peace Corps, and member of the Kennedy family. That August, Drinan was, however, due for another disappointment, and he let the world know how he felt. His *New York Times* op-ed of August 17, entitled, "The Longest Day, 1972," began: "August 10, 1972, was my most depressing day as a member of Congress. On that black Thursday the House rejected 228–178 its last chance in this Congress to set a date for total U.S. military withdrawal from Indochina." As he tried to absorb the shock of this disappointment, his mind went back three years to his visit to Vietnam, where he saw the devastation his nation was inflicting on the Vietnamese people. That was the experience that had changed his whole life.

Determined to do something about the war, he had decided to work "within the system." But, he rudely learned, the system didn't seem to work. Most of the op-ed made personal attacks on his fellow congressmen. "On Aug. 10 old men talked while young men died." During the debate on the legislation, Congressman Richard Bolling of Missouri moved to delete the requirement that the troops be out by the end of the year and declined Drinan's request to pose questions because he was afraid he could not answer them. Drinan could not decide whether the majority leader or the minority leader was "more dangerous or deceptive." Majority leader Hale Boggs said they couldn't get the bill to the president before October 1, because of conventions and vacations—while, added Drinan, "young men die." Minority leader Gerald Ford told the members they could not extend the date from October 1 to December 31; but, said Drinan, Ford was doing this to make the Congress bless, by its silence, the air war, in which Nixon had dropped more bombs than had ever been dropped in history. Drinan's greatest disappointment was the silence of Speaker Carl Albert. On this "issue of all issues," he felt, the Speaker failed to speak or lead.

The only thread of hope was the eloquent plea of Tip O'Neill, the majority whip and a Massachusetts colleague, who for the sixth time urged his colleagues to end the war. This day, O'Neill said, "ended another chapter in my life. The agony of bearing witness to this war which became almost a physical pain after my days in Vietnam remains." He tried "not to be ashamed of being a member of Congress," but history would record that this 92nd Congress went along with this most cruelly waged war, waged from land and sky. He could not look forward to the 93rd Congress. "I am still stunned, numbed, and dismayed."

Nixon

Nixon's strategy throughout these events had been to withdraw American ground troops, so as to satisfy the public's emotional commitment to withdrawal and, at the same time, to accelerate the air war, as if the military goals that eluded the South Vietnamese and American forces on the ground could be won by devastating bombing of the North. In March 1972, Hanoi launched a massive attack in an all-out attempt to conquer South Vietnam. In April, Nixon, declaring that "the bastards have never been bombed like they're going to be bombed this time," ordered both massive bombings of North Vietnamese troops invading the South and B-52 air strikes against the North. In May he ordered Operation Linebacker I, the mining of North Vietnamese harbors, plus bombings of roads, bridges, and oil facilities. In June, Nixon told his aide Charles Colson, "We want to decimate the god-damned place."

Also in June, a helicopter pilot ordered the bombing of the village of Trang Bang, not knowing that refugees had sought safety there. An Associated Press photographer recorded unforgettable footage of children, particularly two nine-year-old girls, naked and standing or running, their flesh seared by napalm blasts. Nixon continued this policy throughout the summer and fall, basically to keep the war going through the election in order to assure his victory by a combination of military and diplomatic moves to convince the public that he, rather than the dovish McGovern, could bring "peace with honor." While Kissinger was continually negotiating a peace accord with the North during the ongoing Paris peace talks, Nixon urged him to stretch the discussion a few months past the election, lest a peace decision help the McGovern campaign.

But, in effect, the end of the Nixon presidency began on June 17, when the five burglars linked to Nixon's Committee to Re-Elect the President (CREEP) broke into the Democratic National Committee headquarters in the Watergate hotel and office complex. The long, intricate attempted cover-up first described in the *Washington Post* ultimately gave Nixon's opponents the new opportunity to remove him from office—impeachment. But during the campaign Nixon managed to avoid or deflect questions about Watergate by stonewalling and accusing the press of bias. As the election approached, Nixon and Kissinger redoubled their efforts at the Paris peace talks. By mid-October they had an agreement wherein U.S. troops would leave Vietnam within sixty days of the cease-fire, North Vietnam would return American prisoners of war, and a tripartite commission would arrange a settlement and administer elections. Kissinger, the week before the American election, announced, "Peace is at hand." Except that South Vietnamese President Nguyen Van Thieu saw that this would allow North Vietnamese troops to remain in the South, and he refused to accept the terms. But the "Peace is at hand" announcement was close enough to election day to have its desired effect.

The Last Laps

At a March 9 meeting of the Newton Democratic City Committee, Drinan had listed as his accomplishments bills he'd introduced on higher-education grants, nursing education, consumer protection, a public works act, cancer research, and environmental protection. Failures included the ongoing war, a loan to Lockheed Aircraft, and Nixon's veto of the Child Development Act.

The congressional campaign, though again a three-way race, would not be a rerun of the 1970 election. Vietnam had faded as an issue; Drinan had to run on his record. His opponent Martin Linsky, a thirty-two-year-old liberal Republican state representative who had worked for Secretary of Health, Education and Welfare Elliot Richardson, had defeated three other Republicans in the primary; and John T. Collins, twenty-seven, an independent conservative, was attacking both Linsky and Drinan from the right. Linsky argued that Drinan was too morally inflexible to work well with others, suggesting that he would be more effective. A *Globe* columnist, David Farrell, on September 7 accused

Drinan of backing away from McGovern when McGovern was perceived as a loser, of adopting a pragmatism of end-justifies-the-means, and of being silent on abortion. He said Drinan had told him that he was against abortion but saw no point in opposing the inevitable liberalization of abortion laws.

Just to cloud the political-moral atmosphere, in Washington John McLaughlin, S.J., who had become a Nixon speechwriter, told Mary McGrory in the September 23 *Washington Post* that—even though he had published a critique of the bombing in the January 17, 1968, *America*—Richard Nixon was the "true peacemaker," that the bombing of North Vietnam was moral, that all the priests he spoke to in Vietnam on his recent visit supported the bombing as "necessary, moral, licit, and upright," and that most of the casualties in the hospitals had been caused by the enemy. He dismissed the recent condemnation of the bombing by the Catholic bishops and said he was thinking of going to Massachusetts to speak against Drinan's candidacy.

By early October, while McGovern led Nixon by only 3 percent in the district, in his own three-way race Drinan led both opponents with 43 percent; Linsky had 33 percent, and Collins had 10 percent, as reported in the *Boston Globe* of October 1. About half the Catholics were leaning toward Drinan, and the Jews split half to Drinan and half to Linsky. While on the popularity index—favorable or unfavorable impression—Drinan led Linsky 53–47, a surprisingly high percentage, one-third, had an unfavorable impression of the priest. The Massachusetts chapter of the Americans for Democratic Action (ADA) gave Drinan and his Massachusetts colleagues James T. Burke, Michael Harrington, and F. Bradford Morse a perfect 100 score on their voting records on thirteen issues—including defunding the Internal Security Committee, school desegregation, funding education, and eliminating funding for the B-1 bomber.

Linsky, less known, invested heavily in TV ads that featured him riding his bike and playing with his family, a subtle way of contrasting himself, always referred to as "Marty," with "*Father* Drinan," who had no children but did have a bike. Drinan spent nothing on TV, relying on free TV coverage of interviews and debates, but focused on radio ads, direct mailings of an eight-page tabloid, a McGovern leaflet, and visits from Ted Kennedy, former Attorney General Ramsey Clark, the comedian and activist Dick Gregory, and Senator Ribicoff of Connecticut to reinforce his credentials with the Jewish community.

By the end of October, with a little more than a week to go, Drinan widened his lead to 51–30 over Linsky, leaving Collins again with 10 percent. Linsky had become better known but was slipping in likability. Both he and Drinan were spending about $200,000 each, while Collins, who had little printed literature and operated out of a rented camper, had a budget of only $25,000. That Drinan was well known worked both ways. Some who got to know him didn't like him. An article published right before the election by Jaime Rosenthal in the November 7 *Phoenix* did its best to portray the Drinan whom people didn't like. The "gawky," "awkward," outspoken Jesuit with "baffling, spontaneous jokes" who had been effective in small groups in 1970 had been replaced with a "breezy line of patter" with a "stream of lofty rhetoric" on the "necessity for a new spiritual vision."

Attempts to press Drinan on details were met with a "flurry of invective"—and "the clincher, 'It's a lie.'" His slick ad campaign, wrote Rosenthal, was marked by a "dash of innuendo and distortion." The writer, who clearly preferred Linsky, gagged at Drinan's slick glad-handing, calling him a baby nuzzler ("'Ah, they're miracles, aren't they? Hel-lo little Lisa'"), one of the gang ("'Vote early and often, men, heh?'"), and a flatterer of middle-aged women ("'Ah, you're too young to vote—let me give you this anyway!'"). He was a "darter of coquettish glances" who persistently made mildly lascivious comments "that make it difficult for a female reporter to spend time within reach." It was all effective, Rosenthal wrote, but "stomach turning"—especially when he made, in the reporter's view, patronizing comments about the people he had just charmed. All this was supposedly at odds with his "projected image."

To compensate for the negative talk and articles, the campaign published a sixteen-page pamphlet filled with anecdotes about Drinan's dealings with his constituents, including the story of the Father roller skating through the halls of Congress.

Drinan's dedication to the Jews predated his candidacy. In his addresses in synagogues while dean of the law school he would dwell on

Christianity's Jewish roots and the Christian responsibility to make sure the Holocaust did not happen again. That June, to follow up on the Soviet Jewry conference in Chicago, he went to Israel, was photographed with Israeli Foreign Minister Abba Eban, and wrote a report for the June 4 *Globe* on his meetings with Soviet Jews who had recently emigrated to Israel. He met with a family that "to my astonishment" had been helped to leave Russia with money from their cousin who was one of his constituents. He concluded his article with the plea that Christian churches meet in Brussels to discuss how they could help Jews move from Russia to Israel. He ended with his often-used quote from the Protestant theologian Reinhold Niebuhr that "no one can be a good Christian until first he is a good Jew."

One of Linsky's primary opponents had been Avi Nelson, an ultraconservative son of a prominent rabbi, who tried to play on fear of the radical Jesuit. Linsky did not go that far, but he did try to garner support on the basis of his ethnicity. After the murder of the Israeli athletes at the 1972 Olympics, some Linsky workers called Jewish voters and asked, "If the Arabs were to overrun Israel tomorrow, wouldn't you feel more comfortable with a Jewish representative in Congress?"

With the presidential election just a few days away, the *Boston Globe*, in a long endorsement editorial, "Who Can Restore Our Spirit?" on November 2, said, "What happened at Watergate was not a caper, but a crime."

> Now more than ever, the President should inspire the nation. He should lift the spirit, give it vision and courage to meet the challenges which face all our people. To restore these honored qualities to a troubled nation as it looks to the future, we believe the United States would be better served by George McGovern and Sargent Shriver as President and Vice President.

The *Globe* reported on November 4 that on the Friday before the election, a poll revealed that Drinan had slipped to 46 percent over Linsky's 35 percent and Collins's 8 percent. Perhaps the Nixon–Kissinger "Peace is at hand" announcement combined with Linsky's intensified campaigning in his home neighborhoods was responsible.

In the Drinan camp this last-minute dip resembled the same dip in the 1970 campaign. Again the election was getting close. On Sunday, November 5, senior *Globe* columnist Robert Healy suggested that just maybe the public could think harder about Vietnam and Watergate and elect McGovern.

As it happened, the only state McGovern carried was Massachusetts. Drinan beat Linsky by 9,000 votes. Collins received about 8,000 votes. If he had not run and those conservative votes had gone to Linsky, the outcome might have been different. According to the *New York Times* of November 9, William B. Anderson of Tennessee, a Democrat, lost his bid for reelection because he had defended the anti-war priests Daniel and Philip Berrigan.

When Drinan entered the ballroom of Newton's Sydney Hill Country Club, where his supporters had gathered to watch the returns and celebrate, he found them all gathered around the television set to watch McGovern's concession from South Dakota. Sensing the mixed emotions in the room, Drinan told the crowd, "Come hell or high water, we will obtain our objective, that supreme objective of everyone here and everyone in this country: peace in the world."

On December 11 the Paris peace talks collapsed and Nixon ordered Operation Linebacker II, in which B-52 bombers over eleven days savaged military targets in Hanoi and Haiphong, dropping more than 100,000 bombs and killing more than 1,600 civilians and losing seventy U.S. airmen killed or captured as fifteen of their planes were shot down.

One of the most perceptive journalists writing about Drinan was a freelancer with a seminary background, Charles Fager, who had first encountered the candidate during the 1970 campaign when Fager and his brother, both with long hair and looking like hippies, observed, from fifty feet away, Drinan campaigning at a Fitchburg shopping center. A voter was castigating Drinan for his alleged support of "radical" youth. When the voter left, Drinan, his balding brow sweating and his voice angry, came over and said, "Why don't you two just go away and leave me alone?" Apparently he felt that their appearance was undermining his message.

Charles Fager told him bluntly, "Father, I have a job to do and I'm staying here till it's finished."

During the 1970 campaign Fager was one of only two reporters to actually read *Vietnam and Armageddon.* He was taken by the message of the book and annoyed that Drinan denied writing what he had truly written. Although Drinan's staff continually gave him the brush-off, Fager persisted and got in-depth interviews and wrote a final essay for an "underground" paper, *Boston After Dark,* that circulated widely in the district, in which he criticized Drinan but strongly rebutted the accusations against the book by his opponents. Drinan told him it was the best article he had read on the campaign. During the 1972 campaign the staff once again was polite but gave Fager no help; nonetheless, he tracked down the candidate, hitched a car ride with him, and kept digging. He concluded in *The Real Paper* on October 18 that while Linsky would make a great congressman, "Drinan is making history." Rather than be too inflexible, he wrote, Drinan had made too many compromises. But, despite his weakness, what stood out was his "determination and brilliance with which he has pursued the mission he has set for himself as a Congressman, and the cogency of the mission itself."

He praised Drinan's attempts to reform the House, his determination to abolish the Internal Security Committee (formerly the Un-American Activities Committee), his attention to constituents, and his efforts to end the war. Fager had perceived Drinan's religious vision, that of the Society of Jesus, at work in his decisions. The government in Washington, Fager concluded, was pagan missionary territory, "and it is just possible that Father Robert Drinan, S.J., can crack it."

9   "My conscience tells me . . ."

One of the cultural icons suggested to represent the 1970s—an age when people turned inward, when personal freedom counted for more than civic responsibility, or when families broke up, and violence in films became more routine and more bizarre—was the William Friedkin film of William Peter Blatty's book *The Exorcist.* The novel and film were based, allegedly, on a true story of a Jesuit priest who drove the devil out of a child in Washington, D.C., years before. That priest from time to time gave lectures to Jesuit novices that included his encounter with Satan. The story, situated in the Georgetown neighborhood, included a renowned exorcist, based roughly on the great French Jesuit paleontologist and mystical theologian Teilhard de Chardin, and local Jesuits trying to help the little girl, who, when possessed, would be transformed into an obscene monster. She vomited green bile, spun her head 180 degrees, and, in a shocking scene, plunged a crucifix into her vagina.

Some have interpreted the film as an allegory about abortion. In this view, the possessed girl was, with the cross as an instrument, mimicking not just masturbation but abortion. The film was released in the same year in which the U.S. Supreme Court handed down its *Roe v. Wade* decision; and both those who supported the right to abortion and those who opposed legalized abortion had something to recognize. Evangelical preachers have argued that sexual promiscuity and abortion can open the door to let the devils in. Traditional Catholics took the film as a parable: Yes, there is a real, living devil, an evil spirit, who can get inside you, take you over, and make you sin. Liberal theologians suggested that Satan is a metaphor for the evil already in our hearts; we need no "outside agitator" to overpower us; our own lust and greed are enough to explain evil in the world. For those threatened by social change, neighborhood crime, and sexual depravity, the film gave the comfort of attributing it to an invading spirit. To liberals, the faults were in failed social structures and in ourselves.

Prior to *Roe v. Wade*, the abortion debate was complex, and many excellent articles and books dealt with the issue's ambiguity. Moralists struggled for formulae that would meet the issues raised by both sides and yet protect some basic human values essential, it would seem, to communities that, at some stage, had taken their values from the Judeo-Christian tradition. After *Roe v. Wade*, for a variety of reasons, the discussion became polarized. For the leadership among the American Catholic hierarchy the argument became centered on the federal government and the U.S. Supreme Court. Their strategy was to elect representatives who would overturn *Roe v. Wade*, either by passing an amendment to the Constitution outlawing abortion or by electing a president who would appoint to the Supreme Court justices committed to overturning *Roe*. Those political leaders who rejected this plan, for whatever reason, especially if they were Catholics, were labeled by the extreme anti-abortion faction as immoral, worthy of being excluded from communion. In their judgment, Father Drinan, because he opposed trying to outlaw abortion in a multicultural society in which the great majority of the population—including 64 percent of Catholic men and 58 percent of Catholic women—believed it must be allowed in some cases, was himself sometimes demonized.

David J. Garrow, in *Liberty and Sexuality: The Right to Privacy and the Making of Roe v. Wade* (1994), traces Drinan's influence, through his writing and networking, on the developing consensus during the decade leading up to *Roe*, on the final decision. The CBS documentary "Abortion and the Law," broadcast nationally on April 5, 1965, featured Drinan as an abortion opponent, a defender of the fetus. The show concluded that there was "little hope" for liberalization of abortion laws, but it stirred debate and increased public interest in changing the law. *The Atlantic, Time, Look*, and other magazines published articles pointing toward change. Drinan wrote that the right of the fetus to be born was the overriding issue, but he warned fellow Catholics that the forces for change were riding high, especially considering *Griswold v. Connecticut*, which was before the Supreme Court at that time and which finally struck down laws that prohibited the sale of contraceptives as an infringement of the right to privacy. In a February 4, 1967, *America* article, Drinan told readers that "the advocates of abortion clearly have the initiative at this time" and suggested Catholics come up with a compromise position that would head off more radical change.

A turning point came in Hawaii in 1969 when state Senator Vincent Yano, a Democrat and a Catholic father of ten, blocked an abortion reform bill to give it more thought. Yano was won over by Drinan's argument, probably in the *Catholic Lawyer*, that repealing an anti-abortion law was preferable to trying to reform it. He had Hawaii's doctors polled, and 96 percent supported liberalization. Then Governor John A. Burns, also a Democrat and a devout Catholic, joined Yano's side. At a Senate hearing in February 1970, sixty witnesses, including a nun, supported Yano's repeal bill, and eighteen were opposed, all of them Catholics. Yano, borrowing Drinan's logic, told the Senate, "Your committee's position for repeal is NOT legalization but rather that we choose not to control or regulate this matter by law, and further that we neither approve nor disapprove of abortion." The repeal passed 17–7; but the conference committee required that abortions take place in hospitals, with a ninety-day residency requirement, and only prior to fetal viability. In his Catholic heart, Burns could not sign the bill, neither could he veto it; so he let it become law without his signature.

Drinan's Position

In 1970, the year Drinan left Boston College to run for office, his abortion stand gained major attention in two scholarly studies: Daniel Callahan's *Abortion: Law, Choice and Morality* (1970) and Germain Grisez's *Abortion: The Myths, the Realities, and the Arguments* (1970). Callahan, a former editor of *Commonweal* in the 1960s, had moved to the Hastings Center for the Study of the Life Sciences; Grisez was a philosophy professor at the Catholic University of America. Both were struck by the manner in which Drinan's ethical stance had evolved from "The Inviolability of the Right to Be Born," published in *Abortion and the Law* (1967) and which appeared in other sources, where he declared that "any change of a substantial kind in America's abortion laws would be a notable departure from that body of Anglo-American law which regulates conduct deemed to constitute a crime against society" to articles, like those in *America*, in which he foresaw the public swing against abortion restrictions and urged Catholics to seek compromise legislation with abortion reformers. Then he moved to the stance where he proposed that, for various reasons, the law should say nothing about abortion. His central point, considered unusual at the time, was that while he maintained that abortion was immoral, the law should say nothing about it, because to legislate the conditions under which a pregnancy would be terminated would be to sanction the termination itself.

Callahan noted the odd phenomenon in which, in America and Great Britain, the movement to abolish capital punishment and the campaign for civil rights paralleled the campaign for less restrictive abortion laws. At the same time, the struggle against poverty, slums, and poor health facilities was stronger than ever. But there seemed to be, he wrote, no convincing evidence that those in favor of restricting abortion also favored the other reforms concerning the value of human life.

Accepting the Model Penal Code's middle-ground restrictions on abortions, said Drinan, would amount to the law's approving of the termination of a human life. Better, said Drinan, that the law say nothing. Callahan called attention to Norman St. John-Stevas, a Catholic member of the British Parliament, who moved from strong opposition to liberalizing abortion laws to a middle ground of accommodation, wherein he did not abandon principles but recognized facts: "[A]bortion is an evil, but it does take place, and a regulatory law that would allow some abortions to take place under proper medical conditions would not be contrary to Catholic faith." A December 9, 1967, editorial in *America* agreed: "The church has never believed that everything immoral should be made criminal."

Boston College yearbook, 1942. (Photo courtesy of Ann Drinan.)

With his parents,
James and Anne,
at Shadowbrook
Seminary, 1942.
(Photo courtesy of
Ann Drinan.)

With his father and
his nephew, Tom
(ten months old), 1949.
(Photo courtesy of
Ann Drinan.)

(Left to right) Tom (Bob's nephew), Bob, Catherine (Bob's sister), James (Bob's father), Ann (Bob's niece), and Frank (Bob's brother), April 1951. (Photo courtesy of Ann Drinan.)

Bob, Tom, and Frank, first communion, 1956. (Photo courtesy of Ann Drinan.)

Backyard politicking during the first campaign, 1970.

With young supporters after winning his first congressional race, 1970.

Meeting the press during the first campaign, 1970.

The Nixon impeachment hearings: Congressman Drinan with Chairman Peter W. Rodino of the House Judiciary Committee, 1974.

(Left to right, front row) Elizabeth Holtzman, Barbara Jordan, and Drinan with their House Judiciary Committee colleagues, 1974.

With Senator Edward M. Kennedy.

With Menachem Begin *(right)*.

Senator Eugene McCarthy, one of Drinan's strongest supporters, addresses an audience at Boston's historic Faneuil Hall as Drinan *(right)* listens.

With Elie Wiesel.

Tom Drinan at an anniversary celebration for his uncle at
St. Ignatius Church. (Photo courtesy of Donna Inserra Worsham.)

With John Kerry.

Visiting a detention camp in Thailand, 1979.

This photo of a typical refugee boat arriving in Thailand, like the next one, dramatizes the desperation of the refugees.

Thai detention camp, 1979.

Drinan cared particularly for the children at the refugee camps.

On the occasion of his receiving an honorary degree from Santa Clara
University, 1980.

(Left to right, rear) Suzy Drinan, Helen Drinan, Ann Drinan, Algis Kaupas (Ann's husband), Betsy Drinan; *(front)* Bob and Jaime Tirrell (Betsy's daughter)—tenth anniversary of *Journal of Legal Ethics*, Georgetown. (Photo courtesy of Ann Drinan.)

Reunion of former staff and volunteers, Boston College, 2006. (Photo courtesy of Maria Plati.)

Summer 1982. (Photo by Gary Wayne Gilbert, courtesy of the *Boston College Magazine*.)

But by 1967 Drinan had said in "The Right of the Fetus to Be Born," in *The Dublin Review* (Winter 1967–68) that he favored the law's withdrawing from regulating abortion. He drew on the writing of John Courtney Murray, S.J., one of the authors of the "Declaration on Religious Freedom" in the documents of Vatican II and author of *We Hold These Truths* (1950), which harmonized the American ideas of freedom with Catholic theology. Murray developed the principle, shared by St. Thomas Aquinas, that, while the moral law is the basis of civil law, civil law need not necessarily be used to enforce the moral law. Murray wrote:

> Law and morality are indeed related, even though differentiated. That is, the premises of law are ultimately found in the moral law. And human legislation does look to the moralization of society. But, mindful of its own nature and mode of action, it must not moralize excessively; otherwise it tends to defeat even its own more modest aims, by bringing itself into contempt. Therefore the law, mindful of its nature, is required to be tolerant of many evils it morally condemns.

Murray believed that the lawmaker must ask to what degree the law can be practically enforced.

Callahan did not mention, however, that, although Murray's formulation might apply to abortion, Murray was writing at the time not of abortion but of pornography and censorship; his was an argument against religious zealotry in censoring objectionable printed matter. Murray concluded that

> Leo XIII is indeed remembered for his revision of the Index of Forbidden Books. But he was not the first Pope to point to the danger of reading bad books. It is his greater glory that he was the first Pope to say, in substance and effect, in a multitude of discourses, that today there is a greater danger in not reading a good book.

Although some who oppose criminalizing abortion may cite Murray's opinion that not everything evil must be outlawed, Murray does not seem to have published anything on abortion itself. He may have believed that abortion is sufficiently evil for the law to restrict it.

In the 1967 article, Drinan had also argued that "the law's concern for the solidarity and the stability of the family as an institution suggests that the law should not forbid parents to terminate an unplanned and unwanted pregnancy." Callahan saw in this a foreshadowing of *Griswold*'s interpretation of privacy rights' impact on future abortion decisions.

Grisez based his criticism on the texts of "The Right of the Fetus to Be Born," a paper delivered at the Harvard–Kennedy Conference on Abortion in 1967 and reiterated at a meeting of the Catholic Theological Society of America in 1968, where Drinan employed an interpretation of Vatican II's "Declaration on Religious Freedom" to strengthen his argument that the state's role in fostering morality is limited. For instance, the Declaration states that "The usages of society are to be the usages of freedom in their full range. These require that the freedom of man be respected as far as possible, and curtailed only when and in so far as necessary." Drinan said that the Declaration ruled out the use of *coercion* in imposing one's religious views upon another.

Grisez pointed out that in this passage the Council was talking about religious freedom and the norms for regulating that freedom, not about abortion. The Declaration says, "These norms arise out of the need for effective safeguard of the rights of all citizens and for peaceful settlement of conflicts of rights. . . . [T]hey come, finally, out of the need for a proper guardian of public morality. These matters constitute the basic component of the common welfare: they are what is meant by public order." Grisez searched the document and found "nothing in it to support the idea that Catholics or anyone else should check their consciences at the door when they enter the forum of debate about public policy." If Drinan was taking "coercion" to mean that a minority cultural group, like Catholics, should not impose its morality of protecting the unborn from being aborted, that is most likely a misreading of what the writers of the Declaration had in mind.

Grisez went on to respond to Drinan's alleged "advantages" of decriminalization. Drinan proposed obligatory counseling that might persuade the woman not to abort. Grisez responded that the counseling might not include that the fetus is a human being with rights and that there is no guarantee of social support if the client does not abort. Drinan said the government would prosecute nonphysicians who performed abortions; but, said Grisez, the government could already do that. Drinan said that legalization would bring abortion into the open where it could be studied as a social problem; Grisez that if it were legal it wouldn't be considered a "problem."

The Court Stops Discussion

The first story Drinan read about himself in 1973 was a page-one *New York Times* article with the headline "Both Sides Gird for Battle on Abortion" (January 2). In 1970, abortion on demand was legalized by the New York state legislature; but in spring 1972 the legislature voted to repeal the law, only to be vetoed by Governor Nelson A. Rockefeller. Now the battle was to be rejoined. Dr. Alan Guttmacher, the obstetrician who led Planned Parenthood, said the other side had "waved fetuses in bottles" at demonstrations, while their side had not sensationalized its case. "Now we may pull off the silk gloves and fight them with bare knuckles." Abortion opponents also took heart in the recent defeat of presidential candidate George McGovern, seeing that defeat as an indication of the strength of their cause. The article named Drinan as a supporter of those who said that abortion was a totally private matter. It also reported that the Catholic bishops of Texas had issued a letter saying, "In our view it would be better, in the ultimate sense, for the laws of the state to be silent on the subject than to lend positive approval to acts that deny the value of life."

Both sides did not have long to wait for an answer. On January 22, the Supreme Court, by a 7–2 majority, handed down long-awaited rulings on the anti-abortion laws of the states of Texas and Georgia in the case of *Roe v. Wade* and its companion case, *Doe v. Bolton*. The state laws involved, said the Court, "violate the Due Process Clause of the Fourteenth Amendment, which protects against state action the right to privacy, including a woman's qualified right to terminate her pregnancy." The decision included guidelines for the three stages of pregnancy: During the first trimester the decision rests with the patient and her doctor; during the second, the state may regulate abortion only to protect the woman's health; and during the third, the state can flatly prohibit all abortions, except those necessary to preserve the woman's health.

The secular press across the country generally endorsed the decision. Conservative and religious scholars and commentators did not. William F. Buckley compared it to the *Dred Scott* decision; the Protestant opinion magazine *Christianity Today* said, "[T]he majority of the Supreme Court has explicitly rejected Christian moral teaching." The legal scholar and judge John T. Noonan Jr. called it "the most radical decision ever issued by the Supreme Court." Daniel Callahan concluded that the Court should have left the matter in the hands of the state legislatures; the *New Republic* agreed with Justice William H. Rehnquist's dissent, in which he denied the application of "privacy" to this case and said the issue of abortion should have been left to the political process.

Perhaps the most damning critique of the thinking behind *Roe v. Wade* came in Noonan's "The Root and Branch of *Roe v. Wade*" (*Nebraska Law Review* Vol. 63: 668–79). Noonan, who was also a professor at the University of California–Berkeley law school, based his argument on the view expressed by Hans Kelson in *The Pure Theory of Law* (1967), in which "a person is simply a construct of the law," which means that "there is no kind of human behavior that, because of its nature, could not be made into a legal duty corresponding to a legal right." In Noonan's view, therefore, as happened in American history, the law turned human beings into property.

The Court in *Roe* shrank from calling the unborn "human." It was "it," or a "theory of life," or "potential life." Subsequent cases were the "branch" that expanded the "mask" hiding the unborn child's reality. In its 1983 ruling *Akron v. Akron Center for Reproductive Health*, the Court said that the state could not require a one-day delay, or a counseling session, or informing the woman "that the being she wished to put to death was a child," or that the remains be "disposed of in a humane and sanitary manner." Noonan concluded with a passage from the *Last Journals* of André Gide. Confronted with and disgusted by "formless fragments of an unborn child's remains," he ordered the gardener's wife to "get rid of that." Rather than discard it like garbage, the woman cleaned and dressed it and placed it in a cradle. Gide was stunned, ashamed of his "sacrilege." "Was I to think that for a few minutes a soul had inhabited this body?" A half century later he could see only its "extraordinary beauty."

Commonweal on February 15, 1973, weighed in with one of its most eloquent editorials. It leveled its denunciation on two houses—the Court and the American Catholic hierarchy—and placed the decision in the context of 1970s morality. "The decision of the United States Supreme Court in favor of abortion is a fair measure of the growing secularization of American society and of the political impotence of the American Catholic Church." The editors granted that laws only imperfectly reflect a society's values and acknowledged the need for reform of abortion laws:

> Yet, what a society values it protects with laws. In that sense civil rights, minimum wage and welfare bills have a moral dimension in that they witness to the national community's concern for every member; and state laws restricting abortion at least testified to some consensus that life in process *is life* and must be protected. . . . [T]he Court has, in effect, determined when life *may* begin. It has diminished the whole concept of what it means to be a person, and succumbed to that cultural elitism that marks cultures content with their values while slipping into decline.
>
> The Court dramatizes what has been clear under other signs for some time: we stand in danger of becoming an abortion culture—one which cringes from the thought of death yet sanctions real death and living death for the convenience of the ruling class. An abortion culture is built on individualism, the right of the strongest individuals to thrive; it sees "privacy" not primarily as a protection of the person but as a system of isolation—withdrawal from the full implications and responsibilities of sex and love. It is a comfortable way of life that settles for the least inconvenient solution to moral dilemmas—like bombing.

The editorial then hit the American Catholic hierarchy for what it saw as its terrible leadership, its loss of credibility on sexual morality because of its dogmatic opposition to birth control, and its comparative silence as bombs fell on Vietnam.

Then *Commonweal* gave Drinan the lead article space to explain the decision. In a way, the decision was one he expected and probably even hoped for, because it, in effect, removed the government from abortion decisions by allowing abortions with hardly any restrictions. But his article listed the balances between privacy and pregnancy. The Court, he said, had not justified the privacy argument in its text. Rather, he surmised, the justices had decided to knock down legal restrictions and landed on privacy as a vehicle with which to do it. The Court, Drinan wrote, "stretches the 'privacy' of a pregnant woman to mean the undesirable consequences which would follow in her life if she were unable to terminate the unwanted pregnancy." Once the fetus can live outside the womb, the Court said, in Drinan's reading, that privacy must yield to the interest the state has in protecting all human life, born or unborn. Drinan was also convinced that the one main reason for the decision was that, in his view, abortion laws are unenforceable. The decision had good results, said Drinan. It cracked down on unlicensed abortionists; it made the medical profession responsible for abortion standards. Now doctors about to abort would have to ponder their traditional role, which has been to save life, not destroy it.

As might be expected, Drinan's analysis did not satisfy all *Commonweal* readers. Monsignor James T. McHugh, director of the Family Life Bureau of the United States Catholic Conference, answered that abortions may still be performed during the first trimester by nonphysicians, granted the concurrence of the women's physicians, and that Drinan's assumption that the medical profession would establish ethical controls was "naïve at best." In the March 10 *New York Times*, Daniel A. Degnan, S.J., then teaching at Syracuse University Law School and later dean of Seton Hall Law School, wrote that he was both shocked by the decision and "oddly diminished by it." In his seminar on law and morality he had explored Thomas Aquinas's opinion that the law should not attempt to restrain all immoral acts, but only the graver ones. Because abortion is considered by so many in society to be a gravely immoral act, one would expect, said Degnan, that the law would reflect some compromise. But the Supreme Court "has decided the moral and legal issues I had thought so serious and so difficult for society." He went on, "If the only question had been the privacy of the woman, we could all have gone home long ago." In Degnan's view, the Court had erected into constitutional law its own theory of fetal life—that it has "only the barest claim to protection (if any) against the woman's right to terminate her pregnancy." Degnan felt that, in effect, the Court had closed discussion on one of the profound issues of our time, and that was why he felt diminished by the decision. "We are not children and the Supreme Court is not our moral arbiter."

Other than pass the moral responsibility to physicians, Drinan did not dwell on the morality of abortion. And, strangely, that same year he passed up an opportunity to rationalize or sum up his own position on abortion as it had developed over the past six years. Immediately after the *Roe* decision, the editors at Case Western Review Press put together *Abortion, Society, and the Law* (1973), consisting of articles that had first appeared in the *Case Western Law Review* in 1971 and 1972 and in *Abortion and the Law* (1967) along with three articles commissioned for this new volume. Drinan simply contributed "The Inviolability of the Right to Be Born" from the 1967 book. Judging from the dates in the footnotes, it was probably written in 1965. Although the purpose of the 1973 volume was to react to *Roe* and it reproduced the full text of the decision, Drinan made no comment on the decision. He concluded with a sentence that could have flown from any right-to-life banner: "It will be a tragedy beyond description for America if the question of legislation on abortion is resolved on sentiment, utilitarianism, or expediency rather than on the basic ethical issue involved—the immorality of the destruction of any innocent human being carried out by other human beings for their own benefit." Lines like that appeared less often as the years went on.

For the time being, abortion took a back seat to other issues. With *Roe* behind him, Drinan plugged through the winter, spring, and summer with his usual full agenda. In January he blasted the Nixon administration for cutting back funding, provided through the Housing Rehabilitation Loan Program, for the redevelopment of a college neighborhood in Fitchburg and the Washington Square area in Brookline. In February, by canceling their hotel reservations, the Soviet Union shot down a visit by religious leaders—including Rabbi Mark H. Tannenbaum; Mrs. Reinhold Niebuhr, widow of the Protestant theologian; Drinan; and others—to investigate the plight of Soviet Jews. The Soviets would deny Drinan himself a visa in August. In March, leading twenty-five other congressmen, he introduced a bill to abolish the death penalty under federal law—the same day that Nixon asked Congress to reinstate it for certain crimes. That month he also revised his strategy for abolishing the House Internal Security Committee (HISC), which he had accepted appointment to in order to close it by transferring its jurisdiction to the Judiciary Committee, where its influence could be smothered. In May he and leaders of Massachusetts medical schools protested federal budget cuts that would deprive Harvard, Boston University, and Tufts of $18 million. The same month the HISC voted 4–1 (Drinan being the 1) to outlaw unauthorized visits by U.S. citizens to countries fighting the United States—an attempt to suppress anti-war activists like Ramsey Clark and Jane Fonda, who visited Vietnam.

In July Drinan filed a bill to end wiretapping under all circumstances and joined Senator John C. Stennis of Mississippi, chairman of the Armed Services Committee, in calling for a full review of the Central Intelligence Agency, of its involvement in the "secret war" in Laos and the developing Watergate scandal. Drinan, a witness before Stennis's committee, criticized Nixon's nominee to head the CIA, William E. Colby, who had supervised a Vietnam pacification program, Operation Phoenix, that had assassinated about 20,000 South Vietnamese, including suspected North Vietnamese agents.

The Move to Impeach Nixon

But the dark, brooding figure and issue at the heart of much of this agitation was President Nixon, who, having won a landslide victory by presenting himself—in the words of the liberal muckraking journalist I. F. Stone—"as Mahatma Gandhi," had kept pouring money into

South Vietnamese President Nguyen Van Thieu's coffers and bombing the countryside. When Thieu met with Nixon and Henry Kissinger at San Clemente, California, Nixon's "Western White House," in early April, some 250 demonstrators marched outside the gate. Drinan, joined by six other Democratic congressmen, referred to Thieu as a "panhandler" and a "pirate" (*New York Times*, April 3, 1973). On May 7, four Massachusetts congressmen—Drinan, Gerry Studds (Cohasset), John J. Moakley (South Boston), and Michael Harrington (Salem)— filed suit in a Massachusetts U.S. District Court to declare U.S. bombing of Cambodia illegal. That same day Defense Secretary Elliot Richardson, recently named attorney general, told Congress that even if they cut off funds the bombing would continue. Drinan was convinced that whatever authority the administration had at the beginning of the military action in Indochina had expired when the troops withdrew and the prisoners were released at the signing of the Paris accords in January.

In January 1973, shortly after Nixon was inaugurated for his second term, the Watergate burglars were tried and found guilty. In April, Nixon aides H. R. Haldeman and John Ehrlichman resigned, along with Attorney General Richard Kleindienst and White House counsel John Dean. It is not clear exactly when Drinan's commitment to impeaching Nixon took seed. His dislike of Nixon was profound and he made no secret of it; indeed, he may have had impeachment in mind when he first ran in 1970.

That spring at the Jesuit retreat house at Gloucester, touring the roads on his bike, Drinan encountered a young Jesuit from New York, also on retreat, walking along the ocean shore. It was before the Watergate matters became dominant, but after the Cambodia bombing. Drinan stopped to say hello and introduce himself. The scholastic, Frank Herrmann, was impressed that Drinan introduced himself, when lots of well-known people simply assume everyone knows who they are. When Herrmann mentioned Nixon, Drinan was quick to reply, "We're going to get that bastard." Herrmann later joined the faculty of Boston College Law School.

The biking congressman was quick to proclaim his disdain for the president of the United States. Yet he and Congressman Michael Harrington both told the press on May 7 that they did not favor impeaching Nixon over Watergate. Nevertheless, between May and late July the drive to get rid of Nixon took hold.

An undated document in Drinan's files, prepared for the final phase of what would have become Nixon's impeachment in 1974, is called "The Theology of Impeachment," as if the concept could be traced to his training at Weston in the early 1950s. Other than the assertion that the concept of impeachment may be derived from the teachings of Judaism and Christianity, there is no theology; rather, the document traces the history of the concept from the fourteenth century to conclude that the essence of impeachment does not require an indictable crime, that the term "high crimes and misdemeanors" does not refer to felonies but to the type of morality concerning misuse or abuse of power by public officials. It is the instrument of the people, thus designed to originate in the House of Representatives. According to this view, Nixon's lawyers' argument that the president had not committed any crime would be irrelevant to the case. Around the same time, June 1974, he would pen a light-hearted *NCR* column on the "moral theology" of impeachment, about the corridors of Congress being filled with politicians buzzing about problems in "moral theology," like the academic exercises at Weston called *casus* (case studies) in which the star student applies the three determinants of morality—the object of the act itself, the actor's motive, and the circumstances—to determine guilt or innocence.

But this is still July 1973, when Congress, which often drags behind public opinion, is too slowly beginning to discover that the public is talking about removing Nixon from office.

The last American troops were withdrawn from Vietnam by March 29. Nixon made a generally unconvincing defense of his Watergate-related actions on May 22. Dean, the former White House counsel, told the Senate Watergate Committee about Nixon's "enemies list" on June 26. Drinan, of course, was on the list. Former presidential assistant Alexander Butterfield revealed to the committee that Nixon had secretly taped all his conversations in the Oval Office and the Executive Office Building.

Although Nixon's secret bombing of Cambodia had been leaked to William Beecher of the *New York Times* in 1969, Congress did not react to the news until the Defense Department confirmed it in July 1973. Somehow this, plus the fact that Nixon had specifically denied it, more than anything else spurred Drinan to action.

We can picture him sitting alone in his office late at night on July 26. Spread on his desk are *New York Times* clippings, including a July 21 report by Seymour Hersh, with paragraphs marked "use." That week the Pentagon admitted that it had secretly authorized 3,630 bombing raids over Cambodia in 1969 and 1970 and destroyed and falsified records to cover up the missions. Senator Harold E. Hughes of Iowa, who had initiated the inquiry, told the *Times*, "Anyone who deliberately lied in relation to this should resign and the committee should call for his resignation." Nixon had lied. Drinan dictated a two-page memo to Jerry Grossman and three members of his staff: "I have today come to the conclusion that I simply must follow my convictions and my conscience and file a resolution for the impeachment of the President."

The "final and overwhelming reason [was] the revelation of the secret war carried on directly and almost exclusively by Nixon in Cambodia for fourteen months prior to his declaration in April 1970 that the United States had 'scrupulously' observed the neutrality of Cambodia up to that point." Yes, there were other reasons—illegal impounding of funds, the White House secret police agency (the "plumbers"), and at least the tolerance of, if not the participation in, various Watergate-related offenses. Drinan was sure there was a case for at least conducting impeachment hearings.

Based on the latest polls, at least 24 percent of the public favored impeachment; in his district, it might be as high as 40 percent. Drinan wanted to send a letter to "the minions" (his term for constituents) on Monday, July 30.

On Tuesday, July 31, 1973, he addressed the House: "Mr. Speaker, with great reluctance I have come to the conclusion that the House of Representatives should initiate impeachment proceedings against the president." Nixon, he said, had told the nation on April 30, 1970, that for the five years prior the United States had scrupulously observed

Cambodian neutrality, while for many months he had ordered thousands of B-52 raids prior to the invasion by ground troops. He explained that impeachment did not require an indictable offense. He reviewed impeachment law, and, because the members of the House are the impeachers in the case, he said he was now just raising questions about the president's conduct. The questions covered the bombing, the taping, impounding funds authorized for health care, and Nixon's secret extralegal security force (again, the "plumbers"). In an ironic conclusion he suggested that impeachment would provide an opportunity for the president to "vindicate himself" and gain an "honorable acquittal" if it were determined he was "unjustly accused."

That summer House majority leader Thomas P. "Tip" O'Neill had been listening to the voters, commissioned a poll, and concluded that "43 percent of the public would vote for a congressman who favored impeachment, while 29 percent would oppose him." As he distributed the results, congressmen who had been extremely reluctant even to touch the issue began to think ahead to the next election. But Drinan's motion to impeach pleased him not at all. He concluded, he wrote in his memoir *Man of the House* (1987), that if Drinan's motion had ever come up for a vote, "[it] wouldn't have had twenty supporters in the House."

"Morally, Drinan had a good case," he wrote. "Publicly, he's always been proud that he was the first member of Congress to file for impeachment. But politically, he damn near blew it." O'Neill knew that if Drinan's resolution had actually come before the House in 1973, it would have been overwhelmingly defeated. A defeat on the issue of Cambodian bombing, in particular, which did not enrage the public, would have made it very difficult to impeach again later on the Watergate offenses. Now, once the resolution had been filed, it could not be withdrawn, and anyone could call it up for a vote. If the White House had thought ahead, the Republicans could have called it up, shot it down (even though they were in the minority), and it would have died. Nixon would have survived. O'Neill's strategy was to station either himself or one of two colleagues on the House floor at all times. If someone called for Drinan's motion, they would immediately call for it to be tabled, meaning it was not open to debate. The bells would ring, and the Democratic majority would rush in to table the motion. Finally O'Neill tired of this exercise. He got along well with minority leader Gerald Ford and got his commitment to keep the motion off the floor. The White House, said Ford, did not want to call attention to the bill in any way. O'Neill could relax and get back to work.

Two other events fortified Drinan's position. In a June primary in Brooklyn, Elizabeth Holtzman, a thirty-one-year-old attorney, defeated eighty-four-year-old Congressman Emanuel Celler, won election in November, and took Celler's place on the Judiciary Committee with Drinan; at the same time, O'Neill's friend Congressman Peter W. Rodino of New Jersey took Celler's job as chairman. Rodino, said O'Neill, was a cautious individual and a reluctant hero. "He doesn't like to move until he knows where he's going." At first Rodino was "scared to death" of the task facing the committee, but he and O'Neill were determined to keep impeachment from becoming a partisan political enterprise. Holtzman, however, thought Drinan was right from the start, and she and like-minded members began talking impeachment among themselves.

Also in June, Drinan, in a long interview with the *NCR*'s Rick Casey, went out of his way to tone down his usual aggressive wit. He turned on his office tape recorder as the reporter turned on his. During their earlier encounters at McDonald's, where Drinan often grabbed his quick dinner, he had referred to Nixon as "King Richard" and read the daily Woodward and Bernstein disclosures in the *Washington Post* with amazement. Now, said Casey, Drinan must avoid appearing the "gadfly." No, he told Casey; he was not reacting to Nixon's including him on his "enemies list." He saw impeachment as a "way to clear the air," because constitutionally there is no other way to determine wrongdoing or punish a president for it. Drinan was not offended that people saw his motion as "premature." "Premature" means a little ahead of schedule. That meant the impeachment would take place.

Drinan's first 600 to 700 letters and telegrams in the first three days after submitting his motion were overwhelmingly supportive. There were also those, he said, who felt that impeachment would "deconsecrate" the nation, because such people have "sacramentalized" the presidency, made the president a "high priest." Most members of Congress, like himself, said Drinan, "hope that the president can be vindicated. No one wants impeachment. We want this thing to go away."

Drinan, of course, had no desire to see "this thing" go away.

As O'Neill said, Drinan was always proud of what he had done. On July 31 he could go home to the Jesuit community at Georgetown knowing that he had struck a glancing blow at a president whose behavior was, in his judgment, clearly immoral. And he had done so on the day of the most solemn feast on the Jesuit calendar, the feast of the founder of the Society of Jesus, St. Ignatius Loyola.

10   The Moral Architect

Thin, medium height, almost totally bald; his skin has a "translucent quality accentuated by the unrelieved black of his clerical garb." His eyes, very deep-set, punctuate his conversation, as they roll around, close as he pauses to reflect, then "dart skyward in mock alarm or dismay." He is controlled in his intensity, yet playful, as he presses his long, thin fingers together in front of him, massages his face, and then jabs them into the air for emphasis. In the fall of 1973 Drinan sat down—when he wasn't jumping up to stalk around his office, or slumping into his chair to swing his feet around and up onto his desk—for a long interview with editor Alan Westin for the *Civil Liberties Review*. "This is a restless man," wrote Westin. "He twists around to add body English to his staccato laugh."

CLR illustrated its interview with a caricature of Drinan by Isadore Seitzer in which Drinan appeared as a mounted medieval knight in armor, with the Constitution on his flag, the Capitol dome as his helmet, and the Bill of Rights in his saddlebags. It was a friendly interview that focused on the work of the Judiciary Committee, and particularly on Subcommittee Three, which concerned itself with prison reform, capital punishment, the newsman's privilege, and repeal of the Emergency Detention Act of 1950, also known as preventive detention, whereby the executive branch had the power to round up and detain people without due process of law.

Echoing his retreat notebook of 1968, in which he exclaimed that he had gone "13 years Without a Voice!" Drinan complained that he had come to Congress in 1970 not only for a "voice"—which he had had as a dean, speaker, and writer—but for a "vote." He discovered, though, that the seniority system, controlled by conservative committee chairmen, prevented him from voting on issues that really mattered to him.

Westin worked Drinan through a host of issues, asking frequently what Congress had actually accomplished in the time during which Drinan had had the opportunity to effect change. The answer was often "Not that much," because of the "structural obstacles Congress throws up against reform"—for example seniority and the narrow Democratic majority with many Democrats from the conservative South. A small caucus of reform Democrats made committee meetings more open, but they changed little. On civil rights, "King Richard" Nixon had begun the year by removing Notre Dame president Theodore Hesburgh from the chairmanship of the U.S. Civil Rights Commission. And the administration was re-segregating schools by cutting funds for busing. To guide future legislation, the committee toured the country investigating prisons and their rehabilitation techniques. In 1972 the Supreme Court had held that capital punishment violated the Eighth Amendment prohibition against "cruel and unusual punishment." The following year Nixon responded with legislation asking that capital punishment be restored for certain crimes. Drinan's response to that was a bill to abolish the death penalty for federal crimes. He knew that the majority of Americans supported the death penalty, but because they were not well informed, the majority, said Drinan, was not to be trusted in certain "basic justice and morality" issues, like busing and prison reform.

The question of the "newsman's privilege"—whether a journalist can be compelled by law enforcement to disclose information he or she has gained in confidence from a source—is a difficult one that would concern Drinan and remain unresolved for years. Drinan in 1973 conceded that someone actually on trial for murder, for example, should be able to call upon a journalist to reveal confidential information that may exonerate him or her; but this was his only exception to what he saw as the journalist's broad right under the First Amendment to serve the public's need for information. In early 1973 Drinan had written to the *New York Times* (February 1) arguing that the same law recognizing the confidential relationships of husband and wife, lawyer and client, and physician and patient should apply to journalists—not as a personal right "but because of the public's right to know, of which the newsman is a trustee." No federal statute should interfere with that public right, Drinan maintained.

Five years later he returned to the topic, in the August 5, 1978, *Nation*, in response to the Supreme Court's *Lurcher v. Stanford Daily* ruling, in which it gave law enforcement officials access, by search warrant, to papers, documents, and files not implicated in criminal activity. The decision would apply to the notes of a reporter. Drinan, with forty-eight co-sponsors, introduced the Press Protection Act of 1978, requiring that such a warrant could be issued only if the news reporter had committed or was committing a crime; otherwise, the intrusion of the law could well have a "chilling effect" on the watchdog role of the press. As the columnist Carl Rowan noted, reporters would commit notes and sources to memory and bury papers in tin cans and empty whisky bottles. Newspapers would shy away from controversy. "One wonders if the Pentagon Papers would have been published or the Watergate affair uncovered if this ruling had existed during those times," Rowan wrote.

An important minor victory in 1972 was the repeal of Title II of the McCarran Internal Security Act of 1950 (also known as the Emergency Detention Act), which allowed the roundup, for emergency detention, of suspects without due process of law.

At the time of the *CLR* interview, Drinan's strong personal desire to abolish the House Internal Security Committee, which for the most part had recently spent time on "frivolous" hearings on allegedly subversive groups like the Black Panthers and peace organizations, remained unfulfilled. Over the years the HISC had gathered files on 752,000 Americans and furnished the information, much of it based on hearsay, to government agencies for the purpose of screening job applicants. Drinan hoped that the reorganization of the House committees would transfer HISC jurisdiction to the Judiciary Committee. He told Westin that he himself was supplying constituents with their own files if they requested them. The following year, 1974, a *Village Voice* columnist, most likely inspired by the *CLR* article, informed *Voice* readers of the service, and seventy-nine readers wrote to Drinan for help;

he passed the requests to the committee staff. "In fact," Drinan told *Boston College Magazine* (Summer 1989), "in those years it became a badge of honor to have an FBI file or HISC file and a disgrace not to."

Missouri Democrat Richard Ichord, HISC chair, saw Drinan's move as "unusual" and "burdensome," and of questionable "propriety," calling a committee meeting to discuss it. Drinan replied on May 31 that he didn't see the problem—and had an impeachment meeting at the same time. When by July 1 his request for the files had not been fulfilled, Drinan threatened to complain to the Speaker and put his complaint in the *Congressional Record*. Ichord replied on July 3 that Drinan was on record as determined to destroy the committee from within. On December 13, Drinan answered that seventy requests were still pending, in spite of the fact that most requests could have been answered by simply stating that no record exists. On December 30 Ichord assured Drinan that, while his goal of interrupting the work of his small and overburdened staff would be achieved if Drinan's request had been given priority, "your many letters have not been forgotten, and all will be answered in due time." By fall 1974 the House Democratic caucus "forgot" to appoint any members to the committee; Ichord himself suggested transferring its work to the Judiciary Committee, where HISC died.

In his commitment to privacy and aware of what he saw as a tendency on the part of law enforcement officials to abuse their power, Drinan objected to some uses of the FBI's arrest records and its 190 million sets of fingerprints, including those of everyone who applied for law enforcement work anywhere or employment in a bank. These records were often made available to state agencies and even private employers. Arrest records themselves, said Drinan, can be misused and misinterpreted, especially given that fewer than 25 percent of arrests lead to convictions.

Two years later, in 1975, Drinan caused a stir when, during a congressional tour of FBI headquarters, he somehow stepped aside from the group and dug out his own partial FBI file, consisting of twenty to thirty 3 × 5 cards with his name on them. Furious, Drinan engaged in a long battle of letters with the FBI, demanding that his whole file be released to him immediately and proclaiming his astonishment and chagrin at discovering "the surveillance of a political nature." In 1973, at the time of the interview, Congress was still working on a version of the Freedom of Information Act, which would give citizens access to their files.

Drinan liked to "blue sky"—think ahead and imagine other good things the government could do, "opening new frontiers of liberty and equality," especially when other "moral" aspects of social policy were clear. He favored "preferential treatment for people who have been victimized by society over a long period." For example, if a company with 2,000 employees had only 1 percent blacks and the community has 10 percent blacks, a better social policy would be employing 10 percent blacks. All other things being equal, Drinan felt, a company should hire a black or minority person before a white person "until the time that the minority has substantially equal right of access to the same job."

Pressed by Westin to describe a recent personal accomplishment in the area of civil liberties, Drinan told the story of a naval "black list," whereby the House Armed Services Committee pressured the services to not send young officers to graduate schools where the universities— including Harvard, Brown, Boston University, and Boston College— were phasing out ROTC. A Drinan letter to the Secretary of the Navy and a House majority whip Thomas P. O'Neill call to the Armed Services Committee swung that around.

The long discussion with *Civil Liberties Review* concluded with the inevitable revisit to the themes that over time would define Drinan's life and congressional career. Unlike other activist priests, he did not demonstrate against the war because he saw his role as "a moral architect urging my opposition on strictly rational grounds." He said he treated the hyphenated priest-congressman question as a "non-issue." On the legalization of abortion, although some Catholic leaders wanted criminal sanctions, its outlawing "was not necessarily binding on Catholics or others," and, in his view, "the greatest evil [was] permitting the government to set standards for who will live or die." And there was some hope that Congress would be fortified in its efforts to protect civil liberties and restrict federal wiretappers because of public revulsion over Watergate. Democrats, he said, should take advantage "of the opportunities presented by a discredited and demoralized Nixon administration."

The Movement for Impeachment Grows

The response to Drinan's July 31, 1973, impeachment resolution came in a flood of letters from all over the country. A random sample of roughly 130 letters received from Wisconsin, Michigan, and Minnesota shows the depth of feeling in ordinary citizens, including two from Jesuit institutions.

Richard H. Lundstrom at the Jesuits' Campion Residential School for Boys wrote on November 3, "I fear this man [Nixon]. He has at his command this nation's enormous military power, the unleashing of which would destroy us all." Daniel C. Maguire, a former Jesuit moral theologian at Marquette University, wrote on November 6, "It does not seem that [Nixon] can be convinced to resign and save the country three more years of unproductive tension." At the same time, eighteen Marquette students and faculty signed and sent Drinan an impeachment petition.

A writer in Madison, Wisconsin, wrote on October 30, "It is my belief that Richard Nixon is a man mad with power, a dangerous man, an unstable man, an evil man." The International President of the Allied Industrial Workers of America, with 100,000 members in the United States, cheered him on. The publisher of *The Progressive*, Mortin H. Robinson, drew his attention to the magazine's "Call to Action" editorial of November 15 calling for the impeachment of Nixon. But the letter that must have touched Drinan most deeply said, "I'm 69, not a Catholic—grateful to you for being someone in government we feel is someone, not self interested, who can be trusted to vote an honest conviction backing a genuine cause." These letters, especially the last, gave him heart. Indeed, the last writer saw him as he saw himself.

In the Judiciary Committee on December 4, 1973, Drinan voted against the nomination of his House colleague Gerald Ford to replace Spiro

Agnew, who had resigned in a bribery scandal, as vice president. Drinan could not accept Ford's legislative priorities and positions. Ford had voted against food stamps, Medicare, federal aid to public schools, rent subsidies, the Voting Rights Act, fair housing, busing, anti-war demonstrators, and migrating Soviet Jews. Ford was for military spending. In Drinan's judgment, he was also complicit in the secret bombing of Cambodia. On December 12, 1974, after Ford had assumed the presidency, Drinan voted against Nelson A. Rockefeller for vice president, because he felt that the former New York governor would not advance the "moral objectives of the American people." According to a Harris poll, 47 percent over 34 percent of the people saw a conflict of interest between Rockefeller's enormous wealth—his family contributed more than $4 million to his 1970 gubernatorial campaign—and the public interest.

In the autumn of 1973, federal Judge John Sirica (who since February had presided over the trials of the seven Watergate defendants); the Senate Watergate Committee, led by Senator Sam Ervin of North Carolina; and Archibald Cox, the independent special prosecutor whom Nixon had been forced to appoint, were all seeking access, via subpoena, to the White House tapes, on which, as Alexander Butterfield had revealed, Nixon had secretly recorded all his conversations in the Oval Office and in the Executive Office Building. On October 20, Nixon, refusing to comply, ordered Attorney General Elliot Richardson to fire Cox; rather than carry out this order, Richardson resigned. Nixon then ordered the deputy attorney general, William Ruckelshaus, to dismiss Cox, but Ruckelshaus also refused and resigned. With these two resignations the solicitor general, Robert Bork, became the acting attorney general, and he fired Cox. Public outrage was overwhelming, and many attribute the beginning of the end of the Nixon presidency to the events that became known as the "Saturday Night Massacre." Congresswoman Elizabeth Holtzman wrote, "I felt as if I were living in a banana republic. The president claims to be beyond the reach of our laws. . . . I wondered if this meant an overthrow of our government as we knew it. How would the other America react?"

* * *

"Mention impeachment to U.S. Representative Robert F. Drinan, and the Gatling Gun volley of words ceases for a moment as he conceals with unconcealed euphoria the possibility that President Nixon's tenancy of the White House may be foreclosed." In a profile on February 27, 1974, Drinan told Charles X. Claffey of the *Globe* that "I ran against Nixon in 1970, but I never thought then that I'd find the most corrupt administration in history."

About Congress, Drinan griped about the seniority system, the entrenched powers, the lack of collegiality, the long recesses—"If you're practicing law, you don't take a vacation in February." The reporter had talked to his critics, who said that Drinan moved too fast and didn't thoroughly examine both sides, that he rankled with his clerical garb—they called him the Mad Monk, claimed he doesn't know enough parliamentary procedure and was "careless with legislation." Drinan responded by referring to himself as a man of integrity. "I don't claim to be 'holier than thou,' but I'm not here to get rich." He was writing a book, he said, that was in part an assessment of his political career and an evaluation of Congress. He was also involved in plans for the General Congregation of the Society of Jesus to Rome next year. Yes, he did relax: reading law journals, books on higher education, and the novel *Seven Days in May*. "And I read this pretty regularly," he said with a wink, holding up his Bible. He played a respectable game of tennis, swam in the House pool, and walked a lot.

On his office door he had posted a card with a quotation from Teilhard de Chardin that a friend gave him during a campaign. It was a quotation popular among progressive Jesuits who shared Teilhard's vision on the origin and destiny of the universe, including his evolutionary views that for many years during his travels and research he was forbidden to publish: "Some day after we have mastered the winds, the waves, the tides, and gravity, we will harness for God the energies of love; and then for the second time in history the world will have discovered fire."

McLaughlin Barks Again

One of John McLaughlin's functions, as he watched his boss's grasp on the presidency slip, was to run interference, travel the country giving speeches and interviews, use his Jesuit training to harass Nixon's critics and detractors, with particular attention to needling the fellow Jesuit who had prayed, played, and studied in the same remote woods of Weston many years before. Because Drinan was several years ahead, and in theology while McLaughlin was in philosophy, they lived on opposite sides of the house and met only on "fusion" days when the classes commingled. In his role as Republican attack-dog, McLaughlin was picking up where former Vice President Spiro Agnew had left off. While they occupied two extremes on the political spectrum, it must have irritated McLaughlin that religious superiors had approved Drinan's political role and not his.

When McLaughlin barked, Drinan had made up his mind to not bite back. But the *Los Angles Times* national correspondent Jack Nelson was able to simulate a debate by talking to them separately in "Two Jesuits at Odds over Nixon" on April 10, 1974. McLaughlin had compared the House Judiciary Committee to William Golding's *Lord of the Flies*, a parable in which schoolboys isolated on an island descend into violence. Drinan, restraining himself, called McLaughlin "more uptight than usual." McLaughlin charged that for Drinan, who had proposed impeachment, to sit on the committee was "a rape of justice." Actually, two other members, Charles Rangel of New York and Jerome Waldie of California, had also introduced impeachment resolutions; and the committee's role is only to rule on referring or not referring the case to the entire House. But Drinan, said McLaughlin, had characterized Nixon's policies as "Hitlerite genocide" and had said, "We will have him out by spring." Drinan replied, "Never said it. Never said it." Yet, Drinan blurted out, "If [McLaughlin] had any goddamn sense of decency, he would not misinterpret my position. . . . But don't quote me on that, I don't want to have anything to do with this. I only talked to you"—Nelson—"because I thought you wanted to talk about impeachment."

Nelson settled in on the topic that, in the long run, would help decide which one represented the priest in politics—lifestyle. Drinan had a room in the Jesuit community, and all such rooms are simple, most of them requiring the Jesuit to walk down the hall to the shower or go to the bathroom. As Drinan had previously told the press, he gave part of his $42,500 salary to the Society for his room, and he had permission to use the other part for the expenses of operating his congressional office. McLaughlin would not reveal his salary, but he said his Watergate apartment was less luxurious than some priests' residences in America and the Vatican. Both said they say Mass. Drinan refused to discuss why he wore the collar, although he had said four years before that it was his "only suit." By now that answer was wearing thin, an example of how he dealt with what he wouldn't discuss. He forgot perhaps that he had told a journalist in 1970 that he wore it to attract attention. McLaughlin said he didn't wear clerics because he didn't want his doing so to be construed as "trading on the collar."

The Committee Takes Hold

On April 30, 1974, Nixon, playing for time, dramatically released not the tapes themselves but, on television, with stacks of binders piled high behind him, heavily edited transcripts. But Leon Jaworski, the new special prosecutor he'd been forced to appoint, took his demand for the unedited tapes to the Supreme Court.

As the weeks went by, Holtzman, smoking one cigarette after another, worked in her office until midnight, until she felt as if she were sinking in quicksand. She had never liked Nixon and thought it pitiful that he had felt it necessary to declare during a press conference, "I'm not a crook." But she was determined to put her personal feelings aside: "We couldn't lightly overturn a presidential election."

On July 24, the Court decided unanimously in an 8–0 ruling (Associate Justice Rehnquist had recused himself because he had worked in the Nixon Justice Department) that executive privilege did not apply and ordered Nixon to surrender all the tapes to Sirica. The Court also asked Sirica to review the tapes to determine which portions should be released to the special prosecutor's office. Thus, Sirica, and eventually the public, learned that, on the unsanitized tapes, Nixon had said to his aides, "I want you all to stonewall it, let [the burglars] plead the Fifth Amendment, cover up, or anything else, if it'll save it—save the plan."

That evening, the House Judiciary Committee, which had been working on impeachment since the previous December, began its public hearings, which were broadcast live on national television.

In previous years the committee had not been considered among the most prestigious. But in the early 1970s it had begun attracting men and women who, like Drinan, were champions of civil liberties and who saw the law as an instrument for reform in issues like civil rights, fair housing, privacy, and women's rights. Besides Drinan, new members included Elizabeth Holtzman, who, like Drinan, had defeated an aging incumbent by referring obliquely to his age—at eighty-four Celler was described as "too tired"—by opposing the war, and by offering a break with "old boy" machine politics. Barbara Jordan, a black woman from Texas, would emerge as one of the committee's most eloquent members. Holtzman appreciated the group's diversity—thirty-eight members, all lawyers, including southerners, a Mormon, three blacks, two women, an Iowa Jew, a Rhodes Scholar, and a Jesuit priest.

J. Anthony Lukas in his Watergate history, *Nightmare: The Underside of the Nixon Years* (1976), divided the committee politically into six groups, according to how they would vote on impeachment: Democratic Firebrands, Probables, and Possibles; and Republican Possibles, Doubtfuls, and Diehards. The Firebrands included Jack Brooks of Texas, John Conyers of Michigan, Drinan, Don Edwards of California, Holtzman, Robert W. Kastenmeier of Wisconsin, and Charles Rangel of New York. Jordan and Chairman Rodino were listed as Probables. The six Diehards included Delbert L. Latta of Ohio, Trent Lott of Mississippi, and Charles E. Wiggins of California.

Rodino had named John M. Doar, a nominal Republican who had led the civil rights division of the Kennedy–Johnson Justice Department, as chief counsel, and the Republicans had selected Albert E. Jenner Jr., a Chicago attorney, as minority counsel. Jenner, in time, would irritate his fellow Republicans by his openness to the idea that Nixon might be guilty. The staff included forty-four lawyers and sixty investigators, clerks, and secretaries. Beginning January 21, 1974, the staff had prepared volumes of research on the history and philosophy of impeachment and analyses of tapes at committee meetings. Doar, to emphasize emotional disengagement, read documents to the committee in a droning voice. At one stage, impatient members, including Drinan, complained that the committee was moving too slowly. Something had to be done, he said, to show that "we're not going to be pushed around." They demanded that the committee subpoena the tapes. But Rodino urged patience; he sensed strategically that the White House was trying to prod the committee into an overreaction so that it could paint the impeachment proceedings as a strictly partisan effort.

By early May the full committee had gained access to a treasure of confidential evidence, including the Watergate grand jury report; in addition, the Internal Revenue Service and other federal agencies had compiled thirty-six notebooks on various topics. By June 21 the committee had completed its closed hearings and was ready to take testimony from witnesses. Rodino knew that the Democrats had the votes to impeach, but he wanted the decision to be as broad and bipartisan as possible. After much squabbling that threatened the cooperative spirit, they devoted the first two weeks of July to hearing ten witnesses, the most important of whom was John Dean, the former White House counsel who had warned Nixon of the "cancer" on his presidency and whose consistency under tough questioning had convinced many in Congress and the public that he should be believed.

Nixon's chief counsel, James D. St. Clair, stuck to the lack of any positive proof—the "smoking gun"—that Nixon had personally participated in the cover-up or, indeed, had committed any impeachable offenses. Other members still clung to the theory of impeachment under which impeachment was akin to an indictment in the contemporary sense, requiring proof of an indictable crime. But for the most part the members understood that "high crimes and misdemeanors," the constitutional language, referred rather to the status of the offender, a "high" official, who had failed to perform the duties of his office and thus needed to be removed by the representatives of the people.

The "Postulate of Tyranny"

The final impeachment hearings, during which the members debated, amended, and voted on five articles and approved three, played out in room 2141 of the Rayburn House Office Building over six days—Wednesday, July 24, through Tuesday, July 30—before 125 reporters in the chamber and 40 million Americans glued to their TV screens. Chairman Rodino rapped his gavel and reminded the committee: "For about 200 years every generation of Americans has taken care to preserve our system and the integrity of our institutions against the particular pressures and emergencies to which every time is subject. . . . Let us leave the Constitution as unimpaired for our children as our predecessors left it for us." As prepared by the subcommittee, the first two articles to be considered were: I, obstruction of justice, the president using his powers to obstruct the investigations of the Watergate burglary and to protect those responsible; and II, the abuse of power, how the president exceeded the "limits which democracy should place on its leaders." Lukas called this "the high water mark of the impeachment tide." Both these articles passed by strong 27–11 and 28–10 majorities, respectively, made possible by a bipartisan "fragile coalition" of seven moderate "men in the middle" who stopped demanding a "smoking gun" and would vote in favor of narrowly drawn articles on cover-up and abuse of power. Article III, on the president's refusal to cooperate with the committee's investigation, passed without the help of the fragile coalition, on a strictly party-line vote of 21–17.

Each member was allowed an opening statement. Drinan did not speak often during the next six days, most likely for two reasons. First, he had already had his moment in the sun a year before on the issue that was, in many ways, his issue, but one that he shared with Holtzman and Conyers—the Cambodia bombing. His files show the most extensive research by his staff on this subject. Although he had intended to bring the issue up again, he had finally decided not to do so, both because it wasn't needed and because he could see it was going to lose.

Second, he was surrounded by thirty-seven other lawyers, most of them senior to him on the committee and with a lot to say. Also, several times he tried to speak but had a hard time getting recognized. In his opening remarks he called up the memory of the Massachusetts delegates to the 1787 Constitutional Convention who opposed including the articles on impeachment; but he separated in this instance from the eighteenth-century founders because of the gravity of the contemporary issue which he saw as paramount, but which his current colleagues rejected. In his words, the committee members were passing over the bombing of Cambodia and focusing on less grave questions because of those issues' capacity to "play in Peoria." While the Cambodians and Vietnamese—everyone except the American people—knew of the bombing, Nixon had "orchestrated a conspiracy to keep the lid on Cambodia until at least after the election of 1972."

How, asked Drinan, could we "impeach a president for concealing a burglary but not for concealing a massive bombing"? He evoked the spirit of the men who fought at Concord—which is in his congressional district—and those who "within 1,000 days" would celebrate the bicentennial of the Declaration of Independence to assure that the impeachment proceedings would either "vindicate the rights of the people against a tyrant" or "acquit one who may be unjustly accused." Holtzman's remarks were, in contrast, based on the Nixon tapes, a day-to-day catalogue of Nixon's violations—"'I want you all to stonewall it' . . . 'Just be damn sure you say, "I don't remember, I can't recall."'" He lied to the prosecutors. He tried to stop the investigations. He tried to buy silence, and he failed to report criminal conduct."

Discussing Article I, on Nixon's alleged criminal activity, Drinan argued partly by induction that "the only possible conclusion that one could come to when you look at the vast amount of evidence" following the Watergate break-in is that Nixon "made it his policy'" to obstruct justice. Later, when Congressman Latta, defending the administration, asked for specifics, Drinan responded with a day-by-day chronology, beginning June 20, 1972, when Nixon lied about the White House involvement in the Watergate break-in and directed Haldeman to instruct the CIA to head off an FBI investigation that would reveal CIA money laundering in Mexico, have the CIA pay bail for the Watergate burglars, and arrange for fundraiser and former Commerce Secretary Maurice Stans and others to testify not before a grand jury but privately to a prosecutor.

The "only possible explanation" for all of this, said Drinan, was a policy to obstruct the Watergate investigation. A little later, Drinan applied the same logic to the activities of the "plumbers," the White House special investigative unit, best known for "Project Ellsberg," because they rifled the files of Daniel Ellsberg's psychiatrist for information that might embarrass the man who released the Pentagon Papers.

One of the more eloquent presentations was that of Congressman Don Edwards of California on Article II, which he and others considered the heart of their deliberations because it focused on the president's alleged abuse of his constitutional powers. Edwards marched through Constitutional Amendments One, Four, Six, and Seven and showed how Nixon had violated each through wiretapping reporters, sending the "plumbers" on illegal errands, using the Internal Revenue Service to harass political opponents, and leaking information unfavorable to criminal defendants. The notion that "national security" warranted putting aside the Constitution, as some Nixon defenders were claiming, said Edwards, was the "postulate of tyranny," the "very definition of dictatorship."

The awesome implication of Article II, said Drinan, moved him to pay tribute to two of his Massachusetts constituents—Democrat Archibald Cox and Republican Elliot Richardson—whose Saturday Night Massacre decision "not to submit, not to go along" should force "every member of Congress and every American citizen to make the same moral decision." In an obvious allusion to Luke 9:25, Richardson, said Drinan, "gave up his entire career rather than tarnish his soul and be part of a cover-up."

Faced with Article III, on Nixon's failure to comply with the demand for his documents, Maine Republican William S. Cohen, one of the fragile coalition, granted that information relevant to the committee had been withheld; he said he was receptive to evidence that Nixon should be impeached and that the administration had degraded the doctrine of "executive privilege," but he hesitated to make this a "matter of law" by including it in an article. Drinan sympathized with Cohen, but he felt that Article III gave strength to the other two. It passed 21–17.

Cambodia Again

In some ways the consideration of Article IV was anticlimactic, although, as its proponents pointed out, what could be more serious— even more immoral—than the abuse of a president's power to initiate

war, especially given that that power was supposed to rest with Congress? Eight members asked to speak in support and thirteen against.
John Conyers, leading off, said the article was more fundamental than
the others because both Lyndon Johnson and Richard Nixon were "casualties of the Vietnam war." He anticipated his opponents by acknowl-
edging that Congress shared in the responsibility because it had
funded the war for ten years and not opposed the president more
forcefully. But this was an opportunity to break with the past. Remember, Conyers said: On March 17, 1969, Nixon secretly ordered the
bombing, which continued until August 15, 1973. Only on July 16,
1973, had Defense Secretary James R. Schlesinger admitted to the Senate Armed Services Committee that the bombing had begun prior to
May 1970, the day of the American ground invasion of Cambodia.

Holtzman enumerated Nixon's reputed deceptions of Congress and
the people and concluded that "if we are to remain a free people" we
have to be able to participate in these decisions. Drinan argued that
this article was not about the merits of the Vietnam War; it was very
narrow in scope. It was only about secrecy. "There is no provision in
the Constitution," he said, for secrecy in the executive branch. Article
IV was rejected by a vote of 26–12, as was a proposed Article V, concerning possible irregularities in Nixon's personal tax returns.

Nevertheless, Cambodia remained Drinan's issue. Though he had
not fought furiously for Article IV in committee, some time later
he submitted supplemental views (undated) for the record. Citing
Holtzman in agreement, he charged that the inquiry staff had declined to do the research required by the issue. He lined up the various excuses offered by the administration for the secrecy—to save
American lives, protect Cambodia's Prince Norodom Sihanouk from
embarrassment, national security, and the alleged sharing of the facts
with thirteen select, but unnamed, congressmen—and shot them
down. The citation of the unnamed congressmen who allegedly had
been consulted was particularly vexing. Both Drinan and Holtzman
wanted that claim investigated, but the staff would not pursue it.
This refusal raised the question of whether there had been an agreement among the leadership of the committee to not pursue certain
questions in order to maintain harmony on the impeachment issues

where there was a consensus. Nevertheless, Drinan's memo concluded: "One can come only to a single and inescapable conclusion"—Nixon's political objective of deceiving and quieting the antiwar movement.

By the time the impeachment hearings were over, impeachment was no longer an issue. Following the Supreme Court's order to surrender all the tapes, Nixon, in San Clemente, had called his aide Fred Buzhardt in Washington to alert him that "there may be some problem with the June 23 [1972] tape." The tape included three conversations between Nixon and Haldeman. Much of it is junk talk—he curses the press; derides old friends, homosexuals, and Jews; and tells Haldeman to "play it tough." And here he is, six days after the Watergate break-in, already knowing well G. Gordon Liddy and E. Howard Hunt's involvement, Attorney General John Mitchell's complicity, and, in contradiction of all he had said in his defense, ordering the cover-up and calling on the FBI and CIA to be accomplices.

While the Judiciary Committee voted its three articles, Nixon listened to the tapes again. As the staff and the Republicans on the Judiciary Committee learned of the tape's content, Nixon's remaining support collapsed, even among the Diehards. The Republican leadership of the House and Senate began to plan Nixon's resignation. As the other House members listened, Ed Koch, a New York Democrat, remarked, "There are a lot of low-class people in that White House." Nixon behaved erratically, spewed out confused, paranoid monologues to his family and cabinet, until he finally gave in, and on August 9 he was gone.

On September 8, President Gerald Ford pardoned Nixon for any crime he had "committed, or may have committed," during his term of office. Barbara Jordan, whom Ford had sent with a delegation to China in what Jordan imagined was an honor, was furious when, on the other side of the world, the news of the pardon reached her. She was convinced that Ford had slipped her out of the country to spare himself her withering, eloquent anger when she learned what he had done.

"The Priestly Zealot"

Like the woman in the Midwest who wrote to Drinan praising him as a moral leader following his impeachment proposal in July, Elizabeth Holtzman was inclined to see Robert Drinan pretty much as he saw himself—as a moral leader, the prescient priest who saw ahead the need to remove the president and whose bold move got other members of Congress talking about a problem they should have faced some time before. Although she did not know him well personally, because they did not share a subcommittee assignment, they shared the same ideals—a devotion to civil liberties and integrity in public life. She remembers that he always carried a little portfolio briefcase, that he was a very nice person, a courageous and passionate man who "loved his calling." In a sense, she knew him from the inside because they were kindred spirits.

On the other hand, University of Massachusetts at Amherst professors John H. Fenton and Donald M. Austern, co-editors of the collection of essays *The Making of Congressmen: Seven Campaigns of 1974* (1976), knew him from the outside as members of a team of scholars analyzing seven 1974 congressional campaigns across the country as the Nixon presidency went down like a flaming fighter plane into the sea. The Drinan campaign was important, they wrote, because he was the "only Catholic priest ever elected to Congress"—not knowing that another priest had just been elected from Wisconsin—and because he was "widely regarded as among the more militant leftists in Congress, occupying much the same radical ground as Bella Abzug of New York." Finally, they said, he was unusual. They classified him as if he were a character in a novel or a film: ". . . in addition to wearing the priestly garb and assuming radical political positions, he looks the part of the priestly zealot to perfection. His eyes bulge as he scolds his opponents, and his rhetoric rings with pronouncements proclaiming the undeniable fact that he is holier than almost anyone else in politics." He could get away with playing this role, they said, because Massachusetts was the most liberal state in the union, founded by Puritans who believed the state had an obligation to promote the well-being of the population.

THE MORAL ARCHITECT | 231

Theirs was a moral commonwealth, a "city on a hill," where a Jesuit priest could play the Puritan moral crusader.

The Fourth District was particularly interesting because of its shape, stretching one hundred miles from the leafy suburb of Newton to the factory town of Fitchburg; its ethnic and economic mix of working-class Catholics, "WASPs," and suburban Jews; its factories dependent on government and military contracts; and its private schools, colleges, and universities. Also, although 19 percent of its voters registered as Republicans and 38 as Democrats, 43 percent were independents; and, because campaigns were frequently three-person contests, the independents could be decisive. As a rule, incumbents have a great advantage and tend to win once they are established.

So Drinan started with the advantage of incumbency, the support of 5,400 campaign contributors, many from outside the state, and 3,000 volunteer workers. In 1974 he spent $178,871, more than twice the amount spent by his nearest competitor. Fenton and Austern saw as strengths his strict morality, his self-description as a "moral architect," his near-perfect attendance record. On the other hand, his weaknesses included his notoriety and radical reputation, along with his temperament and personality. As the 1972 campaign had demonstrated, sometimes to know Drinan was not to like him. His deep-set eyes made him photograph poorly, and his reserved campaign style made him "appear more of a machine than a warm human being." In this campaign the priestly identity again became a problem as the rumor mill again generated questions on whether Drinan "really had permission to run." Also, a series of other priest-related controversies cluttered the front pages for weeks.

Drinan's would-be Republican opponent, former Congressman Lawrence Curtis, perhaps sensing he wasn't going to win, dropped out of the race shortly after his nomination. His replacement, Alvin Mandell, a fifty-three-year-old middle-of-the-road Raytheon electrical engineer, struggled to convince even his fellow Republicans that he was a serious candidate. Drinan's real opponent was a fellow Democrat, Jon Rotenberg, a legislative aide to Tip O'Neill, who had declined to run against Drinan in a primary and now presented himself as an Independent. Unlike Drinan, who was fifty-four, he was young (twenty-six) and handsome, so his campaign took advantage of his appearance in TV ads. Drinan's staff compensated for their candidate's somewhat forbidding appearance with a witty mailing: On the first page it said: "When you elect someone to Congress he should be: (1) honest, (2) hard-working, (3) effective, (4) suave." When voters turned the page over they saw the picture of Drinan with the caption: "Well, three out of four ain't bad."

Meanwhile, during the summer Drinan did his best to both impeach Nixon and run for office at the same time. In his office, stacked high with papers and magazines, some two years old, he entertained a delegation of Girl Scouts from Leominister, took their questions on capital punishment, and told them how to be helpful to handicapped children as state law returned the handicapped to local classrooms. He hustled from place to place, a Coke his only lunch, the pockets of his thin black suit bursting with papers and clippings. Of his 200 letters a day he picked about half to answer himself. In a Marjorie Arons *Newton Times* portrait on April 3, the office buzzed and boomed as phones rang, typewriters clicked, doors opened and closed, "desks [were] crammed together in tiny cubicles, files bulge[d], and stacks of paper spill[ed] out into the hall." Drinnie, a Great Dane belonging to one of the staff, flopped down on the floor.

Directed by Liz Bankowski, the Washington office provided paralegal services for constituents, functioned as ombudsman, and interpreted the law to people in the Fourth District. Arthur Wolf, who left the Justice Department and worked in the McGovern campaign in 1972 and whom Drinan hired on the basis of his résumé without having met him, served as Drinan's special counsel on civil rights and civil liberties and on drawing up legislation for Drinan to sponsor. The interns and volunteers worked, for the most part, without pay—other than the excitement of being in the office and the on-the-job political education, inspired by a man they described to a reporter as sometimes "stiff" or "artificial" but whose work ethic and ideals they were quick to admire.

By the end of the summer, of course, Nixon was gone. With the war and the departed president having faded, the campaign issues seemed bland. Mandell attacked Drinan for neglecting the district because of his obsession with issues like disarmament and impeachment. Rotenberg picked up Martin Linsky's charge from the 1972 campaign that Drinan was "ineffective," saying that he had "never had one bill signed into law that he wrote, that he instituted." Drinan replied that "there is more to being a congressman than giving service to your constituents. I have communicated more than most congressmen and I have listened." He added that he could deal with the great moral issues facing the country. He implied, according to Fenton and Austern, that "he was a rare and morally excellent creature."

Among his Jewish constituency, Drinan had emerged as a fighter for Soviet Jewry and demonstrated, by helping to remove Nixon, his commitment to ethical standards. This time, however, he had two Jewish opponents. And, said the Leventmans, the Jewish couple on the Boston College faculty who were early Drinan supporters, "just below the surface Rotenberg ran an ethnic campaign more extensive than Linsky's." He organized Jewish youth groups who argued that "from one Jew to another," it helped to have a Jewish representative in Congress. It was a "direct appeal to ethnic insecurity." Rotenberg even resorted to recruiting Catholic students in Catholic areas by telling them that Drinan cared about Jews only because they gave money to his campaign. To the Jews, Rotenberg's supporters argued that all Catholics will vote for a priest, so all Jews should "stick together." It didn't work.

Good Priest, Bad Priest?

During the New York Jesuit ordinations at Fordham University a few years earlier, in protest against the Vietnam War, two of the men being ordained interrupted the ceremony to protest the fact that the bishop ordaining them, Cardinal Terence Cooke, was also the Military Vicar and thus an instrument of the government, an enabler in what they saw as an unjust and immoral enterprise.

One of the spokesmen was Joe O'Rourke, a charming and charismatic young man much loved by his close friends but, to many, an imprudent disturber of the peace whose dramatic gestures did more harm than good. His religious superiors in New York tried to both respect his freedom and keep him in check and were unhappy with his leadership role in a group called Catholics for a Free Choice, which saw abortion as a "choice" more than a moral issue. When the pastor of the Immaculate Conception Church in Marlboro, Massachusetts, denied Carol Morreale the right to have her child baptized in the church because of Morreale's stand on contraception and abortion, an abortion activist, William R. Baird, advertised for a priest who would perform the baptism. O'Rourke came forward and, in late August 1974, despite having been ordered not to do so by his religious superiors, baptized the boy on the steps of the parish church before one hundred onlookers, TV cameras, and reporters. Two weeks later O'Rourke was dismissed from the Society.

The same week, by pure coincidence, Reverend Mark Corrigan, a priest of the Boston archdiocese, who had worked as an assistant press secretary and administrator for three years in the administration of Mayor John V. Lindsay of New York City, resigned from the priesthood rather than heed the directive of Boston's Cardinal Humberto S. Medeiros to leave politics and return to Boston and work in a parish. While in New York, he had also angered Medeiros by supporting New York state's liberalized abortion law.

Strictly speaking there was no connection between O'Rourke, Corrigan, and Drinan, other than that all three were priests expressing their priesthood contrary to the public stereotype of a priest. In Corrigan's case, Medeiros was reacting to Corrigan the way he would like to have reacted to Drinan if Drinan had been subject to his authority. O'Rourke and Drinan agreed on Vietnam, but O'Rourke would have agreed with Daniel Berrigan, who protested O'Rourke's dismissal, that a priest does not belong in elective office because there he is inevitably compromised by the power.

A September 6 *Boston Globe* story speculated that O'Rourke's dismissal was a deliberate signal that the Society was cracking down, sending a message to those who had not been taking their vows of obedience seriously enough. The *Herald American* followed on September 21 with an "exclusive" report on an editorial in *SJ News*, the Jesuit newsletter of the New England province, by editor James Hietter, S.J., that Drinan might actually be lacking "an updated, top level, religious permission to be in politics." Drinan snapped back to the *Herald American* that it's a "non-story with the facts all screwed up. . . . I have permission in black and white and I'm not going to get into the question of permission. Some kid wrote that. It's unsigned, isn't it." (The *Herald* added that Hietter was forty-four and had been ordained for twelve years.) Bishop Bernard J. Flanagan said priests didn't belong in politics and he had never given Drinan explicit permission, but he would go along if Drinan's superior approved.

The *SJ News* editorial went on to say that O'Rourke probably thought the obedience would not be enforced; John McLaughlin's "expert handling" of his defense of Nixon surprised religious authorities; a secret document was on its way from the Congregation for Religious, which oversees religious orders, in Rome ordering priests out of politics; Drinan had no explicit permission except Guindon's. The same day the *Globe* ran a column by M. A. Michelson with a story about a parish priest who recently told his congregation to vote against Michael Dukakis for governor because Dukakis was "pro-abortion." Michelson concluded that there was no evidence Dukakis was pro-abortion and pointed out that the parish voted overwhelmingly for Dukakis. His conclusion: Catholics are less dogmatic. "They don't accept as gospel what comes from the pulpit if they don't believe it's gospel."

On September 22 and 23 the *Globe* joined the discussion. Choosing his words carefully, Father Vincent O'Keefe, who had been so instrumental in getting at least passive approval for Drinan to run in 1970, even though Arrupe was against it, told the *Globe* that Drinan had no "explicit" permission and that he needed the permission of Flanagan and Medeiros to run. Finally the New England provincial, Richard T. Cleary, in the Saturday and Sunday (September 24 and 25) *Globe*, made a decisive effort to clear things up: "As his present religious superior, I have granted Fr. Drinan my permission to carry on as a member of the U.S. House of Representatives." He reiterated what had been made known in the previous campaigns: Guindon's permission. The rumored so-called "secret document" was a general statement that did not refer specifically to Drinan. The bishops agreed to follow the judgment of the local Jesuit superiors. The *Globe* interviewed two canon lawyers, one of whom said Jesuits were exempt from the requirement to consult bishops on the law concerning participation in public life, because they were members of an "exempt order"; another said that implied permission constituted permission. According to this theory, if Medeiros and Flanagan knew Drinan was running for office and took no steps to stop him, he had their permission.

Not that the story went away. When Medeiros, who had been in Rome during the controversy, returned, he reaffirmed his conviction that priests don't belong in politics; Drinan declined to comment. The *Globe* editorialized on September 27 that Cleary's clarification was welcome. But it took exception to the other political Jesuit, John McLaughlin, who had defended Nixon's use of obscenity (heard on the White House tapes) as therapy that was good, moral, and sound.

On October 13 the *Globe* reported, again based on a story in Hietter's *SJ News* article, that John McLaughlin had been ordered by Cleary to resign from his White House job. McLaughlin first explained that the reasons were "Jesuit policy reasons," but later he said the main reasons were not Jesuit related but that the new president, Gerald Ford, would want a fresh staff, and that was the main reason for his leaving the job. According to Hietter, Cleary had criticized McLaughlin in May both because of his public statements defending Nixon, which, he felt, reflected negatively on the Society, and because of his style of living—in the Watergate apartments, where a one-bedroom unit rented for $425 to $700 per month (the equivalent of $1,850 to $3,040 today).

A month later, on October 26, Father O'Keefe emphasized to the *Globe* that Rome had never insisted that Drinan "clear anything up." All Drinan had been asked to do was to comply with canon law, and bishops have "lots of ways of giving approval without making a formal statement." Mark Reuver, a former priest and Vatican official who was head of the International Documentation Center, told the *Globe* that the issue of priests in politics had been boiling for years and the Congregation for Religious had been drafting statements but none had reached final form. For them to ban priests from politics would be "a most stupid thing," he said. "That would be saying that religion has nothing to do with life."

Hietter, the Jesuit editor who had written the editorial that triggered the fuss and who had also publicized the internal conflict within the Society over John McLaughlin, was fired—for what Cleary termed "deep differences of opinion on what news is fit to print and what news will further the apostolic ends of this province." He later left the Society.

As the 1974 campaign came to a close, the Jesuit flap did not seem to have damaged Drinan's campaign. In mid-October a *Globe* reporter described Drinan as "appearing invincible, yet vulnerable." He had retained the one-third "unfavorable" rating from the 1972 campaign, and it was possible that that could push Rotenberg ahead. But the strength of Drinan's staff and his attention to constituent needs were profound. His office helped solve a school-funding problem in Ayer when federal funding was withdrawn for Fort Devens's children, and he got federal land for the town of Maynard. He also spent about three times as much money as Rotenberg. In the end, for the first time, he won with a majority of votes cast: Drinan, 77,282 (50.85 percent); Rotenberg, 52,765 (34.71 percent); and Mandell, 21,930 (14.42 percent). As Fenton and Austern interpreted the results, Drinan won because of a very limited set of circumstances: a large Catholic vote, plus a large liberal Jewish vote, plus a growing number of suburban "WASP" liberals, of course all held together by a symbol of moral rectitude inspired by providing service to the community.

11 Around the World

Cngressman Drinan's four-page occasional newsletter to his constituents summed up the achievements of 1974 and outlined the challenges ahead in 1975, celebrating the end of the "dark night" of Watergate and offering hope, based on the arrival of "75 new and generally progressive Democrats" in the House and the "erosion of the seniority rule." This, it was hoped, might lead to a decreased military budget, national health insurance, a coherent energy policy, and antitrust measures against multinational corporations. Drinan was appalled that in five months 50,000 to 100,000 had died of starvation in Bangladesh while 26.6 percent of the administration's Food for Peace budget was earmarked for Indochina. He saw the issues of world hunger, global inflation, and arms control as tied together. Money spent on arms took men and money out of the private sector, where it could increase the volume of consumer goods and decrease prices.

Meanwhile, the U.S. defense posture toward the Soviet Union—which with its re-arming of Arab nations showed it had no regard for international or moral law, in Drinan's view—was based on the presumption that the Soviets would also be foolish enough to trigger a nuclear war with the United States and thereby jeopardize the survival of its own people. He also had problems with the United Nations, where, he said, Communist regimes had helped the Afro-Asian-Arab majority "blackmail" the UN. He did not explain what he was referring to. Meanwhile, he recommended two new books: Congressman-elect Paul Simon's *The Politics of World Hunger* and Lester R. Brown's *By Bread Alone*. Months later, in an interview with the *NCR* on March 14, 1975, he returned to some of these themes. He hoped that Congress would turn its attention back to the cities. Contrary to popular opinion, the civil rights movement was not over, he said; blacks and Spanish-speaking people were not making their place in the world. Watts, South Chicago, and Roxbury, in his native Boston, were in the same condition they were ten years before. He kept hoping that the cause of global hunger would bring the churches of America together. "They want a crusade. They need a crusade."

As the Ford administration continued its support of the failing governments in Indochina and Cambodia, Drinan and his House colleagues continued their protests, including a suit in a U.S. District Court in Boston to halt U.S. military support and advice to Cambodia. In late January, Drinan joined George McGovern, Daniel Ellsberg, Bella Abzug, Pete Seeger, and several thousand others in a candlelight march to the White House. As spring progressed, South Vietnam step-by-step disintegrated while the North advanced. President Thieu resigned and fled to Taiwan. On April 29, with the North Vietnamese army at the gates, helicopters lifted American personnel from the U.S. Embassy roof, and President Ford ordered the continued helicopter evacuation of 7,000 Americans and Vietnamese from Saigon to three aircraft carriers offshore. On April 30 the collapse was complete; in Saigon, a North Vietnamese tank smashed through the gates of the presidential palace and remains there today as a symbol of the North Vietnamese triumph. The war left 58,200 American dead; the Communists listed a million dead soldiers and 2 million dead civilians. By 1983 half a million Vietnamese had fled to the United States.

Another Priest

As the 94th Congress opened in January 1975, one of the seventy-five "new progressive Democrats," Robert J. Cornell, O. Praem., a fifty-four-year-old political science professor at St. Norbert's College in De Pere, Wisconsin, arrived in Washington as the second—some would say "other"—Catholic priest in the House of Representatives. At home he was known as a teacher, administrator, and concert promoter; here he

wanted to be known as a Democratic proponent of economic and welfare reforms. This had been his third try at elective office. He was one
of the swarm of priests who suddenly saw themselves as politicians
in 1970, but he lost both then and in 1972. This time, helped by a
reapportionment of the Eighth District, he beat conservative Republican Harold V. Froehlich, who had served only one term and, as a member of the Judiciary Committee, had voted for Nixon's impeachment
on the first two articles.

Cornell grew up in Gladstone, Michigan, where he converted to
Catholicism as a boy; joined the Norbertine Order, also known as the
Premonstratensians; was ordained in 1944; gained his Ph.D. at the
Catholic University of America in 1957; and taught political science
and history at St. Norbert's for thirty years until his election. He promised Froehlich he would not make impeachment an issue during the
campaign and beat him by a wide margin simply by criticizing Froehlich's positions on taxes and welfare.

Like Drinan, Cornell had been inspired in college and graduate
school by the study of human rights and social justice, and he presented himself as moved by Vatican II to enter a profession in which
he thought he could have an impact in a society that is best served, in
his view, by the application of Christian social principles. The single
incident that triggered his becoming politically active was the strong
negative reaction he received to a talk he gave in 1961 to a group of
Catholic laymen and their wives on "Christian Social Teaching—An
Answer to Communism." After he enumerated reforms, based on the
popes' social encyclicals, that would serve justice, the local pastor invited him to the home of a prominent industrialist where some guests
and the host told him right off how much they disagreed with all he
had said. As word spread, tongues wagged and heads shook: "Where
does Cornell get those crazy ideas? No son of mine will go to St. Norbert's and get exposed to those teachings." This convinced him that
teaching wasn't enough; he needed to work for changes in public policy. A fellow Democratic activist, an atheist, steered him toward running in 1970.

Drinan was among the first to call Cornell with his congratulations.
Though they were colleagues, fellow priests, both Democrats, and they

ultimately co-sponsored some legislation, they were not kindred spirits. Drinan's most admirable quality, to Cornell, was his devotion to the poor; but they went different ways on abortion, specifically on the Hyde Amendment, named for Congressman Henry Hyde of Illinois, which Cornell supported and which would prohibit the use of federal funds for abortion. For Drinan, the issue was legal; for Cornell, it was moral. But asked if he "liked Drinan," Cornell replied, "Not much." Drinan was personally nice to Cornell, but, in general, "not a nice person. He seldom smiled." Drinan invited Cornell to a small dinner, attended by a Supreme Court justice and other distinguished persons, in his honor in the Georgetown Jesuit community guest dining room. But Cornell found it strange that another Jesuit invited for cocktails had not also been invited to join them at dinner. On another occasion, when a Jesuit brother was taking their picture together, Drinan was curt with the photographer. But many other members, especially those on the Judiciary Committee, did like Drinan, said Cornell; and Cornell was very favorably impressed with the support Drinan received from his fellow Jesuits. Cornell was reelected in 1976 but lost in 1978. In 1980 he was set to run again, but, in confusion and ecclesiastical miscommunication, Cornell's religious superiors prematurely believed the pope's order that Drinan not run again applied to Cornell as well, and he withdrew.

The Legislative Record Sheet

A review of 240 bills that Drinan sponsored or co-sponsored during late 1974 and throughout 1975 reveals both a variety of interests and a pattern of emphasis on civil and human rights, the environment, Israel, disarmament, and—as always—the good of his constituents. Among the most significant of the bills he personally sponsored were three that would allow Congress to pay reasonable attorney fees in cases involving civil, constitutional, consumer, and environmental rights.

Arthur Wolf, now a law professor at Western New England College and formerly a Drinan staff member who drafted major legislation, described two important bills in this way:

One of the bills Drinan filed in 1975 would authorize the federal courts to award reasonable attorney fees to the prevailing party in many civil rights and civil liberties cases. His intention was to benefit plaintiffs, many of whom could not afford to bring such cases without the help of this bill. Drinan presided over the Subcommittee hearings on the bill, shepherded it through the House Judiciary Committee, and served as the floor manager for the bill. In October 1976, President Ford signed the bill into law as the "Civil Rights Attorney's Fees Awards Act of 1976." Since its enactment over 30 years ago, the public interest bar and its clients have considered the Act one of the most important pieces of legislation for the advancement of civil and constitutional rights.

Also in 1975 Drinan played a major role in the extension of the Voting Rights Act of 1965, which removed many of the barriers that prevented minorities from voting. Through his efforts the 1975 bill extended the provision of the 1965 legislation and added additional measures. One of the 1975 amendments sought to protect language minorities from voting discrimination by requiring certain bilingual voting materials, including ballots. Drinan also made sure that the 1975 Voting Rights Act extension included an attorney fees provision benefiting successful litigants who advanced voting rights.

The previous year, ecology groups had rated their representatives; in particular, the League of Conservation Voters had evaluated Congress on proposals relating to the Alaskan pipeline, atomic power, mass transit, abortion, pesticides, and support of the United Nations Environmental Fund. Eight House members, including Drinan, achieved a rating of 100; twelve House members, designated as the "dirty dozen," received zero. Drinan backed a measure that would link America by three bike trails: from Atlantic City, New Jersey, to Astoria, Oregon; Maine to Key West, Florida; and Olympia, Washington, to San Diego. He favored laws that would discourage painful devices that trapped animals and birds on federal lands; establish more wilderness areas; end strip mining; and develop into a historic site and national park the home of Frederick Law Olmsted in Brookline, recently added to his district.

He objected to the sale of Hawk missiles to Jordan and Sidewinder missiles to Saudi Arabia, lest they be used to attack Israel. He would vote to send Israel $300 million in foreign military credit, for F-15 fighter planes and electronic countermeasures. Pointing out that cigarettes cause heart and lung disease, he wanted to increase the cigarette tax. But he would amend the Controlled Substance Act to permit any person to possess marijuana, in residence, for his or her own use or the use of another, though not to be sold. The Vietnam Era Reconciliation Act would grant immunity from prosecution and punishment to those who, because they disapproved of U.S. military involvement in Indochina, resisted the draft or went AWOL.

Handguns and Free Expression

Two contentious and complex issues that have long concentrated the attention of political liberals are gun control and the media's right to free expression. Both issues are rooted in interpretations of the Constitution and have been resolved, though not absolutely, in Supreme Court decisions, and both today remain subjects of debate in the media and in Congress. In June 2008 the Supreme Court, by a 5–4 vote, knocked down the District of Columbia's ban on handgun possession, stating that the authors of the Second Amendment referred to the individual's—not merely the collective right, as in the militia—to bear arms. It was a blow to the District of Columbia, which saw the law as necessary if the rate of murders in the community was to be reduced.

The First Amendment issue concerned the role of the government, specifically through the Federal Communications Commission, to regulate radio and television broadcasting in a way that protected the public's right to know by requiring that both or several sides of an argument have equal access to the media. According to the "Fairness Doctrine," the FCC, beginning in 1949 and repeated in 1959, required broadcast licensees "to afford reasonable opportunity for the discussion of conflicting views on issues of public importance." This doctrine is based on the principle that the airwaves, with their limited number of broadcasting frequencies, belong to the public. They are only leased to broadcasting stations; therefore the public should have a right to air its views. Today, the development of cable TV and the availability of higher frequencies have made the Fairness Doctrine and what was known as the equal-time doctrine less necessary, and the FCC has dropped them. But the imbalance of political opinion, especially in daytime talk radio, remains an issue. In 2009 Democrats in Congress considered the Fairness Doctrine's return.

In the spring and summer of 1975, in response to a dramatic increase in crime, especially murders, eleven laws were placed before the House of Representatives for strengthening gun control, including two from Drinan's office. There were 210 million privately owned guns in the country, resulting each year in 25,000 gun deaths—including 12,000 homicides, 10,000 suicides, and 3,000 fatal accidents.

Drinan's Handgun Control Act of 1975 would make it unlawful to own, possess, import, manufacture, sell, buy, transfer, receive, or transport any handgun or handgun ammunition. Exceptions were made for licensed pistol clubs, security guards, and antique collectors. The second bill, the Personal Safety Firearms Act of 1975, required the registration of firearms and licensing of gun owners, and banned the sale or delivery of so-called Saturday night specials. The Federal Gun Control Act of 1968, Drinan argued, was so weak and compromised as to be ineffective. It banned Saturday night specials but not their parts, so individuals could import those parts and sell them to *anyone*— criminal, lunatic, drug addict. He said in his statement to the Judiciary Committee, "Our claim to be a civilized nation cannot be sustained until we enact tough, effective, and enforceable federal gun control laws that will put an end to the tragic and scandalous level of violence that permeates life in America."

In response to an anti–gun control article in the *Civil Liberties Review* (June/July 1975), Drinan the debater took on the author's points in the August/September issue. His bills would not "disarm" the public, he said; they would ban only handguns, which, because they are concealable, facilitate criminal assault. Rifles and shotguns are legal when licensed. Problems with enforcement are inevitable; but, unlike the attempted abolition of alcoholic beverages, this ban would be partial

and "does not outlaw absolutely a very powerful human desire." Difficulty in enforcement could not serve as a rationale for abandoning
the law. "Many existing laws, such as those outlawing larceny or the
possession of heroin, are difficult to enforce, but no one suggests that
for this reason they be rescinded." Handguns are not viable tools for
self-defense, he said. The FBI report for 1973 showed that a firearm
kept in the home for "self-defense" is six times more likely to be used
to deliberately or accidentally kill a relative or friend than an unlawful
intruder.

Drinan often looked for opportunities to show that his political
proposals coincided with the goals of the American Catholic hierarchy.
In September 1976 the Committee on Social Development and World
Peace of the United States Catholic Conference called for "effective
and courageous action to control handguns, leading to their eventual
elimination from our society."

The Supreme Court in 1969 affirmed the Fairness Doctrine in *Red
Lion Broadcasting v. FCC*, a case in which a WGCB Christian Crusade
radio broadcast in Red Lion, Pennsylvania, personally attacked Fred J.
Cook, author of *Goldwater: Extremist of the Right,* and Cook sued for
air time to reply. The Court ruled that the station's license did not
give it a monopoly control over public opinion; and subsequent Court
decisions in 1974 and 1984 supported the rights of persons attacked to
reply. In 1987 the FCC abolished the doctrine. But when Drinan was
preparing his bill repealing the Fairness Doctrine, liberal opinion was
by no means unanimous. Common Cause and the ACLU were not on
board, and three members of Drinan's own staff were "not excited
about the intent of the legislation." Rob Pratt wrote his boss on February 27, 1975, that "From a purist's viewpoint, you are clearly correct in
advocating abolishing the Fairness Doctrine. But many of your traditional allies in the House are not going to go along with you." Washington had lots of media outlets, but, said Pratt, killing the doctrine would
have a greater effect "in the hinterlands where only one or two stations
can be received." In that situation, radio stations and local TV networks "can present any garbage that they want with no citizen input
from the other side."

But Drinan's position was consistent with his position on a reporter's right to confidentiality—fear of the "chilling effect" on journalism. Networks would shrink from taking on controversial topics if doing so meant spending a year fighting lawsuits in which everyone who was criticized demanded broadcast time to present an opposing point of view. Pratt had been dragging his feet on the research because he lacked enthusiasm for the cause; but soon the memos referred to "our" position, and Drinan's presentation to the Senate Commerce Committee, on May 1, was powerful. He cited examples in which both Republican and Democratic presidents had used the doctrine to stifle dissent and argued that 7,785 radio stations and 953 TV stations—compared with 1,749 newspapers, plus the emergence of cable TV, and UHF and more use of VHF broadcast spectrum, plus the future possibility of the TV viewer's having access to 400 channels—were reasons to not compromise the First Amendment, which begins, "Congress shall make no law . . .".

Once Again, the Abortion Battle

But once again the issue that makes Drinan's files smoke is abortion—this year (1975) sparked by another constitutional dispute, the Human Life Amendments, which, in various forms, sought to amend the Constitution by a law protecting human life from the moment of conception; and there was the Hyde Amendment, a rider attached to the yearly appropriations bill for Medicaid, which barred the use of federal funds to pay for abortions. According to the supporters of the Human Life Amendments, which had had at least seven major formulations, since the Supreme Court had interpreted the Constitution to support the right to abortion on the grounds of privacy, only a constitutional amendment would break that legal interpretation. In later years, the simplest formation became the Hatch–Eagleton Amendment (1983), according to which, "A right to abortion is not secured by this Constitution."

A survey of several hundred letters streaming into Drinan's office during 1975 reveals certain prevailing themes. Those in favor of abortion rights thanked him for his stand and urged him to remain steadfast; opponents approached him in various ways. Their goal was to convince the House Judiciary Committee to hold hearings on the amendments so their case could become part of the public debate. Drinan, who responded to almost every letter, usually with a formulaic reply but sometimes by personally engaging the writer, answered that the Senate had already held hearings and there was little evidence that the amendments were going anywhere. Several letter writers emphasized that they were his constituents and they wished to meet with him both personally and in groups to discuss this. Members of the Massachusetts Citizens for Life group reminded him that they were 70,000 strong and wished to meet him during the August recess in whichever local office he preferred. Others offered to meet with him in either Washington or Boston. A staff member warned him that the anti-abortion group's strategy was to have as many meetings as possible, on the basis of being his constituents, to obstruct him by taking up his time. In a memo dated August 27, 1975, the staffer warned that "they are not very pleasant people to deal with, ask the impossible and get nasty when the impossible does not happen."

The tone of some of the letters lends credibility to the staffer's observation. They stressed the number of deaths for which those who don't wish to criminalize abortion were responsible—"hundreds of thousands of human beings being murdered," "900,000 killed unborn human beings" in 1974 alone. At the same time, many of the letters were sincere, anxious pleas from laypersons, doctors, and priests who found it hard to accept that a priest would appear to be an abortion supporter. A couple of letters from fellow Jesuits, as well as from other priests, asked him to please explain his position, because they were reluctant to categorize him as "pro-abortion." Paul Quay, S.J., of the Missouri province reminded him that they met years before and asked why not let the House Judiciary Committee have hearings. Reverend John E. Doran, president of the local senate of priests, asked the same question. To those who asked his position on abortion, he replied, "I am entirely opposed to abortion" but not certain that Catholics should try to amend the Constitution to reinstate criminal sanctions.

Father Patrick Lynch, a parish priest in Annapolis, pleaded with Drinan to use his standing in the Church and in the country to protect life: "We so much need the backing of influential people and most especially influential Catholics. As we see it, you have done nothing." He concluded: "Father Drinan, if you fail in this area of Pro-life issues, we feel that you have failed in a very big area and in the last result you would be better off outside of public office." Drinan replied on October 28: "I thank you for your kind letter and send to you my sincere best wishes."

Dr. Vincent Pattavina, a constituent in Braintree, read a story in the *Herald* about an anti-Drinan protest when he spoke at the dedication of the Creighton University Law School in Omaha. He reminded Drinan that he'd seen him on David Susskind's TV show in the 1960s defending life. What happened? Drinan interpreted this as an assault on his integrity. He replied on September 25, 1975, that the situation had changed. Abortion laws had been nullified by the Supreme Court. It was fruitless to try to amend the Constitution. Drinan's standard reply now to everyone who wanted a change in the law was to recommend that they do what other minority groups—blacks, labor unions, and Jehovah's Witnesses—had done and find cases they could bring to the courts that might expose flaws in the *Roe* decision and litigate them up the line for years if they wanted to get *Roe* overturned.

Richard P. Mori, an Omaha attorney, replied that they had done just that. "We cannot afford to wait for ten or twenty years while the [C]ourt takes the time to change its mind. . . . The lack of your leadership in this area is deplorable." Pattavina on October 9 apologized for any offense in his previous letter. But, he concluded, "Until you, Father, take positive action and help the pro-life forces as you have done on other issues, as the Vietnam War, Watergate, Israel, I am sorry that others will continue to remind you of your unfortunate involvement in this immoral and revolting issue."

That same year, the Hyde Amendment, which would be enacted into law in 1976, was preceded by debate on the Bartlett Amendment, by which "no funds from the Social Security Act may be used to pay for or encourage the performance of abortions, except to save the life of a mother." The proposed act was tabled, which amounted to a defeat. Drinan wrote about the legislation in *Commonweal* on May 9, 1975, emphasizing that it was a discriminatory bill that, according to the U.S. Commission on Civil Rights, would have had an adverse impact only on low-income women, including many racial and ethnic minorities. "It seems to me," wrote Drinan, "that whatever one's view of abortion might be, a law terminating Medicaid benefits for indigent pregnant women who elect to terminate their pregnancies by abortion cannot be justified by any legal or constitutional norm." He granted that it could be argued that under the proposed act a woman would not lose her constitutional right to an abortion, only the right to have the abortion paid for in the exercise of that right. But that wasn't resolved in the Senate debate. The only generalization that could be drawn, he said, was that there was no "Catholic position" on the subject, because, of the fifteen Catholics in the Senate, by a vote of 8–7 they had tabled the act.

The Hyde Amendment was passed by the House in mid-June by a vote of 199–165, and the Massachusetts Citizens for Life were quick to point out that Drinan's vote against it was inconsistent with his 1967 article in which he'd stated that a utilitarian decision on the destruction of any innocent human being would be a "tragedy beyond description for America." Carol MacDonald of Waltham, the group's education chair, told the *News Tribune* on June 28, 1976, that Drinan wrote that before he became a politician.

In the summer of 1977 the *National Right to Life News* published a series of four articles based on interviews with Drinan, presenting what was ultimately a negative evaluation of his abortion position. Drinan, furious at what he considered seven inaccuracies or misrepresentations, wrote an angry reply, including his rejection of the author's observation that he had become nervous and testy when pressed on his abortion views. The *NRLN* (September 1977) printed his full reply but appended four pages documenting his full voting record, a reprint of a long *Commonweal* critique of his article on *Roe*, and a catalogue of quotes from fellow congressmen, including several Catholics, who said they resisted a hearing on, or had voted against, the Human Life Amendments because Drinan had convinced them to do so.

Soviet Jews

Drinan did not take well the two rebuffs, in 1973 and 1975, from the Soviet Union in which he and an ecumenical group of American religious leaders, when first their hotel reservations and then their visas were canceled and their plans to visit Soviet Jews who wanted to emigrate were crushed. In his view, a foreign government's canceling the visa of a member of Congress was unacceptable. So he obtained another visa through the State Department and headed across the world on his own, with an itinerary that would include Leningrad, Moscow, Romania, Israel, and a later trip to Brussels. He had made Soviet Jewry his special ministry, perhaps because it combined issues and personal elements that jelled with his character—human rights, international law, Jewish culture and values, an emotional link with his constituents, and a chance to show compassion for underdogs, both old and young. His method was to meet with groups of Jews, listen to their stories, confront the Soviet bureaucracy with challenging questions and criticisms, and then write articles for the *Globe, NCR, Christian Century*, and the *Jewish Advocate* reporting on his trips and calling on Christians to support the rights of the Jews.

The background is the Helsinki Accords of 1975, in which thirty-five states, including the United States and the Soviet Union, signed a ten-point declaration designed to improve relations between the Communist bloc and the West. It included respect for human rights and fundamental freedoms; respect for freedom of thought, conscience, religion, or belief; and fulfillment in good faith of obligations under international law. One result was that those who lived under oppressive governments that signed the accords used them to justify their dissent. The Jackson–Vanik Amendment, named for Senator Henry Jackson of Washington and Congressman Charles Vanik of Ohio, denied most-favored-nation trade status to countries that restricted emigrants' rights. It was aimed at the Soviet Union, which put a "diploma tax" on would-be emigrants, who had been educated at government expense, to force them to pay for their education. Its purpose was to stop the "brain drain" of well-educated Soviet Jews' wanting to move to Israel or the West. "Refuseniks" were Soviet Jews who wanted to leave, but, allegedly because they had served in the military, worked in nuclear or defense laboratories, or had other access to confidential information, were considered security risks and were not allowed to go.

In Leningrad (now Saint Petersburg), Drinan "was appalled to learn of the humiliation and indignities which are inflicted on every individual who makes public his desire to go to Israel." They lost their jobs, their phones were disconnected, their children were humiliated in school, and their lives were frequently placed under surveillance by the KGB. The official Kremlin ideology treated a person who desires to leave the Soviet Union as a traitor or a nonperson.

He told one forty-year-old refusenik engineer about his own canceled visa. The man had never in his life heard that any Christian was interested in his plight. Drinan procured a list of seventy-nine refuseniks and transmitted it to the National Conference on Soviet Jewry in New York, which would try to get persons or organizations to "adopt" a refusenik. Drinan challenged the "top" immigration officer, who was courteous but insisted that 98.5 percent of all Soviet Jews who wanted to emigrate received visas. According to Drinan, the official refused to acknowledge another 100,000 more Soviet Jews applying for visas (*Jewish Advocate*, September 11, 1975).

In Moscow, Drinan sat and talked with the "troubled and lonely" renowned dissident Andrei Sakharov for more than an hour. The wife of the famous nuclear physicist had gone to Italy for eye surgery, and their two-year-old "handsome grandson, recently threatened by blackmailers, rested on his grandfather's lap," suffering from a mysterious illness caused perhaps by a criminal assault. Sakharov hoped that his daughter Tatyana and her husband would be able to leave Russia and accept a fellowship offered by MIT in 1973. His own wife had been able to get a visa only through the intervention of King Baudoin of Belgium and Berlin Mayor Willy Brandt. He married her, after the death of his first wife, after having met her at a protest vigil. She was half-Jewish and the daughter of a woman who had spent sixteen years in a Stalin-era prison camp. Drinan speculated that she must have been the one responsible for having radicalized and "religionized" her husband. He told Sakharov his visa story, and the scientist replied with stories of those, including Christians, who were imprisoned and didn't get the support they needed to continue the fight. Drinan left disquieted with his "concern about the future of this beautiful human being." Would the Kremlin keep his wife outside of the Soviet Union and thereby induce her husband to follow? "Would [Premier Leonid] Brezhnev hope that the prophetic voice of Sakharov be allowed to remain in Moscow where each day his stature grows as prophet?" (*Globe*, September 13, 1975).

Anatoly Malkin, a twenty-year-old student at the Moscow Institute of Steel and Alloys, applied for a visa to Israel, only to be suddenly conscripted by the army. Furthermore, his parents had denied him permission to go to Israel; but this was only because they feared that the government would retaliate and they would lose their jobs. During Drinan's visit, he said, Malkin was "on trial," although this may have meant that he was appealing his draft status in the courts. If Malkin submitted to the draft, that would mean two years of active service, followed by five years during which his army service would categorize him as one possessing state secrets and thus ineligible for emigration. One guest at a lunch table of dissidents was the twenty-seven-year-old chess genius Anatoly (Natan) Sharansky, who had not seen his wife, who was in Israel, for two years. Drinan was happily able to present the young man with a photo of his wife with author Elie Wiesel. Sharansky, denied a visa, joined Sakharov's movement, was arrested in 1977, convicted of spying for the United States, and sent to a Siberian labor camp. Freed in 1986 as a result of a campaign led by his wife, he moved to Israel, where he entered politics and became known for a hardline attitude toward the Palestinians.

In his encounter with the top Soviet official for immigration, Drinan told him he "[did] not want to hear the usual proclamation that there is no problem, that 98.5 percent of all Soviet Jews can emigrate, etc., etc." The official admitted that there really were no standards by which a person's access to classified documents should bar that person from emigrating. And the official conceded that the Helsinki Accords meant that the Soviet Union had no right to charge $55 for every repeated application to emigrate. Although there were increased requests for visas, the Moscow visit did not give Drinan much hope for increased emigration. But he left Moscow for Bucharest inspired by the heroism of the city's 178 refuseniks, one of whom had given him a final desperate quote that the journalist Drinan could use several times: "In this nation I cannot be a good Russian and I cannot be a good Jew."

In Bucharest, Drinan spent almost two hours with Romania's chief rabbi, Moses Rosen, a man known for his cooperation with the government but who also had preserved for Jews some measure of religious freedom. The rabbi could not predict how many of the remaining 60,000 Jews in the country would leave for Israel, where Romanians were the largest ethnic group. But he was also concerned about freedom of worship for the 60,000 Jews in Hungary and the 8,000 to 10,000 in Czechoslovakia. Finally, what Drinan enjoyed most on the trip was the company of fifty Romanian Jews, young and old, on his plane, singing for joy, on the way to their new homes in Tel Aviv.

In Israel, Drinan was happy to hear from those in the Ministry of Finance that the bill he had filed in Congress "to eliminate the insidious effects of the Arab boycott" of Israel was considered the most promising. (He was referring to a suit by twenty-five House Democrats accusing two government departments of encouraging American companies to violate the 1965 Export Administration Act, which requires the United States to oppose restrictive trade practices against other countries friendly to the United States.) On a long drive he visited the Golan Heights, imagined what it must have looked like when Syria massed 1,200 tanks there before the October 1973 Arab–Israeli Yom Kippur war, and came away convinced that Israel must have defensible borders. Yet, of the scores of former Russians he met in Israel, the most moving, he said, was seventy-five-year-old Bertha Rashkovsky, mother-in-law of Vladimir Slepak, a Moscow dissident whose visa had been delayed for six years. She toured England and the United States, though she knew little English, speaking on behalf of Soviet Jews, and even convinced members of the British Parliament to send bar mitzvah greetings to her grandson.

Drinan punctuated his articles with constant negative judgments of the Soviet Union. He even uttered his sometimes belief "that Russia would do to its three million Jews what it did to the people of Czecho-slovakia in 1968." (At that time the USSR used Soviet tanks and 650,000 Warsaw Pact troops to crush a Czech "socialism with a human face" reform movement that had allowed a free press, an independent judiciary, and religious tolerance.) He nevertheless concluded his report with a maxim some erroneously attribute to St. Ignatius Loyola, "that we must work as if everything depended upon us and pray as if everything depended upon God."

Drinan told his *NCR* readers on October 2, 1975, "I would like to write that there are signs of hope for religious freedom in the USSR. I cannot. Some 500,000 Christian Baptists have a state-sponsored religious group. But some 100,000 Christian dissidents operate underground, with an estimated 300 of their activists in jail." Then he concluded, "Perhaps the Kremlin knows that American Christians, haunted by profound guilt at their silence during the holocaust, may be prepared now to heed the early warning signals which Soviet Jews are sending out to the world." The Leventmans, in their study of Drinan's relations with his Jewish constituents, concluded: "Here Drinan had finally joined the issue, the conversion of Christians back to oneness with their ancient Hebraic origins and a reawakening of responsibility for the welfare of their Jewish brethren. Drinan is fond of quoting Reinhold Niebuhr's observation, 'One cannot be a good Christian unless one is first a good Jew.'"

Drinan followed up his Soviet travels with the Second Brussels Conference on Soviet Jewry in late January 1976, notable for the participation of forty Christians. The Soviet Union's concern about the influence of the conference, he reported, prompted them to "plant" seven Soviet Jews in Israel, in order to have them return to Russia and proclaim at a press conference that they had made a mistake in leaving and that Russia was a much better place after all. Participants at the Brussels conference asked why Russia, now the home of one-fourth of all the Jews in the world, with its strong economy and 250,000,000 population, still insisted that its 3 million Jews, less than 1 percent of its population, could not emigrate to Israel. While in Brussels Drinan also met with Elie Wiesel, author of *Night*, perhaps the most-read Holocaust memoir, who volunteered just as Drinan was about to ask for his help in his coming reelection campaign. Wiesel was leaving New York for Boston and, in fact, would live in Drinan's district. Drinan quoted the closing address of Golda Meir, the former Israeli prime minister, who asked Russia, "The second greatest power in the world—what are you gaining from this policy?" She concluded, "We refuse to disappear. No matter how strong and brutal and ruthless the forces against us may be—here we are. Millions of bodies broken, buried alive, burned to death. But never has anyone been able to succeed in breaking the spirit of our people" (*Jewish Advocate,* February 2, 1976).

Reelection in the Bicentennial Year

In early 1975 Drinan read a squib in *Newsweek* that sent him through the roof. In the January 27 issue, the magazine maintained that "Jesuit activists like Daniel Berrigan, Massachusetts Congressman Robert Drinan, and former Nixon aide John McLaughlin have skirted the letter of Jesuit law. Others, like Joseph O'Rourke, who was expelled last year for performing a baptism forbidden by his superiors, have openly defied it." He called an editor and demanded a retraction. *Newsweek*, though, had a custom of never admitting to error; the only way to "correct" an allegation was to send a letter. Drinan offered a letter which included a demand that "*Newsweek* regrets its error." *Newsweek* offered a statement that its allegation had been based on the fact that his running had been the occasion for some controversy: "*Newsweek* did not allege that Father Drinan acted improperly or is acting improperly now." Drinan replied that to say he "skirted the Jesuit law" was unjust and untrue, a "calumny."

In retrospect it seems clear that, unlike Drinan, *Newsweek*'s editors did not know the distinction between Jesuit law and canon law. The press had covered the public surface of the story, in which the ecclesiastical authorities were obviously reluctant to have him in Congress and the Jesuit authorities in Rome were insistent that Drinan fulfill canon law by getting local ecclesiastical approval, but finally, through the provincial, the Society gave him strong backing. Drinan was not, in fact, skirting specifically Jesuit law, but he was—and this is not a pejorative term—finessing canon law, in which the bishops' failure to absolutely forbid his running in 1970 constituted legal permission to run and then to keep running. Drinan gave up on *Newsweek* and consoled himself by telling the story to his readers of the *NCR* (February 14), which would be the liberal priest's equivalent of letting off steam to his family.

Now, a year later, as he prepared to run his fourth campaign, he knew he would have to go through the whole split-level routine again—running against the political opponent he could see in the Fourth District and against unseen, but present in their letters, authorities in Rome and throughout the American Church who did not want him in Congress.

For the first time in four races he had only one opponent, Arthur Mason, a young (thirty-five) attorney from Brookline, a former Democrat who was associated with the Nixon administration as a member of Nixon aide and Watergate co-defendant Charles Colson's law firm; he had also served as Colson's attorney during his disbarment proceedings before the Virginia Supreme Court. Mason had graduated from Cornell University in 1963 and Boston College Law School in 1966 and served as a captain in the Army in Vietnam, where he had won a Silver Star. It was hard to escape the irony of a young man who had looked at Father Drinan as his teacher and dean for three years and was now determined to remove his former teacher and dean from the national scene.

Mason's theme: Congressman Drinan was the wrong man in the wrong place at the wrong time. "I am running for Congress," he announced, "because Robert Drinan is part of the problem. . . . The issues of 1976 do not involve the great moral questions but a series of difficult pragmatic choices [that] pose the common dilemma of having no right or wrong answers, no simple moral solutions." As he moved through the district introducing himself as a candidate, he emphasized what had long been a criticism of Drinan in Congress, that he was grabbing headlines on "moral issues" to the detriment of constituent interests such as jobs (*Globe*, April 26, 1976). Mason was also Jewish. He knew he could not question Drinan's support of Israel, but he identified America's defense policy with Israel's security and argued that because Drinan opposed many Pentagon policies, he put Israel's security at risk.

The Drinan camp had begun laying out its strategy in January, three months before. Fundraisers were to include a casino night at which celebrities would work the gambling tables and cash bar; a "sink the deficit" party on the waterfront with a nautical motif, with political celebrities like Bella Abzug and Elizabeth Holtzman; a performance by the Panovs, a Russian ballet couple who had emigrated to Israel; and smaller parties in private homes. As usual, the family was on board. Dr. Frank and Helen Drinan were donors and committee members, and nephew Tom Drinan, who had been a student at Boston College when his uncle was first running for office and had gone on to Suffolk University Law School, would conduct a "Stick Up for Drinan" day. Jerome Grossman and John Marttila were again active. A Hart Research Associates survey showed that Drinan's position was strong. Rating his job performance, as judged by religious groupings, 65 percent of Jews rated him excellent or good, 59 percent of Catholics and 37 percent of Protestants. Divided by economic groups, 53 percent of those making more than $15,000 judged him excellent or good, 49 percent making between $10,000 and $15,000 and 59 percent of those making under $10,000.

Again, because they did not employ television, a major element in the strategy was the clever, well-designed pamphlet. Because Mason portrayed himself as a hardworking pragmatist devoted to local issues, Drinan's brochures dropped the moral issues and stressed economics. A sixteen-page pamphlet gave seven two-page presentations on constituent letters thanking Congressman Drinan for his help; bills introduced to prime the economy; government reform, particularly stopping the FBI's surveillance of private citizens; health care; services for older Americans; tax reform; and energy, like the Solid Waste Energy and Resource Recovery Act. The health care page begins, "Talking to Drinan on the state of health care is hazardous to his health. The man's face turns red. Blood pressure rises to dangerous levels. You think maybe he should see a doctor.—But he'd have to pay for it himself. His insurance doesn't cover doctor's visits."

One of Mason's flyers referred to him as a hard worker, so the Drinan camp published an outsized brochure that opened, "It's eleven P.M. Do you know where your Congressman is?" This was followed by a photograph of Drinan, in clerics, toiling away in the glow of his desk lamp, papers piled high behind him.

"We hold these truths . . .": 1976

On July 4, 1976, the 200th anniversary of the signing of the Declaration of Independence, America was like a shipwrecked sailor washed ashore, not on a desert island but on the beach of a rich man's estate. It had been traumatized by the twin storms of Vietnam and Watergate, but it had survived. It was still shaken, but it was telling itself that the "system had worked," that the scandal had been an aberration, not due to a fundamental flaw in the American character. If President Ford's post-Nixon proclamation "Our long national nightmare is over" was literally so, the past decade had not really happened at all; it had just been a bad dream. On July 3, a warm, sunny day in the nation's capital, a crowd of 500,000 had cheered a parade of 10,000 marchers, 50 bands, and 60 marching units, led by Vice President Nelson Rockefeller and the singer Johnny Cash, while President Ford prepared for a city-hopping ordeal the next day by playing golf at Burning Tree Country Club in suburban Maryland.

"Political leadership has rarely been so undistinguished and so determined to proclaim its inferiority," wrote the columnist Joseph Kraft in the *Washington Post* on July 4. "'A Ford, not a Lincoln,' the president says of his own qualities. His two leading competitors, Ronald Reagan and Jimmy Carter, define themselves as simple men of common sense, untainted by experience [in], not to mention mastery over, national government." America, Kraft concluded, had pushed its egalitarianism too far. Fellow columnist David Broder called attention to two statues beneath the Capitol dome—those of Abraham Lincoln and Ulysses S.

Grant: "What a fine reminder, in this time of national back-patting, that just as our people and our politics are fully capable of producing men of sublime genius and saintly character, so also they produce men of surpassing mediocrity and moral obtuseness. And both kinds become President." Nevertheless, "The American people showed that once they had the facts, they were prepared to render a judgment against a Chief Executive who had overstepped the bounds of his power and forced him to yield the office that they had but recently and by large majority entrusted to him."

In New York, as hundreds of thousands of people lined the shorelines, 52 warships from 21 nations cruised under the Verrazano-Narrows Bridge up into the harbor at the mouth of the Hudson River, followed by 250 tall-masted sailing vessels, under 30 flags, some constructed in the nineteenth century. As the day progressed, an estimated 5 to 7 million people swarmed into historic lower Manhattan, where George Washington was inaugurated and where he prayed in St. Paul's Chapel and where Alexander Hamilton is buried in the Trinity Church graveyard. President Ford flew to Philadelphia for a ceremony at Independence Hall, then to Valley Forge, where 200 wagons from five separate wagon trains had crossed 17,000 miles of the country to convene and celebrate. Then the president landed on the deck of the *USS Forrestal* to watch the tall ships, surrounded by scores of small boats, move majestically up the Hudson.

The *New York Times* editorial said, "The words of the Declaration, ever renewed, take on pointed significance when we apply them to the realities of the present age, to the gaping holes and strident deficiencies in our society, to the injustices and inequities that still exist and in some cases are even intensifying, to the erosion and the corrosion of public life and private standards of morality." The *Boston Globe* editorial asked whether the King George whom the Declaration overthrew had been replaced by corporate America, the federal judiciary, or the "imperial presidency": "The truths once supposed to be self-evident are being challenged to prove themselves as social classes, races and sexes battle each other for equal standing in a manifestly unequal society."

Where was Congressman Drinan as Boston celebrated? He and his brother, Frank, were at historic Faneuil Hall, where Samuel Adams in revolutionary fervor had proclaimed James Otis's phrase "Taxation without representation is tyranny," to give the main address at a conference sponsored by a Jewish group. He spoke of the similarities between America's beginning and the Jewish colonists in Israel.

As the election campaign moved into October, the press described the tone as getting tougher, repeating the observation that Drinan's problem was not recognition but polarization. Voters either loved him or hated him. Mason, campaigning in a Framingham neighborhood club after a Newton debate, met a registered Democratic roofing contractor at the bar who hated Drinan with a passion because, he said, priests and politics don't mix. A gym teacher seated a few stools away had voted for Drinan before, but not this time, because of the slipping economy, which, according to Mason, Drinan had not done enough to save. The national Republican Party had marked Drinan as one they would most like to beat (*Globe*, October 11, 1976). Mason also hoped to attract voters who had sent Drinan to Congress to oppose the war but did not expect that, as a priest, he would hang on. Mason, because he had a more quiet delivery but knew how to raise his voice, while Drinan talked too loudly and fast and droned on, pressed for more debates.

But the vast majority of people who met Drinan in small groups liked him, and, in spite of Mason's charges, he had a good record of dealing with constituent problems. When the Defense Department decided to close the local Army base, Fort Devens, Mason pushed that as a sign that Drinan's "anti-military" policies were responsible; but the Drinan camp responded with a four-page brochure documenting Drinan's efforts, based on legal research on a similar case in Kentucky and backed by Tip O'Neill and the Massachusetts congressional delegation, to require a comprehensive economic-impact study, measuring the anticipated effects on the community before closing the fort.

As the end approached, the Drinan camp hoped for a big win. By October 18 Mason had spent $108,744 to Drinan's $88, 537. If that trend held, this would be Drinan's cheapest campaign. Mason was

backed by several notable Republicans: then–Commerce Secretary Elliot Richardson, one of the heroes of the Saturday Night Massacre;
Massachusetts Senator Edward W. Brooke; and New York Senator
Jacob Javits. Drinan had Holtzman, Peter Rodino, and Elie Wiesel, who
spoke at a fundraiser. The clincher would be the *Globe* endorsement
on October 24: "It is perverse to argue, as his opponent does, because
the Vietnam War is over and Richard Nixon is gone, that Drinan has
passed his prime. The argument suggests this country will never again
face a moral crisis, that all we need is the nuts and bolts service of
chasing down federal jobs."

But What About Rome?

Was Drinan an obedient priest? This issue was passed over during the
Bicentennial—in Boston. But in January 1976 as the campaign committee planned the fundraisers, the leaflets, and the platform, Drinan
knew that shortly after the 1974 election, Father General Arrupe had
written to him and told him not to run again. On August 29, 1975,
Arrupe wrote to Father Robert Mitchell, president of the American
Jesuit Conference, annoyed that Drinan had not answered his letter
and calling upon either Mitchell or the New England provincial, Richard T. Cleary, to settle this matter soon. Arrupe had been strengthened
in his decision by consultation with prudent American churchmen like
Cardinal Joseph Bernardin of Chicago, Cardinal John Krol of Philadelphia, papal envoy Archbishop Jean Jadot, and Monsignor George Higgins, a most highly respected progressive social action priest and
writer. Arrupe had become convinced that the Society was doing harm
by allowing Drinan to remain in office.

Prompted by Cleary, Drinan finally replied to Arrupe's original letter with a four-page defense of his apostolate, listing the Catholic universities that showed their support for him with honorary degrees, a
Red Mass here, an address to a convention of Catholic educators there,
his work on the visiting committee at Harvard Divinity School and his
trusteeship with Bread for the World, as well as his popularity with
Jewish groups. He did not "compromise" his principles, he said; he

voted his conscience. He advocated the reforms of the U.S. Catholic Conference on immigration and amnesty.

He argued that removing him would interfere with other priests and nuns who run for office. His clincher: "I am more influential in a moral and spiritual way now than I was during the dozen years that I was Dean of Boston College Law School." He argued, as would Cleary, that the general owed Drinan his reasons for removing him. To withdraw the permissions he had always had without convincing reasons "will bring scandal to the Church and to the Society." Not a word on abortion.

Cleary replied to Arrupe on September 27, 1975, that, first of all, Drinan's failure to respond had been based on a misunderstanding; he had been led to believe that the question would be handled by Cleary. And Cleary did handle it with a forthright and powerful, though respectful, argument that Arrupe was wrong. Drinan, he said, had a position of moral influence on "faith and justice," emphasized by the recent Congregation of the Society of Jesus, "superior to that which most other Jesuits can attain." Cleary would accept Arrupe's decision, "even though it will be one I shall not be happy to execute." But he also suggested that, according to No. 80 of "Our Mission Today" from the Congregation, it was left to the provincial to "give or refuse the permission" concerning political office. In short, he was saying that the general may have been exceeding his authority. Also, Arrupe, he said, should give Drinan in detail the reasons for his decision—something Arrupe had not yet done even with Cleary. Cleary concluded that he intended no disrespect, but that "such honest communication is essential among brothers in the Society, all in the context of the obedience which we have vowed."

In January 1976 Drinan met an old Jesuit friend on the Georgetown campus, and rather than just blurt hello and keep running, which was his usual manner, he paused to chat. They sat on a bench and Drinan said how happy he was with the way things were going. Was he under pressure from Rome? "None at all." All the storms had blown over, he insisted. The friend knew better. The friend, who had experience as a religious superior and was well informed about what went on between the United States and Rome, was among those who fully expected a letter to arrive any moment shattering Drinan's illusions about the "storm" over him having subsided. Was Drinan just in denial? The friend, foreseeing a crisis, suggested that Drinan find himself a spiritual adviser, or a Jesuit friend to whom he could talk about spiritual things. Drinan was not turned off by the suggestion.

Six months passed, and Arrupe wrote Cleary that he would not insist on the implementation of his November 1974 letter to Drinan at Georgetown. But he could not offer positive encouragement. He asked Cleary to find a convenient way to have Drinan withdraw, but he left the timing to Cleary. He was not judging Drinan's record, which, he'd heard, is "generally good." He just didn't think priests should hold elective office.

As a follow-up to the correspondence with the general and also to the literally hundreds of letters he had received from Catholics who could not understand how a priest could be "pro-abortion," Cleary had a long talk with Drinan, who, in response, drew up a twelve-page report on what he had written and said about abortion from 1959 to 1976. This convinced Cleary and other leading Jesuits that Drinan was sincerely opposed to abortion on moral grounds but opposed, for various practical and constitutional reasons, to an attempt to re-criminalize it or amend the Constitution to ban it.

The twelve-page report to the provincial, dated May 20, 1976, contains few surprises. Above all Drinan insisted that his position over seventeen years had been consistent. At the end, he summarized his points: (1) He accepted Vatican II on abortion. (2) *Roe* was a result of profound movements against abortion laws. (3) Anti-abortion amendments to the Constitution won't work. (4) Opponents of abortion should rely on education rather than law. (5) Abortion should be viewed in perspective with other global problems.

One novelty was his statement that the answer be in educating physicians and other health care professionals on the evils of abortion—an idea he never promoted in his public life. Relevant today is his citation of a January 2, 1976, *Commonweal* editorial on the hierarchy's position. "In staking their prestige on the abortion issue . . . and overestimating their influence with their constituents—[they] have promised a vote they can't deliver." The bishops "had been had. . . . With shepherds like this, is it any wonder their flocks have wandered away?"

Central to his thinking, he said, was his argument that the Model Penal Code, by outlawing abortion but allowing hard-case exceptions, thereby made the law responsible for the deaths of the hard-case fetuses; *therefore,* according to Drinan, there should be no legal limits on abortion. It should be pointed out here that all the leading moral theologians rejected that argument at the meeting sponsored by the Kennedys when Drinan was still dean of Boston College Law School. Drinan seemed to overlook the fact that the purpose of the Code's formula was to protect that vast majority of the fetuses who would be destroyed simply because, under abortion by request, they would be considered an inconvenience to the mother. Drinan was a lawyer, not a moral theologian, and his logic, though consistent, seems strange.

Why did Arrupe, who obviously felt strongly that Drinan did not belong in Congress, repeatedly give in when his decisions were challenged? Most likely it was because Arrupe was a holy and humble man who was moved by the rational arguments of men whom he had appointed to high positions and was thus obliged to take their advice seriously. This was especially so when one of Drinan's defenders was Father Vincent O'Keefe. Arrupe was contemplating resigning from what had always been a lifetime position, and O'Keefe was a most likely successor. And, on a larger map, something else was going on. A bottom-up theology was taking hold in the grassroots. Americans, for the time being, at least, were saying they wanted *this* priest to lead them, and it would not be wise to silence them.

In an October 30 *America* article, timed to appear right before election day, "Governor Carter's Commitment to Christian Concerns," Drinan, though originally a supporter of Congressman Morris K. Udall of Arizona for the Democratic presidential nomination, wrote that he and Jimmy Carter shared the same moral reasons that brought him to Congress and the spiritual concerns that Catholics have for the morality of the nation. By "moral issues" he meant the social and political issues about which the American bishops had expressed their concerns. These started with the dangers of a nuclear holocaust and extended to the world economy, freedom of the seas, environmental quality, food supply and safety, population, and the reduction of world armaments. "We cannot have it both ways," said Carter. "Can we be both the world's leading champion of peace and the world's leading supplier of the weapons of war?" Yet, Drinan suggested, there might be a contradiction in Carter's support for the "new Trident submarine, capable, with its missiles, of destroying any nation on earth." And, as he saw it, neither Ford nor Carter was clear on the possible nuclear first strike with nuclear weapons strategic or tactical.

Unlike Ford, Drinan continued, Carter saw the government as an instrument to help the poor and the victimized. While Ford saw taxes as a means to stimulate capital formation, Carter would use them to more equitably distribute the financial burden. The U.S. Catholic Conference positions on gun control, tax reform, food, health, and the arms race were much closer to Carter's than to Ford's. Drinan concluded the article by urging readers to vote on the "ultimate issue"—the arms race—which is "impoverishing the underdeveloped nations and threatening the entire universe with a war of incalculable tragedy."

Ironically, these international issues, which Drinan saw as paramount when he addressed a national readership, were not the ones he stressed in his own campaign. Sensitive to his opponent's characterization of him as someone more concerned with lofty moral issues than with the bread-and-butter concerns of his constituents, he tailored his message to their needs. He knew what he was doing. He won his first one-on-one race 109,238 to 100,562, with 52 percent of the vote to Mason's 48 percent. Today, Mason, a Washington lawyer, remembers Drinan as a good teacher and a man of integrity.

At the Newton victory celebration on November 2, Drinan returned to the motif of the moral issues that the people must resolve. He spoke of the "bond of love" that had brought so many hundreds of his followers there that night, a bond that "descends profoundly into the transcendental and spiritual hunger of the soul of man." He recalled the themes of the Bicentennial, America's "uniqueness," and the American dream. He quoted Carter, Franklin Roosevelt, Eisenhower, and Wiesel and told his audience that the next day he would fly to Argentina, as a representative of Amnesty International, to investigate the religious and political oppression in the nation ruled since March by a military *junta*.

12 Latin America, Israel, and the Last Campaign

Drinan's expedition to Argentina was in the tradition of his 1969 flight with an investigating committee to Vietnam—a team of concerned human rights activists, this time representing Amnesty International, who wanted to talk to presidents and prisoners, visit scenes of alleged crimes, and question the victims as well as those responsible. They wished to alert the larger world to a local crime that demanded global attention.

It was also a foreshadowing of a major direction his life and career were about to take. What he learned in Argentina he would reinforce the next year in El Salvador, and the following year in South Africa and Southeast Asia again, and finally a return to El Salvador and other countries in Central America during what would become his last year in office. But the combined impact of all these experiences would transform him into one of America's leading apostles for human rights, both in and out of office.

The situation in Argentina at the beginning of what was called "the dirty war" was in some ways more difficult than that in Vietnam. In Saigon the government was a U.S. client, under pressure to treat the investigators cordially. But in Argentina their host was a military *junta* that had seized the presidency from the widow of Juan Perón only the previous year and acted in absolute secrecy. The remote origin of this crisis period, which lasted from 1976 to 1983, was the return in 1973 of former army officer and president Juan Perón from his eighteen-year exile in Spain, after having been driven from office in a coup in 1955. Though reelected to the presidency, he died in 1974, to be succeeded by his third wife, the former dancer Isabel Martinez de Perón. Her inability to govern led to her removal and replacement by the military government of Jorge Rafael Videla in a year.

Although state-sponsored violence, including assassinations, had been a control tactic since 1973, during the *junta*'s dictatorship from 1976 to 1983, called the "National Reorganization Process," all basic civil rights were revoked and up to 30,000 people "disappeared." In the government's estimation, a "civil war" was going on and extraordinary methods—including the suspension of political parties, kidnapping, arrest, long imprisonment without being charged, the imposition of military tribunals, torture, murder, and the denial of civilian attorneys—were required to deal with subversives, "Communists," and guerrilla activity.

To an extent the military modeled its campaign on the Battle of Algiers, in which the French colonial army, from 1954 to 1962, divided Algiers into zones and systematically tortured captives in order to wipe out the infrastructure of the rebels. Meanwhile, in Argentina, both right and left political factions were divided among themselves. Extreme right-wing groups, which included reserve officers and pro-Nazis among their leaders, had heavily armed death squads that enjoyed immunity from police interference. They considered the government too moderate and opposed its diplomatic relations with the Soviet Union and Cuba. According to the *New York Times* of November 27, 1976, Videla had authorized the visit of Drinan's Amnesty International group with the hope that it might issue a moderate report dealing with both the repressive excesses against the people and the subversive violence that had caused 1,300 deaths that year.

The Amnesty delegates were Lord Avebury, a member of the British House of Lords and of the Human Rights Commission; Father Robert Drinan; and Patricia Feeney, a British member of the International Secretariat of Amnesty International. They were to investigate the identities and number of political prisoners, allegations of torture, the alleged complicity of police and military in illegal and violent abductions, and the nature and effects of legislation enacted since the coup. During their stay, November 6–15, they failed to get an interview with President Videla but did talk with nine members of the government, from the offices of foreign affairs, justice, and the interior. At least twenty plainclothes policemen followed them everywhere and questioned, intimidated, and in some cases detained a number of people with whom the committee met. The police often declined to identify themselves and pursued the committee, armed, in their Ford Falcons around the city. The final report supplemented its immediate discoveries from government and private individuals with previous testimonies from prisoners and the relatives of missing persons.

According to the *Report of the Amnesty International Mission to Argentina*, the death squads were financed by the Ministry of Social Welfare and responsible for a large proportion of the 1,500 assassinations which occurred in the 18-month period following Perón's death. The left-wing organizations, developed during the military governments from 1966 to 1973, were responsible for ten incidents in 1976, mostly bombings, that killed 48 and injured more than 100. The right-wing extremists in 1974 alone were responsible for 300 murders and in the last quarter of 1976 were responsible for 15 abductions a day.

The *Report* described the State of Siege, declared in 1974, which allowed the temporary suspension of the constitution in a period of internal unrest or external aggression but which, in this case, had disregarded the constitutional restrictions on its powers. Other decrees changed a minor breach of the peace into a major federal crime; set up military "summary" courts with no civilian lawyers for any offense related to "subversion"; imposed the death penalty for anyone who killed or injured a member of a security force; declared forty-eight organizations illegal; and authorized firing squad execution within forty-eight hours of conviction, five- to twelve-year sentences for "illicit associations," "summary pre-trial" arrest for anyone subject to "strong suspicions or half-conclusive proofs of guilt," and ten-year sentences for anyone who divulged news that lessened the prestige of the armed forces.

The authorities refused to reveal the names or the number of the imprisoned, but the committee's other sources estimated at least 4,610 held in four prisons in preventive detention by executive decree. Amnesty further believed that, at the time of writing, January 1977, there were between 5,000 and 6,000 political prisoners, two-thirds of whom had not been charged but were being detained indefinitely. The request to interview twenty-six prisoners was refused, and permission was granted to visit only one prison. Lord Avebury went to Villa Devoto and was struck by stories of maltreatment and torture.

However, most of the information on torture and prisons came from statements of former prisoners. For example, a twenty-six-year-old farm laborer, being transferred to another prison, was grabbed by a guard in the middle of a physical exam and dragged naked into the courtyard where ten employees beat him all the way to his cell. There they kicked his teeth out, dragged him out naked, and beat him again. Another reported being stretched out on the floor naked and kicked, beaten, and questioned about trade unions and political parties. One was stabbed in the kidney by a bayonet. Another's entire body was covered with bruises; several times a day and during the night, the guards amused themselves by running the points of their blades in his wounds. The more systematic torture included electric shocks to all parts of the body; cigarette burns; withholding of food, drink, and sleep; being plunged into ice-cold baths; hooding (using large hoods to blindfold prisoners); and, for the women, rape and being beaten into miscarriages. Carlos Baros, a member of the Communist Party Youth Federation and a doctor, described how he was abducted, stripped, tortured for hours by electrical prods on his testicles, thorax, mouth, and other body parts, then pitched into a barrel of water while hanging from his legs, four or five times, until he lost consciousness. Then again he was tortured with the electric prods.

As with other statistics, the government and Amnesty disagreed on the evidence of the "disappeared." Amnesty said the most frequently quoted figure was 15,000 and concluded that the problem was getting worse, while between May and August 1976 the government was receiving, it said, ten complaints a day. As reports mounted, the government put a cap on reports at forty per day. According to the official line, the "missing" had gone "underground," emigrated, or been killed in clashes with the security forces. One recent disappearance, according to the *New York Times*, was that of a twenty-five-year-old student of architecture, Josefa Martinez Cordoba, not long after she had met with Drinan, and later with Amnesty International.

The fifty-page, single-spaced *Report* concluded that "there is overwhelming evidence that many innocent citizens have been imprisoned without trial, have been tortured and have been killed. The actions taken against subversives have therefore been self-defeating: in order to restore security, an atmosphere of terror has been established; in order to counter illegal violence, legal safeguards have been removed and violent illegalities condoned." Amnesty submitted eight recommendations to the Argentine government in February 1977. The first was to invite the United Nations to send a mission to investigate the situation of human rights in Argentina at an early opportunity. The others included: protect refugees, publish a prisoner list, punish the armed groups of murderers, implement the UN rules against torture, and end the State of Siege.

But the military rule continued, introducing the new brutality of executing "enemies" by taking them in helicopters out over the ocean and tossing them out the door. In 1982 the *junta*, in a desperate move to rally patriotic support, invaded the nearby Falkland Islands, a territory of the United Kingdom that the Argentines historically had claimed sovereignty over and called Malvinas. The British declared war and humiliated them. The *junta* was replaced by the moderate Raúl Alfonsín, who to some degree prosecuted those responsible. President Videla was sentenced to life in a military prison, later moved to house arrest. Citizens painted enormous arrows on the street pointing to his house with a sign: "30,000 disappeared: Assassin on the loose."

Argentina's Jews

Drinan personalized the visit by seeking out Jews about whom he could report to his Jewish constituents at home. The State Department and the American Jewish Committee convinced a reluctant prominent Jewish journalist to allow Drinan to visit while remaining anonymous. So he headed out on a rainy morning. Determined to shake off the six police guards, he hustled up a one-way street where they couldn't drive their Falcons, ducked into a subway station, and emerged two blocks away, where he grabbed a cab—only to see the Falcons right behind him again.

The Falcons didn't bother his host, "Michael," because he suspected that every conversation in his office was already being recorded. Michael, in discussion with Drinan, maintained that the level of anti-Semitism had really not increased since Videla had taken over. Michael did not want the world to think that anti-Semitism in Argentina was on the rise. If that happened, he said, the authorities would begin to blame their economic problems on the Jews. The oppressive tendencies of the government, he said, were not due to anti-Semitism but to the government's paranoia. When Michael's nineteen-year-old son, "David," entered the conversation, the father suggested that the son not be "on record" with his opinions.

Drinan left the meeting perplexed. He had been steered away from what he saw as the problems of the 400,000-member Argentine Jewish community. That evening he visited an Argentine Jewish industrialist who, like "Michael," did not want anti-Semitism mentioned in an article. Political repression, he said, was necessary in order to curb left-wing guerrillas. Drinan left convinced that "Anti-Semitism in Argentina is not blatant; it is insidious." The greatest danger, he concluded, "is silence."

In a December 2, 1976, paper that is either a talk or the draft of an article on the Jewish community and the Argentine *junta*, Drinan wrote he could sense in Argentina that since the *junta* took control anti-Semitic activity had increased. Proof, he said, was the record availability of anti-Semitic literature available in the kiosks in Buenos Aires. Drinan favorably cited the Buenos Aires daily, *La Prensa*, which called for shutting down the publishers of the anti-Semitic literature, just as Germany had recently forbidden pro-Nazi literature "for moral reasons." Indeed, the military government of Argentina had issued a decree banning anti-Semitic books as not compatible with Argentine values. He left Argentina, he said, convinced that anti-Semitism was worse there than the Argentine Jews realized.

On November 13, 1976, Josefa Martinez Cordoba visited the Amnesty group and talked about her experiences. The next day she disappeared. Drinan had missed the Amnesty meeting, but he felt responsible for Josefa. He badgered the U.S. Embassy and the Papal Nuncio, but there was no information until December 15, when she was released. Monica Mignone, a schoolteacher in a poor neighborhood, daughter of Dr. Emilio Mignone, former commissioner of education, was kidnapped by four military men in May 1976. When Drinan left she was still missing.

One well-informed citizen told Drinan that in his opinion there "is not one courageous person in all of Argentina." On July 4, 1976, three priests and two seminarians were murdered. The government could discover the murderers if they wished, Drinan was told, but they would prefer to have the assassinations "out there" in order to intimidate the Church. Drinan concluded his *Commonweal* report (February 18, 1977) with the judgment about the disappearances of Josefa and Mignone. This treatment, of course, could not be morally justified. But he had to quote the bishops of Brazil (November 18, 1976) for a Church statement to support his side. This kind of anti-Communism "is sacrificing freedom, suppressing individual guarantees and leading to state abuses, arbitrary punishments, torture and the loss of freedom of thought."

The Middle East

On August 4, 1970, as Drinan was in the home stretch in his first congressional race, Senator J. William Fulbright of Arkansas, chair of the Senate Foreign Relations Committee, addressed the Senate, in a speech that was considered a key document of the 1970s, on what he called the "Old Myths and New Realities in the Middle East." He argued that some of the operative myths were roadblocks to reconciliation and peace. One such myth, Fulbright said, was the religious myth of the land being "holy." Jerusalem has the Wall of the Temple and the Dome of the Rock. As in the days of the Crusades, he said, religion can exaggerate an issue and beliefs can smother the humane ethics of each religion.

Then, Fulbright said, there were the myths of mutual victimization. Jews fear a repeat of the Holocaust and Arabs indulge in extravagant talk about "holy wars" and driving the Jews into the sea. Israel saw itself as insecure, exaggerated its vulnerability, yet possessed military superiority. "The status of the Palestinians and the question of the occupied territories are the critical issues for peace in the Middle East," said Fulbright. Just as Israel feared being surrounded by Arab states, the Arabs feared that there were no bounds to Israel's territorial aspirations. Fulbright proposed a double initiative to bring peace and stability to the Middle East: Both the United Nations and, independently, after that, the United States, would guarantee Israel's security, following a settlement according to UN Resolution 242, which required that Israel return to its pre-1967 boundaries, as required by international law. The United States, Great Britain, the Soviet Union, and France, as permanent members of the UN Security Council, would have major responsibility for enforcing the peace terms. Plus, the United States by treaty would guarantee Israel's security within those borders.

Fulbright's idea set the tone for many subsequent discussions on the Middle East, but there is little evidence that Drinan shared his views. Drinan placed in the March 5, 1975, *Congressional Record* what he described as an "exceptionally perceptive article" about Israel. It was a long editorial from the *New Republic* that argued against the utility of "guarantees," emphasized Israel's smallness and vulnerability, and barely mentioned any claims of the Palestinians who had been deprived of their property.

Why Israel?

Drinan's dedication to Israel and to the Jewish people was genuine and profound, yet its roots are obscure. Again, because he declined to talk about his early life, it is difficult to pinpoint, say, an early Jewish friend or school experience that might have provided the roots for his later dedication. The easy "political" answer proposed by many is that his devotion was pragmatic, because Jews were strong among his congressional constituents. It is also true, however, that he and his brother, Frank, were raised in a family atmosphere free of prejudice, open to fellowship with Jews and black people from the beginning. During his fifteen years as a young priest and dean, Drinan was especially friendly with Jews, speaking in synagogues and hiring them as law professors, before he decided to run for office. As a Boston College undergraduate he was exposed to a culture that offered glimpses of anti-Semitism; if he was struck by that and rebelled against it, he did not tell us. The only article concerning Jews in the small Weston seminary journal that Drinan co-edited argued for their conversion. And the atmosphere at Georgetown Law School in the early days was overwhelmingly Catholic.

James Malley, S.J., who was a lawyer when he entered the Society in 1957 and who later worked as a chaplain at Georgetown Law, is convinced that Drinan's affinity for Jews was consistent with his feelings about black people and anyone who had been the victim of injustice. Malley believes that Drinan was reacting strongly to the anti-Semitism he witnessed growing up in Boston. He was convinced that the purpose of the law was to protect the rights of the underdog. Though he appeared cerebral, Drinan, he said, acted from his "gut," his heart. In the same line of thought, Jerome Grossman saw Drinan's commitment to his Jewish brethren as coming from his "ecumenism." Again, the moment of his first ecumenical insight is unrecorded, but it is reasonable to suggest that his teacher Bill Leonard may have had something to do with it, beginning with his student days. Furthermore, his human rights expeditions to Vietnam and Latin America were ecumenical, not specifically Catholic, ventures.

Another word might help to explain Drinan's devotion to Israel—"love." Besides being moved by the most basic Christian virtue, it is clear in his writings that Drinan, who as a celibate priest had no immediate family of his own, gained emotional satisfaction both from working with his younger staff and in serving groups whom he perceived as vulnerable. His Jewish constituency gave him loyalty and devotion, and he reciprocated.

Nevertheless, Drinan had a complex and highly compartmentalized mind. His strong emotional commitment to one downtrodden group, in the judgment of admirers who supported his other politics, did not always carry over to a neighboring group. When he published "An Open Letter to the Pope on Israel" in the *NCR* of July 20, 1973, asking why the Holy See had not officially recognized Israel and calling for the pope to back the emigration of Soviet Jews to Israel, two readers responded, one on August 17 and the other on August 31. The latter, Simon Smith, from Brighton, Massachusetts, had just returned from Israel, Lebanon, Syria, Jordan, and Egypt. His contacts were the "little people"—workers, local clergy, refugees—in those countries. He listed what he considered the brutal effects of Israel's expansion beyond its borders. He concluded, "I would have expected a man of your legal background, theological training and current national responsibility to have displayed more awareness of the complexity of the issues, particularly since your voting record on Third World issues so far has demonstrated admirable integrity and sensitivity to complex issues."

Drinan's book *Honor the Promise: America's Commitment to Israel* (1977) is many things: a condensed history of the relationship between Christians and Jews; an analysis, from one point of view, of American foreign policy in the Middle East; a fervid sermon—some would say a *fervorino*—on America's moral obligation, particularly Christian America's obligation, to commit itself to Israel's well-being, no matter what the cost to America. He summed the history up this way:

> It has been the central thesis of this volume that America's commitment to Israel cannot and will not be kept unless Christians, contrite over the unbelievable sins of Christians through the centuries against Jews, recognize that the Christians of this generation—especially in America—are called upon by their religion and by their government to undertake whatever extraordinary remedies might be necessary to protect Israel, a nation made necessary by the holocaust acquiesced in by most of the world's Christians.

It is difficult to read a 1977 book on the Middle East in the present day with the more recent history of that sad land still fresh: the two invasions of Lebanon, the building of the Wall, the Israeli withdrawal from Gaza, the checkpoints, the separate highway system, and the retaliatory war on Gaza killing at least 1,500 persons. Drinan was responding to what he saw as a critical situation for Israel: The Soviet Union was arming the Arab nations. The United States was aiding

Israel but not, in his judgment, enough. The Arabs had a chokehold on the West by virtue of their ability to control the flow of oil—America didn't want to offend the Arab world and lose its oil source. But, because of Christian guilt over anti-Semitism, America, perceived by many to be a Christian nation, *owes allegiance to Israel no matter what.* Rhetorically, Drinan entitled some chapters as questions: "Can Christianity and Judaism Coexist in Peace?" "Can Zionism Be the Basis of a Modern State?" "Does Arab Hostility to Israel Derive Ultimately from the Moslem Religion?"

His writing method, according to those who witnessed it, was to dictate material from his head or from a particular book that he would cite in the text; but there is no bibliography, no footnotes, no way of tracing many quotations to their sources. His chapter on whether the Church resisted the Holocaust during World War II resembled the convoluted logic of some of his abortion articles in the 1960s, where he presented what might have been controversial ideas by attributing them to others or expressing a proposition in a double negative rather than affirming it: "There are also not a few observers who wonder whether the militarism which was indispensable in 1947 and 1948 has engendered attitudes in Israel which may tend to exaggerate the indispensability of military force as a weapon of survival" (87).

He relied heavily on Gordon C. Zahn's *German Catholics and Hitler's Wars* (1962) and Guenther Lewy's *The Catholic Church and Nazi Germany* (1964) and concluded that "the silence of Catholic bishops in Germany was reprehensible." But he left us with the impression that Pope Pius XII might have done all he could to help the Jews, or might have done more than previous popes. But he didn't do enough for Israel after the war.

There's a chapter on the Palestinians; however, the reader does not get the message that the Palestinians are victims of an injustice, that the refugee problem is the fundamental burning issue in the Middle East that explains why Arabs states do not respect America, or that Israel is obliged under international law to retreat from land it acquired in war.

In two passages in the book (pp. 167 and 175) Drinan speculated that if Israel didn't get enough military aid from the United States, it might be inclined to develop nuclear weapons to give itself a feeling of security against the Arabs encircling it. He said, in his roundabout way, that Americans might view this with horror, but if it came to pass it would be America's fault for not giving Israel enough arms. The Drinan who wrote *Vietnam and Armageddon* strongly criticized the American bishops for not absolutely condemning *any* use of these terrible weapons. Yet he declined to condemn Israel for adding them to its arsenal. Before publication he had offered the manuscript to the Israel lobby American Israel Public Affairs Committee (AIPAC) for review. The AIPAC editor praised the manuscript but asked that any reference to Israel's development of nuclear weapons be removed. In the edited manuscript those passages are crossed out. But nevertheless Drinan left them in the book. It is ironic that he referred to Israel's nukes as a mere future possibility. Did he not know by 1977 that during the Yom Kippur War in 1973 Israeli fighter-bombers armed with nuclear warheads were on the alert, ready to be called into battle?

Reviews, mostly in religious opinion magazines, many of which published his articles, were generally supportive. In *America* (September 9, 1978), Donald Herzberg wrote, "A difficult book, yes. But to ignore Drinan's challenge is to invite disaster—disaster not only for Israel, but for all that America has stood for." In *Commonweal* (July 21, 1978), Wilson Carey McWilliams observed that "For Drinan, Israel is intimately bound up with Western culture and religious life, so that our attitudes toward Israel are a reflection of our spiritual health." In the politically conservative Jewish journal *Commentary* (January 1978), Michael Ledeen wrote, "There are moments when one has the sensation of reading a latter-day Theodor Herzl." (Herzl, a Zionist [1860–1904], was considered one of the inspirational founders of Israel.) In *Christian Century* (October 18, 1978), John C. Raines said, "The modern state of Israel is for [Drinan] God's 'answer' to the Holocaust, a visible sign of continuing faithfulness to God's chosen people." *Library Journal* (November 15, 1977) dissented: "Rather than a thoughtful, research examination of the topic, this book is merely propaganda. Based almost exclusively on pro-Israeli works, it repeats uncritically the pro-Israel 'line,' its material being selected and skewed to conform to it, its aim to arouse emotions, not inform."

278 | LATIN AMERICA, ISRAEL, AND THE LAST CAMPAIGN

Frank

Robert Drinan was on one level simple, obvious, out front. He projected a strong public persona that was drummed out, recycled, proclaimed, and repeated both in person and in the various media—speeches in school halls and synagogue meeting rooms; testimony in Congress and insertions into the *Congressional Record*; interviews and articles in the Catholic, Jewish, and Protestant press; op-eds in the *Globe* and letters to the editor of the *New York Times*. Wiretapping is wrong. Israel is right. Abortion is wrong, but it must be legal.

Yet his personality was complex, erratic, sometimes explosive, with moods ranging from infinite kindness to peevish anger. How he behaved often depended on where he was and whom he was with. The Jesuit communities knew him, with some caricature allowed, as the man who ate his meals standing up. Always on the move. No time to sit and talk. A minority disapproved of his politics, and, though Jesuits in general are collectively more liberal than other clerics, many would part ways with him on abortion. Some found him dogmatic, but Jim Malley describes him as always generous with Jesuits, including those who did not agree with his positions. But Malley and Drinan were not close friends. Drinan was a workaholic without time for close friendships, says Malley.

But the Bob Drinan who, on his working weekends in Newton or especially on holidays like Christmas and Thanksgiving, drove out of St. Mary's Hall, down to Beacon Street, west toward Newton center and then left on Lake Street and right along Crystal Lake—at most a ten-minute trip—to his brother Frank's house was someone else. Here he was a different man. Sometimes he would bring some Jesuit friends for Thanksgiving dinner. Off came the omnipresent clerical collar and old black suit. On with the sports clothes. With his brother, Frank, and sister-in-law, Helen, surrounded by his three nieces and a nephew, and sometimes with his sister, Catherine, visiting from Germany, his humor, playfulness, and affection let loose. When the children were small he would wrestle with them on the floor and join them in crawling under the dining room table.

Frank's was a large brick house from the 1920s, on an urban lake in Newton, that still had the remnants of a buzzer system connected to what used to be the servants' rooms upstairs; and Drinan, either playful or clumsy, would deliberately or accidentally step on the buzzer under the table. The family shared his intellectual interests and political life as well. Frank and Helen joined a theology discussion group at their Sacred Heart Parish, along with the pastor, Father John Connelly, and several other couples. All the family at one time or another helped in the campaigns. The oldest niece, Ann, then twenty, worked in the 1970 campaign and took off from college at the University of Wisconsin to work again for her uncle in 1972.

After graduation from Boston College in 1940 and Tufts University School of Medicine in 1943, Frank joined the Army and was sent at the end of the war to Japan, where, as a captain in the Medical Corps, he was responsible for the health care of a large area. While there he wrote to Helen every day; but, when he returned, for some reason he never talked about his experience in Japan. He even stopped eating rice. But Bob mentioned his brother's experience in Japan as a credential, proof that he knew that life there was hard, when he volunteered to be a missionary there during his studies at Weston. Frank told his family he was proud that during his time in the service he never fired a gun.

Back home, as an internist, he became known for his devotion to the poor, passing up opportunities for a more comfortable lifestyle to devote his energies to the Catholic Interracial Council and the social action committee at Sacred Heart. It was through his early friendship with a black fellow internist at City Hospital that he learned what redlining—the surreptitious designation of a neighborhood to remain all white—was. Besides his family practice he became a medical school professor at Tufts, served on the staff of several hospitals, and was a research fellow at Boston's Pratt Diagnostic Center. He also served as a consultant to the Jesuits, who sent all their prospective novices to him for examination before they were accepted.

But Frank failed to take proper care of his own health. He smoked even on his way to the hospital. He became more gaunt. There was speculation in the family that perhaps in Japan he had been contaminated by the radiation from Hiroshima and Nagasaki. When a pain in his leg was diagnosed, his physicians found that cancer had spread to the bone and metastasized to the whole body. He died on November 11, 1977, at the age of fifty-eight, and was buried from the Sacred Heart Church on Tuesday, November 16, at 8:00 P.M. The church today looks as it did when it opened in 1891, with its high, flat, Italian-decorated ceiling and hard wood floor, and the sanctuary elevated only a foot above the floor. So there's an inescapable intimacy to the liturgy. Because the funeral, unusual for those years, was at night, there was an outpouring of former patients and friends to say goodbye. Although Drinan played the role of principal celebrant, it was no secret to his friends that, because he was not a pastor and had been saying a private early morning Mass, he had said so few public Masses in his life that he had not mastered the new liturgy, some of which had changed since Vatican II. He was, as one priest colleague described him, a "liturgical anarchist." Father Connelly and his old Boston College classmate Joe Nolan hovered nearby, signaling what page to turn to and which prayer to intone. Drinan left the principal homily to Connelly but read his own statement to introduce him. He said:

> Of all his qualities Frank was most of all gentle. In an essay on suffering which he discussed with a friend, he liked particularly this thought: "Gentle people become so sensitive that they never stop growing in compassion; they can love the world in pain."

The next morning's cortege to the cemetery consisted of more than one hundred cars.

Frank's death, like any loss of a brother, left a special void in Drinan's life. One political friend suggested that Frank was Drinan's "conscience." But a family member said rather that they looked up to each other. His brother's death altered in some ways his relationship to the family. He felt more responsible for them; but, like many celibates in the 1970s who weren't in tune with women's liberation, he knew little about how the day-to-day life of a family operated. He did not take care of his clothes and asked women friends to sew buttons on his shirt as if that were the women's role. To contribute to the holiday meals, without consulting, he would buy groceries at random—marinated mushrooms, dozens of eggs, and ice cream—with no sense of what or how much might be needed. Which, in the end, made him all the more lovable and vulnerable, in a way his other friends seldom saw.

Between the summer of 1977 and December 1978, aside from his fourth reelection campaign, Drinan's major Washington efforts were to convince President Jimmy Carter not to support the costly B-1 bomber program; prevent the sale of sixty F-15 supersonic fighters to Saudi Arabia; put strict limits on police searches of newspaper offices; curtail government wiretapping of telephone communications; and extend the deadline for ratification of the Equal Rights Amendment. Also, there was probably some amusement in Washington when the historian Allen Weinstein, with a special research interest in the Freedom of Information Act, in a *New York Times* op-ed essay (January 18, 1978) recommended Drinan to be the next director of the FBI.

El Salvador

On March 16, 2009, the FMLN (Farabundo Martí National Liberation Front), the leftist party in El Salvador, which years before had represented the guerrilla movement, democratically won the presidency of El Salvador. It defeated the right-wing Arena Party, which in the 1970s and 1980s was held responsible for the murders of a group of Jesuits, four nuns, and Archbishop Óscar Romero. The FMLN, in a peace agreement, laid down its weapons in 1992 and turned to politics. During the civil war some 75,000 people died and an estimated 8,000 disappeared. As in Argentina, some deaths were the result of guerrilla raids and terrorist attacks, but most were due to the government's preoccupation with an imagined Communist threat to its power and its use of both the regular military and right-wing death squads, organized under a 65,000-member group called ORDEN (Democratic Nationalist Organization).

Founded by Carlos Humberto Romero (unrelated to Archbishop Romero), soon to be elected president, it called itself "Christian," its symbol, a yellow and white torch, representing papal gold and white anti-Communism. Drinan, in his official visits and later *NCR* columns and books, tracked El Salvador's trials and progress. The 2009 election would have granted him some satisfaction.

He saw how El Salvador resembled Argentina, as the same claws of a dictatorial totalitarian regime were squeezing human rights and basic freedoms out of the political body. And the corpses of the "disappeared" cluttered the city dumps. It was a poor Central American country the size of Massachusetts, with a population of 4.2 million, where a poor laborer earned $100 a year, whose main product was coffee, controlled by a handful of rich families and a military *junta* that had not permitted a fair election since 1931. Its then leadership took control in 1961 and went through four presidents, leading to the then occupant, General Carlos Humberto Romero, who, after a fraudulent election, took office on July 1, 1977. Alternate candidates, including José Napoleón Duarte, who actually won the popular vote in 1972, were exiled.

The year 1977, prior to the arrival of the three-man Unitarian Universalist Service Committee team—Drinan, the historian Thomas Anderson, and John McAward, director of the international programs of the Service Committee, who had prepared their interviews—had been a bloody mess. By coincidence, President Romero and Archbishop Romero were selected for their new offices around the same day, February 20. The new archbishop, however, considered a moderate, had not been the first choice of his priests; and, after six days of vote-counting, 40,000 to 60,000 citizens swarmed into Plaza Libertad to protest General Romero's election. At midnight, troops cordoned off the plaza and ordered the remaining 6,000 protestors to leave. Then they opened fire on the 1,500–2,000 who remained. Protests continued through the 28th, with troops killing, the government said, eight; others estimated as many as 300. Archbishop Romero immediately came into town to minister to the victims.

On March 12 Rutillo Grande, a young Jesuit friend of the new archbishop, who was working with thousands of peasants, using the Scriptures to give them a sense of their own aspirations, was driving with an old man and a small boy to a little town to say an evening Mass. At 5:30, as they passed through a field of sugar cane, high-powered bullets fired from the roadside slammed into the car and killed them all. On May 10, also at 5:30, four men entered the rectory of the Resurrection Parish in San Salvador and shot down the young pastor, Alfonso Navarro, who had said a public Mass during the assembly in Plaza Libertad, and a fourteen-year-old boy. In early August, General Romero invited Archbishop Romero to his residence for a conversation.

The president was wearing his mask of moderation. Why could not the church and the government cooperate? he asked. The archbishop, meeting weekly with his advisers over several months, had prepared a three-stage memorandum for the encounter. First, the government must explain what happened to the persons who disappeared, investigate the Grande and Navarro murders, bring back the priests who had been expelled, and stop the defamation of the Church in the media. Second, set meetings with the high-level military officers during which the Church could explain its teachings about the poor and discuss how to improve the lives of the poor farm workers known as *campesinos*. Third, change how wealth in El Salvador was distributed. In November the government created a security law, similar to the State of Siege law in Argentina, strictly limiting civil liberties. By the time Drinan's committee arrived, the situation, which the new administration had promised to improve, had deteriorated. General Romero's promise of a "clean slate" had prompted the United States to allow a loan giving El Salvador $90 million for a San Lorenzo Dam project to pass through the Inter-American Development Bank. The U.S. State Department called this a "carrot and stick" policy in dealing with a problematic regime. The Service Committee had come to test that assumption.

During its January 7–12, 1978, visit, the committee met with the clergy, the president, the vice president, families of the disappeared, peasant groups, union leaders, and the ministers of justice and the interior. Archbishop Romero and Cesar Jeres, the Jesuit provincial for Central America, and other prominent churchmen during the clergy session talked mostly about the deplorable conditions of the peasants paid less than the living wage, the repressive tactics of ORDEN, and the religious persecution. In response to a Drinan question, they said most U.S. aid went to the military. The next morning Drinan was invited to concelebrate and preach at Romero's Mass in the cathedral, where 800 people crowded in to celebrate and people all over the country would hear the Mass broadcast over the church's own radio station.

It was the feast of the Epiphany, and the homily compared the congregation to the three kings who followed the star that led them to their destiny:

> The people of El Salvador do not want communism or Marxism. To suggest that they are following communist influence in their attitudes is an insult to their intelligence and to their integrity.
>
> The people of El Salvador want the flowering of their human rights as the Gospel proclaimed them and as the legal institutions of their nation are committed to implement them.
>
> Some persons in El Salvador who are afraid of the equality and the human dignity made possible by Christian beliefs seek to silence or even eliminate priests or others who enunciate these views.

After meeting with the families of the disappeared, the group concluded that as many as 200 persons had disappeared while in government custody during the previous two years. The final report included a list of 111 names, nearly all of whom had been detained, beaten, disappeared, tortured, or shot and left for dead. It included one man beheaded, another castrated; two sisters, one twenty-two and the other ten, raped by the same corporal; a man tortured for eight hours; a man hacked up by ORDEN machetes who saw fourteen in his family disappeared. The list of twenty-five exiled, expelled, abused, tortured, slandered, or assassinated priests included eight Jesuits and members of three other religious orders. At the presidential palace, Drinan sat down alone for an hour with General Romero as U.S. ambassador Frank J. Devine took notes.

The interview did not go smoothly, and Drinan did not shrink from confrontation. The president said Drinan should get out and see the beautiful countryside, implying, perhaps, that such committees as Drinan's typically speak to only a select few. Drinan replied that he had been out in the countryside, adding:

I have talked with dozens of people in the countryside and they tell me a grim tale of intimidation and harassment by forces responsible to the Government. As a matter of fact, it is intimidation of the Catholic Church. The National Guard and ORDEN tell people not to attend Mass or go near the priests.

Romero replied:

If you have gone to Aquillares and Paisnal and heard these things, I think you should go to other places and other churches where the people of ORDEN themselves have suffered and where FECCAS and UTC [guerrilla groups] commit degradation and intimidate the people. Some people have even been killed.

To each Drinan charge Romero claimed Drinan had only biased information; he should talk to different groups. Drinan said, "You are harassing the archbishop." Romero said, in effect, Prove it. Drinan showed him propaganda material denigrating Archbishop Romero and labeling certain priests Communists. The general said the government would not sink to that level and that he in fact had provided security for the Jesuits. Drinan tried to explain that the priests had been trying to live up to the declarations of Vatican II and the recent meeting of Latin American bishops, which put the Church on the side of the poor. "It is modern Catholicism," says Drinan. "It is not going to change." And General Romero's government could not tell these priests what to teach or not to teach.

The general objected that a local priest had placed a photo of the slain Rutillo Grande on his altar. Drinan replied: "Because he is a martyr. He was killed, and the government of El Salvador has never investigated his death."

Later, at a meeting with union leaders, when Drinan asked what could be done to improve conditions, the leader of one group declared that "the United States must send out a signal that it believes in democracy in the whole world."

When they sat down at the end of their visit, the investigators had four points:

There has been no real improvement since the July 1 inauguration
of President Romero. High-profile figures, like priests and opposition party leaders, were not murdered, but the grass roots cate-
chists were now the targets.

Because of its social role, the Church has been singled out for
persecution.

The government, through ORDEN and suppression of the national
university, has created a closed society.

This government does not respect the laws.

It is hard to imagine that the results of their visits gave the three
men much satisfaction. Things would get worse. Beginning in December 1979 the Unitarian Universalist Committee was back in Central
America, to be joined by representatives from Americans for Democratic Action, for a survey study of Guatemala, El Salvador, and Nicaragua. In March 1980 Archbishop Romero was gunned down in the
middle of Mass. And on December 2, 1980, four American religious
women—Ita Ford, a Maryknoll Sister who worked with the poor and
refugees; Maura Clarke, M.M.; Jean Donovan, a laywoman; and Dorothy Kazel, O. So. U.—were ambushed, raped, and killed in El Salvador
by members of a military death squad. In 1989 six Jesuits at the University of Central America, along with two laywomen who worked
with them, were taken out by the Salvadoran army in the middle of
the night, spread out on the lawn, and had their brains blown out.

Norman Walker

The 1978 election campaign began to take its unusual shape in April.
If the 1976 race had been unusual in that it was Drinan's first two-
man–two-party faceoff, the 1978 race was the first in which Drinan's
only challenger would come from within his own party, with its show-
down on primary day, September 19. Norman Matthew Walker, forty-
one years old, far from the law school dean–writer–eight-year congressman he was challenging, was a Newton North High School English

teacher and football coach, married for twenty years to Phyllis (Glea-son) with eight children—Diane, Julie, Heather, Norman, James, Janet, Mel, and Jennifer. He had graduated from Williams College in 1959, got a Harvard teaching M.A., and done postgraduate studies at Boston College, Boston University, and Suffolk University. If Drinan had a list of recent honorary Ph.D.s, Walker had a list of coaching and teaching awards. Over 6'2" tall, he had a way of gently filling a room when he walked through the door. He also taught swimming; coached basket-ball, baseball, and wrestling; and sang in the church choir.

He began his first prospectus, "I am running for Congress in the Fourth District because the economic and cultural survival of middle income families is at stake. Families of both blue and white collar workers find it almost impossible to cope with the soaring cost of living." He went on, "Our working people, our fathers and mothers, the elderly, the students and all our young need a representative in Washington. In my role as educator and as a parent I have had first hand experience with their problems. I can truly represent them." But as he ran through the issues—government spending, energy conserva-tion, development of solar power, opposing the Arab oil embargo, sup-port for Israel, and so on—it became clear that the gap between his policies and his opponent's was not wide. He was really running be-cause of one issue—abortion. He had been encouraged to run by four people, whom he named: John R. Longo of Leominster, Dr. David J. Greenblatt of Newton, Barbara Rockett of Brookline, and Reverend Richard G. Philbin, S.J., the Jesuit brother of the longtime congress-man, recently deceased, whom Drinan had defeated in 1970. Norm Walker was a longtime admirer of Robert F. Drinan, but Walker was very much against abortion. The Drinan camp took Walker's candidacy seriously and proceeded with its usual elaborate, clockwork campaign preparation as if it were running against a well-financed Republican lawyer rather than a high school football coach.

The first step was the canvass, marking prospective voters on the census with a pink highlighter if they were identified as Drinan "posi-tives" and with a yellow one for the remaining registered voters, all coded by professions—educators, salaried professionals, and retired,

then white-collar and blue-collar Democrats, self-employed professionals and businessmen and "others." As the "yellow" voters were reached
by their callers, they were marked with a blue ink check. In the last
two weeks of August up to the primary day, the staff called the posi-
tives, sent them letters signed by local opinion leaders and friends
from "good-guy" organizations (tax reformers and consumer groups),
and arranged rides to the polls. The "personal letters," which went out
in early September, were eighteen slightly altered mailings personalized to the needs of each town, all beginning "Dear friends, We would
like to offer some thoughts about" etc., starting with what Drinan was
doing for Fitchburg, Waltham, and so on and describing him as a national leader on tax reform and human rights. Then, "But we see the
other side," which emphasized his visits to the district, involvement in
local affairs, availability in his office. Each was signed by from two
to twelve local names most likely to be recognized by most of the
recipients.

Then there were the celebrity letters, signed by fifty prominent
artists or John Kenneth Galbraith; Barbara Jordan; Robert Meserve,
president of the American Bar Association during Watergate; and Carl
Sagan, and finally the full-page letter from the novelist Leon Uris, author of *Exodus*, who had been deeply moved by *Honor the Promise* and
Drinan's work for Soviet Jews, calling him a "moral force too valuable
to lose." Then, fundraising letters, like the one from Bert Rabinowitz
sent to 4,000 Jews both in the district and across the country, praising
Honor the Promise and the support of Soviet Jews. A letter from Florida
Congressman Claude Pepper, of the House Committee on Aging, told
the voters that Drinan helped him abolish the mandatory requirement
for retirement at age sixty-five. A review of a list of approximately
1,400 campaign donors reveals very few gifts of more than $100. One
of the more generous gifts was $250 from the comedian Steve Allen,
along with $100 from former Congressman Emanuel Celler of Brook-
lyn, who had lost to Elizabeth Holtzman in a primary in 1972. A high
proportion of givers were teachers, professors, physicians, and retired
people, ranging from $1 (six gifts) and $2 (about twenty) through a
median of about $20 to a few in the hundreds. Although Drinan had

spent $202,000 running against Arthur Mason, he was planning to take on Walker with only $90,000.

Endorsements came from fourteen labor unions that included their mailing lists and provided letters addressed by their leaders to thousands of members active and retired. Press attaché Mark Gearan, who had biked to his first campaign at the age of twelve, made sure local newspapers like the *Worcester Telegram and Gazette,* the *Newton Graphic,* and the *Leominster Sentinel* sent reporters and photographers to the country club gatherings, wine and cheese parties, and youth club meetings in July.

Walker's campaign was necessarily more low key. Interviewed in his office by a reporter from the *Globe* (September 14) right before the primary, he quoted Dante's *Divine Comedy* to his questioner: "'By their malediction one is not so lost that Eternal Love cannot return as long as hope have still a speck of green.'" The role of government, he said, was to bring people hope, and that's what he was trying to do. He was better known as a coach, he acknowledged, but he was proud to have been a successful teacher for twenty years. When TV reporters interviewed him, they did so on the practice field with the players working out in the background, but Walker did not allow his players to work on his campaign in order to avoid the appearance of a conflict of interest. Although he borrowed $50,000 and his main contributors were Williams College alumni, he planned to spend under $20,000. His most successful promotion event was his daughter Julie's actually running the whole length of the district—ninety miles—in August. "I tried to talk her out of it," he said. Presumably she did not run it all in one day.

Because Walker was a devout Catholic layman with a large family, in a way that the average Catholic voter might feel attracted to him, religion as an issue was ever present but seldom openly discussed. On two occasions the parish Sunday bulletins, distributed at Mass, touched on the campaign. In July the St. Camillus Catholic Church Bulletin called on its parishioners to "write to Drinan and tell him to STOP voting for federal funding for abortion on demand. 300,000 unborn children need your help." The Drinan staff asked the pastor to print a clarification stating that this "was NOT in any way to express opposition to Drinan's campaign." And the Sunday before the primary,

St. Leo's Church in Leominster inserted into its bulletin, on blue paper, the voting records of all the candidates on abortion.

The campaign included one ugly clash between the candidates. One morning Walker rose early and went to a local factory entrance in the traditional campaign ritual of greeting workers when they were changing shifts, shaking their hands and handing out campaign litera-ture. While Walker was greeting the workers, Drinan pulled up in his car and accosted him, saying he had no right to be there. This was "his" morning, reserved. Drinan called the superintendent, got him to check the schedule, and demanded that Walker leave. Walker recalls it as his scheduled time to be there. He insisted on his right to stay and did so, giving out pamphlets with Drinan there. Drinan "blew up," he says, got mad, yelled, and stormed away.

As early as April, when Walker first announced his candidacy, the conservative but venerable *National Catholic Register*, published in Denver, ran an article on him and recounted the story of when Drinan, speaking at a Holy Name Communion breakfast of seven combined parishes, rebuffed pro-lifers who questioned him about his abortion record. Drinan acknowledged to them that in eight years as a member of Congress he had never made a pro-life speech to educate his fellow congressmen. Through his access to prominent Catholic laypersons, the article said, he tended to neutralize much pro-life activity. Walker told the *Register* that he first heard Drinan, then dean of the law school, in 1968, when he spoke against abortion on a radio program. When he saw Drinan's record in Congress, he "felt betrayed."

Around the same time (April 25), Drinan received a memo from a staff member expressing concern that when addressing the abortion question in small groups Drinan applied his roles as a lawyer and theo-logian, but not as a politician, often leaving his listeners feeling uneasy. A recent weekend at the Colonial Inn, the staff member said, might be a "watershed" in dealing with opponents who charged that Drinan "abandoned his earlier positions out of political expediency." Accord-ing to the staffer's interpretation, Drinan at that meeting stressed his consistency with Vatican II and Catholic moral theology. And Drinan said he had opposed the Hyde Amendment saying that it did not con-form to Catholic moral theology because "it would have prohibited federal funding of abortion in any and every instance."

Catholic theology, Drinan is remembered to have said, approved abortion in "cases of rape, incest, life of the mother, medical necessity (such as an ectopic pregnancy)." Chances are that the staff member misunderstood Drinan. An ectopic pregnancy case, in which a fetus is developing in a diseased Fallopian tube, requires that one accept the death of the fetus as an unintended secondary effect of the diseased tube's necessary removal. The other cases, at least in standard Catholic theology, do not allow for abortion, although there are very likely moral theologians who, out of compassion, would not make a hard judgment in certain circumstances.

Drinan also reportedly said that "the ONLY effective way to reduce the number of fetal deaths is to provide programs which will encourage mothers to go full term." The staff member then encouraged Drinan to enumerate his efforts to reduce abortion by these means. (This line of argument developed in Catholic intellectual circles especially during the 2008 presidential campaign. If Drinan pioneered this idea thirty years before, this was not well known at the time.)

Drinan does not seem to have reacted to the staff member's suggestion on the abortion question, but he did react strongly to the *Register* article. On May 3 he sent a memo to three staffers telling them to "accentuate the Catholic background and Catholic activities in which I participate." In view of the fact that "about 70 percent of the voters in the Democratic primary on September 19 will be Catholics we should stress the following Catholic and religious activities in which I have engaged." These included his honorary doctorates from Villanova University and St. Joseph's College; he attached the citations, which he found "magnificent" and "truly impressive." Also included was his Red Mass sermon for lawyers and judges in Omaha at Jesuit Creighton University. Two years before, invited by Bishop Walter F. Sullivan, he had given a talk in Richmond, Virginia, and in April of the current year the annual Paul Hanly Furfey Lecture at Catholic University. He also included a talk at the University of San Francisco, at a "relatively prestigious conference" on reform of the federal criminal code, and finally a talk at Holy Cross.

He then added the ecumenical activities: his position on the visiting committee at Harvard Divinity School; his trip to El Salvador; his service on the board of the National Conference of Christians and Jews;

his book about Israel; articles for *Commonweal, America,* and *NCR*; and appearances at local Catholic high schools. All these, he urgently recommended, should be "exploited" in campaign publicity. He suggested getting a long list of Catholic names, priests and nuns, to endorse him. He recalled his 1970 address at Regis College in Weston and suggested enlisting Regis in the campaign by getting an on-campus "agent" to invite him to the college and line up campus persons to endorse him.

This was a list of accomplishments that he would attempt to swing into battle a year and a half later. As it happened, he did not need them in the fall of 1978. He beat Walker two to one—40,297 votes to 21,375, or 65 percent to 35. The next day Drinan called Walker to ask if he was "all right."

Two years after his defeat, Walker sat down and wrote a memoir of the campaign and on Drinan's influence in his life. Today Norman Walker can say without affectation, "I loved Bob Drinan." But how a man of Drinan's caliber and in his role as a priest could take the stand he did on abortion remains at least a half-mystery to him. Walker had begun the campaign to the right of Drinan on defense issues; but, during the campaign, as he was teaching John Hersey's *Hiroshima* in English class, and as his students were shocked at the effect of nuclear weapons on the lives of people like themselves, he read them passages from Drinan's *Vietnam and Armageddon* on unilateral disarmament. The students rebelled against Drinan's proposals: "He's crazy!" "We could never do that!" Walker found himself arguing in class for his opponent's position, and he saw the weakness in his own "macho" response. Walker wrote:

> Macho is first learned when a little boy's father makes him go back out to face the neighborhood bully (who just beat him up). We all hope that one day the little boy can grow up to master the bully and, even better, to one day embrace the opponent after a victory or defeat on a field of competition. . . .
>
> Who will write the poem or novel about the failure to embrace after the nuclear war?

There will certainly be no images of John Wayne, Alan Ladd, or Gary Cooper riding into the sunset to the swelling strains of orchestra music. And the laughter generated by the famous anti-heroes of the '70s who railed against Establishments won't do us much good. The best hero we can hope for is a mad Dr. Strangelove with his Doomsday Machine or his blue counterpart, Slim Pickens, riding the bombs down to Earth with a wild "Yee-haw!"

There will be no music and no laughter. After Slim Pickens is through yelling, there may be only an uproarious silence or perhaps "in the last dying sunset . . .".

Only Robert Drinan has offered a solution to the problem of nuclear Armageddon. His idea is not really original; he has simply updated an old message. That idea was proposed about 2000 years ago as a way for individuals to cope with the problem of violence in the world; some moderns, notably Mahatma Gandhi and Martin Luther King, demonstrated the viability of the solution, not just for individuals but for nations.

After the election, in late fall, after Drinan had been a guest speaker at Newton North High School, Walker followed him outside and asked him how he, a Catholic priest, author of "The Inviolability of the Right to Be Born," could vote for the right to kill the unborn.

Drinan began to give his usual answers: The votes to outlaw abortion aren't there. Walker looked into Drinan's eyes, which seemed far away, as if to say, "There's no way I can explain it to you because you haven't been where I have been, but I have to vote the way I do . . .".

But how could Drinan, with his stature, in a position to influence others, vote the way he did, Walker insisted on knowing. Drinan again gave a stock answer: A human life amendment won't work. You have to change hearts . . . and so on.

Walker knew he was losing him. He imagined a lecture in which Drinan would ask how he and his friends could devote so much energy to this question when children were starving, abused, and enslaved all over the world. It was true, Drinan would say, that abortion ranks among the most vile of human acts; but most who do it are just thoughtless people pressured by forces within and without, who deserve our empathy. Beyond this is the spectacle of "nations armed to the teeth against every child alive . . .".

Walker asked himself later whether Drinan was saying that if he were to direct his energies and talents to opposing abortion he would lose those whom he counted on to support him in his crusade for human rights. Was Drinan's abortion stance a tradeoff?

In 1986 Walker's daughter Julie, who had run the ninety miles to raise money for his campaign, died and was buried in Newton Cemetery. Years later, after a visit to Julie's grave, Walker heard on the car radio that Drinan was celebrating the fiftieth anniversary of his ordination at St. Ignatius Church. Walker hurried down Commonwealth Avenue, arriving just in time—because Drinan himself was late—to find Drinan tying his shoes in the back of the church before going up the aisle. "Hello, Father, congratulations on your fiftieth," he said.

"Hello, Norm. Thanks for coming."

In 2001, when one of Walker's granddaughters was applying to Georgetown, he asked Drinan for a recommendation. Drinan asked for her records, examined them, and wrote a superlative recommendation She got in and graduated in 2004.

13   "Hurt, bitter, and confused"

In many ways, the travels of Drinan's last two years in Congress were trips that summed up the pattern and goals of his life. The persona of the advocate for the oppressed—particularly black people, immigrants, refugees, and victims of dictatorial governments—was first implanted on his 1969 trip to Vietnam, where he employed the research method of listening to a cross-section of the society, from prisoners to presidents, then returning home to paint the shocking scene he and his committee had experienced and to ask what the American citizens and their religious leaders were going to do about his discoveries. In 1979–80 he alone or with congressional or ecumenical colleagues flew to South Africa in February; to Hong Kong, Thailand, Indonesia, Malaysia, and Hanoi in August; and finally to Guatemala, Nicaragua, and a return to El Salvador in December and January. He reported his findings for *America*; or, in twenty-nine-page co-written reports, he fingered guilty foreign leaders and recommended changes in national policy.

Apartheid was the legislated separation of the races imposed in 1948 in South Africa by the African Nationalist Party headed by Daniel F. Malan—into whites, black Africans, coloured (mixed), and Asians. Whites ruled. Each race was relegated to a particular territory, and blacks, who had been allocated only 13 percent of the land, could not leave their area without a pass. In urban areas, for example Johannesburg and Cape Town, black neighborhoods were often sprawling, terrible shanty-town slums. Blacks toiled in the gold and diamond mines, the men separated for months and years from their families, and they were forbidden to strike in protest of their wages or working conditions. By the time Drinan arrived, a significant political resistance had formed. In 1960 the government had killed 69 peaceful protesters in black Sharpeville; in 1963 young Nelson Mandela, head of the African National Congress, was sentenced to life in prison; in 1977 police killed at least four children in a crowd of 10,000 demonstrating in black Soweto township, setting off a bloody ongoing battle that killed more than a thousand; police arrested and most likely caused the death of student organizer Stephen Biko in prison. The Catholic and Anglican churches were supporting the struggles of their faithful.

Drinan, as was his method, focused on one victim and publicized his case. The Louvain-educated Reverend Samangaliso Mkhatshwa, thirty-two, secretary of the bishops' conference for eight southern African nations, had been "banned"—which meant he could not preach, teach, write, or speak to the media—for five years. Mkhatshwa, who had been jailed for six months following the student riots in Soweto, had advocated that American corporations disinvest in South Africa in protest against the policy of apartheid. Rather than shut up, Mkhatshwa used his victim status as a springboard for continuing his attacks on the government to visiting spokesmen like Drinan. His basic message: "It is simply immoral for four million white people to segregate and brutalize 19 million black people" (*America*, February 3, 1979).

The president of the Southern African Bishops' Conference, Archbishop Joseph P. Fitzgerald, urged Drinan to alert world opinion to their plight. Drinan's reply was to ask *America*'s readers to write to Mkhatshwa in support, and above all to bombard South Africa's ambassador to the United States with protests.

America's readers did so. Ambassador David B. Sole showed up in Drinan's Washington office one day, March 30, 1979, though not yielding an inch, to make his case. On January 28, 1979, said the ambassador, Pope John Paul II, addressing the Puebla, Mexico, Conference of Latin American Bishops, had gone out of his way to state that Jesus was not a political activist involved in the class struggle. "This conception of Christ as a political figure, a revolutionary, as the subversive of Nazareth, does not tally with the Christian Catechesis." Jesus, the pope had said, "does not accept the position of those who mix the things of

God with merely political attitudes." Drinan interpreted this line of argument as the ambassador's manipulating the words of the Holy Father to suggest that they applied to Reverend Mkhatshwa, who was asserting himself on behalf of the victims of apartheid. To a degree, Drinan was correct. The pope's statement may not have applied strictly to Mkhatshwa. But in the pope's mind it may have applied to Drinan himself. Several times in his 1979–80 trips Drinan must have seen his own career mirrored in the lives of the activist priests where he and his committees flew in and listened to the grassroots talk.

Meanwhile, back in New England and Rome, Jesuit superiors could read John Paul II's words as applying to their man in Congress.

Desperate, the South African ambassador said that Drinan should consult a South African prelate who agreed with the government, but, of course keep the prelate's identity secret. Drinan concluded a second *America* article (June 9, 1979) by repeating his plea that readers send their protests to Sole at the South African Embassy and to Mkhatshwa in Pretoria. Mkhatshwa went on to have a distinguished career that involved several arrests, including one for having a gun and ammunition in his home; two meetings with John Paul II; and receipt of the Stephen Biko Human Rights Award in 1990. By that time his struggles were being rewarded. Nelson Mandela, at the age of seventy-one, was released from prison in 1990 and addressed the nation from the balcony of the Cape Town City Hall. In 1994 Mandela was elected South Africa's president. Apartheid was over, but the struggle for peace and social justice in South Africa still had a long way to go.

The Refugee Crisis

Many of Drinan's writings, particularly in his books, can bog down, trudge along; but his "Asia's Refugees, the World's Conscience" (*America*, September 15, 1979) makes the reader wonder: What if Drinan had not left Congress at the end of 1980 and had remained to become chairman of the committee on immigration? Would the United States, to a radical degree, have opened its arms to a greater influx of "huddled masses yearning to breathe free"? The causes of the mass exodus, or rather reshifting of populations, in the late 1970s were both complex and interconnected. In 1975 the governments of Vietnam, Cambodia, and Laos collapsed. China briefly invaded Vietnam in 1979, and Vietnam, following a series of border clashes, invaded Cambodia and removed the government of Pol Pot in 1979. (For some reason, Drinan does not give credit to Vietnam for ending the mass genocide of the Khmer Rouge.) Each invasion forced thousands of refugees onto the roads. In Drinan's view, the phenomenon was, for the most part, a consequence of U.S. policies in Vietnam. America's prolonged intervention had destabilized the whole area, Drinan believed, triggering a series of economic and political upheavals that forced more than 400,000 refugees into a series of camps where he and eight congressional colleagues systematically made their inspection tour. "Our trip revealed," he wrote, "the agony and the tragedies of one of the largest mass migrations in modern history." He continued,

> The boat people out of Vietnam now number over 300,000. Another 200,000 Vietnamese have gone to China while thousands of Cambodians and Laotians continue to move into the countries bordering the South China Sea. The immensity and the immediacy of the problem are overwhelming, but there are few quick solutions. Countless people in Vietnam—especially the 1.4 million ethnic Chinese—have concluded that life is so intolerable under the Hanoi government that in order to avoid it, they will lose their fortunes and risk their lives in a quest for a new life.

Hong Kong responded to the crisis generously: "No one is ever turned away or towed out to sea." Eighty-three percent of the 15,000 refugees in one Hong Kong camp were ethnic Chinese who had chosen to live outside Vietnam or China, but they would not be invited to live anywhere else. "Indonesia became involved with refugees like Simon of Cyrene," said Drinan. "There was no way to refuse to carry the cross." Ethnic Chinese made up two-thirds of the "boat people" who drifted onto the isolated islands of Indonesia. Thailand was harboring 180,000 from Cambodia and Laos in twenty camps. Half were Laotian or Hmong (Meo) tribal people fleeing the extermination program of the Communist Pathet Lao, and many were among the thousands who had acted as surrogate soldiers in the CIA's secret war in Laos. Drinan observed that Thailand might soon join a storm of voices in Malaysia, Indochina, and Hong Kong demanding that the United States take all 400,000 refugees scattered throughout Southeast Asia to a camp in the United States. In Malaysia the problem was so bad that one official threatened to shoot boat people who tried to land on their shore. On Malaysia's Bidong Island, a square mile housing 32,935 refugees, Drinan met a Vietnamese Catholic priest who had received his degree in education from Boston College, and he was inspired by the joy of those who had broken with the past to have hope for the future. But his "weary and bewildered" delegation found Hanoi depressed, overcome by a pathological fear of China and desperate about its own economic situation.

At one stage Drinan's tendency always to say what he thought almost torpedoed his trip. While he and his colleagues were in Hong Kong, Drinan said that the "new development zones to which Hanoi [had] been sending refugees to cultivate rice [were] really 'concentration camps.'" He said that Vietnam was "engaged in one of the most fundamental violations of human rights seen in this century." If that was the way the Americans felt, if they had come to criticize rather than to help, said Hanoi, then Drinan and his delegation could turn around and go home. The situation was saved by Richard C. Holbrooke, assistant secretary of state for East Asia and Pacific Affairs, who asked Hanoi to re-invite the delegation (*New York Times*, August 9, 1979).

What was America to do? It should at least lift its trade embargo against Vietnam, said Drinan, expedite the emigration from Vietnam of the relatives of the 220,000 displaced then in America, and use some diplomatic initiative to heal the breach between Vietnam and China. But the fundamental problem, as Drinan saw it, was that America had not established a fair immigration policy of its own. In a sentence that could have been written today, Drinan said, "Congress has been unable or unwilling to resolve the status of an estimated five million undocumented aliens now residing in the United Sates." He concluded:

The drama of the boat people may soon disappear from the television screen, but the agonies of 400,000 homeless Vietnamese, Cambodians and Laotians will go on. Vice President Walter Mondale expressed the historic challenge that confronts America in these closing words of his eloquent address at Geneva on July 20, 1979: "History will not forgive us if we fail. History will not forget us if we succeed."

Chaos in Central America

In the conclusion to its report on Central America, following the investigation sponsored by the Unitarian Universalist Service Committee, led by Drinan and joined by John McAward and Dr. Thomas P. Anderson, the team warned that the United States at the end of 1979 had been so preoccupied with the Iranian revolution and the Soviet invasion of Afghanistan that it had neglected the potential explosion in its own back yard, where national policy for too long had been one of complicity with dictatorships that operated behind a façade of "democracy." If we failed to focus on Central America at this point, Drinan warned, we "might find ourselves with an 'Iran' in Guatemala or Nicaragua . . . a 'Cambodia' in El Salvador." Since Drinan's recent trips to Argentina and El Salvador, conditions in Latin America had only gotten worse.

After McAward and Anderson did advance preparations in all three countries, Drinan, accompanied by Bruce Cameron of the Americans for Democratic Action (ADA), representing Congressmen Tom Daschle of South Dakota, Tom Harkin of Iowa, and Howard Wolpe of Michigan, joined them in Nicaragua on January 4, 1980. Although his colleagues had spent a week in El Salvador, the situation became so chaotic there that Drinan himself was limited to a series of interviews in the airport on January 7. After five days in Guatemala together, they returned to the United States on January 12 and held a press conference on the 14th. The team members were encouraged in their project by the Carter administration's new emphasis on human rights, but they were handicapped by what they judged was the inaccurate reporting from U.S. embassies, whose ambassadors and staffs were not well enough informed on what was happening under their noses and thus weren't providing Washington with the information it needed to make wise decisions.

When the team arrived in Nicaragua, the Sandinista revolution had finally driven the Somoza dynasty, which had ruled since 1937, from office, ending a civil war that left an estimated 40,000 killed, 100,000 wounded, 40,000 children orphaned, and 60 percent of the people unemployed. Father Miguel D'Escoto Brockmann, the foreign minister, explained the four principles on which the revolution had been based: nationalism, democracy, Christianity, and social justice. Land reform, encouragement of foreign investment, and especially the literacy campaign, led by Father Fernando Cardenal, S.J., were seen as keys to an economic revival.

Some dangers: 500 to 1,000 revenge murders followed the fighting's end; publication of a conservative newspaper was suspended because it didn't "serve the revolution"; and Robert Villavicencio, a Nicaraguan-born U.S. Air Force retiree arrested for allegedly helping the National Guard, was being held as a political prisoner—one of very many. As soon as Drinan protested, the minister of the interior led him immediately to the old Somoza headquarters where Villavicencio was being held and released him on the condition that he leave the country within forty-eight hours. For the team, this exemplified both the minister's decency and his totally arbitrary power. The committee concluded that Nicaragua's future was promising, that it probably would not become "another Cuba"; but it was essential that the United States support the process with economic aid.

It may have been heartening for Drinan to see two fellow priests, a brother Jesuit (Fernando Cardenal) and a Maryknoll father, the order Drinan almost joined (Miguel d'Escoto Brockmann), in cabinet positions, as affirmation of his own belief that political office can be a means to do the work of the gospel. He would learn differently within the year; and in 1983, during Pope John Paul II's visit to Nicaragua, the pope would pull his hand away rather than allow Father Ernesto Cardenal, the minister of culture and Fernando's brother, to kiss his ring. In November 1983, a new, stricter canon law, Art. 285, specifically barred priests from public office, and in 1984 Fernando Cardenal chose to leave the Society, while retaining his residence and close relations with his fellow Jesuits, rather than give up his post.

In Guatemala, where the group spent the largest share of its time, the members reported that "politics [had] settled into what has become a familiar routine." They said:

> Behind every government is the military, fully screening candidates and sometimes rigging presidential elections. Despite the fact that there is no one ruling party, such as the PCN in El Salvador, there is a close inter-dependence of the agricultural oligarchy, military men, and three major right wing parties . . . all dedicated to blocking reform. The army chooses its candidate for the presidency and secures the cooperation of one or more of these parties, which are given a candidate whose victory is assured. Each president crushes any democratic opposition or worker-peasant movement that in any way would risk the victory of his chosen successor. . . .

Both the left- and the right-wing groups had their terrorist organizations, and their rivalry led to an estimated 20,000 politically inspired deaths in the previous decade. Each year, the holdings of the wealthy grew, and those of the poor, especially the Indians, shrank to the point where a mere 1.9 percent of the population owned 80 percent of the land. The report suggested strongly that the 2,000 political murders in the previous year and a half were linked to the government of the fraudulently elected president General Romeo Lucas García: "It is as though Guatemala were a country governed by the Mafia." The Church was of no help; only three of the fifteen bishops had spoken against the government. On the final day of the committee's visit, January 10, 1980, the Jesuits of Guatemala, joined by the provincial for Central America, charged publicly that the repression "[equaled] the worst known in the recent history of Guatemala." The government accused the Jesuits of fomenting revolution and, on January 23, the secret right-wing terrorist group threatened to kill all Guatemalan Jesuits.

The committee's report, *Central America 1980* (Unitarian Universalist Service Committee), concluded, "a savagely repressive government hides behind a façade of democratic reforms. Since the mid-fifties, the response of the Guatemalan elite to any threat of social change has been a reign of terror carried on not only by private para-military organizations, but by the army and police as well." In the view of the writers of the report, the United States should dissociate itself from the Guatemalan state.

Criminal Code Reform

Congressman Drinan's last legislative challenge, which spread over al-most two years, was an ordeal, a grind, a noble effort, and only a partial success: the reform of the federal criminal code. Depending how its time is measured, the project was initiated by President Lyn-don B. Johnson in his March 9, 1966, message to Congress, "National Strategy Against Crime," in which he asked Congress to review all federal criminal laws, "make the punishment fit the crime," and bring order to what he called the "crazy quilt patchwork throughout the criminal code." According to the House *Report of the Committee on the Judiciary, Criminal Code Revision Act of 1980* (September 25, 1980), the committee was to deal with four general problems: (1) uncertainty and uneven application of legal norms, which lowers respect for laws; (2) confusion in the defining of federal crimes, where the federal con-nection to the event is distinguishable from the other elements—for example, in a fraud case it may depend whether a phone or the mail was used; (3) an inconsistent sentencing structure—for example, twenty years for robbing a federally insured bank, ten for robbing a post office; and (4) absence of a comprehensive federal sentencing policy. In short, the lack of clarity, consistency, and comprehensive-ness "[tended] to undermine the very system of justice of which it is the foundation."

The reform attempts of the 1970s began with the national commis-sion, known as the Brown Commission, named for its chairman, Cali-fornia Governor Edmund G. "Pat" Brown, which issued its final report, known as Title 18 of the United States Code, to Congress in 1971. The Justice Department drew up bills acting on the Brown Commission's recommendations and submitted them to both houses of Congress. None of the bills introduced in the 93rd Congress (1973–75) got out of committee. Nor did the 94th Congress act decisively, although in the House several congressmen introduced re-codification bills.

During the 95th Congress, in May 1977, Senators John McClellan of Arkansas and Edward M. Kennedy of Massachusetts, with the cooperation of Attorney General Griffin B. Bell, introduced a compromise bill in both the Senate and House, and the Senate passed it 72–15 on January 30, 1978. Meanwhile, the House had been hearing extensive testimony. The Subcommittee on Criminal Justice finally reported that the current reform proposals, including the McClellan–Kennedy Senate bill, were seriously flawed and that an "omnibus" reform wouldn't work; it recommended an "incremental" approach through small groups of separate legislation. By January 1980 the Kennedy Senate bill had been revised and renumbered as 1722 and approved by the Senate Judiciary Committee. The House, meanwhile, had rejected the "incremental" idea and opted for a middle ground between "incremental" and "omnibus" approaches.

Under Drinan's leadership the House subcommittee held seventy-four public meetings, plus ten more days in September and October 1979, taking testimony from more than forty organizations. In March 1980 it offered House Resolution 6915 to the full Judiciary Committee, which for various reasons didn't report it out till July 2, 1980. In "The Federal Criminal Code: The Houses Are Divided" (*American Criminal Law Review*, 1980–81), Drinan concluded his efforts and highlighted some of the bill's accomplishments. A few examples:

> On the question of *mental state* of the accused in determining *culpability* in a crime, the Model Penal Code uses four terms: purposely, knowingly, recklessly, and negligently. The Senate bill says "reckless state of mind" is sufficient. The subcommittee decided to require *knowledge of conduct, circumstances, and results*. Thus, said Drinan, "the reduction of complexity advances the prospect for reform."
>
> Under *prohibiting physical interference with specified government functions*, the subcommittee, wary of terminology that expanded the government's discretion in making arrests, lest any

prosecutor impede any large demonstration on federal grounds, listed specific offenses that would apply.

Whereas any *false statement*, sworn or unsworn, written or oral, made to a government employee might be penalized as a felony, the subcommittee would not penalize simple oral false statements, except when a written statement was unavailable or in special circumstances, like emergencies.

On *sentencing,* the subcommittee agreed the foremost problem was sentence disparity, they would not increase prison time, there was a need for objectively determined facts in sentencing, and artificially high sentences should not be meted out. They considered abolishing parole but feared this might lead to longer sentences.

Given the opportunity to add supplemental or dissenting views to the report, Drinan was pleased that the subcommittee had not approved the government request to appeal sentences on the grounds that they were too lenient. Democratic Congressman Robert W. Kastenmeier of Wisconsin, an original member of the Brown Commission, voted no on the bill because the subcommittee had hurried through its work in the last weeks. Like a work of art, he says, "the test is not whether it is better than other works of art but whether it is worthy of the civilization it represents." This work "[did] not quite make the grade."

His Democratic colleague John Conyers of Michigan did not wholly approve of the decision to abandon the "incremental" approach. The federal law, Conyers said, was not a unified body of statutes. The laws should have been dealt with separately, with thorough consideration. Drinan's method, said Conyers, was like constructing a bill by "a sort of multiple choice selection process." How many like the Model Code on this issue? How many side with the Brown Commission's report? The Code of Hammurabi? Furthermore, they should have repealed the Logan Act, a 1799 law that makes it a felony to speak without authority to the representative of a foreign government. Congressman Harold L. Volkmer of Missouri said Drinan and his subcommittee deserved praise for their heroic efforts, but "they bit off more than they could chew." Don Edwards of California, with others, opposed the deletion of the section of the code that allowed counsel to accompany a witness appearing before a grand jury.

Drinan tried to end his report on a positive note. The remaining obstacles to reform, he said, were more political than philosophical. Staffs met, compromises were possible, but the fall elections and other problems interfered. Congress ran out of time. There were now two proposals, the House's and the Senate's, "each with significant virtues"; "Congress should be able to enact legislation which would be acceptable to all but the most extreme critics of criminal code reform."

Yet reform didn't happen. Ronald L. Gainer reported in his lengthy history of code reform, "Federal Criminal Code Reform: Past and Future" (*Buffalo Criminal Law Review*, Vol. 22, 1:45), that the Senate bill sank when three conservative senators announced that they would offer approximately sixty amendments and engage in extended debate on each. In the House, Conyers succeeded Drinan as chairman of the subcommittee, but, following the Senate defeat, the House supporters turned their attention to other issues. Gainer concluded: "The dynamo pushing a code toward enactment in the previous Congress, a Roman Catholic priest, had withdrawn from politics at the request of the Vatican."

The Last Days

A talk by Pope John Paul II, who assumed office in 1978, to the Latin American bishops at Puebla, Mexico, in January 1979, a harbinger of his removal from office of four priests in Nicaragua, was also a signal to Drinan's Jesuit superiors that the clock had run out on the string of permissions that had kept him in Congress for five terms. At a meeting of the American provincials in October 1979, the new New England provincial, Edward O'Flaherty, S.J., and Gerald Sheehan, S.J., General Pedro Arrupe's American assistant, had several cases to talk about. One was that of Father William O'Callahan, a women's rights advocate, who had been ordered to return to Boston from the Quixote Center, which he had founded in Washington, and to be silent on the issue of women's ordination. The other was the need to "do something about" Drinan. Arrupe had told O'Flaherty's predecessor, Richard T. Cleary, that he wanted Drinan to leave Congress, but he left it to Cleary to determine the timing. O'Flaherty realized that the time had come.

Several factors were at work. One was the personality of this new pope. His predecessor Paul VI was also both concerned by what he saw as the liberalizing tendencies of the Jesuits and opposed to priests' holding political office; but he was also sympathetic toward the Society and was willing to allow more freedom because of his abiding trust. The new Polish pope, while he toured the world attracting huge crowds of worshippers, was quick to use his power to discipline and silence those he considered dissident or influenced by Marxism. The *New York Times* (May 6, 1980) reported that in September 1979 the pope had directed Arrupe to remedy the "regrettable shortcomings" of Jesuits around the world who had "secularizing tendencies" and did not practice "doctrinal orthodoxy." And many noticed that the pope's reaction was reserved when, on March 24, El Salvador's Archbishop Óscar Romero was assassinated in the middle of his Mass and crowds at his funeral were shot down.

Another factor, difficult to measure, was the growing determination by leaders in the American "pro-life" movement to remove Drinan from office. Because he was now apparently unbeatable in a congressional election, their only means was an end-run to ecclesiastical authorities—first to Boston's Cardinal Humberto S. Medeiros and then to the pope in Rome. The conservative Congressman Robert Dornan, a California Republican, was one of Drinan's most outspoken critics. In May 1978 he approached Drinan and said, in effect, "Father, please do not cancel out my vote. Why are you doing this when it is against our Catholic training and the teaching of our Church?" Drinan made no reply, turned, and walked away. Dornan approached as many bishops as he could, including Medeiros, and told a friend that he had succeeded in getting a letter he had written against Drinan on the pope's desk. It is entirely possible that the Drinan issue was raised by Drinan's critics with the pope when the pope visited Boston in 1979.

That Cardinal Cushing would have approved Drinan's political ambitions makes sense. When Drinan was a young lawyer-priest-dean,
Cushing would sign his notes to him, "Your devoted admirer." Medeiros, on the other hand, had given many signals over the years that
he did not believe priests should be in Congress, and this included
Drinan. At the same time he wanted to avoid a public fight with the
Society of Jesus and he did not want to take public responsibility for
removing the people's elected representative. That aspect of the situation didn't bother the pope.

Drinan seems to have been able to file away the issue of the three-
way relationship between abortion, his priestly identity, and his role
in Congress in the bottom drawer of his consciousness, while in other
minds—for example, Arrupe's—this issue came to the fore. On April
10, 1979, Drinan wrote Arrupe a long letter trying to convince him
that he was a "very important moral influence" in Congress, using the
word "moral" six times on the first page. He described his work on the
criminal code as an opportunity to introduce into law a higher morality
with regard to crime. His role as a congressman had led to his board
membership at Bread for the World, an international organization
working against world hunger; his book *Honor the Promise* had received attention because he was a congressman; and he had been invited to China and would use the opportunity to inquire about
returning the Society of Jesus to that country. He suggested that he
was doing in Congress what fellow Jesuit Matthew Ricci had done in
China centuries before. He enclosed the citation on his Villanova honorary degree. On February 5 Arrupe wrote to O'Flaherty agreeing to
allow Drinan more time to extricate himself from Congress; but he
couldn't understand Drinan's position on the federal funding of abortion or how Drinan resolved in his conscience the scandal caused by
his position.

On Sunday, April 27, 1980, the Roman headquarters of the Society
of Jesus called O'Flaherty with the news that John Paul II had ordered
that Drinan withdraw his candidacy for a sixth term. O'Flaherty informed Drinan immediately but also agreed to appeal. To Rome O'Flaherty repeated the familiar argument that this would be perceived as
Vatican interference with American politics and pointed out that the

date for filing a candidacy was May 6, just over a week away. On Monday night Jerome Grossman had dinner in Washington with Drinan. He sensed that something was bothering Drinan, that he was not himself; but Drinan told no one. He kept it all to himself. On Saturday, May 3, the Vatican said its decision was final.

The Long Weekend

As Drinan drove from Dottie Reichard's house a few blocks away late Saturday afternoon back to his gloomy little room in St. Mary's Hall, he had a lot to do. He had a personal meeting with O'Flaherty coming up the next day, but it was to prepare for Monday's press conference. He had known this was coming for a week, but it is very likely that he entertained the fantasy that somehow the provincial's appeal would work its magic as it had every two years before. On the surface the decision was simply the application of canon law; in reality it was part of a pattern of decisions by the pope to silence what he saw as dissident voices and thereby to strengthen the "true faith."

Now Drinan had a day to prepare himself to face the press and explain why he would not simply break away, serve the people, as so many Jesuits had done in recent years. What would he say? We can be confident that as he turned in to Boston College with St. Ignatius of Loyola Church, where he had said his first Mass, a few yards away, his mind raced back to 1942, when he had decided to become a Jesuit. Now that vow of obedience was depriving him of what he most loved—that job in Congress where he was doing so much good. But if he had not gone to Boston College and become a Jesuit and then dean of the law school, would he ever have had a chance to be where he was today? Now he had to reach deep down into the spirituality the Society had given him and find God's will in this most terrible moment of his life.

That Sunday morning in Washington, Ken Bresler, who was twelve when he first worked on Drinan's 1970 campaign and was now his legislative assistant, had just four more weeks to go in D.C. before returning to Boston for the 1980 campaign. He was dressed and about to leave for the office to get a head start on the week's work when the phone rang. It was Clark Ziegler, Drinan's administrative assistant, to tell him: "Rome says Drinan can't run again."

As he headed down the corridor of the Rayburn House Office Building, Bresler kept telling himself it was a joke. But it was no joke. Drinan had played a special role in his life; for him, Drinan was a unique link between the Christian and Jewish people. Personally he knew that the Jesuit motto was "AMDG," the Latin abbreviation of "For the greater glory of God," and so he felt that in working for Drinan he too was doing "G-d's work." In the office the staff had already begun to gather. The mood was glum and the faces were filled with hurt. Word had spread the night before as Jerry Grossman and Dottie Reichard had begun calling the Boston politicians—like Michael Dukakis and John Kerry—who might want to pick up the baton and run in Drinan's place. David Frank, the press secretary, heard the news on National Public Radio and called his brother Barney, who immediately decided to move from Boston to the Fourth District and make the run. Within 48 hours, 12 candidates had collected 2,000 signatures each in order to qualify for the race.

One staff member, a Catholic, announced, "I'll never set foot in a Catholic church again. It's a darker day for the Church than it is for Drinan." Bresler and another staff member, Ranny Cooper, went to the storeroom to collect data to compile a quick biography of their boss. They found a document from 1970, when Bresler had thought all the quibbles about priests running for office had been put to rest, in which Drinan had written, "Sometimes I have depressing moments when it appears that the two most precious qualities of my life are a hindrance to the work I now desire to do. Those most precious—those priceless gifts—are my priesthood and the honor I have to be a member of the Jesuit Order."

The office filled and the phone rang wildly. Two staff members flew to Boston. On the wall, overlooking their toil, was a beaming photo of John Paul II, which Drinan had mischievously signed, "To Bob from JPII." That evening as the news clips came in Liz Bankowski wept. She had known Drinan since she had worked in the Boston College Law School Library at eighteen, and he had baptized her daughter that recent Christmas. When they finally closed shop, a Catholic staff member drove Bresler home, but she stopped first at Georgetown to make an appointment with a priest to discuss whether she would remain in the Church. She had skipped Mass that day because she knew it would include a prayer for the pope.

Maria Plati, who had joined the Drinan followers at the age of fourteen to hand out leaflets in the 1970 campaign and had returned to work in the local office after college, read the story in Rome, where she was on a journalism fellowship. When she called Drinan, he said, "I know why you called. You talked to the Pope and you got my job back." Almost two months later she sat down and wrote a long letter, though not knowing to whom she should send it, in which she "resigned" from the Catholic Church. She concluded her handwritten rough draft with the proclamation that "I can no longer believe—I can not justify this decision—I can no longer give credence to a _____ that tells us that our role as Christians means abstinence from our social political duties as members of the brotherhood of man."

In the *Boston Globe* office Sunday night the page-one editor decided to run "Vatican Tells Drinan Not to Run Again" as the lead story, and he juxtaposed it with a large photo of the pope in Kinshasa, Zaire, perched on a high wooden throne, shaded by a thatched palm. He had ordained eight African bishops and told his audience to "leave political responsibility to those who are entrusted with it: the role that is expected of you is another, a magnificent one: You are leaders in another jurisdiction as priest of Christ." Nine people had been trampled to death and sixty-nine injured in the rush to see him.

Bresler and the others returned to the office at 8:00 A.M. Monday and read the newspapers. Someone in the Waltham office pressed a radio, which was broadcasting the 10:00 A.M. press conference from the Marriott Hotel in Newton, against a WATS line so the Washington staff could hear it over the phone.

That morning, May 5, before an audience of thirty reporters, plus friends and supporters, as Arrupe issued a statement thanking Drinan for his loyal compliance with the directive reflecting the "expressed wish" of the pope, O'Flaherty gave the background facts. Drinan, in a short statement, asserted that he had spent ten of his twenty-seven years as a priest as a member of Congress, and that "I am certain that I was more influential as a priest in those 10 years than in my 14 years as dean of the Boston College Law School." He listed his travels to Argentina, Russia, and Southeast Asia and looked forward to flying to Amsterdam the coming Sunday for a conference to liberate Anatoly Sharansky from prison.

> I am grateful to have had these opportunities as a moral architect. I can think of no other activities more worthy of the involvement of a priest and a Jesuit.
>
> I am proud and honored to be a priest and a Jesuit. As a person of faith, I must believe that there is work for me to do which somehow will be more important than the work I am required to leave.
>
> I undertake this new pilgrimage with pain and prayers.
>
> Global hunger and the arms race have been the two interwoven agonies of mankind which have disturbed me more profoundly than any other problems confronting the human race, I hope that in God's providence I may be given an opportunity to work to alleviate world hunger and to stop the arms race.

An unintended casualty of the drive to remove Drinan specifically was Wisconsin priest Robert J. Cornell, who was campaigning to recapture his seat in the House, lost in 1978. His bishop, Aloysius Wycisio, told him that the apostolic delegate had informed him on Monday that Rome's directive applied to "any priest," and that an all-inclusive policy document was in the works. This turned out to be false. The apostolic delegate denied that interpretation of the call. But Cornell withdrew, only to find that in fact the directive was tailored for Drinan alone. Several nuns in political office across the country said bluntly that it did not apply to them.

After the press conference, Drinan flew back to Washington. When the staff gathered, he shook hands with the men and kissed the women and apologized to everyone again and again. He still seemed dazed, so Liz Bankowski suggested that some Jesuit friends take him out to dinner. In the office the phones were still ringing, and Bresler, as praises poured in, was still choked up. He wrote to the pope and told him, "I hope you will be forgiven for removing one of the finest and most moral Congressmen." On Thursday Drinan flew back to Boston College to support the kickoff of Barney Frank's campaign. In the judgment of the interview committee, consisting of Drinan's colleagues, Frank was the one most likely to continue Drinan's ideals. Bresler wept, and the inner circle retired to Dottie's house, where the party continued till 3:30 A.M. Drinan responded to the many letters about his firing with a simple "God's ways are not our ways."

When Drinan got back to the Georgetown Jesuit community and made one of his customary late-night entrances into the Georgetown Room, he found that a few of the men, including James Walsh and Joseph Sebes, had been watching his press conference on the TV news. Sebes had advocated "taking the gloves off" during the Vietnam War and bombing the enemy harder, and Drinan and he were on different planets politically. But he rose to welcome Drinan warmly and to say how proud he was to know him.

Fred Enman, a young Jesuit novice, a lawyer, at Georgetown for his novitiate "trial," where the new men get a taste of different aspects of Jesuit life, asked Drinan how he felt. Drinan replied, "Hurt, bitter, and confused." Enman went on in the Drinan spirit to become an assistant dean at Boston College Law School and run a project building houses for the poor.

The Wake

Over the next few days the media commentary built and dealt with Drinan's limitations as well as his gifts. In the *Times*, Marjorie Hunter observed that "Except for a few liberal friends, Father Drinan was always something of a loner on Capitol Hill. He was widely regarded as somewhat eccentric, in part because many of his colleagues had difficulty accepting a priest in political vestments but also because of the outspoken, sometimes didactic way he had of challenging them." She also observed the "awkwardness of manner" that showed up in his political campaigning back home. Asked by a reporter to source a scripture quote Charles Colson used during the attempt to impeach Nixon, Drinan rushed to his office to dig out his Bible but found only one written in Swahili (*New York Times*, May 6, 1980). Also in the *Times*

314 | "HURT, BITTER, AND CONFUSED"

(May 11), Kenneth Briggs concluded that this move was but one step in clamping down on Jesuits as a whole. In an interview with Francis X. Clines of the *Times* (May 17), Drinan toyed with the reporter, jibing, "Don't you have any better questions than that?" as a way of not answering any pointed queries. But Father Richard McBrien, a Boston College theologian on his way to Notre Dame, had no doubt that Drinan's vote in favor of abortion funds for the indigent had been the decisive factor in his destruction. The pope, he believed, deliberately timed his decision, right before the filing deadline, for maximum worldwide impact.

The *Globe* (May 7) did man-on-the-street interviews that displayed the usual split between lovers and haters. A man at a bar in Newton Corner said, "I'm surprised the Pope took so long to knock him off"; a Boston College law student said, "What this says to me is how concerned is the church with social welfare? Where's the church's place in social reform?" The Catholic historian Garry Wills, who had once been a Jesuit, observed that ever since the pope's Mexico trip he had been trying to "restore clericalism in the modern world, which is strict separation of clerical and lay roles in the world. . . . Historically clericalism was imposed on the priesthood to increase its hold on the conscience of laymen and put that hold beyond question."

> If this Pope had studied Western history a little more carefully, he would have found that clericalism has led inevitably to anticlericalism. Father Drinan used to be a symbol that anticlericalism had become obsolete—just as President Kennedy's success signaled an end to anti-Catholicism. But the Pope seems bent on reviving many obsolete things, and that strange effort will undo more important matters than Robert Drinan's political career.

When the smoke and dust cleared, perhaps the best commentary was the *New York Times* editorial of May 7, in which the editorial writer pointed to the irony that the current pope was among the most political popes of them all.

> If politics and the priesthood are really incompatible, would there be in this day a Polish Pope? . . . It would seem to be not politics that the

Pope wants priests to abandon, but only elective office, and perhaps only at the national level, and maybe in only some countries. Why? . . . He helped display a Church that is multifaceted. And now his acceptance of its direction reveals still more of the complexity of the man.

Drinan's withdrawal recalls the poetry of Gerard Manley Hopkins, also a Jesuit, torn by other conflicts:

> Glory be to God for dappled things
> .   .   .   .
> All things counter, original spare, strange;
>   Whatever is fickle, freckled (who knows how?)
>   With swift, slow; sweet, sour; adazzle dim;
> He fathers-forth whose beauty is past change;
>   Praise him.

Epilogue: Resurrection

Once Pedro Arrupe had carried out the very unpleasant task—unpleasant for both Drinan and himself—of removing Drinan from office, he turned his attention to two major items on his agenda. Like Drinan, he had been struck in his travels through the Third World by the pathetic sight of thousands of refugees, including the boat people fleeing the after-effects of the Vietnam War, as they made their way through the world, from one unwelcoming port or beach to another. Because he knew the history of the various Jesuit houses in Rome, he knew that in the early days of the Society, when Ignatius and his first companions arrived in Rome, they were confronted with a similar sight—thousands of people driven out of their small towns by famine, disease, poverty, and cold. Within one year the early band of Jesuits cared for 3,000 refugees from a total population of 40,000, giving them shelter, clothing, and food. So Arrupe sent a letter to twenty major Jesuit superiors asking how they could respond to the contemporary crisis. His answer was to found the Jesuit Refugee Service. By 2005, though pastoral care, advocacy, social services, education, companionship, and the recruitment of volunteers, this new service would touch more than a half million lives in fifty countries.

Arrupe, seventy-two, had also made up his mind to resign his office. Because the generalship of the Society is by institution a lifetime job, like the papacy, John Paul II would not allow him to quit. Most likely it is because John Paul II feared that Arrupe's successor, perhaps his vicar general, Father Vincent O'Keefe, would be elected and continue Arrupe's policies with renewed vigor. Then, on August 7, 1981, descending from a plane at the Rome airport, Arrupe suffered a cerebral thrombosis. Barely able to speak, he gathered his staff and appointed O'Keefe to run the Society. But John Paul II, rather than allow the Society to elect Arrupe's successor, appointed his own man, conservative and nearly blind Father Paolo Dezza. The members surprised John Paul II by not rebelling, but it was eighteen months before the Jesuits were allowed to have their congregation and govern themselves. Father Peter Hans Kohlvenbach, from Beirut, was elected and continued Arrupe's policies, while Arrupe, partly paralyzed and eventually rendered mute by his stroke, lived on in the infirmary, silently "carrying his cross" until his death in 1991.

After Drinan completed his fifth term and left Congress in January 1981, Georgetown Law quickly offered him a professorship, and he returned to a modest room in the ancient Mulledy Hall and a very challenging and satisfying new life. For the most part, this gave him every opportunity, comparable to his congressional influence, to work for the goals of what he had come to consider essential during his "best" ten years. A Jesuit who knew Drinan fairly well observed that, while he could be "snarky" as a congressman, he mellowed in his new life. But this mellowing took time. One of his good woman friends, Ellen Griffin, who came to him at Boston College Law School for spiritual guidance during her college years at Wellesley, kept in touch with him for the rest of his life. He performed her marriage ceremony, comforted her during her divorce, and called her every New Year's Day after she moved to Florida. She could see that it was taking years for him to accept the blow of leaving Congress. She also sensed in him during these years a touch of loneliness, a yearning perhaps for the married life he had forsaken to become a Jesuit.

But much of what he did during the congressional years he kept doing.

He wrote seven books, many journal articles and reviews, and a regular column for the *National Catholic Reporter*, which gave him every opportunity to reach a large Catholic and ecumenical audience with his political views. And he wrote regularly for *America*, the magazine that had given him his start. Between 1993 and 2006 he also wrote twelve articles for the respected British Catholic periodical *The Tablet*.

His *America* articles were often on the same topics as his *NCR* columns, but they were longer, often on legal issues, less frequent, more academic, and less personal. These articles, as well as occasional op-ed pieces for the *Boston Globe* and other papers, were often nostalgic, in that they took their inspiration from turning points in his life— the 1969 trip to Vietnam; his campaign victories; the drive to impeach Nixon; his trips to the Soviet Union, South Africa, and Southeast Asia. But they were not sentimental. The past was called up by a recent headline, a death, an execution, the anniversary of an event we have yet to adequately appreciate or understand. Many of the journalism articles that appeared first in the *NCR, America, New Catholic World, Christian Century*, the *New York Times*, and the *Boston Herald American* were republished in *God and Caesar on the Potomac: A Pilgrimage of Conscience* (1985), and many of the articles concerning human rights were developed more fully in *Cry of the Oppressed: A History and Hope of the Human Rights Revolution* (1987). *The Mobilization of Shame: A World View of Human Rights* (2001) is both a study of the development of the human rights policy the United Nations has carried on since 1945 and a reflection on the eight-day conference in Vienna in 1993, the UN World Conference on Human Rights, in which Drinan participated, and the declaration and program that the conference published.

He served as board member or sometimes president of several political and public-service organizations: the Americans for Democratic Action (1981–84), Common Cause (1981–87), the World Presidents Association, Bread for the World (1974–82), People for the American Way (1986–2007), Lawyers Committee for Human Rights (1981–94), Council for a Livable World, NAACP Legal Defense and Educational Fund, Holocaust Memorial Commission (1980–86), Lawyers Alliance for Nuclear Arms Control (1981–86), Helsinki Watch Committee, Union of Councils for Soviet Jews, American Civil Liberties Union, American Academy of Arts and Sciences, American Bar Foundation, International Committee for the Release of Anatoly Sharansky, National Conference of Christians and Jews (1981–84), National Inter-religious Task Force on Soviet Jewry American Law Institute, and PeacePAC.

Drinan's FBI file reveals that in May 1994 he was being considered for an appointment by the Clinton White House requiring Senate approval and so underwent a full FBI investigation. He is described as six feet tall, weighing 160 pounds, with brown hair and blue eyes. The agents questioned all the editors of the *NCR* in Kansas City, prominent Washingtonians, and most of the Jesuits in the Georgetown community. All proclaimed him a man of impeccable integrity. What the position would have been, we know not. But the extraordinary praise heaped upon him during the vetting process is a sign that, thanks to the devotion of his family, friends, and colleagues, the wound of having to leave Congress was beginning to heal.

Teaching law again, this time in the school where he had learned his law, he gained an extraordinary following among the faculty, many of whom enabled him to extend his Jewish friendships, and he earned the devotion of another generation of young men and women. The opportunities for kindness gave him a way to express those profound paternal feelings that had long been a major emotional force in his life.

Teaching again also kept him in the center of political action. As one example, with his membership in the Council for a Livable World (CLW), led by Jerome Grossman and John Isaacs, and the Council's offshoot PeacePAC, he worked to elect to Congress candidates who would fight for arms control and the abolition of nuclear weapons. At the CLW today Drinan's portrait hangs proudly in the front hall, and each year a Drinan Award is made to arms control advocates.

Isaacs describes him at CLW meetings as "brilliant, irascible, and unforgiving." The members greeted his bad moods with benign neglect and overlooked his short temper because much of it was attributable to his frustration with his declining hearing. Dan Koslofsky had the double perspective of knowing Drinan at the law school and at Peace-PAC. Koslofsky eventually left Washington because he hated seeing what it did to corrupt the personalities of ambitious politicians. Drinan was one exception. At both the law school and at the board meetings of PeacePAC, Drinan may have had his eruptions of temperament, but he remained a simple, humble man. Being famous didn't go to his head. Georgetown and other law schools had the reputation for hiring "big names" from outgoing presidential administrations, whether or not they could teach, cared about students as human beings, or had been involved in ethically dubious activity like approving torture or promoting an unnecessary war. Drinan was the rare famous man who would give a student all the time in the world. Koslofsky's strongest impression of Drinan was of a man joyously throwing himself into what he most loved to do.

NCR

NCR editor Tom Fox was the man who, as a worker for the Catholic Relief Services in Vietnam, first smoothed the way for Drinan's visit in 1979. *NCR* had been publishing him for years, but when Drinan left Congress, Fox saw an opportunity to make him a full part of the team. From 1980 on, Drinan wrote an average of almost twenty articles a year; many consisted of only a few hundred words, but some were longer. Read collectively today, the columns suggest that Drinan had carte blanche. Editorially it was a prudent decision, in that over the course of twenty-seven years, they took a variety of journalistic forms, the first of which was repeated political analyses of the same issues he had pursued as a congressman—gun control, opposition to the death penalty, prison reform, international arms sales, Latin America (El Salvador, Guatemala, Argentina), human rights, Soviet Jews, Just War Theory, world hunger, refugees, and his own opposition to tobacco and gambling. There were occasional returns to church–state controversies lingering from the 1950s, like school prayer, which he opposed, and whether "under God" belonged in the Pledge of Allegiance. (He thought it didn't.) These columns also allowed him to write occasionally about things that the priest-congressman had seldom talked about, like his piety, his prayer, and finally his past.

The candidate who told reporters that he "didn't have a childhood" visited his family's graves and shared an occasional reminiscence from a buried childhood. And when a beloved friend or relative whose newsworthiness might not have rated a headline died, Drinan shared his sorrow with his readers and made a good but lesser-known person much better known.

In 1996, for example, at the family graves in St. Patrick's Cemetery in Cambridge, he recalled the burial of his mother, who died suddenly after surgery in 1946 at the age of fifty-eight. His father's was his first funeral Mass, in 1954. His brother and nephew are there too—along with Drinans who migrated from Ireland in the nineteenth century. The mystery of death as a fact of life, for him, remained a constant puzzle. In his view, "God is in control of the universe" and "arranges the lives and deaths" of the thousands of Catholics buried in those graves (*NCR*, September 20, 1996).

As the American bishops prepared for their annual meeting in November 1982, Drinan reminded his readers that in his *Vietnam and Armageddon* he had called for a Vatican III to deal precisely with whether Just War Theory permitted nations to possess nuclear weapons for deterrence even when their use either offensively or defensively could never be morally justified. This and the related question of world hunger, as 2 billion more people would be added to the then-current world population of 4.2 billion in the next eighteen years, were what the bishops must discuss, Drinan wrote in the *NCR* of July 2, 1982.

On November 2, 1983, the United Nations General Assembly voted 108–9 to rebuke the United States for its invasion of the tiny island of Grenada. The vote, wrote Drinan, was unprecedented and correct; it represented the "voice and conscience of humanity." The intrusion of the U.S. massive military might into this underdeveloped country with only 110,000 citizens "[looked] incongruous, uncalled-for and cruel. We lost eighteen marines and killed 38–69 Cubans and at least 20 civilians. Nowhere is this justified in international law" (*NCR*, December 9, 1983).

What About the "Seamless Garment"?

In 1983 two Catholic events seemed to make ideal subjects for *NCR* columns or *America* articles. First, on May 3 the National Conference of Catholic Bishops (NCCB) published *The Challenge of Peace: God's Promise and Our Response*. They followed this with *Economic Justice for All: Pastoral Letter on Catholic Social Teaching and the U.S. Economy* (1984–1986). Both documents, products of years of research and public hearings, were landmarks in modern Catholic teaching. *The*

Challenge of Peace strongly condemned nuclear war, forbade the targeting of enemy populations, and strongly questioned even the possibility of a "limited" nuclear response. At the end, it carried its pastoral discussion to "reverence for life" and connected taking human life in warfare to taking life through abortion. The documents say all life issues are one.

The same year, on December 6, Cardinal Joseph Bernardin of Chicago delivered the lecture "A Consistent Ethic of Life: An American Catholic Dialogue" at Fordham University. Building on the letter on war and peace, Bernardin extended the "right to life" to "quality of life" issues—hunger, homelessness, unemployment, and undocumented workers. He later introduced the image of the "seamless garment," worn by Jesus and stripped from him at the crucifixion, as a metaphor for the linkage between abortion, capital punishment, euthanasia, war, and all the other "life" issues.

In 1983 and 1984 Drinan wrote on his usual topics—Latin America, capital punishment, Soviet Jews, world hunger—but he passed on the Bernardin "consistent ethic." However, in the *NCR* of August 31, 1984, he did deal with the connection between abortion and nuclear war in his analysis of the NCCB's August 9 statement on religion and politics for the fall 1984 elections. He was puzzled by the bishops' rejection of the idea that "candidates' personal views should not influence their policy decisions." Most, if not all, legislators did let personal views affect policy, Drinan wrote, but they also "[had] the right and duty to not impose their views on others." His example was the Catholic who votes for the poor woman's right to have Medicaid fund her abortion. And he did point out correctly that Church authorities did not condemn the politician who favored using nuclear weapons. Drinan granted that abortion was a big problem—55 million a year, 45 million of them in the Third World. It was a problem, he said, "that cannot be solved without massive education and a sharp reversal in public opinion."

The reader must conclude that Drinan resisted the strict across-the-board application of the "consistency of human life" principle—at least in politics.

* * *

In 1987 Drinan returned to Argentina, where eleven years before he had visited with the Amnesty International human rights investigators, at a time when the Church was "struggling to find its role" while hundreds of people were killed or kidnapped by the Argentine government. He had a long lunch with Emilio Mignone, author of the recent *Church and Dictatorship*, which argued that the Church had not done all in its power to save lives during the "dirty war." Drinan reported that there were two sides to that story, but he told his *NCR* readers on May 1 that the bishops of Argentina opposed nine human rights groups' meeting with Pope John Paul II during his recent visit, that bishops are paid wages equivalent to those of higher-ranking civil servants, and that certain religious objectives are subsidized by the state.

Young Tom

On January 20, 1987, Drinan dictated a letter that, like nearly all his letters, was short. He told *NCR* editor Tom Fox, "I attach herewith an article which is somewhat different from the items which I usually write." It was about his nephew's death. "There may well be reasons why you feel that this particular article should not be published. Please feel free to make whatever judgment seems best."

In the February 6 edition, Fox gave the nephew, Thomas J. Drinan, a large picture and a full-page spread, headlined: "And Death Shall Have No Dominion: My Only Nephew—The Nearest Thing I Had to a Son—Was Gone."

Young Tom Drinan graduated from Boston College High School in 1966 and from Boston College, *cum laude*, in 1970, in time to help his uncle run for Congress; and after his father's death, he served on his uncle's local advisory committee. At Suffolk University Law School he was editor of the *Law Review*. Married to Diane Biohm, he first worked five years as a trial lawyer for the Massachusetts Defenders Committee, then became a prosecutor, as a specialist in tax cases. U.S. Attorney Robert S. Mueller, later director of the FBI, told the *Globe* on December 31, 1986, that Tom Drinan was "what a prosecutor should be. He was tough, hard-nosed, fair and compassionate." He pursued tax evaders and marijuana smugglers. When a bank robber sentenced to more than one hundred years was paroled, Tom Drinan discovered that he had returned to his criminal lifestyle and sent him back to jail. In his spare time he helped Boston College and Harvard Law students stage mock trials.

On December 30 at 4:35 A.M., Father Bob Drinan's phone rang. The quiet voice of his sister-in-law, Helen, said, "I have some terrible news. Tommy just died." Tom, thirty-eight, had never been sick. He'd had no warnings. He just suffered a convulsion, an aneurysm, and was gone. Two days before his death Tom and his uncle had discussed his future. "His career was blossoming. Some day he might be a Federal judge or other important Federal official."

For several days Drinan was stunned, wordless, trying to make sense of the event, as if God was using this moment to send a message to him and to the family. Frank and Helen had named their son for Thomas Aquinas. Tom was not outwardly devout, but he was committed to justice and fairness. Tom had been present at all the high and low moments of his uncle's career. It was he who drove him to the airport after that final press conference at the Marriott seven years before; and of all the letters Bob received following his retirement from Congress, Tom's meant the most. At the funeral at Sacred Heart Church, the same church from which his father had been buried, Drinan struggled to find the right thing to say. At the gravesite, confronted with the tombstones of all his family, as the wind and snow howled around the mourners, Father Drinan suddenly understood for the first time in his life the doctrine of the communion of saints. The buried loved ones were all praying for the family and for him. They were the church triumphant pleading before the Trinity for the church suffering and church militant.

A few minutes before, he had ended his remarks in the church with a Cardinal John Newman quotation from Frank Drinan's memorial card: "He does nothing in vain. He knows what He is about. He may take away my friends. He may throw me among strangers. He may make me feel desolate, make my spirits sink, hide my future from me—still He knows what He is about."

The following year, the family and friends established at Suffolk University Law School the Thomas J. Drinan Memorial Public Interest Fellowship, which funds the ten-week summer employment for law students in the criminal justice field, working in a public office in the prosecution or defense of criminal cases. In 1989, speaking at a reception for the donors to the fund, Drinan described the fellowships as the vanguard of a new movement in legal education, the integration of *pro bono* work into the training process. "It is an exciting time to be a lawyer in America," said Drinan. "I have never seen any moment in my life when the bench and bar were as alive to ethical standards and aspirations as they are now. It may be that we are living in the golden age of the legal profession in America."

By the end of 1988, Drinan had another "stab of sorrow." In 1970 Lonni Stern, at the age of twelve, became briefly famous when many newspapers and magazines, including *Time*, ran the picture of her holding high the large placard at the post-midnight party celebrating Drinan's election to the House. The sign read: "Our Father Who Art in Congress." The slogan caught on, and in 2007 a senior at Brown University won an award for an honors thesis about Drinan's first campaign with that as his title. Lonni went on to run marathons but was devastated with cancer. When Lonni's mother was pregnant she had taken Diethylstilbestrol, or DES, a chemical compound designed to prevent miscarriage; but by 1971 it had been discovered that thousands of children born to women who had been given DES would be afflicted with cancer. Nothing could be done for Lonni, and she died at thirty. Drinan struggled again to make sense of the loss of a young life. He drew on the Book of Job and *When Bad Things Happen to Good People*, written by one of his constituents. But nothing worked. All he could do was tell his readers that "In another and better world" we will understand how "Lonni's sufferings and our compassion contributed to the glory of God" (*NCR*, December 14, 1987).

In *The Jesuit Factor: A Personal Investigation* (1990), Peter Rawlinson, a British politician and writer, described his worldwide tour in which he interviewed selected Jesuits in order to present a collective portrait of an organization that, in his judgment, had lost its moorings—its emphasis on obedience to papal authority—and drifted into an era of "dialogue" and "pluralism," embodied in its emphasis on "justice," particularly in Latin America. After talking with Fernando Cardenal in Nicaragua and Father Peter Henriot, of the Center of Concern in Washington, by telephone, he visited Drinan (whose first name he rendered as Richard) in his Georgetown Law School "well-equipped studio" basement office. Drinan told him that his congressional service was the "natural flowering of all the things I had done as a priest, a Jesuit, an educator and a lawyer." Although he had difficulty thinking of any war that is just, he said he had no doubt that the defense of Israel is. He decisively dismissed any suggestion that his support of government-funded abortion was "anomalous," because *Roe v. Wade* had settled the question. When Rawlinson asked him whether a priest should set certain conditions that might lead him to break with his political party, Drinan twice refused to answer: "I have no position on that."

When the conversation shifted to personal spirituality, wrote Rawlinson, "the personality of the man appeared to change." The politician fending off the interviewer gave way to the priest who spoke of Ignatius and Augustine and the Spiritual Exercises as the "essence of my entire life" and his image of the Church as "the Mystical body of Christ which is the extension across time and through space of Christ himself." When the interviewer brought up the memorable correspondence between John Adams and Thomas Jefferson, in which Adams—having learned of the restoration of the Society, which had been suppressed by the papacy and European governments worldwide in the 1770s—wrote, "I do not like the resurrection of the Jesuits. Shall we not have swarms of them here? In as many shapes and disguises as ever King of the Gypsies assumed?" Drinan, apparently unaware of the context, had a strange reply. "Those," Drinan said, bridling, "those are the myths made up by the English people."

When nuclear weapons came up, he launched into a lengthy statement on a topic that disturbed him deeply: "And my country, God forgive us, has thirty thousand nuclear weapons seeking to exterminate millions of people."

For the interviewer, the pious priest had disappeared. As Rawlinson packed his recording equipment, Drinan told him that this was "the darn'dest right-wing interview" he had experienced in many a year. From Washington, Rawlinson flew to St. Louis University, first to meet John Padberg, historian and director of the Center for Jesuit Spirituality, whom he liked more than most of the Jesuits he had met so far, then to talk to St. Louis University historian James Hitchcock, who "spoke of the Society with unrelieved criticism." Author of *The Pope and the Jesuits* (1984), which included strong disapproval of Drinan's role in Congress, Hitchcock suggested that the new emphasis on "justice" may stem from the Jesuits' own crisis of faith: "If you are uncertain about eternal life, if you are uncertain about life after death, if you are uncertain about what the real Christian gospel means, then you tend to say that if Christianity has any meaning we should be building the kingdom of God on earth."

Drinan's good news in 1990 was the realization that, after twenty-seven years of struggle, every Jew who wished to leave the former Soviet Union was now free to do so (*NCR*, June 15, 1990).

The Gulf War

In 1991 the *NCR* pulled out all the stops in its coverage of the first Gulf War, wherein President George H.W. Bush rallied America with civil religious rhetoric and the help of prominent religious leaders, plus a coalition of allies, to repel Saddam Hussein's army from tiny Kuwait, where, among other territorial goals, Iraq claimed a port to give it access to the Persian Gulf. A number of other religious leaders opposed the war. Drinan, in a television debate on CNN's "Crossfire" (January 29, 1991) with Jerry Falwell, television evangelist and leader of the Moral Majority, argued that most of the criteria for a just war had not been met: It was not being waged as a last resort, and the bombing strategy put innocent lives at risk.

He debated again on CNN (February 8, 1991) with Dr. Robert Grant, president of the American Freedom Coalition, and warned that the after-effects of the war would be "devastating and tragic." Between

January 25 and March 15, he turned out five powerful political–moral analyses, immediately condemning the war as unjust in a meticulous analysis of Just War Theory, spelling out his prayers for peace, and reviewing the war's opportunities and pitfalls. Disappointed with how members of Congress "sleepwalked" into the war, he asked on January 27, "What happened in the souls of members who fought together with me in the House to stop the war in Vietnam?"; in his prayers he said on February 1, "No one condones the aggression of Saddam Hussein, but can it be moral to say that the answer is to destroy Iraq and Kuwait in order to 'liberate' Kuwait?" The casualties disturbed him the most. "Will the people of America ever learn—or even care to learn—how many Iraqis or Kuwaitis were killed?" In an amazingly astute prediction of some of the first Gulf War's effects, he wrote, "It is a serious possibility that Americans will now assume that other situations can be rectified by a quick military fix."

When Pope John Paul II visited the tiny island of Gorée, the former center of the African slave trade off the coast of Senegal, he used his visit as a symbolic occasion to ask forgiveness for the sin of slavery. Drinan used his column of March 13, 1992, to promote the U.S.-based Gorée Historical Trust Society's efforts to create a museum and archives on the history of the island. When California carried out its first execution in twenty-five years on April 21, Drinan reminded his readers that "events are moving against 2500 people on death row." He asked why those many Catholics opposed to abortion did not also fight against the death penalty (May 1, 1992). He left the bishops' conference that November "angry, perplexed, melancholy," because they had failed to approve their pastoral letter on women. He had never criticized bishops before now, he said. He had praised their positions on immigration, civil rights, and poverty. "But will all that be obscured by the bishops' failed crusade to re-criminalize abortion? And by their unfortunate, collective stumbling on the question of the rights of women?"

Abortion, Again

In the debate over the morality of abortion, the most extreme and shocking example of the "evils" of abortion used by its opponents is the practice of so-called partial-birth abortion. In the description, the late-term fetus is pulled feet-first from the birth canal. The head, which is still inside the mother, is pierced with scissors, and a tube is inserted so the abortionist may suck out the brain in order to collapse the skull and complete the extraction. Abortion opponents hoped the public would see what it viewed as the obvious barbarism—indeed, the immorality—of this procedure and, by extension, of abortion itself. In April 1996, President Bill Clinton, a prominent Georgetown Law alumnus, who had said abortions should be "safe, legal, and rare," vetoed a bill outlawing this procedure, arguing that it did not contain a provision taking into account the health of the mother. For reasons that are not entirely clear—very possibly an attempt to be consistent with other things he had written about the morality and legality of abortion, but to others a loyalty to friends in the Clinton administration— Drinan took the opportunity to write two defenses of Clinton's decision. The first appeared in the *NCR* on May 31, the second in the *New York Times* on June 4.

The two texts come to the same conclusion but are adapted to their audiences. Drinan told his *NCR* readers that "Those opposed to abortion have the right and duty to urge public officials to work diligently to make abortion 'rare.' . . . But opponents of abortion cannot reasonably or responsibly fault Clinton for his April 10 veto of a bill that would have criminalized certain late abortions." To the *Times* readers he said, "The indignant voices of the pro-life movement and the Republican Party will likely reach new decibels in the campaign to urge Congress to override President Clinton's veto of the bill banning so-called partial-birth abortions. But Congress should sustain the veto. The bill does not provide an exception for women whose health is at risk, and it would be virtually unenforceable."

In the *Times* version, his second paragraph was the one that most angered Church authorities and Catholics who had studied his record: "I write this as a Jesuit priest who agrees with Vatican II, which said that abortion is virtually infanticide, and as a lawyer who wants the Clinton Administration to do more to carry out its pledge to make abortions rare in this country." To the basic secular or religious reader without a sophisticated understanding of the debate, here was a Catholic priest saying partial-birth abortion was acceptable.

Drinan argued that such abortions were extremely rare, that only one-half of 1 percent of abortions take place at or after twenty weeks. This procedure, called "dilation and extraction," was safer than other procedures. He said Clinton was sincere in asking only for an exception regarding the woman's health. Convictions of doctors who performed the procedure would be hard to get, and the bill would sanction "intrusive enforcement by requiring Federal officials to keep informed about doctors who performed later term abortions."

Was Drinan tone-deaf in not foreseeing the avalanche of opprobrium that was to descend on him? On the far right was the right-wing Ignatian Society at Georgetown—including member William Peter Blatty, author of *The Exorcist*—which had already called for the removal of Jesuit president Leo O'Donovan for his public friendship with President Clinton. They petitioned Washington's Cardinal James Hickey to remove Drinan's priestly faculties in the Washington archdiocese until he publicly withdrew his support for Clinton's veto. According to *The Georgetown Academy* (August 1996), a conservative journal, twelve Jesuits felt compelled to send Father Drinan a letter of protest.

Unfortunately for Drinan, rebuke came from three sources where he might have presumed support for whatever he had to say.

The Boston Pilot, which had published some of his first attempts at journalism, zeroed in on his self-identification as a priest who agreed with Vatican II, saying, "From there on, it is all downhill; a shocking, schizophrenic and even scandalous reflection on the role of law without further reference to his identity as a Catholic, a priest and an avowed supporter of the teachings of Vatican II, which specifically called abortion and infanticide 'abominable crimes.'" The Clinton "health risk," they averred, was meaningless, because the Supreme Court had defined "health" as anything that might disturb one's social, emotional, financial and familial 'well being.'"

New York's Cardinal John J. O'Connor penned his regular column in the *Catholic News* (June 6, 1996) as a sad remembrance of the young Jesuit law dean in the 1950s who gave him good advice on a problem and who wrote the 1965 article "The Inviolability of the Right to Be Born." Something had happened on the way to Congress, the cardinal felt. O'Connor went through Drinan's justifications and shot them down: If the number of partial-birth abortions was low, how many were acceptable? Since when should the federal government not interfere with the practice of medicine? Was that not the role of the Food and Drug Administration? What about the requirement that doctors be licensed? About Drinan's assertion that the law would be unenforceable, O'Connor asked, Do we not prosecute wife-beating, arson, rape, theft, murder—all hard to enforce? He concluded, "You could have raised your formidable voice for life, you have raised it for death. Hardly the role of a lawyer. Surely not the role of a priest."

Finally, for the first time, the New England provincial could not support what Drinan had done. Father William Barry required him to retract his judgment. It took some time. In May 1997, the Washington archdiocese released a statement, reported in the *Boston Globe* (May 17) and elsewhere, that Father Drinan retracted remarks made a year before: "Drinan has issued a statement on May 12 saying that his remarks were used in a way he did not intend." Drinan himself said, "I withdraw those statements and any statement that could be understood to cast doubt on the church's firm condemnation of abortion—a doctrine that I today accept." New information, he said, rendered his statements on partial-birth abortion factually incorrect. . . . "I stand ready to promote laws and public policies that aim to protect vulnerable human life from conception until natural death." His statement was carefully worded in a way that would allow him to say he had been consistent all along; but having to issue it was a humiliation. And it was the springboard for Hitchcock's long article in *Catholic World Report* asserting that, based on letters in the provincial archives, Drinan had apparently run again and again for public office without the approval of Church authorities.

His loyalty to Clinton, however, did not flag. When the House Judiciary Committee in 1998 was considering Clinton's impeachment, Drinan and other members of the committee from 1974 came to the president's defense in the *New York Times* of October 1. Drinan wrote another defense for Clinton in the December 6 *Washington Post*.

Moments of Self-Revelation

More and more, Drinan's guaranteed space in the *NCR* gave him a chance to open up personally on religious and emotional issues that he had supressed over the years. He recalled the sermon he heard at Christmas Midnight Mass following the attack on Pearl Harbor in 1941; reading Cardinal Newman in college and the spiritual writer the Abbot Marmion in the novitiate; and teaching in prisons during his days at Weston. He was humbled by incomprehensible mysteries like the Trinity and how God could have allowed His son to suffer not just the crucifixion but the scourging on Good Friday.

His old college friend and Boston College priest-theologian Joe Nolan felt that Drinan should have resisted the opportunity to write extensively about theological topics, because, as he saw it, Drinan was out of his element. The theological training in Weston in the late 1940s and early 1950s was not up to date in Nolan's view, and Drinan, although he was aware of John Courtney Murray and Teilhard de Chardin, had not educated himself on the recent Scripture scholarship. As a result, Nolan thought, he treated the events in Exodus and the infancy narratives in Luke and Matthew as literal history. In an article on devotion to the Blessed Virgin Mary, he described Luke's perhaps interviewing Mary on the details of the virgin birth and Jesus's youth, unaware that the infancy narratives are a literary form, not a literal record, in the contemporary sense (*NCR*, May 16, 1990). In 1995 Drinan gave a retreat in Puerto Rico, and a young Jesuit who participated got a look at Drinan's retreat notes. The pages were yellow and crumbling. The custom in the "old Society" had been to use tertianship to prepare *the* retreat one might preach for many years. In short, Drinan had not kept up on modern theology.

When he wrote about his own retreats he reflected on the lives of his fellow Jesuits—the 2,500 departed members of the combined New York, New England, and Maryland provinces, whom he remembered at daily Mass; John Courtney Murray; Teilhard de Chardin; John La-Farge; and the recently departed Joseph Sebes, an expert on the Jesuits in China. He wrote again and again about the six Jesuits at the Jesuit University in San Salvador who were massacred in the middle of the night by government troops on November 16, 1989, and the slain Rutillo Grande and Óscar Romero. Because U.S. foreign policy subsidized the regime, he wrote on October 19, 1990, American complicity in their slaughter was undeniable. When Pope John Paul II visited San Salvador in February 1996 and "turned his back" on them, did not visit the scene of the murders, and gave only perfunctory, last-minute attention to Romero's tomb, Drinan felt "almost personally rebuffed" (March 8, 1996).

His Lenten reflections were often grim. For example, on March 5, 1993: "We know, most of the time, that consciously or otherwise we are running away from God. The hound of heaven pursues us, but he will not compel our attention if we, as we so often do, separate ourselves from God by addiction to secular information or trivia. . . . Nothing can keep away on a permanent basis those moments of quiet desperation that, without faith and prayer, can dominate our lives." On April 9: "It is theologically correct to say that if my sins were less serious, the sufferings of Christ in the agony of the garden would have been less acute. Jesus undertook unbelievable sufferings to demonstrate in a dramatic way that every sin of every child of God caused pain and suffering to God himself." The feast of Pentecost cheered him: "If we treat the Spirit with courtesy, we will find on Pentecost the world is again new and dazzling." Some of these musings in his later years help put in context the retreat reflections in 1968.

From 1990 until his death he wrote, in *America*, the *NCR*, and the *Globe*, about his annual spiritual retreats, made with groups of Jesuits at various retreat houses, and his anniversaries as a Jesuit. Jesuits are required to make an eight-day retreat every year. They may do so in groups, led by a director who delivers daily conferences. Or they may do so individually, consulting a spiritual adviser for direction. Drinan usually joined a group.

In his forty-eighth year as a Jesuit he worried about the Society's shrinking manpower. There were 36,000 Jesuits worldwide in the 1960s; in 1990, there were 24,000. He prayed that Cardinal Newman would be named a saint. On his fiftieth anniversary he said, "At Boston College I was challenged by the twin goals of St. Ignatius and the Jesuits: deepen your spirituality and intensify your scholarship. They go together." He had entered into secular positions because of Ignatius' core teaching, "Find God in all things" (*Globe*, June 28, 1992). In his retreat with forty-two others at Fairfield University in Connecticut, he worried about the future of Jesuit schools: "Will the 28 Jesuit colleges and universities and the 46 Jesuit high schools drift into an orientation of secularism, with a touch of prayer and piety in the catalog and at graduation?" In the library he picked up a brochure featuring pictures of 320 Jesuits in the province who had died between 1972 and 1990. The pictures "stabbed" him. With some he had played handball; others he had taught. But he had forgotten them. Was it Voltaire who said that "young men enter the Jesuit order uninvited, live unloved and die un-mourned" (*NCR*, September 10, 1993)?

In 1999 he made his retreat at a Trappist monastery and said the divine office with the monks. He left in awe of those monks who have given up everything in order to be in the presence of the Trinity at all hours of the day. In 2002 he made a Zen retreat, directed by Robert E. Kennedy, S.J., who is both a theologian and a Zen master. Each day there were thirteen meditation "sittings" followed by eight minutes of walking in unbroken silence. In 2006, in what would be his last retreat, with fifty-two other Jesuits at the former novitiate at Wernersville, Pennsylvania, he was depressed, sensing a dismay and lessening of hope among his fellow retreatants. He worried and wept at the state of the Church. Was this the hour, in the words of Francis Thompson, "of the church's unqueening"? (Thompson's "Lilium Regis" compares the Church to an Easter lily that dies and is reborn.) On the other hand, statistics portrayed a vibrant Church worldwide. The Church now had 1,086,000,000 Catholics—15 million more than the year before (*NCR*, February 24, 2006).

Georgetown Law School

On December 18, 1980, Drinan was cleaning out his congressional office. His spirits were low. He had notionally but not emotionally accepted the fact that his career in public office was over. He was tempted to skip the annual White House dinner-dance for members of Congress, but he liked and respected Jimmy Carter. When he arrived at the White House, President Carter, who had been defeated for re-election the previous month by Ronald Reagan, took him aside and said,

"Father, God wants us both to do something different next year, and it will be more important."

When now-Professor Drinan walked into his first classroom at Georgetown Law School in 1981, the school had come a long way from the one that gave him his law degree in 1949. When the American Bar Association accreditation team visited Georgetown Law in the spring of 1978, they praised its dean and faculty, select and diverse student body, and clinical programs and declared Georgetown "on the threshold of greatness."

When David McCarthy was named executive vice president for the Law Center Affairs, he set up a process that led in 1978 to a long-range set of goals for the coming decade. Thus, the 1980s became the school's "renaissance" decade. The first step was to enlarge the full-time faculty, which grew from fifty-four in 1977 to seventy-two, including the newly integrated clinical instructors, in 1983. Among the new stars—who included Martin Ginsburg (husband of future Supreme Court Justice Ruth Bader Ginsburg), who had been a professor at Columbia; Eleanor Holmes Norton, who had been chair of the Equal Employment Opportunity Commission (and would later become the House of Representatives' nonvoting delegate representing the District of Columbia); and the sociologist Norman Birnbaum from Amherst College—was former Congressman Drinan.

By 1983 three-quarters of the faculty had received their legal training outside Georgetown, and many had interdisciplinary credentials. In 1988–89 more than 90 percent of the faculty published: monographs, textbooks, book chapters, and scholarly articles. In 1987 the median LSAT was 42, minorities were 25 percent of the class, and women were almost as many as men at 48.2 percent. A goal close to Drinan's heart was to ensure that every student, through interdisciplinary courses, seminars, and clinics, learned to confront the problems of society.

One admiring student won a competition to become Drinan's research assistant. Terry Berg, as a Georgetown undergraduate, had gone to Central America as a member of the John XXIII Program, volunteers who worked in Nicaragua for a year building community. From 1984 to 1986 he handled Drinan's correspondence and researched human rights, particularly the Carter administration's efforts to integrate human rights into American foreign policy. Berg had at the beginning sought Drinan as a possible role model, but three weeks of working for him adjusted that dream. Here was one man writing for *America*, the *NCR*, law journals, and books, teaching full time, lecturing, and moving in political circles! Berg told himself, "No man can do what this man is doing."

In 1986 Drinan received gifts from the American Bar Association and several law firms to establish the *Georgetown Journal of Legal Ethics*, the first of its kind, which made its first appearance in June 1987 with articles solicited from distinguished professors throughout the country.

Among Drinan's courses during his twenty-six years as a professor were International Human Rights, Arms Control, Constitutional Law I & II, and Professional Responsibility. His large lecture halls had a capacity of 150, with, in some years, as many as 119, 146, or 136, seated, spread out before him, the center-front seats empty, each student sitting according to the chart on the professor's rostrum. He quickly became known for his generous willingness to teach more courses; one semester he had five.

Charlie Kelly, a Fordham University undergraduate who had Drinan for Ethics at Georgetown Law in the spring of 1986, began his professional career as a journalist in Pittsburgh, then, like a number of journalists, switched to law, and later ran unsuccessfully for Congress. In 1986 he was in his third year and was taking Ethics, which had about twenty to thirty students, a required course designed to "ensure that our technical skills would be applied within the framework of an ethics base that was both legally correct and morally rigorous." He remembers Drinan as fastidious in appearance, punctuality, and decorum. He was "a bright star among a legion of stars," someone "to take," along with Sam Dash, the former counsel to the Senate Watergate committee, and Robert Pitofsky, the Federal Trade Commission chairman. "They brought passion to the classroom" to show that law is social policy to be used to achieve what is a social good. A typical case study asked about the lawyer who discovers that his client is "participating in fraudulent or otherwise illegal conduct and must determine when he must report this to the court." The *Paper Chase* analogy, says Kelly, does not do justice to third-year courses that focused not merely on "the law" but on "human conduct," how we treat our fellow men. Dash was "full frontal"—he wanted to wield the law to protect individual rights, and he said the students, because of their privileged backgrounds, had an obligation to be "keepers of the law." Pitofsky had a "soaring intellect," with all the facts of a case at his fingertips, inspiring the students to "aspire to stunning scholarship." Both stressed the case method. Drinan, in some ways, was "a conscience leading with a moral compass, putting him squarely *in situ*—a Jesuit teaching not only contemporary legal issues, but eternal truths in an institution devoted to both."

In 1995, Charlotte Bruce Harvey, writing for *Boston College Magazine* (Spring 1995), interviewed Drinan and sat in on one his classes. Her Drinan was "tall and sharp-shouldered, built like a knife." His "overcoat is so chafed it's hard to tell whether it started out navy or black, his pants are rumpled; there are crumbs on his shirtfront." If Drinan, Harvey observed, "thrills in the company of children, he is pained by adult small talk and dullness." Back in his office, when she asked a routine question, he rolled his eyes. "You can do better than that," he snapped, crossing the room to switch on the old rabbit-eared Sony next to his desk. "Wanna see how O.J.'s doing?"

She took a seat in his Constitutional Law class. Drinan applied de Tocqueville's term the "tyranny of the majority" to a Texas law that limited the percent of personal income that could be taxed for education. As a result, poor school districts, which tax their residents to the maximum, could raise only what half the rich districts spent per child on education. A student objected: "Where is there a constitutional right to equal quality of education?" As the discussion heated up, Drinan invoked the concepts of fairness and justice. Harvey wrote, "Juxtaposed against the tight legal verbiage and logic of his students, his words sound old-fashioned, even quaint. He's making a truth claim. They want logic." During the break a student complained to Harvey that Drinan was "too emotional." Her friend had transferred to another, happier class, one based on reason. "In here, everything comes down to right and wrong. The class on abortion was awful; people were yelling at each other."

Elizabeth B.L. King, now the assistant director of the Center for Human Rights and International Justice at Boston College, took Drinan's Human Rights course in 2001–2002. Why? He was a legend. The students knew he was old and wouldn't last much longer, so it would be best to get him now, before it is too late. Although he had once described himself as six feet tall, she estimates he was 5'9". His method: He would walk in, come to the lectern, take a deep breath, and talk for an hour or two without notes. "He just knew a tremendous lot of things." There was little discussion. The students listened to him.

Student course evaluations are an odd literary form: highly subjective, contradictory, perceptive, and sometimes cruel. A survey of several hundred pages of Drinan's from 1984 and 1995 reveals a familiar mix of praise and gripes. The positive comments laud his experience, warmth, concern for students, humor, wide knowledge, and openness to the ideas of others. Critics say he was politically biased, was not sufficiently analytical, cut off students in mid-sentence, and was lax in not sanctioning those who were scheduled to recite on certain days and just didn't show up. Just as listeners found his campaign speeches twenty years before rambling and unfocused, so did some of his law students find his classes.

At Boston College Law, students are graded on a curve; at Georgetown they are not. In a Human Rights class in 1984, thirty out of sixty-two students got A's or A—'s. In Constitutional Law the same year, out of thirty-one students, grades were broadly distributed from A to C. The final exam in a Professional Responsibility class was a three-hour open-book test consisting of five questions. Typical questions concerned what a lawyer must do when he or she sees actual or projected perjury; what regulations a state may impose on TV and radio ads by attorneys; and what level of moral integrity should be required of those who seek admission to the bar.

In October 2006 the Law Center established the Robert F. Drinan Chair in Human Rights. By then he had been a visiting professor at four American law schools and had received twenty-one honorary de-grees, written twelve books, and received the American Bar Associa-tion Medal in 2004 and the Congressional Distinguished Service Award in 2006.

In his last major book, *Can God and Caesar Coexist? Balancing Religious Freedom and International Law* (2004), Drinan reminded us that the right to practice the religion of one's choice is very new in human history and asked whether, if this new right were enforced, would the world be spared the savage wars caused by the clash of religious beliefs.

He worked his way across the world, dropping in on the United Nations and other international bodies, reviewing perennial American controversies like prayer at public events and vouchers for faith-based schools, confronting issues raised by the status of the Koran. Does the official designation of a national religion per se discriminate against the followers of other religions? What if Muslims, Hindus, Christians, and others around the world agreed that abortion should be prohib-ited—how would Americans react? What about the rights of nonbe-lievers who assert that the protection of religious freedom for all puts them in a second class? If we protect the rights of all to practice their religion, what about those religions whose beliefs subjugate women? What of China's rule that each family is limited to having one child? As a result, female fetuses are disproportionately aborted. What if Chi-nese couples protested to an international court that their fundamental right to manage their family life had been violated? Can the world community require China to expand its habitable areas or permit more Chinese to emigrate?

In response, the *St. John's University Law Review* (Vol. 45:11) pub-lished a symposium on the book's themes, including three responses to Drinan from other scholars, with an introduction by the author an-swering the three scholars' essays. Reviewers found it a "book of ques-tions," short on solutions but provocative enough to merit reviews in the *New York Times Book Review* by John T. Noonan (March 13, 2005) and by Greg Kalscheur, S.J., in *Theological Studies*.

Drinan Faces Death

One day in his last years Drinan escorted *NCR* writer Arthur Jones and his wife on a Georgetown campus walk following lunch in the Jesuit dining room. It was the fiftieth anniversary of his mother's death. They stopped at the ancient Jesuit graveyard. As they passed by the tombstones, Drinan, clearly in a sad, even morose mood, declared, "Georgetown gets my body and New England gets my money." It was a rare acknowledgment of his own mortality.

Because he did not like to talk about, or even acknowledge, his age, Drinan would not allow celebrations of his birthdays, so his family and best friends had to come up with other excuses—like the anniversary of his 1970 election—to get together and celebrate the bond that had held them together for almost forty years. About thirty of them gathered for brunch at Boston College Law School in November 2006, just two months before his death. The festivities took the form of a "roast," recalling embarrassing moments and laughing a lot, and Drinan shooting down critics with his wit. But he was failing physically, looked old and thin, and they could see the pacemaker, which he never acknowledged, protruding from his chest under his shirt.

Robert Frederick Drinan died of pneumonia and congestive heart failure in Sibley Memorial Hospital in Washington, at 3:00 on Sunday afternoon, January 28, 2007. It was a cloudy, windy day. The day before, hundreds of thousands of anti-war demonstrators had filled the streets of Washington, and his niece Betsy had briefly left his bedside because she was sure he wanted her at the demonstration. Two days before, Senator Russ Feingold of Wisconsin opened a Judiciary Committee hearing on ending the war in Iraq by using the power of the purse, and three days before, Congressman John Conyers of Michigan, chairman of the Judiciary Committee, set hearings on President George W. Bush's use of "signing statements" putting conditions on laws he signed.

Drinan had collapsed in the classroom about a week and a half before; and for his religious superior, John P. Langan, S.J., Foreign Service School philosophy professor and holder of the Joseph Cardinal Bernardin Chair of Catholic Social Thought at the Kennedy Institute of Ethics, it was a struggle to get Drinan to admit he was sick and must see a doctor. "I don't rest in the daytime," said Drinan. So Langan had his class canceled to stop him from going. Meanwhile, he was losing weight dramatically. On Martin Luther King's birthday he finally went to the hospital.

Since the deaths of his brother and nephew, he had been traveling back to Newton to celebrate memorial liturgies for the family. Now the family—his sister-in-law, Helen; her daughters, Ann, Betsy, Diane, and Susan, and their husbands and Tom's wife, Donna; loyal friend Judith Gilbert, who had moved from Boston to Washington; Jesuits John Langan and Ladislaw Orsy were present toward the end. Ed Leahy, now a prominent Washington lawyer, whom Drinan had plucked from Scranton to be a star student at Boston College Law School and whose wife had been Drinan's Law School secretary, came by several times. When their son had died at eight years, Drinan had consoled them.

Drinan's last column for the *NCR* (published February 2) opened with a happy lede: "Of the 192 members of the United Nations, 185 countries have ratified the U.N. Convention on the Elimination of All Forms of Discrimination against Women. It provides that women receive equal pay with men, are free to choose their own marriage partners, and have the same social, economic, and cultural rights as men." He lamented that in the United States only thirty-five of the required thirty-eight states had ratified the proposed Equal Rights Amendment to the U.S. Constitution.

In a photo illustrating an article by Tony Mauro, "Our Father," in *Legal Times* (November 27, 2006), Drinan is sitting in what appears to be a darkened room, an EXIT sign above his head, with a sub-headline reading "At 86 Robert Drinan . . . Is Going Strong." His eyes, set deeper in his head, are staring ahead, his hands wrinkled. Mauro joined him for lunch in the new Jesuit residence on the Georgetown campus, where his room was more comfortable than in the previous early-nineteenth-century brick building and he had his own private bathroom. The house's modern architecture has a high-ceilinged elegant simplicity in the front parlor which also signals that the community welcomes guests. Some of their conversation was surprising. The law professor seemed at least theoretically open to torturing someone who had "kidnapped your child" or "who knows where the nuclear bomb is and when it's going to go off." Drinan liked Senator John McCain of Arizona because he'd heard that his second wife is a Catholic and had put their son in a Jesuit high school; and talk of a presidential candidacy by freshman Senator Barack Obama of Illinois struck him as premature: "He hasn't done anything. I mean, who is he?" The reporter asked Drinan how he would be remembered. "Drinan allows himself one self-referential moment. Maybe it's been good for the church to have a priest who has brought some glory to the church. . . . But, no one can be a judge in his own case."

Drinan had two funerals—one at St. Aloysius Church, right next to the Capitol, on Thursday, February 2; the other, two days later, at St. Ignatius Church at Boston College, where he had said his first Mass and celebrated his anniversary. In Washington, House Speaker Nancy Pelosi, Senator Edward M. Kennedy, and Georgetown President John DeGioia gave eulogies, and Father Langan delivered the homily. Langan did not shrink from the abortion controversy:

> For the most part, his advocacy of human rights harmonized with the social and moral teachings of the Catholic Church. But it must be acknowledged that on the immensely painful subject of abortion there was a sharp conflict, a conflict which I wish neither to minimize nor to revisit but only to put into a larger context of common concern for the well-being of women and children in a society wracked by moral disagreement.

Through his 86 years he both learned and gave us much, said Langan.

> As a result, so many of us mourn him and look to him as an iconic and exemplary figure, a man in whom the religious and political issues of our age came together fruitfully, if not always happily. We salute a life well lived for the good of others. We recognize a Catholic son of New England, who learned Protestant virtues and institutions and who came to share Jewish joys and sorrows, and who in consequence became more comprehensively Catholic and more universally human.

At Boston College, while a half-dozen protesters stood across the street brandishing anti-abortion slogans, Governor Deval Patrick, Senator John F. Kerry, and Representative Edward J. Markey stood in their pews as the coffin arrived. Eulogist Barney Frank, who had succeeded Drinan as congressman representing the Fourth District, called Drinan an exemplar of "what the moral approach to politics really means"; Yale Law Dean Harold Koh said, "He was not one of those lawyers who [love] human rights but can't stand human beings." Retired Judge Mary Beatty Muse, at whose home Drinan had set one of his first campaign events, recalled his student and dean days at Boston College. Father William McInnes, S.J., in the homily, recalled meeting Bob three months before, late at night, as many did, when he stopped by the *haustus* room. Bob had been reading the autobiography of another Jesuit and was asking whether he should write something like that himself.

> To some he was an icon; to others he was seen as politically naïve. But no one ever questioned his moral passion for justice. He made new friends through his position; he also accumulated enemies. He sometimes found himself in the no-man's land between partisans of a rigid moral absolutism and—on the other side—uncompromising secular advocates of the separation of church and state who were scandalized at the sight of a Congressman dressed in clerical garb.

McInnes admired how Drinan moved in the highest circles of Washington but always returned to the companionship of the Georgetown Jesuit community, and how whenever he returned to Boston he made the trek to Weston to visit the sick and the old. "Bob never lived to write his own history. But he lived the mystery. Like all of us, he leaves this world with business unfinished. We inherit the mystery."

Georgetown Law School honored him with forty-eight pages (http://tiny.cc/Drinan) of tributes from faculty and students—including classroom anecdotes, eating habits, weddings, funerals, bar mitzvahs, reciting the Kaddish, visits to the sick, "a constant presence of committed goodness," a changed vote in Congress to help a colleague, his digital timer counting down the seconds until President

George W. Bush would leave office, the man without children with a talent for talking with children, the instinctive mentor who gave advice that led a young lawyer to take on the case of a Guantánamo detainee.

Mark D. Gearan, the boy on the bike, had gone on to work as communications director in the Clinton White House, lead the Peace Corps, and become president of Hobart and William Smith College. He wrote in the *Boston Globe* on February 2, 2007, that, for him and for others, Drinan was above all a mentor who, like a parent, loved his staff unconditionally and molded his followers without their realizing he was doing it. In a moral jam, they would ask, OK what would RFD do?

Liz Bankowski wrote to her fellow staff members about what made his absence so felt: "I think it is the loss of his voice in the world and in our hearts."

Three Perspectives

The broader public evaluation of Drinan's career might fall into three groups: the "haters" and severe critics; the devoted followers, most of whom worked closely with him or took his classes; and the admirers, who respected him as a champion of human rights but had serious reservations on his abortion position. This last faction felt that if human rights are universal laws, why could not the law do at least something to protect the lives of those soon to be born? There were also those who found Drinan's moods and mannerisms irritating or offensive; but his devoted friends accepted these as if they were the quirks of an eccentric uncle, and others applied the "nobody's perfect" rule and learned to deal with his faults because they had to deal with him and admired his goals.

Of those who strongly disliked him, most did so because of his abortion position; they were one-issue pro-life, often more concerned for life in the womb than for the starving children of the poor throughout the world, the victims of war and torture, and prisoners on death row. The tone of their dislike bordered on hatred and can be sampled on right-wing Web sites.

Among his devoted supporters, although Drinan is best known for his early Nixon impeachment resolution, his lifelong commitment to human rights around the world is the unifying idealistic glue of his public life. They value him as an advocate more than as a legislator and accept his self-description as a moral architect, one who by his writings and presence raised moral issues, specifically justice issues, that might have been neglected had he not entered public life. They accepted his distinction between abortion as a moral issue and a political issue where the decision is properly left to only the mother and her doctor. For many of his admirers, Catholic and non-Catholic, he represented a brand of Catholicism they could most respect— ecumenical, pluralistic, justice-based, yet still branded with his personal piety, the retreats, his friendship and multiple kind deeds.

Other admirers would follow him on the other justice issues and even accept the general principle that not all immoral activity can be controlled by law, but they remain puzzled by what they consider his inconsistency on abortion, his shift from defending the right of the fetus to be born, his describing abortion as "infanticide," to what was, in effect, abortion on demand. He was both inconsistent with his earlier position and inconsistent with what Cardinal Bernardin called the "consistent ethic of life," the "seamless garment" analogy, based on Jesus's garment that the soldiers who crucified Jesus could not cut, which wove together and protected every human life from the womb, through birth, education, marriage, work, sickness, even prison, war and peace, to one's final hours. There is a genuine sadness in some of the letters Drinan received from anti-abortion advocates asking him to use his public pulpit to speak for the value of unborn life. Many who otherwise supported him found his line of reasoning against the Model Penal Code—that legislation limiting abortion to specific hard cases (rape, incest, the deformed fetus, etc.) was wrong because it "approved" those deaths—misguided. The purpose of the Penal Code argument was to protect the lives of those who might otherwise be killed on strictly arbitrary grounds. Drinan ended his chapter on marriage and abortion in *The Fractured Dream: America's Divisive Moral Choices* (1991) with:

Those who see the true horror of abortion and realize that it is virtually the same as infanticide will hope that sometime in the future the nation and the world will realize that the legalization of abortion was a dreadful deviation from the majestic rule of law in the United States. When that moment of recognition comes the world will be grateful to those who kept alive the noble ideal that the life of an unborn child must be respected as a precious gift from God. (50)

If he had spoken like that in Congress, would it have made a difference, would he have been reelected? There are indications that he himself was not entirely at peace with the formula he had embraced. But he put that aside and postponed facing the issue to that "sometime in the future" when somehow the nation would realize what it had done.

To what degree had Drinan answered the question: Can a priest successfully be an elected politician? Drinan would say yes. The pope said no. Jerome Grossman, the man perhaps most responsible for Drinan's being in Congress, says today that the answer is no—the roles are basically incompatible. Except for Drinan. He was a special case, chosen for a special mission—to stop the Vietnam War. He did a great job, said Grossman, but he should be the last of his kind.

The Last Word

In the summer of 2008, when I drove out to Drinan's grave at what was once the Weston seminary, where he studied philosophy and theology, but which is now a retreat center and infirmary, I stopped by the Campion Health Center room of Father Francis J. Nicholson, born in 1921, for a long while Bob Drinan's fellow lawyer, good friend, and companion through every stage of the course. When I asked him for a word or two that, in his judgment, best summed up Bob, he made a thoughtful tent with his fingers, meditated for a few silent minutes, and then looked up and said, "Go!"

Partly because I had celebrated my own fifty years as a Jesuit the year before, I turned to Drinan's fiftieth-anniversary Mass at St. Ignatius Church on Sunday, June 28, 1992, for a few words that might sum up where his heart and mind would be at the end. In his homily, he thought of the 5,000 future lawyers he had taught at both Boston College and Georgetown, then focused on the companions and supporters—often referred to as the Drinan "mafia" or "minions"—who had stuck with him since 1970: "I have never seen such a group of individuals who loved each other so much and who cherished the ideals they shared together." "The tender bonds between them" were a gift of God. As a Jesuit he had always felt challenged to do "more" for the glory of God, and he felt frustrated that his shortcomings in sanctity and his limitations in producing first-rate scholarship kept fulfilling his ideals always "beyond one's grasp."

But Drinan had always sought to "love God by discovering him in the persons he created." He gave his final words to the poet William Butler Yeats: "Think where man's glory most begins and ends./And say my glory was I had such friends."

Notes and Sources

Abbreviations

BC   Boston College
BCA   Boston College Burns Library Archives
GDA   Woodstock College Drinan Collection at Georgetown University
NEA   New England Province Archives at Holy Cross
PA   Pedro Arrupe, S.J.
RAS   Raymond A. Schroth, S.J.
RFD   Robert F. Drinan, S.J.

There are three major archival collections of Robert F. Drinan, S.J., material. The most extensive and open is the Robert F. Drinan, S.J., Congressional Papers 1970–1981 in the Burns Library Archives at Boston College. This consists of 17 series divided into 421 boxes. I used these, plus a box of pre-congressional papers and speeches, selectively, concentrating on the major themes of this study: his congressional campaigns, samples of his legislative initiatives, correspondence with constituents on Vietnam and abortion, the drive to impeach President Nixon, his travels on behalf of Soviet Jews and human rights in Latin America, and the reform of the U.S. Criminal Code. The collection also contains very useful scrapbooks, including local press coverage, on RFD's campaigns, compiled by his brother, Frank Drinan. These files are used frequently in both undergraduate and graduate research projects. All of my files used in writing this book have been given to the Boston College Archives.

The second potential source is the Archives of the New England Province of the Society of Jesus at the College of the Holy Cross in Worcester. Access here is limited. I was able to use information on the academic and daily life of the Jesuit scholastics at Weston College in the 1940s and 1950s when Weston was the philosophy and theology seminary of the province. Professor James Hitchcock of St. Louis University shared with me his copies of some of this material that was otherwise unavailable.

The third potential source is the collection of RFD's papers from his post-congressional career at Georgetown University Law School from 1980 to 2007. These consist of sixty-two boxes listed generally according to contents but not yet catalogued or open for research. I was permitted to use them to check on a few specific issues. A most useful tool is *Father Robert F. Drinan, S.J. Scholarship 1950–2007*, published by the Georgetown University Law Center, April 12, 2007, following his death in January of that year. It lists all his books and nearly all his scholarly and journalistic articles.

Throughout the book I have given the names and dates for all relevant magazine and newspaper articles in the text and included the more significant magazine articles in the bibliography.

Introduction

The story about Anthony LoFrisco's hearing RFD and going to Mississippi was told to RAS by LoFrisco both in person and in writing. Bill McNichols's story was told to RAS. The story of RFD's visit to Robert Blair Kaiser's apartment was sent by Kaiser to RAS. Paul Rothstein sent his reflections to RAS in September 2007 and published them in the *Georgetown Law Journal*, Vol. 95, August 2007. Jeff Thielman both told RAS his story and sent it in writing. The Rockhurst College dean told to eat his hamburger was RAS. Others are among the anecdotes RAS received by letter following the notices in *America, Commonweal*, and the *NCR*.

This book contains several descriptive analyses of RFD's personality. Unless otherwise indicated, they are based on interviews with several people who knew RFD at various stages of his life.

1. A New Beginning

The description of the Chestnut Hill neighborhoods is based on the explorations of RAS. For the early history of BC, the construction of the buildings on the new campus, and so on, see Charles F. Donovan, S.J., David R. Dunigan,

S.J., and Paul A. Fitzgerald, S.J., *History of Boston College, from Beginnings to 1990*, Chapters 13–17; James O'Toole, "This Old Man" and "The Operator," in *Founding Fathers: Six Boston College Presidents and the University They Built*, ed. Ben Birnbaum; and Thomas H. O'Connor, *Ascending the Heights: A Brief History of Boston College from Its Founding to 2008.* The description of the original Drinan home in Hyde Park comes from RAS's visit to the house and its environs and conversation with the current owner, Joseph Murphy. The material on early family life and BC life comes from interviews with and letters from Helen Drinan, Betsy Drinan, Ann Drinan, William Drinan, Joe Nolan, Velia DiCesare, Ted Griffiths, Frank Donovan, and Robert and Mary Muse. The grammar school information comes from RFD's *NCR* recollection and RAS interview and correspondence with Sister Anne Susan Zilla. The portrayal of Hyde Park High School, which today has been recently subdivided into three sections concentrating on various vocations, comes from a visit to the school and reading the *Postscript* and *Bluebook* from the archives in the school library. The documentation for the early BC curriculum comes from the contemporary BC catalogues and RFD's college transcript. RFD's article on Father Shea is "His Words Changed My Life," in *Boston College Magazine*, Fall 1981. For background on the status of Jesuit education in the 1930s, see RAS, *The American Jesuits.* The story of Lou Montgomery comes from the *Heights*, the yearbook *Sub Turri*, and Reid Oslin, *Tales from the Boston College Sideline.*

2. Breaking out from a World Frozen in Time

William Leonard's *The Letter Carrier* is an excellent interpretation of the social history of the Church in the 1930s and 1940s. The description of troops moving into St. Mary's Hall is in a Jesuit newsletter in the NEA. There is an account of Shadowbrook's history in *The American Jesuits* and *Woodstock Letters* Vol. 51. The articles on the building and opening of Weston are in *Woodstock Letters* Vol. 51 (October 1922) and Vol. 59 (June 1930). At Weston I am grateful for the hospitality and research information provided by Paul Holland, S.J., the rector, and Ron Wozniak, S.J., the minister. RFD said, "I couldn't wait to get out" to Joe Appleyard, S.J. The story of the Zacheus Maher report is in *The American Jesuits.* The information on what periodicals were available, life at the villa, the daily life of the scholastics, and the *Weston Quarterly* is in

"Beadle's Diary" in the NEA. Daniel Berrigan, S.J.; George Drury, S.J.; Charles J. Dunn, S.J.; and Paul Kelly described to RAS life at Weston during those years. Also see Daniel Berrigan's *To Dwell in Peace: An Autobiography*. Correspondence concerning RFD's writing for *America*, his desire to be a missionary, his request for summer studies, the letter from his father, and his ordination is in the BCA pre-congressional box. For the history of early Georgetown Law School, see Daniel R. Ernst, *The First 125 Years: An Illustrated History of the Georgetown University Law School*, 94–164.

3. Moving Up

For the developments at BC, see Donovan, *History* (270–409) and Ben Birnbaum's interview with Michael Walsh, S.J., "The Walsh Tapes," in *Founding Fathers*. RAS also knew Walsh. Paul Kelly told RAS in an interview and in writing his story of meeting RFD again and Drinan's leadership style. *BC/Law*, the Boston College Law School magazine (Spring/Summer 2007), contains thirty-one articles in a tribute to RFD. Those most pertinent to this chapter are Hon. Francis J. Larkin, "Drinan as Dean," which provides the framework for that section of this chapter; Edward R. Leahy, "An Authentic Lesson"; Sanford N. Katz, "Enduring Fairness in Family Law"; and Frank R. Herrmann, S.J., "Defining the Catholic, Jesuit Mission." Harold Hongju Koh, "Father Drinan's Revolution," is in *The Georgetown Law Journal*, Vol. 95, August 2007. Judge Henry W. McCarr told his story to RAS both personally and in writing. Interviewed for the Law School and BC passages were Sanford N. Katz, Richard G. Huber, John Flackett, and James A. Woods, S.J. John H. Robinson's observations are from correspondence with RAS. The texts of the address to CORE and the early talks on abortion are in the BCA BC 03–056, Letters and Speeches While Dean of BC Law. The reflections on his retreat are in an untitled scholastic notebook in BCA early papers. They are also referenced in Casey Bohlen, "'Our Father, Who Art in Congress.'"

Because RFD recycled talks, including those on abortion, the best references are to the published versions referred to in the text and notes herein. For the reader's convenience, these are Drinan's main writings on abortion, in chronological order, based on both the Georgetown University Law Center's "Father Robert F. Drinan, S.J. Scholarship 1950–2007" and RAS research referred to in the book. "Inviolability of the Right to Be Born," *Western Reserve*

Law Review, 1965, 464–79; "Strategy on Abortion," *America*, February 4, 1967; "The Right of the Fetus to Be Born," *Dublin Review*, Winter 1967; "The Morality of Abortion Laws," *Catholic Lawyer*, 1968, 190–98; "Reflections on New York's Commission on Abortion," *Catholic World*, September 1968; "Abortion and the Law," in *Who Shall Live: Medicine, Technology, Ethics*, ed. Kenneth L. Vaux, Fortress Press, 1970; "Jurisprudential Option, Abortion," *Theological Studies*, March 1970; "The State of the Abortion Question," *Commonweal*, April 17, 1970; "The Abortion Decision," *Commonweal*, May 8, 1973; "Abortion as Medicare?" *Commonweal*, May 8, 1975.

4. "The World Turned Upside Down"

Most of the background on the Catholic Left is from Francine du Plessix Gray, *Divine Disobedience: Profiles in Catholic Radicalism* and Charles A. Meconis, *With Clumsy Grace: The American Catholic Left, 1961–1975*. The full title of RFD's report from Vietnam is "Findings on Trip to Vietnam, U.S. Study Team, May 25–June 10, 1969," for the U.S. Study Team on Religious and Political Freedom in Vietnam. The basic source for Jerome Grossman's role is his own memoir, *Relentless Liberal* (22–75), but he also appears in Tom Wells, *The War Within: America's Battle over Vietnam* (328–30) and Nancy Zaroulis and Gerald Sullivan, *Who Spoke Up: American Protest against the War in Vietnam, 1963–1975* (esp. 270–72). RAS also interviewed Grossman and other participants, conversed with hyphenated priests, and personally reported on the riots at the Democratic Convention in Chicago in 1968 and other protests in the 1960s.

5. A "New Politics" Candidate

In general, the political narrative structure is based on all references to RFD in the *New York Times* and *Boston Globe*, added to which are details from local coverage available in or suggested by the scrapbooks in BCA, Boxes 413–15, and documents from Campaigns 1970–1978, Boxes 358–67, with emphasis on surveys, election analysis, activities, and strategies. Concerning the selection of Drinan as a candidate, see Grossman, *Relentless Liberal*. RAS interviewed both Grossman and Arthur Obermayer, who supplied all the major documents concerning the caucus. Nearly all the discussion of Drinan's obtaining permission to run as a Jesuit priest is based on RAS interviews with those responsible for granting him permission over the years—Vincent O'Keefe, S.J.; Paul T. Lucey, S.J.; Richard T. Cleary, S.J.; Edward M. O'Flaherty, S.J.—and on the correspondence between Father General Pedro Arrupe, S.J., and William Guindon, S.J., members of his staff, and subsequent provincials and RFD. RAS received copies of the correspondence from James Hitchcock, who used it in his 1996 article in *The Catholic World Report.* Lucey's assessment of Guindon is in his interview with Richard W. Rousseau, S.J., in the autobiographical pamphlet series *New England Jesuits Oral History Program*, Vol. 67, May 2008. Paul Mankowski, who originally obtained the correspondence from the archives, has a thirty-seven-page unpublished memorandum (2007) in which he summarizes the documents and maintains that the material he copied was not confidential but already reviewed to be used by historians. He feels that if his interpretation of the material was true he should be congratulated.

6. The "Miracle" Election

William Tobin described the "Barry Farber Show" events to RAS both in an interview and in writing. Interviewed concerning the campaign were John Marttila, Jan Attridge, Judith Gilbert, John Hurley, Ann Marie Goggin, Christiane Joost-Gaugier, Robert and Mary Muse, Thomas Kiley, Maria Plati, Dorothy Reichard, Thomas Vallely, and Elizabeth Bankowski. Mark D. Gearan published his account in the *Boston Globe* after RFD's death. Of the several in-depth studies of the 1970 campaign, the most thorough are Vincent A. Lapomarda, S.J., "A Jesuit Runs for Congress: The Rev. Robert F. Drinan, S.J., and his 1970 Campaign," *Journal of Church and State* 15 (Spring 1973), 205–22, and Bohlen, "'Our Father Who Art in Congress.'"

7. The Age of Less-Great Expectations

The Annals of America: Détente and Domestic Crisis, Vol. 19, 1969–1993, an anthology of key documents published by the Encyclopedia Britannica, is the source for several of the documents in these chapters, beginning with the Harris survey of popular attitudes toward the government and the Senator

William T. Fulbright address on the Middle East. The picture of resistance within the Catholic Church is from James O'Toole, *The Faithful* (258–65). Some of the culture analysis of the period is from Bruce J. Schulman, *The Seventies: The Great Shift in American Culture, Society, and Politics*. The historical analysis follows James T. Patterson, *Grand Expectations: The United States, 1945–1974* (743–91). The invitation to write for the *NCR* is from the *NCR* files, sent to RAS. The description of the Georgetown Jesuit community is based on RAS recollections of living there 1967–69, and during 1995. The bills described among RFD's legislative efforts in 1971 are in BCA Box 1 and Box 2. The story about the young Jesuits' draft cards is in the *Washington Post*, July 10, 1971, and from RAS interviews with participants.

8. Close Calls

The incident at John Carroll University is from two letters from Mark Kay Katz to RAS. The letters from constituents on Vietnam are in Legislative Correspondence, BCA Box 20. The Nixon quote to "decimate the god-damned place," according to BBC, March 1, 2002, is in the White House tapes of the first half of 1972. Nixon is proposing a nuclear strike to Kissinger. This reinforces Grossman's assertion in 1970 that Nixon was considering a nuclear strike on Vietnam.

9. "My conscience tells me . . ."

David Garrow's references in *Liberty and Sexuality* to Drinan's cooperation with Planned Parenthood and his interest in birth control and abortion legislation are on 228–303, 312–13, 412–14, 421. He explains the influence of Drinan's writings on the Hawaii decision to decriminalize abortion. Tip O'Neill's story on his opposition to Drinan's impeachment resolution, for reasons of strategy, recounted in his *Man of the House*, is anticipated in Jimmy Breslin's memoir of the impeachment proceedings, *How the Good Guys Finally Won*. This narrative of public events leading up to impeachment still relies on James T. Patterson's *Grand Expectations*. The undated paper on "The Theology of Impeachment" is also in Box 314, but RFD was more motivated by news reports on the bombing of Cambodia rather than by Watergate. The correspondence replying to his decision to call for impeachment is in Box 318.

10. The Moral Architect

Mary Callahan tells the HUAC story in "Dear Congressman Drinan, Dear Mr. Chairman," in *Boston College Magazine*, Summer 1989. A portrayal of the atmosphere in RFD's office in these years is Marjorie Arons, "Drinan Sets Place in D.C.," *The Newton Times*, March 27, 1974. For the most part, the description of the Nixon White House and the chronology of the impeachment process in this chapter is based on J. Anthony Lukas, *Nightmare*, Chapters 15 and 16; and on Stanley I. Kutler, *The Wars of Watergate*, 421–533. The transcript of the debate on articles of impeachment is in BCA Box 309. RFD also published his "Resolution of Impeachment of President Nixon"; "Nixon Bomb Defense Inadequate," on the bombing of Cambodia (first published in the *NCR*, October 19, 1973); "Analyzing Watergate Issues" (first published in the *Congressional Record,* September 24, 1974); and "Watergate: A Sickness that Strengthened a Nation" (first published in the *Boston Herald American*, July 11, 1982) as appendixes in *God and Caesar on the Potomac: A Pilgrimage of Conscience.* Elizabeth Holtzman's participation is from her memoir, *Who Said It Would Be Easy?* and her interview with RAS. Barbara Jordan's reaction to Ford's pardon of Nixon is in Mary Beth Rogers, *Barbara Jordan: American Hero*, 225. The description of the Judiciary Committee is a combination of Holtzman and Lukas. The Fenton–Austern analysis in *The Making of Congressmen* is notable in its emphasis on RFD's self-description as a "moral architect." On the "permission" controversy RAS did a follow-up interview with Father Cleary.

11. Around the World

Father Robert J. Cornell, O. Praem., tells his own story in his memoir, *Is There a Priest in the House?* He was interviewed by RAS in 2008 and died in May 2009. The Drinan-sponsored and Drinan–co-sponsored legislation for the 93rd and 94th Congresses discussed here is in Boxes 9, 10, and 11. The abortion letters are in Box 108. The status of Soviet Jews appears in several references in the various RFD archive boxes. This chapter used material in Box 399 as well as press clippings and interviews with the Leventmans on the role of Jews in RFD's elections. The material on the 1976 campaign is in Boxes 364–67. Again, on the "permission" issue, we have the stories in the public press, the Arrupe–New England Jesuit Provincial correspondence, and RAS interviews with Cleary. The twelve-page memo that RFD wrote for Cleary on his abortion position, "Abortion and the Law," May 20, 1976, is a unique summary of the development of his policy and is in Box 390. The contemporary comment of Mason on RFD is from a brief RAS telephone interview with Mason.

12. Latin America, Israel, and the Last Campaign

The nature and motivation of RFD's devotion to the Jewish people is much discussed; and the observations here are based on interviews and conversations with those who knew him well, including Jerome Grossman; James Malley, S.J.; Sanford N. Katz; the Leventmans; and others. The pages on Frank Drinan are based on the published obituary and interviews with family members and family friends Father John Connelly and Father Joseph T. Nolan. The details on the trips to Argentina and El Salvador come from the published reports on the trips mentioned in the bibliography and the text, RFD's published articles, and James R. Brockman's *Romero: A Life.* According to a knowledgeable Argentine Jesuit, the anonymous Jewish journalist was Jacob Timmerman. Norman Walker's account of his candidacy is from his interview with RAS and his unpublished essay. The 1978 campaign reports are in Boxes 366 and 367. Several of RFD's speeches and writings from 1971–80, including the El Salvador report and the manuscript of *Honor the Promise*, are in Boxes 386 and 387.

13. "Hurt, bitter, and confused"

Although the material on the reform of the criminal code is voluminous, this chapter relies primarily on those articles cited in the text. The account of the weekend in which RFD received the final order to leave Congress is based on interviews with Dottie Reichard; Edward O'Flaherty, S.J.; Kenneth Bresler; Frederick Enman, S.J.; James M. Walsh, S.J.; Maria Plati; and Elizabeth Bankowski.

Epilogue: Resurrection

For the Jesuit background in 1980 see RAS, *American Jesuits*. Ellen Griffin's story is from an RAS interview and letter. The summary of RFD activities is based on the Law School's *Father Robert F. Drinan, S.J., Scholarship 1950–2007*. The story of Thomas Drinan is based on the published obituary, the RFD papers in the GDA (Woodstock Library), and discussions with the family. The discussion of the partial-birth abortion op-ed is based on the *New York Times* and *NCR* versions and files in the GDA, and an RAS interview with William Barry, S.J., who was RFD's provincial at the time. R. Emmett Curran, author of the two-volume history of Georgetown University, most generously made available the pages of the about-to-be-published second volume concerning the status of the Georgetown Law Center during the early 1980s, when RFD returned. The picture of RFD as a teacher comes from interviews and/or published statements of Terry Berg; Elizabeth King; Charles Kelly; Charlotte Bruce Harvey; Daniel Koslofsky; Jeff Thielman; Kevin Quinn, S.J.; and material in GDA. Information on RFD's last days comes from the family, Judith Gilbert, Maria Plati, and John Langan, S.J. The fact of Drinan's teaching five courses is from Kevin Quinn, S.J.; of his Puerto Rican retreat, from José Luis Salazar, S.J.

Bibliography and Interviews

Books, Selected Articles, and Interviews

The Annals of America: Détente and Domestic Crisis, Vol. 19, 1969–1973. Chicago: Encyclopedia Britannica, 1976.

Berrigan, Daniel, S.J. *To Dwell in Peace: An Autobiography*. San Francisco: Harper & Row, 1987.

Berry, Jason. *Amazing Grace: With Charles Evers in Mississippi*. New York: Saturday Review Press, 1973.

Birnbaum, Ben, ed. *Founding Fathers: Six Boston College Presidents and the University They Built*. Chestnut Hill, Mass.: Linden Lane, 2008.

Blum, John Morton. *Years of Discord: American Politics and Society, 1961–1974*. New York: W. W. Norton, 1991.

Bohlen, Casey. "'Our Father, Who Art in Congress': The Political Beginnings of Father Robert F. Drinan, S.J." Honors thesis, Brown University, 2008.

Brennan, Joseph Gerard. *The Education of a Prejudiced Man*. New York: Charles Scribner's Sons, 1977.

Breslin, Jimmy. *How the Good Guys Finally Won: Notes from an Impeachment Summer*. New York: Viking, 1975.

Brockman, James R. *Romero: A Life*. Maryknoll, N.Y.: Orbis Books, 1989.

Callahan, Daniel. *Abortion: Law, Choice and Morality*. London: Macmillan, 1970.

Cleary, William, ed. *Hyphenated Priests: The Ministry of the Future*. Washington: Corpus, 1969.

Cormier, Robert. "Going His Way: A Priest in Congress." *St. Anthony Magazine*, May 1971.

Cornell, Robert J., O. Praem. *Is There a Priest in the House? A Memoir*. Self-published, undated.

Criminal Code Revision Act of 1980, Including Additional Comments. Committee on the Judiciary, House of Representative, September 25, 1980.

Curran, Charles E. *Catholic Moral Theology in the United States: A History.* Washington: Georgetown University Press, 2008.

Debate on Articles of Impeachment. Hearings of the Committee of the Judiciary, House of Representatives, 93rd Congress, 2nd Session.

Donovan, Charles F., S.J., David R. Dunigan, S.J., and Paul A. Fitzgerald, S.J. *History of Boston College, from Beginnings to 1990.* Chestnut Hill, Mass.: Boston College, 1990.

Doyle, Brian. "My Lunch with George." *Boston College Magazine,* Spring 1991.

Drinan, Robert F., S.J. *Can God and Caesar Coexist? Balancing Religious Freedom and International Law.* New Haven, Conn.: Yale University Press, 2004.

———. *Cry of the Oppressed: The History and Hope of the Human Rights Revolution.* San Francisco: Harper & Row, 1997.

———. *The Fractured Dream: America's Divisive Moral Choices.* New York: Crossroad, 1991.

———. *God and Caesar on the Potomac: A Pilgrimage of Conscience.* Wilmington, Del.: Michael Glazier, 1985.

———. "His Words Changed My Life." *Boston College Magazine,* 1985.

———. *Honor the Promise: America's Commitment to Israel.* Garden City, N.Y.: Doubleday, 1977.

———. *Religion, the Courts, and Public Policy.* New York: McGraw-Hill, 1963.

———. *Vietnam and Armageddon: Peace, War and the Christian Conscience.* New York: Sheed and Ward, 1970.

Drinan, Robert Frederick, John J. McAward, Thomas P. Anderson, and Bruce Cameron. *Central America 1980. Nicaragua, El Salvador, Guatemala; Findings of an Investigative Mission.* Boston: Unitarian Universalist Service Committee, 1981.

Drinan, Robert Frederick, with John J. McAward and Thomas P. Anderson. *Human Rights in El Salvador—1978.* Boston: Unitarian Universalist Service Committee.

Drinan, Robert Frederick, with Michael E. Ward and David W. Beier III. "The Federal Criminal Code: The Houses Are Divided." *American Criminal Law Review,* 18, 1980–81.

Drinan, Robert Frederick, et al. *Central America, 1980: Guatemala, El Salvador, Nicaragua 1980.* Boston: Unitarian Universalist Service Committee.

Ernst, Daniel R. *The First 125 Years: An Illustrated History of the Georgetown University Law Center*. Washington: Georgetown Law Center.

Fager, Charles E. "Priest, Law School Dean, Candidate." *The Christian Century*, September 9, 1970.

Fenton, John H., and Donald M. Austern. "The Case of the Priestly Zealot: The Fourth District of Massachusetts," in *The Making of Congressmen: Seven Campaigns of 1974*, ed. Alan L. Clem, pp. 93–106. North Scituate, Mass.: Duxbury Press, 1976.

Finding on Trip to Vietnam. U.S. Study Team, May 25–June 10, 1969. U.S. Study Team on Religious and Political Freedom in Vietnam.

Friedman, Elliot. "How to Win a Primary by Really Trying." *Boston Sunday Globe*, October 18, 1980.

Fullerton, Adelyn Kaye. "Out of the 'moral thicket': The American Christian Religious Leaders and the Persian Gulf War (George H.W. Bush)." Ph.D. diss., Purdue University, 2001.

Gainer, Ronald L. "Federal Criminal Code Reform: Past and Future. *Buffalo Criminal Law Review*, 2, 1998.

Grant, Philip A., Jr. "The Election of Father Robert F. Drinan to the House of Representatives." *Historical Journal of Massachusetts* 14 (June 1986): 114–21.

Gray, Francine du Plessix. *Divine Disobedience: Profiles in Catholic Radicalism*. New York: Vintage, 1971.

Grisez, Germain. *Abortion: The Myths, the Realities, and the Arguments*. New York: Corpus, 1970.

Grossman, Jerome. *Relentless Liberal*. New York: Vantage, 1996.

Harvey, Charlotte Bruce. "Absolute Drinan." *Boston College Magazine*, Summer 1995.

Hitchcock, James. *The Pope and the Jesuits: John Paul II and the New Order in the Society of Jesus*. New York: National Committee of Catholic Laymen, 1984.

———. "The Strange Political Career of Father Drinan." *The Catholic World Report*, July 1996.

Holtzman, Elizabeth, with Cynthia Cooper. *Who Said It Would Be Easy? One Woman in the Political Arena*. New York: Arcade, 1996.

Jonsen, Albert R. *The Birth of Bioethics*. New York: Oxford University Press, 1998.

Katz, Sanford N. "Enduring Fairness in Family Law." *BC Law Magazine*, Summer 2007.

Kennedy, Kerry. *Being Catholic Now: Prominent Americans Talk About Change in the Church and the Quest for Meaning.* New York: Crown, 2008.

Kennedy, William, "Father Runs for Congress." *Look*, September 22, 1970.

Killen, Andreas. *1973 Nervous Breakdown.* Edinburgh: Bloomsbury, 2006.

Koh, Harold Honaju. "The Activist." *Boston College Magazine*, Spring 2007.

Kutler, Stanley I. *The Wars of Watergate: The Last Crisis of Richard Nixon.* New York: Alfred A. Knopf, 1990.

Lapomarda, Vincent A., S.J. "A Jesuit Runs for Congress: The Rev. Robert F. Drinan, S.J., and His 1970 Campaign." *Journal of Church and State* 15 (Spring 1973): 205–22.

Larkin, Francis J. "Drinan as Dean." *BC Law Magazine*, Summer 2007.

Leonard, William, S.J. *The Letter Carrier.* Kansas City: Sheed and Ward, 1993.

Leventman, Paula Goldman, and Seymour Leventman. "Congressman Drinan, S.J., and His Jewish Constituents." *American Jewish Historical Quarterly* 66 (December 1976): 215–48.

Levey, Robert L. "Father Drinan: Freedom's Advocate." *Boston Sunday Globe*, October 29, 1967.

Lukas, J. Anthony. *Nightmare: The Underside of the Nixon Years.* Athens: Ohio University Press, 1999.

McCormick, Richard A., S.J. *The Critical Calling: Reflections on Moral Dilemmas Since Vatican II.* Washington: Georgetown University Press, 2006.

McGreevy, John T. *Catholicism and American Freedom.* New York: W. W. Norton, 2003.

Meconis, Charles A. *With Clumsy Grace: The American Catholic Left, 1961–1975.* New York: Seabury, 1979.

Murray, John Courtney, S.J. *We Hold These Truths: Catholic Reflections on the American Proposition.* New York: Sheed and Ward, 1960.

Nolan, Joseph T. *A Life in Liturgy: Rediscovering the Mass.* New York: RJ Communications, 2008.

O'Connor, Thomas H. *Ascending the Heights: A Brief History of Boston College from Its Founding to 2008.* Chestnut Hill, Mass.: Linden Lane, 2008.

O'Neill, Thomas P., with William Novak. *Man of the House: The Life and Political Memoirs of Speaker Tip O'Neill.* New York: Random House, 1987.

Oslin, Reid. *Tales from the Boston College Sideline.* Sports Publishing L.L.C., 2004.

O'Toole, James M. *The Faithful: A History of Catholics in America.* Cambridge, Mass.: Belknap, 2008.

Panarella, Christopher. "Father Robert F. Drinan, S.J.: His Life and Views on the Church–State Issue," Senior Thesis, American Studies Program, Georgetown University, April 24, 1991.

Patterson, James T. *Grand Expectations: The United States, 1945–1974.* New York: Oxford University Press, 1996.

Rawlinson, Peter. *The Jesuit Factor: A Personal Investigation.* London: Weidenfeld and Nicolson, 1990.

Report of Amnesty International Mission to Argentina, 6–15 November 1976.

Riegle, Donald, with Trevor Armbrister. *O Congress.* Garden City, N.Y.: Doubleday, 1972.

Rogers, Alan, and Lisa Rogers. *Boston. City on a Hill: An Illustrated History.* Sun Valley, Calif.: American Historical Press, 2007.

Rogers, Mary Beth. *Barbara Jordan: American Hero.* New York: Bantam, 1984.

Rosenthal, Jamie. "Three in the Third: Drinan, Linsky & Jack." *Boston Phoenix,* November 7, 1972.

Rothstein, Paul. "Glimpses of the Priest as Dean, Legislator, and Friend." *Georgetown Law Journal,* Vol. 95, August 2007.

Rousseau, Richard W., S.J., ed. *Paul T. Lucey, S.J.* The New England Jesuits Oral History Program, 2008.

Schroth, Raymond A., S.J. *The American Jesuits: A History.* New York: New York University Press, 2007.

Schulman, Bruce J. *The Seventies: The Great Shift in American Culture, Society, and Politics.* New York: Free Press, 2001.

Walbert, David F., and J. Douglas Butler, eds. *Abortion, Society, and the Law.* Cleveland: Case Western, 1973.

Wells, Tom. *The War Within: America's Battle over Vietnam.* Berkeley: University of California Press, 1994.

Westin, Alan F. "'I Gave Up Beating on the Justice Department for Lent': Conversation with Congressman R. F. Drinan." *Civil Liberties Review* 1 (Fall 1973): 75–95.

Zaroulis, Nancy, and Gerald Sullivan. *Who Spoke Up? American Protest Against the War in Vietnam, 1963–1975.* Garden City, N.Y.: Doubleday, 1984.

Principal Newspapers and Periodicals

America

Boston Globe

Boston Herald

Boston Pilot

Commonweal

National Catholic Reporter

New York Times

Interviews

Jan Attridge

Elizabeth Bankowski

William A. Barry, S.J.

Terry Berg

Daniel Berrigan, S.J.

Jason Berry

Edward W. Bodnar, S.J.

Michael Boughton, S.J.

Ken Bresler

Richard T. Cleary, S.J.

Father John Connelly

James L. Connor, S.J.

John Conyers

Robert J. Cornell, O. Praem.

Velia Di Cesare

Sam and Mary Anne Donnelly

Frank Donovan

John Donovan

Ann Drinan

Betsy Drinan

Helen Drinan

William Drinan

George Drury, S.J.

Charles Dunn, S.J.

James Fallon

Maurice Fitzgerald, D.M.D.

John Flackett

Barney Frank

Judith Gilbert

Ann Marie Goggin

Ellen Griffin

Ted Griffiths

Jerome Grossman

Robert Hanlon, S.J.

John Haughey, S.J.

Paul Heffron

Elizabeth Holtzman

Richard G. Huber

John Hurley

John Isaacs

Christiane Joost-Gaugier

Sanford N. Katz

Paul Kelly

Thomas Kiley

Elizabeth King

Daniel Koslofsky

John P. Langan, S.J.

Seymour and Paula Goldman
    Leventman

Paul T. Lucey, S.J.

James B. Malley, S.J.

John Marttila

Arthur D. Mason

Henry W. McCarr

William McNichols
Daniel Morrissey
Robert and Mary Muse
Francis J. Nicholson, S.J.
Joseph Nolan
Arthur Obermayer
Edward M. O'Flaherty, S.J.
Vincent T. O'Keefe, S.J.
Frank J. Parker, S.J.
Maria Plati
Kevin Quinn, S.J.

Dorothy Reichard
James W. Skehan, S.J.
William Tobin
Terrence Toland, S.J.
Thomas Vallely
Norman Walker
James P.M. Walsh, S.J.
Arthur D. Wolf
James A. Woods, S.J.
Donna Worsham

Index